Y0-ECI-952

No. 846
$9.95

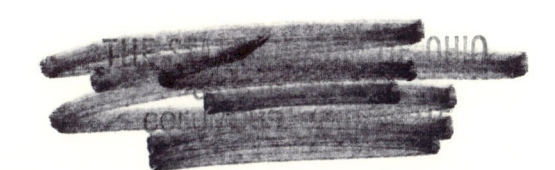

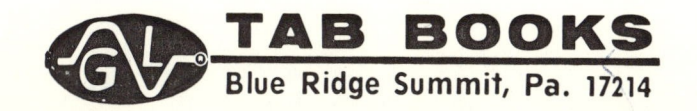

THE BICYCLER'S BIBLE
BY PAUL DEMPSEY

TAB BOOKS
Blue Ridge Summit, Pa. 17214

FIRST EDITION

FIRST PRINTING—JUNE 1977

Copyright © 1977 by TAB BOOKS

Printed in the United States
of America

Reproduction or publication of the content in any manner, without express permission of the publisher, is prohibited. No liability is assumed with respect to the use of the information herein.

Library of Congress Cataloging in Publication Data

Dempsey, Paul.
　The bicycler's bible.

　Includes index.
　1. Bicycles and tricyles.　2. Cycling.
GV1044.D45　　　796.6　　　77-5602
ISBN 0-8306-7846-8
ISBN 0-8306-6846-2 pbk.

Contents

	Preface	7
1	**A Brief History**	9
	Early Development—The Peak Years—Decline—Technological Debts—the Bicycle Today	
2	**Bikes in the Urban Environment**	34
	Bikeways—Parking—Bikes and Mass Transit—Action	
3	**The Heart of the Matter**	44
	The Dublin Study—The Missing Ingredient—Conditioning Methods—How to Get Started	
4	**Touring**	56
	Touring Bikes—What to Carry—Planning—Bikeways—Sleeping Accomodations—Cooking Out—Preflight Inspection—What to Wear	
5	**Buying a Bike**	70
	Bicycle Technology—Warranties—Where to Buy—Which Brands—Which Bikes—Components—Appearance—Before You Buy	

6 Bike Safety 94
Riding Defensively—Reflexes—The Bicycle—Helmets—Bike Security

7 Rim Brakes 113
Side Pull vs. Center Pull—Adjustment—Brake Levers—Cables—Stirrup Brakes

8 Derailleur Transmissions 127
Gear Ratio—Shifting—Nomenclature—Freewheels—Cluster Removal and Disassembly—Freewheel Body Overhaul—Rear Changers and Control Levers—Front Changers Derailleur Chains—Cable Adjustments—Rear Changer Adjustments—Chain Jumps—Overhaul

9 Crank and Hub Transmissions 157
Operating Principles—Installation—Transmission Teardown—Cable and Twist Grip Replacement—Troubleshooting—Planetary Transmissions—Sturmey-Auto-Torq Dana Three Speed—Planetary Transmissions—Sturmey-Archer—Sturmey-Archer Hubs—Other Makes—Dynohub

10 Hub Brake 204
Bendix Coaster Brakes—Bendix Automatic Transmission-Brake Combinations—Bendix Red Band Two-Speed—Bendix Yellow and Blue Band Brakes—Sturmey-Archer S3C—Shimano 3.3.3—Shimano Disc Brake—Forks

11 Hanger and Headsets 248
American Pedals—Continental Pedals—American Cranks—Cottered Cranks—American Headsets—European Headsets

12 Wheels and Tires 271
Hubs—Spikes—Rims—Wheel Repairs—Wheel Alignment-Repair—Wheel Buliding—Tires

Index 294

Preface

The bike has been acclaimed as the most efficient means of transportation yet devised. They are so ingrained in our everyday lives that their very existence has become a part of our vocabulary. Their uses range from adolescent toys to conditioning devices to serious hobby machines; from practical transportation to the big-time sport of professional racing. And, reasonably so, their construction, suitability, and maintenance varies just as widely.

So, the content of this book necessarily varies as much as the construction and uses of bicycles. The level of maintenance required varies from bike to bike—the more sophisticated the bike, the more maintenance required. The level of maintenance actually *given* to a bike varies even more—from absolutely none to downright coddling.

You can always have the dealer perform the necessary service. But in some parts of the country dealers are scarce and almost nonexistent in others. And the level of dealer service is not always satisfactory. Some dealers do a magnificent job; others look on the service department as a necessary evil. What this all comes down to is that you will probably use your tool kit sooner or later. This book will help. It includes just about everything you need to know about bike maintenance and repair. I have tried to include everything—from choosing and improvising tools to transmission overhaul. The most troublesome and most difficult to understand systems receive special emphasis.

This is also a hobbyist's book that will increase the enjoyment of being a cyclist—from what equipment to take along on a tour to just plain enjoying being on the road in the sunshine doing what you love to do.

Just about everybody knows how to ride a bike. It is my fondest hope that this book will let you learn how to truly enjoy this mechanical marvel.

Paul Dempsey

1

A Brief History

When did man first learn he could balance upon two wheels? Historians are not certain. There is evidence that the ancient Egyptians and Romans amused themselves with scooter-like vehicles, although the evidence is blurred. It can be argued that these machines had three or four wheels and thus were no more than small wagons. A stained-glass window in Stoke Poges Church, Buckinghamshire, England, dated between 1580 and 1642, is sometimes said to be the first picture of a man riding a bicycle. Unfortunately, the artist did not supply a plan view. It may be that this vehicle had paired rear wheels (Fig. 1-1)

A most remarkable drawing has come to light with the recent publication of "lost notebooks" by Leonardo da Vinci (1452-1519). Actually, the notebooks were not lost, they were merely misfiled for a couple of centuries. Leonardo's usual genius for things mechanical is exhibited with drawings of antifriction bearings, power transmissions, and other elements of machine design, centuries ahead of their time. But the really interesting drawing is pasted to the cover of one of the notebooks. It is not in Leonardo's hand, and is believed to be the work of one of his students. It clearly shows a bicycle complete with chain drive. The front wheel can move through a small arc and the rear-wheel stays are triangulated. All that is missing to make this a truly modern bike is the diamond-center frame and the steering head.

Fig. 1-1. A sketch of the stained glass windows at Stoke Poges. (Courtesy Raleigh Industries Ltd.)

EARLY DEVELOPMENT

We do not know if this machine was constructed. The first prototype bicycle to be actually built, as far as the records show, was the *Celerifere* by Comte de Sivrac in 1791 (see Fig. 1-2). It may have been modeled upon an abortive attempt by Jean Theson a century earlier, but probably was the development of a popular child's toy of the period. These machines, renamed *Velociferes* had no steering or propulsive mechanism. The rider moved it crab fashion with his feet. These adult toys were quite popular with the French upper classes and at least one race was held on the Champs-Elysees. When one recalls the events of the last years of the 18th century in France, one has a certain sympathy for this urge to play.

An improvement on the basic design was made by Nicephore Niepce in his *Celeripede* of 1818. At least one version could be steered. About the same time Baron Karl von Drais de Sauerbrun invented a similar vehicle. It too was steerable and was intended to be used for practical transportation. The Baron traveled about extensively in his work as an engineer and had no love of horses. The *Draisienne* became well known in Europe, without however becoming a threat to horseflesh, and was copied in England and the United States under the name hobbyhorse or dandy horse (see Fig. 1-3). Both terms were pejorative: a "hobbyhorse" means a somewhat silly fixation and "dandy" meant what it meens today—an idle, over-dressed young man. And this was the class that the Baron's vehicle appealed to. Denis Johnson, a noted coach maker, built deluxe models for this clientele. The machines featured adjustable seats, improved steering, and dropped frames for lady riders. Riding academies were opened to teach mastery of the new vehicle.

In 1839 a Scottish blacksmith, Kirkpatrick Macmillan, added a propulsion mechanism to the hobby horse. The pedals drove the rear wheel by means of wooden treadles and iron connecting rods, locomotive fashion as shown in Fig. 1-4. The wheels were wood, shod in iron. Macmillan thought nothing of riding 14 miles from Courthill to Dumfries and, in 1842, gained another distinction. He was the first bicyclist to be hailed before the magistrate. It seems that he struck a child in Glasgow at the end of a 40-mile run. His defense was that the crowd mobbed him, but the judge was unsympathetic and fined him five shillings.

The next development was unfortunate. Rather than continue with a geared drive to the rear wheel, Pierre Michaux and his son Ernest added a crank to the front wheel. The family operated a small tricycle factory and repair shop in Paris, and made this modification to a customer's machine which was in for repair. We do not know what the customer's reaction was, but the public was enthralled. Within four years the Michaux family was building 400 *velocipedes*, or boneshakers, a year and were unable to fill all orders (see Fig.

Fig. 1-2. The Celerifere of 1791. (Courtesy Raleigh Industries Ltd.)

Fig. 1-3. The hobbyhorse, circa 1818. (Courtesy Raleigh Industries Ltd.)

Fig. 1-4. Macmillan's bicycle, the first to be driven through pedals. (Courtesy Raleigh Industries Ltd.)

1-5). Years later, Ernest wrote that the idea had come from cranks used on grindstones.

Pierre Lallemont was the mechanic who had actually installed the pedals on the first velocipede and was convinced, rightly or wrongly, that the inspiration was his. Unhappy with the treatment he was receiving, he emigrated to the United States in 1866. In collaboration with James Carrol, Lallemont patented the velocipede. It was the first bicycle patent granted in this country.

The Michaux boneshaker continued to be manufactured until about 1872, but lost much of its initial popularity to French and English competition. The *Phantom* by W. F. Reynolds was typical of this new breed. It featured a metal frame triangulated for strength and steel spokes. The spokes were threaded into the rims and flanged to the hub. They could be tensioned by moving the hub flanges apart. This bicycle, designed in 1869 and marketed the following year, represented the first commercial use of the suspension wheel which had been invented by G. F. Bauer at the turn of the century.

Fig. 1-5. Ernest Michaux with his "Velocipede". (Courtesy Raleigh Industries Ltd.)

The first bicycle show was held in Paris in 1869. Exhibits featured contracting brakes, variable-speed transmissions, and several freewheel mechanisms. This same year saw the first organized bicycle race. It was held between Paris and Rouen and was won by James Moore, an Englishman.

The most significant event of the late 1860s was the entry of the Coventry Sewing Machine Company into the market, or more exactly, the entry of their shop foreman, James Starley. The story begins in 1868 when the firm's Paris agent returned to England with a Michaux velocipede. He showed it to the company directors and suggested that they go into bicycle production to meet the needs of the French market. Along with the bicycle the agent brought orders for 400 machines. The directors agreed and changed the name of the firm to the Coventry Machinist's Company.

Starley was then 39 years old. Self-taught, he left home at the age of 15 to make his fortune in the world. His first job was as a gardener in London. He used his spare time to design and build a sewing machine. The machine served as Starley's entry card into the factory world of Coventry, although no manufacturer wanted to produce it. Starley took out other patents which, to a great extent, have determined the shape of modern sewing machines.

Starley oversaw the production of the first consignment of velocipedes. There was no question of design improvement—the directors had taken a gamble and they needed receipts. Apparently there was no concern with possible patent infringement. These bicycles were delivered and new orders were accepted. In the meantime Starley had designed his own bicycle which was called somewhat melodiously the *C-Spring and Step Machine or Coventry Model*. Few of these "springers" were sold, but in 1870 he designed the Ariel which was marketed under license by Haynes and Jeffries of Coventry. The drawing in Fig. 1-6 hardly does justice to the spiderly beauty of the machine. As preserved in several museums around the world, the Ariel gives the impression of taut energy and grace which very few objects made of metal ever achieve. In terms of the implications of its design the machine is finished. There is nothing superflous or incomplete about it.

The Ariel could be fitted with a speed gear which turned the wheel twice as fast as the crank. These spokes were adjustable in a fashion not too different from modern rims. But the major feature of the machine was its large front wheel. Starley recognized that few purchasers would be willing to pay 50% more for a gear train. Real speed could only be obtained

Fig. 1-6. James Starley's Ariel. (Courtesy Raleigh Industries Ltd.)

by increasing the drive wheel diameter. These bikes were popularly dubbed pennyfarthings after the large British farthing and diminutive 1/4 cent piece. The drive ratio was fixed but comparison between models could be made by wheel diameter. We use the same system today, complicated by sprocket ratios.

The size of the drive wheel caused new problems. Torque developed in braking and acceleration tended to twist the hub relative to the rim. The braces shown in the illustration were a stopgap measure intended to counteract these forces. Starley solved the problem for his next model without additional parts and weight. Instead of attempting to compensate for hub rotation, he turned the hub before the wheel was laced. Spokes crossed out of the hub fore and aft so that they formed a series of triangles.

Hub-to-rim movement was resisted by the spokes in tension rather than in compression. For either part to be displaced, the spokes had to stretch. Radial spokes as used on the Ariel merely bend. Today almost all bicycle wheels have tangent spokes. Most are cross three although a few heavy-duty wheels are laced cross four for added strength.

Pennyfarthings, also called ordinaries, were not the lightest of machines. Typically they weighed 50 pounds or so, although track models were built which tipped the scales at slightly more than 20 pounds. A certain J. Moore rode a standard Ariel with a speed gear 14 1/2 miles in one hour in 1873. In the same year four young men cycled from London to John o'Groats—a distance of 690 miles—in two weeks of furious pedaling.

Of course Starley was not alone in producing bicycles. There were many manufacturers in Great Britain, France, and the United States turning out ordinaries in the '70s and into

Fig. 1-7. The crank-driven Facile of 1869. (Courtesy Raleigh Industries Ltd.)

the '80s. Some of these machines had ingenious features. The Kangaroo has paired chain drive to the front wheel; the Facile (Fig. 1-7) used a system of cranks and levers. And the American Star, a racing bike of some note, reversed the wheel configuration. The rider sat directly over the drive wheel and steered a small front wheel through a universal-joint arrangement.

But even at its best the ordinary left something to be desired. It was difficult to mount and dismount and was dangerous for even experienced riders. "Headers" or tumbles over the handlebars were routine. Like judo trainees, novice bicyclists first had to learn how to fall. Front wheel diameters of 40 to 60 inches meant that speed was impossible unless one had long legs. Bicycles were the province of the young and the male.

In an attempt to attract more customers, Starley and other builders added one, two, or three additional wheels. Tricycles, quadricycles, and pentacycles were hardly exciting, but did offer safe, reliable transportation. The first of these multiwheeled machines to become commercially successful was Starley's Conventry Lever tricycle. As the name indicates, it was driven through a lever mechanism. The large drive wheel was mounted on the side, Mississippi steamboat fashion, and the two smaller wheels were connected so that both steered in response to the tiller. In 1878 he further improved it by adopting a chain drive, developed earlier by H.J. Lawson. This improved model, the Conventry Rotary tricycle is illustrated in Fig. 1-8.

Starley was nothing if not prolific. In the early '70s he built a prototype quadricycle. Two large wheels mounted amidships provided the traction while steering was split between the smaller leading and trailing wheels. The machine required two operators, seated side by side, each pedaling his own drive wheel. While on a test ride with his son William, the machine suddenly pivoted and pitched the inventor headlong into a bramble. Obviously something had to be done to equalize the torque going to each wheel.

He solved the problem by reinventing the differential which had first been conceived in the 16th century and forgotten for lack of an application. The differential gear split the torque evenly between each wheel and allowed the pedals to be combined on a single shaft. In turns the inside wheel slowed so that the vehicle tracked without slippage, or damage to Victorian lawns.

Production models dropped the rear wheel and were sold under the name Salvo. The Queen purchased a pair of them

Fig. 1-8. Starley's Coventry Rotary Tricycle. (Courtesy Raleigh Industries Ltd.)

(henceforth the name would be Royal Salvo) and in a ceremony at Coventry, presented the inventor with a gold watch. This model is shown in Fig. 1-9.

Ball bearings and tubular frames had become standard by the end of the '70s. The former reduced friction and the latter made possible radical reductions in weight without penalizing strength. The new interest in frame materials was accompanied by a better appreciation of the principle of triangulation. Ideally the frame should consist of structural members in tension or compression; bending or torsional (twisting) loads should be avoided. A perfectly triangulated frame would not need welds. Under stress the members would butt themselves together more securely. Of course this kind of perfection is not seen in the real world, but the principle is valid.

Meanwhile, H.J. Lawson's chain drive was a way around the impasse presented by the ordinary's large front wheel. All that was required was to mount a crank hanger at the center of the frame and take the drive out through the rear wheel. Lawson built such a bicycle in 1873. It employed a chain in place of the rope which he had used for the prototype. Figure 1-10 illustrates the commercial version with its atavistically large front wheel. Few were built and Lawson reaped little profit from his efforts. Indeed he became a kind of ghost, haunting his competitor's factories and begging them to build Lawson bicycles under license. This was not to be done, since it was easy enough to design a "safety" bicycle around Lawson's patents. Nor was the Lawson bicycle difficult to improve upon.

Early chains were made on the pattern known today as the pin chain. There were no rollers between the pins and the sprocket teeth (Fig. 1-11A). About the time of the American Civil War, James Slater fitted rollers to the pins, a design which reduced friction by converting sliding motion to rolling motion. However Slater's roller chain was less than ideal since wear was concentrated on the side plates. Hans Reynold

Fig. 1-9. Starley's Royal Salvo tricycle. (Courtesy Raleigh Industries Ltd.)

Fig. 1-10. H.J. Lawson's technically important, but commercially disappointing, Bicyclette. (Courtesy Raleigh Industries Ltd.)

solved the problem with the roller bush chain. As can be seen in Fig. 11-B the roller has a bushing superimposed upon it. The contact area is enlarged, and rubbing speeds are lower. The ends of the bush bear against the side plate, distributing thrust loads over a large surface. Reynold's chain was perfected in 1880, just in time to be used in the second generation of safety bicycles.

English and European bicycles were in prominent display at the Centennial Exposition in Philadelphia. The Cunningham Company purchased the unsold demonstrators and thus

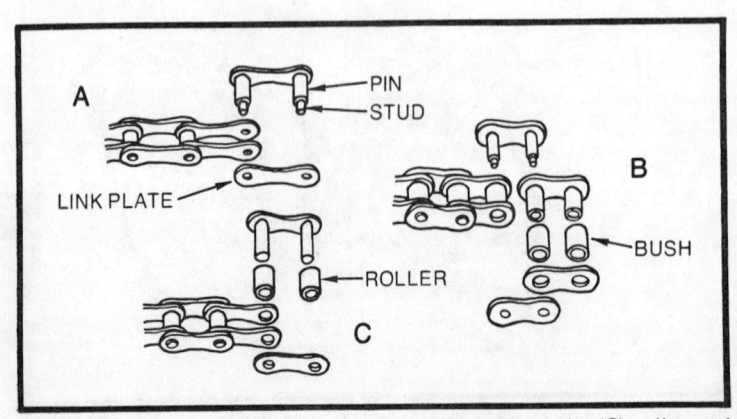

Fig. 1-11. Chain evolution. (A) pin chain, (B) roller chain, (C) roller and bushing.

became the first American firm to specialize in bicycle imports. The company was based in Boston, a city which would soon become a center of the industry. Colonel Albert A. Pope, part showman, part speculator, and a business manager of the first rank, began producing high-wheeled Columbia bikes in Hartford. From the very first, Pope was committed to mass-production, a technique invented by the Harper's Ferry Arsenal and perfected by the American sewing-machine industry. One of his employees was Pierre Lallemont, whom we have met earlier as a mechanic in the Michaux shop.

Not surprisingly, the first commercially successful safety bicycle was built by John K. Starley, nephew of the inventor. In some respects the Rover was surprisingly primitive, although it did have a triangulated frame, racked steering (for directional stability), adjustable wire spokes, and pneumatic tires. The frame was heavy (which accounted for the 37 lb all-up weight) and the seat was flimsily supported by the stays which also had to bear propulsive, braking, and joust loads. Nor were the forks set to align the center of steering with the tire contact area.

Many bikes of this era, as characterized in Fig. 1-12, did not employ a diagonal tube between the seat and pedal hanger, but supported the rider's weight on the stays. Within a few years the familiar diamond frame consisting of two triangles joined at the seat and pedal hanger would be standard.

Fig. 1-12. A safety bicycle of circa 1890. It is believed to be a Rudge-Whitworth or a Humber. (Courtesy Raleigh Industries Ltd.)

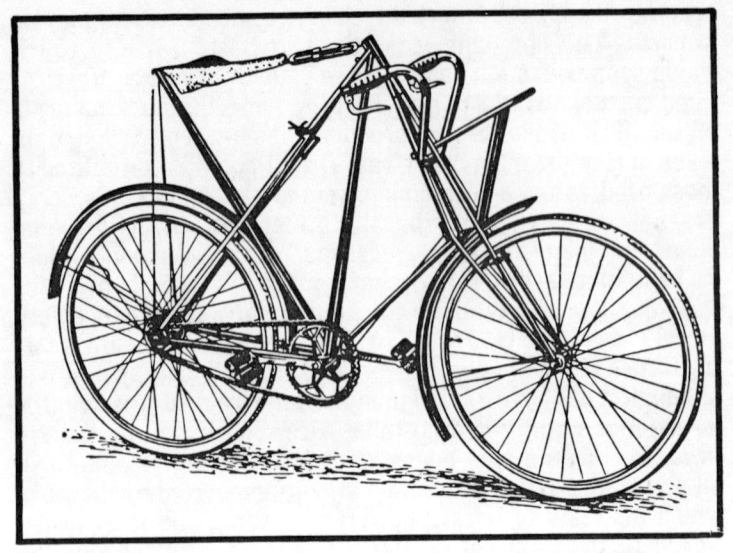

Fig. 1-13. The Dursley Pederson deluxe bicycle. (Courtesy Raleigh Industries Ltd.)

Other manufacturers made more or less direct copies of the Rover or experimented with frame geometry. One of the happiest experiments was the Dursely Pederson (Fig. 1-13) which had been patented in 1893. Our drawing shows an early twentieth-century model. Depending upon which historian you consult, these machines weighed between 13 and 21 pounds. The latter figure seems more reasonable and compares favorably with the best efforts of contemporary builders.

Soon, however, the era of experimentation ceased and the double-diamond frame became standard fare. This frame consists of two triangles joined at the seat tube. While not as theoretically perfect as some of the more exotic approaches, it does have the advantage of ease of construction, reliability (from the reduction in the number of joints), and esthetic appeal. Careful choice of materials and skilled workmanship have fairly well overcome the limitations of the design. The only serious challenge to the double diamond in recent memory was the Moulton with its pressed steel backbone construction.

Another area of progress was the brakes. Ordinaries were fitted with spoon brakes on the rear wheel. The illustration of the Ariel in Fig. 1-6 shows the typical arrangement. Front wheel braking was the responsibility of the rider's leg muscles. With the introduction of the freewheel mechanism in the late '70s, a better system was needed. The first development was the stirrup brake which bore against the inner circumference of the rim. Later, caliper brakes became popular primarily because they allowed rapid wheel changes. A few manufacturers preferred the positive action of the drum brake which, although a heavy mechanism, was in its final form impervious to water and dust. Brake actuation was via rods or cables, devices which are still found on some European and Oriental utility bikes. But by the end of the century, quality machines were braked through flexible Bowden cables. The sheath is made a coiled spring stock; the inner or control wire is stranded. As the brakes are applied, the inner cable acts in tension while the sheath is under compression. The inventor, Frank Bowden, went on to found Raleigh Industries, Ltd.

In the United States matters were simplified by the adoption of the coaster brake, operated by the chain. Much ingenuity was expended on these devices. Nearly all coaster brakes worked from a drive screw in the hub. At one extreme of travel the sprocket was clutched to the rim for forward travel. At the other extreme the hub was braked by metal shoes or discs. The middle position disengaged the hub from the sprocket for freewheeling or coasting.

Lighting was another area that exercised the ingenuity of early cyclists. The first successful headlamp was introduced by Joseph Lucas, Ltd., for the high-wheel trade. It was an oil-burning affair with a reflector and lens. Part of the reason for this lamp's success was the clever mounting arrangement. Instead of brackets and stays, Lucas simply hung the lamp on the inside of the front wheel with a leather strap over the hub. The weight of the lamp kept it upright.

Oil lamps continued to be used well into this century when they were replaced by acetylene flares. Richard Weber of Leipzig patented the first dynamo for bicycles in 1886. By the 1920s these friction-drive AC units had become a world standard. In 1936 Raleigh improved the design by mounting the alternator (an AC generator) in the rear hub where it was shielded from the elements. Later this unit was combined with three-and-four speed Sturmey-Archer transmissions. A more recent development was to combine a battery with a dynamo (DC generator). At low speeds, in city traffic and the like, the lamp is powered by the battery. As the cyclist pedals faster or chances upon a steep hill going his way, the generator automatically cuts in, saving the battery.

A fixed-speed bicycle is at a disadvantage in any but ideal conditions because the human engine works best at about 60 revolutions per minute and quickly fatigues at other speeds.

This disadvantage compounded by the tall ratios fitted to nineteeth-century sporting bikes. Riders were more concerned with top speed than with endurance or hill climbing ability. Almost from the first it was recognized that a bicycle should be driven through some sort of variable-speed transmission.

The English thought in terms of a planetary gear train concealed in the hub and triggered from the handlebars. A fixed sun gear or annulus turns with the hub and is meshed with epicyclic or planetary gears which are mounted in a cage. Three ratios or speeds are provided as explained in Chapter 9. A planetary transmission is light for the power it transmits and since the gears are always in mesh, it requires only a brief interruption of power flow to make the shift.

Frank Bowden had marketed a machine with a replaceable gear wheel in the late '80s. The rider had to dismount to change ratios, but it was better than pushing. In 1902 Henry Sturmey, a school teacher, and James Archer, an engineer, approached the industrialist with a model of the first practical planetary transmission. It was an immediate success and remains popular in middle weight touring bikes for reasons of durability and ease of adjustment. Three, four, and five-speed models have been offered as well as a three-speed with a coaster brake. The most desirable Sturmey-Archer, the three-speed close-ratio model, is no longer in production.

The disadvantages of the planetary transmission are the power losses entailed in the indirect speeds and the severe limitations on ratios. One has only three or at the most five speeds to choose from and these ratios are fixed by geometry. There is no question of tailoring the box to individual needs.

An alternative to the hub gear was to use variable-ratio sprockets. The Whippet gave four speeds by means of an expanding chain wheel. Back-pedaling opened the wheel and reduced its working diameter. E. H. Hodginson's Gradient of 1889 employed a derailleur which moved the chain laterally over three ganged sprockets. It was mechanically ingenious, but expensive to build and troublesome to maintain.

At the turn of the century Paul de Vivre, or Velocio as he was known to the readers of his magazine *Le Cycliste*, was experimenting with multiple ratios. His first attempts were crude. Paired chain wheels and sprockets gave four speeds to his La Gauloise, but the chain had to be moved by hand. He saw a Whippet with its protean transmission and although somewhat put off by its complexity, realized that the chain could be lifted by mechanical means. In 1906 Velocio devised a jockey and wheel arrangement which could be moved laterally over the rear sprocket. The cage which contained the mechanism was in the form of a parallelogram. Velocio never bothered to patent his derailleur and within two years it was copied by several French manufacturers.

The inventor was accused of undermining the moral fiber of cyclists by making it easier for them to negotiate hills. Racers resisted them, in spite of the fact that the current French champion Edouard Fischer, was humbled by a derailleur-equipped newcomer. And Henri Desgrange, founder of the Tour de France and publisher of the influential journal, *L'Equipe*, conceded that the derailleur was of some utility for those over 45, but, as for himself, he would remain true to the single-speed. "Isn't it," he asked rhetorically, "better to triumph by muscular force than to give way to the temptations of mechanical artifice?" Velocio didn't think so and the battle raged in the French sporting papers for almost 30 years.

In contemporary form the derailleur gives 10, 15, or 18 speeds, depending upon the number of chain wheels. Six-sprocket clusters have enjoyed recent popularity although they require extreme wheel dish and a wide-capacity cage such as the Shimano Crane or the Compagnolo Nuovo Record.

In concept the derailleur is elegant, but the hardware is complex and requires frequent adjustment. Its action is brutal—engineers have been known to blanch when they encounter a derailleur for the first time—and hardly positive. The wheel stays flex, the chain stretches as it wears, and the cable lengthens with use. Add to this the number of pivots and shock-loaded bearings and it is a wonder the device works at all. But it does work and, in the more expensive versions, works relatively well.

The pneumatic tire was invented early in the 19th century by R.W. Thomson who had intended it for horsedrawn carriages. It was forgotten until rediscovered in 1888 by John Boyd Dunlop. A veterinarian by profession, Dunlop became interested in the problem because of complaints by his small son. The child's tricycle was too difficult to pedal. The pneumatic tire Dunlop constructed from surgical tubing reduced pedalling effort. *Consumer's Reports* in test on contemporary tires established that the pneumatic tire has a third of the rolling resistance of the solid types and gives up to 15 percent superior braking traction. Dunlop recognized the value of this invention and took steps to get it in production. Popular acceptance was aided by the racing successes of the DuCross brothers who used the new tires to roundly trounce the solid-tired competition.

The first Dunlops were puncture-prone and subject to blowouts. Repairs were difficult since the tire was glued to the rim. Charles Welsh added a wire-reinforced edge and William Barlett further refined the design with a molded lip or bead. These tires were held in place by means of air pressure. Another important development of the period was the use of cords rather than fabric. Cotton cords were wrapped diagonally around the tire to give strength to the sidewalls and were sandwiched between sheets of rubber to reduce chafing. By the end of the century solid tires were almost a curiosity.

THE PEAK YEARS

The late 1800s saw the peak of bicycle popularity. There were an estimated 10 million bicycles in the United States, which at that time had a population of 100 million. England had a similar bike-to-people ratio.

Feats of derring-do caught the public's imagination. Stunt riders were a stock fare at carnivals and circuses, but special fame was reserved for long distance cyclists.

One of these was Thomas Stevens who pedaled eastward out of San Francisco in the summer of 1884. Stevens rode, pushed, and dragged his high-wheeler across the California Sierras, the Nevada desert, through the forbidding emptiness of Utah, over the Great Divide and east across the prairie. There were almost no roads and few people in this part of the west. In Carson, Nevada, Stevens was obliged to perform for a group of cowboys in the local saloon. Prodded by their pistols he managed a few laps around the pool table, "almost," he recounted later, "braining myself on the chandelier."

He continued through Omaha, across the Missouri, and deep into the Iowa farm belt. He was lost for days among the sand dunes and scrub grass on the banks of Lake Michigan. The police jailed him in Cleveland for riding on the sidewalk. One hundred and three days after leaving San Francisco he ended his journey in Boston.

In 1896 Margaret Le Long started west from Chicago on a new safety. Friends and relatives predicted a fate worse than death at the hands of cowboys, Indians, and the drifters who hung like smoke along the tracks of the transcontinental railway. It was a lawless country as desolate as any place on earth. She pedaled through Illinois, the rich farm lands of Iowa, and into eastern Nebraska. In her account of the journey, Miss Le Long said that eastern Nebraska seemed like "the other place." There she traveled along smooth, graveled roads, flanked on either side by sod houses, abandoned, with their windows broken and doors flapping in the wind. Occasionally she would pass a windmill, its tattered sails turning slowly in the prairie wind. Nebraska was dead land, killed by the locusts and the Panic of '73.

In Wyoming she was able to depend upon the hospitality of the ranches for food and, in one instance, for medical care after a nasty fall. Once she encountered a heard of cattle which, instead of giving way, began to crowd her. Miss Le Long frantically searched for her revolver, buried somewhere in the bottom of her tool kit. She found it as the animals were literally breathing down her neck. With eyes shut she fired five shots into the air. When she opened them the cattle were gone. She crossed the desert, following patches of wagon road and the more reliable telegraph lines. The last stretch from Reno and across the Sierras to San Francisco was almost anticlimatic.

Nor were these long distance endurance feats limited to the United States. In the '90s several intrepid souls toured the world by bicycle. Annie Londonberry managed the journey without a dime in her purse. She earned steamship fares by lecturing on the benefits of cycling to awestruck crowds. Two young graduates of Washington University, Thomas Allen and William Sachtelben, crossed Asia and were guests of the Manchu Emperor. Fannie Workman and her husband spent a decade on two wheels, visiting the more remote and wild parts of the world. On one epic trip they transversed the Sahara.

Racing was part of the picture from the start. Perhaps the greatest racer was Arthur Zimmerman. This legendary figure won both the one- and ten-mile events in the first American World Championship races held in 1893 and won the bloody six-day race at Madison Square Garden. This race was so brutal that further events of the kind were banned until 1972 when the Garden hosted another six-day marathon. Earlier, Zimmerman had set the world record for the 1/2 mile—1 minute, 10 3/4 seconds. His machine was a high-wheeler which weighed a staggering 70 pounds. That Zimmerman would use such a mastodon for a world-record run was typical of his approach to the sport.

He liked a drink or two (or ten) and preferred the dance halls to the practice track. He won hundreds of races here and in Europe and was, without doubt, the champion of the world. No other racer has approached his record of total performance, a fact which irks some modern bike racers who train with monastic discipline.

The absolute speed record was held by Charles "Mile-a-Minute" Murphy with the help of the Long Island Railroad. Murphy rode behind a coach and locomotive that had been modified for racing. Boards nailed over the ties were his track. At one point he lost slipstream and had to pedal back into it. At the end of the run the engineer shut the throttle too quickly and "Mile-a-Minute" collided with the coach. A quick-thinking brakeman hoisted him to safety. The record was actually a little better than his nickname and stood for 42 years. In 1941 Alfred Letourner bested it behind a racing car.

Bicycles became associated with the cause of health, much in the way that they have in our time. Dr. Charles Stables published *Health upon Wheels* in 1881. It was a tribute to the curative power of the bicycle. Ten years later Dr. Harold Clark in *Hygenic Bicycling* repeated the message—man is an anagram of mind and body—a healthy mind is the result of a healthy, well-exercised body—the bicycle is the ideal means of exercise, combining as it does practicality with access to the wonders of nature. Other books were written in the same vein, as well as hundreds of articles and personal reminiscences.

While certain elements of the medical community opposed bicycling—chiefly on the grounds of overstress to young, undeveloped muscles and secondarily because of the casualty rate—the most determined opponents were in the clergy.

"Those who ride bicycles will soon come to a place," intoned one New England preacher, "where the roads are never muddy." To judge from surviving sermons, the opposition was centered upon the freedom the bicycle gave young people. Instead of attending worship services, they were, the clergy feared, up to mischief.

The response of the legislative authorities also was hostile. They were quick to pass restrictive laws in England and in the United States. In England the Highway and Railway Act of 1875 transferred regulatory power over the highways from the Crown to the local jurisdictions.

In effect this meant that cyclists could be excluded from public roads on whim. In 1899 Lady Harbeton was refused service at the Hautboy Hotel because her clothing, quite conservative even by comtemporary standards, typed her as a bicyclist. In this country the pattern of discrimination centered around the use of public parks and turnpikes. The League of American Wheelmen was founded in part to fight these restrictions, by the '80s made its clout felt, although the court fights were time-consuming and expensive.

Other forms of discrimination were more difficult to cope with since they originated with individuals. Country folk considered it great sport to nudge a high-wheeler, sending its rider over the handlebars. Another passtime was to wait for cyclists at a narrow part of the trail and push sticks through his spokes. How much of this went on, we do not know. But it is a common theme in the reminiscence of cyclists of the era.

Consequently, part of the motivation for forming clubs (the first one in this country was founded in Boston in 1879) was self-protection.

We can only hazard a guess at why bicycles were considered threatening while other inventions of that most prolific period met with instant approval. No one passed laws against the phonograph or went about breaking light bulbs. Samuel Colt of Hartford, whose plant was not far from Colonel Pope's bicycle factory, was considered a kind of hero, although one could argue the social utility of his products. The reason had little to do with technology, although some romantic thinkers, such as John Ruskin, made their denunciations on this basis. Ruskin saw the bicycle as a barrier to man and the natural world, substituting steel and India rubber for honest shoe leather.

Cyclists evolved into a kind of subculture. They created a language to describe their activities and learnedly discoursed on rakes, treads, hollow and forged forks, bearings, and cones. A few made themselves noticed by "scorching" the highways, frightening horses, and generally wreaking havoc on the quite tenor of rural communities. On or off their bikes they could be identified by their dress. Women's clothes changed radically in response to the demands of the bicycle and to the new freedom it represented. The "pinched look", achieved with stays and crinolin, gave way to simpler, more utilitarian styles. Knickers, a modified bloomer, became popular along with simple hats and split skirts. This fashion change, in hand with the demonstrated athletic prowess of female cyclists, according to some historians, was the beginning of the women's liberation movement.

The League of American Wheelmen campaigned for better roads. Other elements in the society—farmers, businessmen, and the budding construction industry—also agitated for improved roads, but could not match the evangelical fervor of the League. Lobbies were organized in state capitols and in Washington. League-sponsored newspaper and magazine articles extolled the virtues of a transportation network. The tone of these pieces can be gathered from a typical title—*The Gospel of Good Roads*. In 1892 *Good Roads* magazine appeared. The Chicago World's Fair in 1893 was a "media event" which received national press coverage. The League used it as forum for further agitation and propaganda. Meanwhile, the redoubtable Col. Pope made speeches and, at one point, circulated a petition for better roads which was delivered to the Department of the Interior with 150,000 signatures. He also persuaded the Massachusetts Institute of Technology to offer courses in road building.

> # PHYSICAL CULTURE.
>
> One aid—the best aid—to physical culture is recreative exercise.
>
> In no way can this be gained so well as on a bicycle.
>
> The best bicycle for ladies' use is the
>
> ## Columbia Ladies' Safety.
>
> **POPE MANUFACTURING COMPANY,**
> **77 Franklin Street, BOSTON.**
>
> BRANCH HOUSES:
> 12 Warren Street, NEW YORK.
> 291 Wabash Avenue, CHICAGO.
>
> FACTORY, HARTFORD, CONN.

Fig. 1-14. A typical Columbia ad, circa 1892.

Sparked by the cyclists, other pressure groups entered the picture. The National League for Good Roads was founded in 1893. A few years later, the American Highway Association, whose influence extends into the present, was organized. The federal government established an Office of Good Roads in the Department of Agriculture before the century was out, but actual construction was state business. New Jersey instituted a revenue-sharing scheme to apportion funds to the counties. Many states set up rock-crushing facilities to convert mud roads to macadam. In the South convict labor was used, instituting the era of the chain gang.

By 1916 there was a program of federal aid to the states for road construction and improvement. Later, in the postwar period, grants-in-aid took on massive proportions and were supplemented by the sale of cheap surplus military-surplus trucks and tractors to the construction industry.

By means of skillful propaganda and direct political pressure, bicyclists made the creation of a first-class road network a national imperative. That they would hardly benefit from the program and, three generations later, would have to fight for bikepaths on the margins of superhighways, is one of the ironies of history.

DECLINE

By 1900 the boom burst. The League of American Wheelmen lost 90 percent of its membership and, in this country at least, it was impossible to sell a bicycle to anyone over 12 years old. Englishmen and Europeans were more faithful to their bikes, but the excitement was gone, upstaged by the automobile and the motorcycle. Bike racers, men such as Barney Oldfield and Tazio Novolari, quit pedaling and bought motorcycles.

Bicycle technology stabilized and seemed to stagnate. What improvements there were centered on production techniques. Raleigh perfected a method of mass-producing the bottom bracket. This part had been difficult to make because of the tolerances required—four holes had to be bored at precise angles and locations and the inner diameter turned to accept the crank bearings. Under the Raleigh method all these operations were done simultaneously. The same firm introduced dip brazing in place of hand brazing.

But even in the darkest years, there were always a few racing bikes. Racing remained popular in southern Europe and there was a small, but steady, demand for high-quality competition bikes. The derailleur was finally practical, aluminum rims became standard, and frame materials improved. Reynolds Tube progressed from high carbon steel, through manganese steel to the current manganese molybdenum 531 alloy. Like improvements have taken place in antifriction bearings and in tires.

TECHNOLOGICAL DEBTS

The bicycle was responsible for key elements of auto and aircraft technology. The responsibility was so pervasive that we could almost call the automobile the direct descendent of the bicycle, differing only in the power source, number of wheels, and in the requirement for weather protection. The direct influence of the bicycle on the automobile is evidenced by the use of:

- the pneumatic tire
- ball and other types of antifriction bearings in the running gear and steering mechanism
- steel-spoked wheels
- bush and roller chains
- tubular members at points of stress concentration such as the transmission shaft and frame cross members.
- external expanding and internal contracting drum brakes
- control cables
- planetary transmissions

The most familiar example of the latter is the Model T Ford and this type of transmission is used today in conjunction with torque converters. Tricycles were responsible for certain concepts in steering geometry and for the differential gear.

Pioneer airplanes seem to be built from bicycle parts. For example, the Wright machine of 1903 employed bicycle chains, hangers, and seats. The structural principle of its wings was essentially that for bicycle wheels. Guy wires were rigged in tension against each other and braces.

This indebtedness to bicycle technology was not accidental. Many of the men associated with the development of powered vehicles had been involved in the bicycle trade. The Wright's bicycle shop supported their experiments with heavier-than-air flight. Glen Curtiss had been trained as a bicycle mechanic and, after work with aircraft powerplants, combined both skills to build the world's most powerful motorcycle. Henry Ford, R.E. Olds, Charles Duryea, William Morris, George N. Pierce, and H.A. Lozier made the transition from bicycle manufacturer to automobile builder. Colonel Pope and the Starley family did likewise. Firms which supplied accessories and cycle parts often succeeded in doing the same for autos. Perhaps the most famous of these is Joseph Lucas Ltd., that continues today as a major builder of automotive electrical equipment. Coventry, once a center of British bicycle production, is now the British equivalent of Detroit.

THE BICYCLE TODAY

In 1960, 3.7 million bikes were sold in this country. Ten years later the figure almost doubled to 7 million. In 1973 sales hit an unprecedented 15.3 million. 1972 was a milestone year—for the first time since 1897 bikes outsold automobiles.

In the summer of '71 AMF had four times the orders it could fill. Bicycle demand exceeded all American and European production capacity by a factor of three. Schwinn worked a 17-hour shift.

No one is quite certain what caused the bicycle boom or why it was timed to go off in the early and middle '60s. Some theories have been advanced, one of the most popular being that bicycling is a kind of counter-culture thing, akin to long hair and faded jeans. Most other counter-culture values were being accepted by the dominant culture, so it was not surprising that the bicycle became a kind of status symbol connoting that its owner was an aware, alert, living human being.

Another possible reason was the concern with cardio-vascular disease by the federal government and by the media. Circulation problems were identified as the major killer of Americans, accounting for more than half the deaths in 1968. Dr. Paul Dudley White and other authorities argued that moderate, regular exercise could reduce this toll.

At the same time the automobile was under concerted attack—the first it had faced in its 75-year history. Environmentalists pointed to the sociological costs of the automobile and consumer groups wondered where the quality had gone. The attack was telling enough for Henry Ford III to publically lament the end of the love affair between Americans and their cars.

Bike use was given additional impetus by the recent fuel shortage. However, it appears that the halycon days are over. The fad has passed and those who wish to be current will have to do something else. In addition bike prices have hit the stratosphere. Only a few years ago, the Schwinn Paramount sold for $250. Today it goes for $540. Other brands show even steeper markups. These price increases have not been accompanied by increases in quality.

But most people who have thought about the question feel that the bike is here to stay; it has become an integral part of a way of life for several million people who use a bicycle for serious transportation and recreation. And there has been at least some social response to this fact. The bike has been accepted by some city planners, the money is there for bikeways along the interstates, Amtrac and other carriers are making provision for bikes, and motorists don't seem quite as uptight as they used to be.

Bikes in the Urban Environment

The automobile is being challenged by the bicycle in the cities. While no one believes that like the monster in children's fables, the auto will be banished from the kingdom, its role will shrink.

The automobile, in its present proliferation, is a most dubious blessing. Nearly 50,000 Americans per year are killed in auto accidents and eight times as many suffer permanent injury. In 1970, the year of the EPA pollution index, autos generated some 1470 megatons of carbon monoxide, 195 megatons of hydrocarbons, and 117 megatons of various and sundry oxides of nitrogen. The cost of ownership per family has been conservatively estimated at $1800 a year per family. Other side effects, such as the disruption of urban living patterns, cannot be measured.

Mass transit offers hope for the future, but this hope is slow in being realized. Most existing rolling stock is worn out and new technologies have, for the present at least, been disappointing. BART is down every weekend while its technicians chase "bugs" in the computer; other systems do not seem to fare much better. The railroads, our best existing mass transit system, were described as "depressed" by Dr. Robert Nelson, chief of the federal Office of High Speed Ground Transportation. He ascribed this situation to the lack of resources and talent. "Bright young men have not gone into it."

And new systems, even granting technical viability, are slow in building. Metro is a typical example. Supposedly the system would involve some 38 miles of track in the District of Columbia and 60 miles in Virginia and Maryland. It was to be a one-shot proposal with a single investment from all parties. The fact is the system will require annual infusions of 100 million dollars for the next twenty years to defer construction and operating costs. As it stands now, Metro is less than half completed and the directors have little idea where the construction funds will be found.

Autos are impossible and mass transit flawed. What then is the answer to the transportation problem? Bicycles are at least part of it. Imagine that the bicycle was just invented. It would be hailed as the wonder of the age. A zero-pollution vehicle capable of burst speeds of up to 30 mph with an effective range of more than ten miles, and all of this in a package weighing 25 pounds and the cost averaging less than $200. The mechanism is simple enough so that most servicing can be done by the owner. And, with all of this, the bicycle is more adaptable than any other known vehicle. No tracks, monorails, or tunnels are needed. If necessary the operator can portage his bike up and down stairs and over obstacles that would stop anything short of a goat.

City authorities should embrace the bicycle as the hope of the century. A probike city council in Davis, California, has done just that. The mayor of Grenoble, France, has gone on record in support of bicycles as a prime means of transport and has banned motor vehicles from the central city. State and local groups have sponsored some probike legislation, perhaps most successfully in Oregon and most ambitiously in Illinois.

BIKEWAYS

The first modern bikeway was opened in Homestead, Florida, in 1962 as a "safety route" linking schools, shopping centers, playgrounds, and recreational areas in the city. (See Fig. 2-1 for bikeway nomenclature.) Other communities followed suit and today there are more than 15,000 miles of officially approved bikeways in this country. Dade County alone has more than 100 miles including bike routes through Miami. Colonial Williamsburg provides rental bikes and has banned autos from the main street. In the north, Ottawa has spent some three-quarters of a million dollars on bike paths through the suburban greenbelt.

The Federal Government is also responding to the need for bicycle facilities. The Park Service has established a series of campsites known as "hiker-biker overnighters" in areas under its jurisdiction. A string of overnighters connects Harper's Ferry, West Virginia, with Cumberland, Maryland. Bike

BIKE ROUTE

STREET OR HIGHWAY — PED WALK

UNPROTECTED BIKE LANE

STREET OR HIGHWAY — BIKE LANE — PED WALK

PROTECTED BIKE LANE

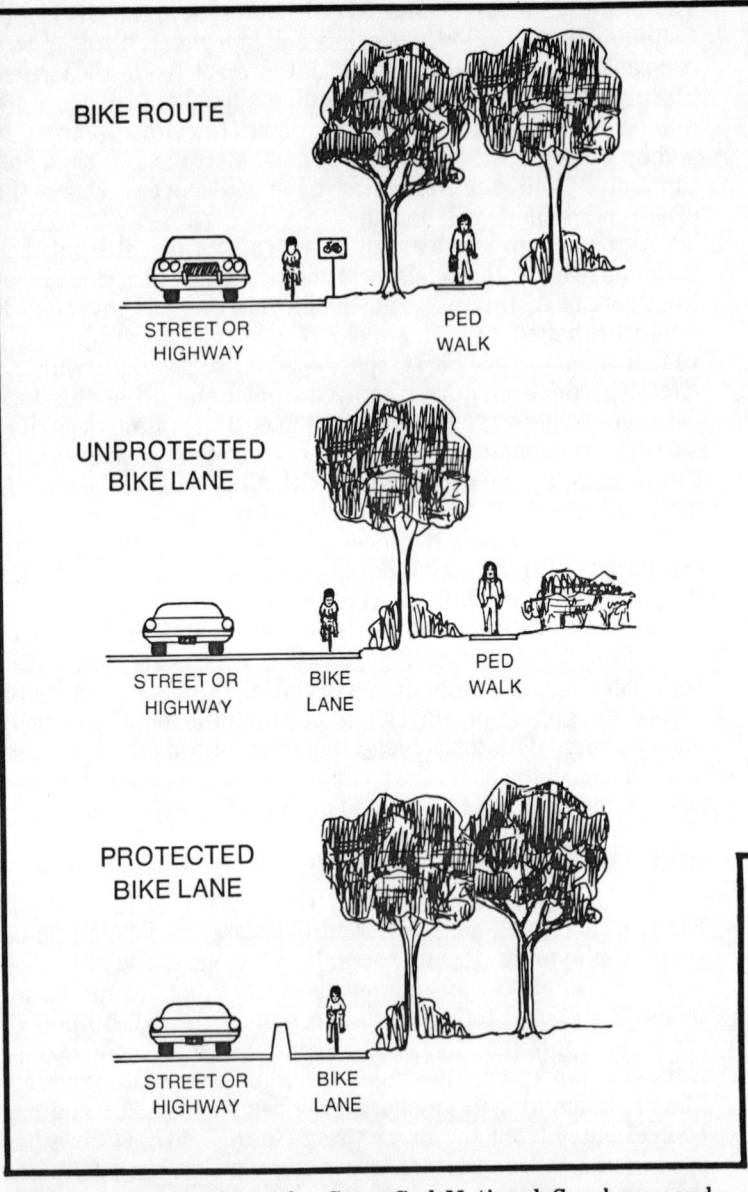

STREET OR HIGHWAY — BIKE LANE

routes are open along the Cape Cod National Seashore, and follow the mule path of the Chesapeake and Ohio Canal. The Federal Highway Act of 1973 allocated 120 million dollars for construction of bike paths flanking interstate highways. And the Environmental Protection Agency considers bicycles an integral part of its plan to clean up the air in major cities.

BIKE TRACK

STREET OR HIGHWAY · PED WALK · BIKE LANE

BIKE TRAIL OR PATH

Fig. 2-1. Bikeway nomenclature.

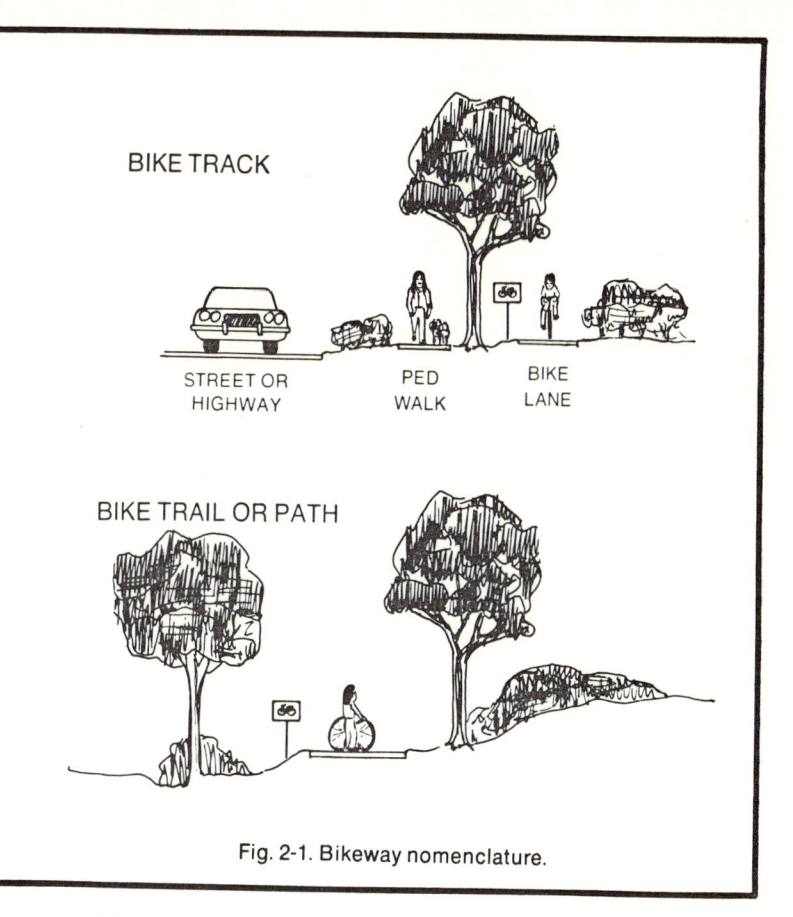

The interest in bikeways is heartening, and in light traffic the situation is all for the good. But much needs to be learned about the bicycle-auto nexus, particularly on city streets.

At one time it was believed that the bicycle could be integrated into urban life by constructing segregated bike lanes on the curb sides of city streets. All major cyclists' organizations and publications supported this strategy. The justifications were subjective and, to an extent, based upon research on bike accidents in Denmark and France. Studies showed that protected bike lanes reduced bike-related fatalities by almost half.

However, in the implementation of the study results, several problems were uncovered. First, there is the question of priority. Many cities simply cannot afford to strangle major arteries further than they have already been by the proliferation of motor vehicles. Building bike paths on the rights of way is expensive and in some cases impossible. Another problem and the locus of attack on the bikeway concept by men like John Forester and John Williams (former "bike czar" of San Luis Obispo) has been the original European studies. While these studies did show a decrease in fatalities, the cross-traffic fatalities actually went up a bit. Forester suggests that the reason for the slight increase in this category was European experience with bicycling. In the United States cross-traffic fatalites could be expected to increase dramatically if cyclists are usually segregated from the traffic flow.

Obviously a completely hermetic system of bikeways would solve the problem. But such a system is not possible until autos are restricted. Bikeways, no matter how extensive, begin and end at an auto traffic nexus. In practical terms the integrity of bikeways is further compromised by intersections and driveway accesses. Both of these intrusions are quite hazardous to the cyclist. He must, if confined to the right of the traffic stream, make illegal left-hand turns and is vulnerable to motorists making right-hand turns. Driveways are subject to less traffic, but half of it is during backing—the most dangerous mode of vehicle operation.

A study by the California Department of Public Safety indicates that a full 66% of bike fatalities occurred during these cross-lane interferences.

John V. Williams suggested a hierarchy of bikeways, graded in terms of safety:

- *bike trails:* ideal but impractical in heavily urbanized areas.
- *bike tracks* and *bike lanes*: segregated by markers or cordons are compromise solutions, neither as safe or as secure as they might appear.
- *marked bike routes*: the best solution—a system that allows the cyclist full use of the road, but is planned with a view toward minimum auto traffic and road debris.

As a footnote, Davis, California, "Home of 18,000 Bicyclists," tried protective bike lanes and abandoned them.

If the bicyclist is to be given a Magna Carta in the form of full and equal freedom to use downtown streets, he must be trained to cope with traffic. A recent study by the Institute of Highway Safety has shown that 78 percent of all bicycle/auto collisions were caused by the cyclist. This study was heavily weighted toward young riders. Almost 70 percent of those over 25 were victims of careless motorists.

PARKING

Convenient, secure parking is as important to urban commuters as access to the streets. Chicago has a privately-operated parking lot for cyclists. But in most cases the city will be charged with this responsibility. One approach is to weld U-brackets on the sidewalk side of parking meters. Large concentrations of bikes can best be stored in racks, and thought has been given to rack technology to reduce the possibility of theft. A particularly intriguing design is by the Patterson-Williams Co. of Santa Clara, CA. Marketed as the Bike Safe, this rack consists of an upright and paired steel arms. One arm is fixed and the other slides. The bike is sandwiched between the arms and locked. Studs prevent removal of the frame and wheels.

Bike racks should be located well clear of traffic lanes. In parking lots shared with automobiles, the racks should be buffered on concrete pedestals.

BIKES AND MASS TRANSIT

It's very desirable to make space for bicycles on buses and planes without inconveniencing other passengers. Airlines offer the least difficulty: most will gladly ship a bike if the handbars are turned and the pedals removed. BART allows bike riders during nonpeak hours. A limit of five bikes is carried in the last car of each train. An ID card ($3) is required as well as a brief pretrip inspection by BART police (to keep crud-covered bikes off the trains). The PATH system, connecting Newark, Jersey City, Hoboken, and New York City has a similar procedure. Bikes can be transported in the luggage cars of Amtrac trains.

Buses could be designed with bike-storage bays, although at this point trailers seem more practical. David M. Eggleston has made a study of the feasibility of bus trailers under the auspices of San Diego University and concludes that the idea has merit. At least one jitney service already has adopted the idea. Van and trailer combos carry cyclists to the beach area in Suffock County, L.I.

ACTION

Bicyclists are organizing to attain their goals and, for the most part, are doing so in very intelligent and effective ways. Morgan Groves, now Executive Vice President of the League of American Wheelmen, almost single handedly organized a Bike-to-Work Day for Dallas. He sent a memo to his boss, suggesting that the building superintendent be asked to provide parking for bikes. His boss responded suggesting that he uses his energies more constructively. Groves was not easily deterred, and after a long bike ride came up with the idea of a city-wide promotion to make Dallas aware of the existence of bike commuters and to publicize bikes as an available alternative to gas-guzzlers.

Groves and his friends enlisted the cooperation of the mayor, local organizations, traffic officials, and the media. The mayor led the caravan through the downtown district with a police motorcycle escort and full news coverage by the local TV stations. As Groves is quick to point out, nothing spectacular happened. Dallas went on as usual, with as many autos on the streets as before. But it was a beginning. The downtown YMCA arranged parking facilities and the city traffic department surveyed the interest in bikes. Cyclists were at least on the map in Dallas.

Things took a slightly different turn in New York City. Former Mayor John V. Lindsay led a bike caravan to dramatize the ecological potential of the bicycle. In the euphoria of the event, he announced that the city would establish experimental bike lanes. However, a year passed and nothing happened. In the interim, four riders were killed on New York streets.

Harriet Green and her husband, Barry Fishman, hadn't forgotten the mayor's promise. And they did something about it. Ms. Green became an expert on bicycling and the urban environment. Soon she was being interviewed on the local TV talk shows and by the newspapers. Her husband led a small group of riders once a week from Central Park to their offices to demonstrate that cyclists were here to stay. The couple organized a broad movement known as Bike for a Better city, and promised a rally in Central Park on the first anniversary of Lindsay's well-televised bike ride.

Approximately 300 cyclists showed up amid TV sound trucks and newspaper reporters. Ms. Green explained the position of BBC and their disappointment at the Mayor's hollow pronouncements. He was not on hand for this demonstration. On a signal the cyclists massed and rode to City Hall where they were met by one of Lindsay's aides, who had expected a petition. Instead he found himself listening to a prepared statement and subject to a polite, but edged, cross-examination. He made another promise, this time reassuringly vague and left the stage with the frowning look politicians have when their organizations begin to flake.

Both of these actions—one soft, tinged with humor and fellowship, the other with a bit of implacability in it—show the politicians that there is already a cycling constituency that hopes to be increasingly recognized by the public.

The Texas Cycling Committee, led by John Gaynor of Houston, has used these and other techniques. It is an umbrella group with a nucleus of University of Texas students, representatives from a variety of bike clubs and with some shop-owner participation. They see themselves as a legislative lobby and as a clearing house for information concerning cyclists.

TCC is a new organization, but has already met with some success. For example, they have obtained equal rights for cyclists at Garner State Park (previously one could be fined for carrying a bicycle through this monument to a politician) and have quelched a move by the city of Austin to prevent cyclists from using the city streets.

The TCC is pushing three bills in the state legislature. One is to overthrow the ban on bicycle racing. The current law prohibits "contests of speed, acceleration, or physical endurance" on state roads by drivers of vehicles. Trial law has expanded this statute to include cyclists. The second is the current law concerning bicycle registration, similar to most states. Cities are allowed to enact ordinances in the matter and are charged with keeping the records. Obviously this is insufficient. The TCC wants statewide registration with the Department of Public Safety keeping the records and issuing the license indicia. All new bikes sold in Texas would have serial numbers stamped on the frame by the manufacturer. The licensing requirement would be a matter of city or county option. If such ordinances were enacted on the local level, all bikes in the jurisdiction would have their serial numbers recorded and license indicia affixed. Altering either of these numbers or knowing possession of a bike so altered would be a misdemeanor, punishable by a $1000 fine, a year in jail, or both.

The third and major goal of the TCC's legislative reforms is to enact the Bikeway Fund bill. The state has not applied for federal monies for bikeway construction, even though these funds are available through the Federal-Aid Highway Act of 1971. The reason for this reluctance is that money spent on bikeways would be subtracted from grants for highway projects.

The Bikeway Fund Bill would establish a $5 million annual allocation for building bikeways throughout the state. All classes of bike thoroughfares are included in the term *bikeway*—bike routes, lanes, tracts and trails. Three broad classes of users would get priority:

- students and faculty at public schools and state-supported universities

- commuters and shoppers on their way to community and recreational centers
- families and riders of all abilities touring scenic areas

Scenic and recreational bikeways would be unpaved and of indeterminate length or paved and at least 20 miles long.

The state Highway Department would administer the program and establish standards for bikeway construction. It would have authority to accept funds from private sources for the construction of bikeways and to purchase land. The Highway Department would have condemnation powers. A somewhat similar law has been passed in Oregon. One percent of the state's highway funds is allocated for bicycle and hiking trails.

The activities of the Philadelphia Bicycle Coalition are legion. They lobby—both the Philadelphia City Council and the legislators in Harrisburg—pass on information through their breezy and always pertinent newsletter *Bike On!*, work with organizations that share similar goals such as Zero Automobile Growth and the Pennsylvania Alliance for Returnable Containers (fewer no-deposits, no-returns mean fewer flats), conduct bike repair and urban riding classes, and somehow seem to have a lot of fun. Recently PBC has published a bicycle map of the city showing the best and most direct bike routes. Two categories are included in the map: *preferred* and *preferred but difficult*. The former are those which bear little traffic (or are wide enough to accommodate bikes), are relatively litter-free, and direct. The preferred but difficult routes are traffic- and fume-ridden, but included for the sake of mobility. The map also indicates parks on the routes and major bike shops. Another map is coming soon which will include the Philadelphia suburbs as well as routes to Camden. A monthy regional cycling magazine called *Bike Power* is the offing.

The League of American Wheelmen has suffered all the vicissitudes of bicycling in this country. They fought the battle to open the roads to cyclists, and in the 1880s were the strongest voice for better roads. By 1898 LAW membership had grown to 102,636. Then the bike boom collapsed. Four short years later League membership fell to 8,629 and continued to slide until the early 1940s. War brought a brief resurgence to bicycling, but the movement crumpled as soon as the veterans were demobilized. The last national convention was held in 1955, and there the LAW voted to end its existence.

But a few Wheelmen didn't forget and in 1964 a reunion hosted by Joe Hart in Chicago resulted in the rebirth of the organization. Every year since 1965 has seen a LAW convention—now called Roundups—in different parts of the country. Membership has grown apace with cycling and by 1973 counted 10,000 cyclists from all 50 states.

As befits a national organization, the LAW is interested in the broad aspects of cycling. Their program—the LAW calls it their platform—includes:

- comprehensive cycling education in the schools, stressing safety and emphasizing that the bike is a *vehicle*
- education of motorists and pedestrians to make them more alert and responsive to the presence of cyclists on the road
- efforts to encourage touring by bike as well as tour-planning assistance and the creation of a net of cycle routes across the continent
- comprehensive program for urban cycling. The bicycle must be included in transportation planning. This means street maintenance, provision for bike facilities in areas such as bridges and narrow overpasses, parking and security facilities, and encouragement of transit companies to carry commuters' bicycles
- efforts to convince manufacturers to build utility bikes capable of carrying heavy loads under a variety of weather and lighting conditions
- continuing practical and technical information for members through the LAW Bulletin

3

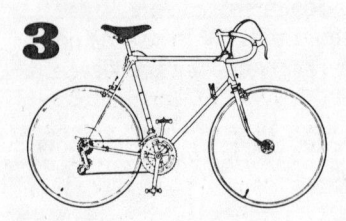

The Heart of the Matter

In 1967 cardiovascular diseases—diseases of the circulatory system—were responsible for 46.2 percent of worldwide deaths. In this category heart disease accounted for 22.3 percent of deaths. Cancer ran a poor second with 15.2 percent. The same tabulation, prepared by the World Health Organization indicates that cardiovascular diseases are increasing in frequency, and striking earlier. WHO terms them "the worst epidemic mankind has ever faced." Sir William Ostler (1849-1919) was one of the most capable diagnosticians of his age. Among the many thousands of patients he examined, he met only a handful of cases of angina pectoris, an ailment which every doctor is depressingly familiar with today.

The primary problem is the narrowing of the coronary arteries that supply blood to the heart. In nearly all of these cases the restriction is due to atherosclerosis, a general disease of the large arteries. The disease has a strong predilection for those arteries in the coronary tree. While the exact cause of atherosclerosis is unknown, its progress is quite well understood.

Over the years the arteries collect streaks (plaques) of fatty matter, particularly at the branches where the direction of blood flow is interrupted. These plaques have a tendency to cluster and develop by slow accumulation. The system compensates in part and can even grow alternate supply routes to get oxygen to the heart muscle. But, as is so often the case, the rate of fat deposit increases beyond the ability of the system to correct. The artery narrows dangerously. Blood supply may slow and stop as a direct result of the fatty obstruction, or a small clot may block the narrowed artery. The result is coronary thrombosis—the classic heart attack.

Contrary to popular belief, exertion is not in itself a major immediate cause of heart attacks. Only about five percent of heart attacks are triggered by sudden strain. Indeed, 50% of the victims are stricken while asleep in bed. Other diseases, particularly those associated with the respiratory system, and surgical shock may initiate the attack, as well as a heavy meal or violent emotion. More predictive factors, in part because they can be relatively easily controlled, are high blood pressure, obesity, diabetes, and cigarette smoking.

It has been found that atherosclerosis is particularly prevalent in industrialized countries such as the United States and parts of the Soviet Union. American men under 65 are twice as likely to die of a heart attack than men living in Norway and Sweden. Coronary atherosclerosis is responsible for more than half the deaths in the United States and the loss of over 1 million work days a year. The toll is almost as high in Germany.

Genetic factors seem to be important to the likelihood of one falling victim to the disease. Certain families have a high-risk history in this regard. High blood pressure is also a predisposing factor—some 25 percent of the men with coronary heart disease and half of the women so afflicted suffer elevated levels of blood pressure. Diabetes is another fellow traveler, and can produce complications in fat production. Many people would be better off if they avoided sucrose and dextrose.

Most physicians believe that atherosclerosis is, to one degree or another, associated with high cholesterol levels, although data is sometimes contradictory. But patients who already have the disease show higher than average cholesterol counts.

Obesity has also been identified as a contributing factor to the development of atherosclerosis and to early heart attacks. Studies have shown that deaths from cardiovascular disease are twice as frequent among the overweight.

Occupational factors also seem to be important. A study carried out by the Myasnikov Institute of Cardiology determined that of 200,000 workers in Moscow, high blood pressure was found most frequently among engineers, supervisory personnel, and technicians as compared to shop personnel who had limited and well-defined responsibilities. Noise and vibration in the work place also predispose toward high blood pressure: bus and taxi drivers are especially affected.

THE DUBLIN STUDY

The Harvard School of Public Health and the School of Medicine, Trinity College, Dublin released a joint report on the causes of heart disease in the closing months of 1970. No other investigation has been so extensive and so effectively rules out genetic variables.

Cardiologists, nutritionists, and other specialists from both schools located 570 pairs of brothers, half of whom had remained home in Ireland while the others emigrated to the Boston area. These men were from 30 to 65 years of age and all had lived in Ireland during their adolescent years. The reason for immigration seemed entirely a function of economic circumstances and chance. There was no discernable "immigrant personality" to cloud the test results.

To reduce further the possibility of experimental error, control groups were set up on both sides of the Atlantic. Reports of autopsies performed in Boston and Dublin were tabulated, with particular regard for evidences of atherosclerosis.

Each brother was studied in terms of the amount of exercise he engaged in, the amount and kinds of food he ate (with particular attention to the cholesterol intake), and in terms of his physical condition. The major emphasis was, of course, upon the cardiovascular system. Nearly every test known was administered to the heart and arteries.

The results? Post-mortem examinations showed that Irish hearts were, on the average, decades "younger" than American hearts. And comparative examinations of the living brothers showed that those who remained in Ireland had hearts that were twice and even six times healthier than those who had emigrated. Irish brothers also had lower blood pressure and lower cholesterol counts.

The latter finding was remarkable since the rural Irish diet is exceptionally high in butter, cheeses, meat, eggs, and other sources of saturated fats. And the Irish were thinner, even though they consumed significantly more calories a day than their American counterparts.

While heavy consumption of alcohol has been shown to be a critical factor in the development of heart disease, alcohol was of less importance in this study. Both American and Irish brothers drank about the same amount, although the Americans favored hard liquor over warm beer and ale. Smoking also seemed to be of lesser significance. The Irish did not smoke as much as Americans, perhaps for economic reasons. But smoking was common.

Stress is very difficult to evaluate since no one has been able to measure stress with scientific exactitude. Most of the American group were city dwellers and subject to the assaults of an urban environment. The Irish were predominately rural. But both groups found themselves having to work for a living. The Irish workday in the countryside is almost medieval, with 14 and 16 hour days not uncommon in the summer months. Vacations, sick leave, and other amenities which one would suppose reduces stress, are arranged informally, if at all.

Coffee drinking had recently been associated with coronary disease, and this is one habit which is almost entirely the province of Americans. The Irish drink tea, which conceivably could reduce the tendency for arterial deposits.

But the real difference, according to Dr. Fredrick J. Stare of Harvard who cochaired the study with Dr. W.J.E. Jessop of Trinity, is the high level physical activity of the Irish. On the basis of this study it would seem that physical activity is the major preventive medicine for coronary disease.

Most medical experts agree that physical activity is important, although the emphasis given to this and other predisposing factors—cigarette smoking, diet, high blood pressure, stress, and diabetes—varies with the study and, to some extent, with the locale. One of the many anomalies in this field is the high rate of coronary disease in parts of Finland. Again, middle-aged men are the primary victims, although the population is very active, generally lean, and aware of dietary and other risk factors. But exercise is the one active measure we can take against heart attacks and other side effects of aging.

THE MISSING INGREDIENT

The President's Council on Physical Fitness and Sports estimates that some 50 million Americans live a completely sedentary life with no real physical activity from the time they leave school. Theodore G. Klumpp, consultant for the Council, identifies much of the current coronary epidemic as caused by the replacement of food and related physical activity as the central source of energy. This has developed in the United States as perhaps in no other country in the world. Machines have invaded every sphere of activity from harvesting crops to playing golf. The automobile has almost completely displaced walking, even for distances of a city block or less. And the evolution of the automobile has been consistently toward less muscular effort—power steering, power brakes, automatic transmissions, and the like have measurably reduced the caloric output of automobile drivers. Heavy labor, labor of the kind that Adam was cursed and blessed with, has become an anachronism. Few of us still earn our bread by the sweat of our "faces" as the Hebrew has it. And, of course, this same tendency for physical inertia affects the children as well. One third of American boys and girls are estimated to be overweight. And of a random sample of 12 year old boys, nearly a third could not perform a single pull-up.

While Americans at all age levels are growing taller, we are also growing broader of beam. To accommodate this, theater seats are wider than they were at the turn of the century and the Air Force has recently had to broaden the seats in its jet fighters for our rotund pilots.

Exercise Programs

In recent years, doctors practicing in technologically developed parts of the world have given a great deal of attention to the need for exercise. Because of the urgency of the matter and because most human beings work better in groups, the emphasis has been on developing programs. The nature of these programs varies from the Chinese habit of massed calisthenics on apartment roofs in Peking to Soviet physical culture organizations. These have a claimed membership of 50 million people, or more than one quarter of the population. Industrial plants are often operated in conjunction with a preventorium program. Workers may spend from four to six weeks there under the supervision of medical personnel who examine the patient, with particular attention to the detection of cardiovascular diseases, and prescribe treatment which often involves strenuous physical exercise. The Vita Parcours program has spread throughout most of Europe. Vita Parcours (in loose translation, "the racecourse of life") is simple and logical, requiring very little in the way of trained personnel or physical facilities. A short jogging track is laid out with areas for group calisthenics. The participants exercise and, at frequent intervals, monitor their heart beats. A rate of 160 beats per minute is considered maximum. Switzerland, the country of origin, has nearly 200 Vita Parcours installations and is building more.

In the United States the President's Council on Physical Fitness and Sports promotes efforts at improving the physical condition of the population by means of publicity, research, and information sharing. The most comprehensive programs are organized and supported by the YMCA, and include those which aim at generalized fitness as well as the "Run For Your

Life" and other single-activity programs. That YMCA programs work was documented by Dr. Lenore Zohman, cardiologist at Montefiore Hospital, New York City. Patients who had already suffered one heart attack were encouraged to volunteer for a carefully designed regimen of exercise. Dr. Zohman stress tested heart functions with the aid of a stationary bicycle before the program commenced and repeated the tests at intervals. For those who continued to take part, heart functions showed definite improvement. The best news was that only two out of the 38 cardiac patients suffered a second attack during the first year. Statistically, five should have.

Dr. Kenneth Cooper has published two popular books on exercise. The first volume *Aerobics* discusses the motivation and the techniques used to design the program; the second, *New Aerobics*, expands the concept to include most forms of physical activity. Dr. Cooper's approach to the subject is rigorously scientific and has been tested in repeated experiments. As such it is more convincing than those programs designed from anecdotal or experimental information.

The basic concept can be paraphrased as this: the efficiency of the human engine depends, in the final analysis, upon its ability to use oxygen. Exercise will demonstrably increase the level of oxygen consumption and at the same time improve circulation. But the kind of exercise is important. Early in his researches Dr. Cooper found that mere exercise is not enough. Men which had histories of jogging three miles a day would be in very different physical condition. The rate of work is as important as the amount of work.

Aerobics is based on a point system. After the individual is in reasonable physical condition—calculated by the time required to run a mile—he or she should make 30 points a week. Various exercises can be used to meet the quota. The most efficient in terms of time spent is running, followed by swimming and bicycling.

A 20-mile bike ride has these point values:

TIME	POINTS
2 hrs plus	13
1 hr 59:59 to 1 hr 20 min	18 1/2
1 hr 19:59 min to 1 hr	28 1/2
less than 1 hr	38 1/2

What Exercise Can Do

Exercise, done correctly and faithfully, can make profound changes in the individual. These changes can even involve the personality structure but are most marked in the circulatory and respiratory systems.

Circulatory System. At one time doctors believed in a phenomenon called *athlete's heart* and considered it a predisposition toward disease. What they had seen was the large, slowly beating heart typical of athletes. The heart is a muscle and responds to exercise by growing larger and stronger. Most medical opinion today is that a heart which has enlarged due to physical activity and not some other cause is healthy and should function longer, simply because it works less. The typical heart beat of 70 a minute means that the heart contracts and relaxes 100,000 times a day, 36 million times a year. Any reduction in its rate is welcomed if only to lessen the wear and tear on the pump. It has been reported that Eddy Merckx, Tour of France winner in 1969, '70, and '71, is endowed with a heart that beats no more than 60 times a minute under racing conditions and 40 times a minute at rest.

In addition to making the heart stronger, exercise will open the major arteries and help relax the walls for a lower level of blood pressure. And exercise will actually cause additional arteries to branch from the coronary tree. The leg muscles, as Doctor Paul Dudley White pointed out some years ago, assist in circulation by forcing the blood up and against the pull of gravity. Exercises like cycling and jogging will strengthen these muscles and reduce the load on the heart by a very significant amount.

Respiration. It is a well established fact that vigorous exercise will improve the quality of respiration, both in terms of raw oxygen consumption and in terms of the muscular effort needed to operate the lungs. Dr. Henry Bass of Boston demonstrated this quite convincingly with patients suffering from chronic bronchitis, emphysema, and other lung blocking disorders. He had his patients exercise on a stationary bicycle for ten minutes, three times a day, for 18 weeks. The results were carefully tabulated: improvements in heart rates, oxygen consumption, and carbon dioxide production. To return to Eddy Merckx, his lung capacity measures between six and seven liters. The average is no more than five liters.

Weight Loss. One of the quickest ways to get rich in the United States is to write a book telling people how to painlessly lose weight. Dr. Herman Taller published his immensely successful *Calories Don't Count* in 1961. But six years later, a federal jury found him guilty of violations of Food and Drug Administration regulations, conspiracy, and mail fraud. The ancient Romans guarded their waistlines with vomitoriums—after a meal they simply regurgitated. More modern techniques have involved the use of appetite depressents such as Dexedrine or canned meals such as Metrecal.

The advantages of reducing are many. Insurance company statistics—which are comprehensive and available, but which can be faulted—show that men who are 10 percent overweight have a 13 percent higher mortality rate than their thinner fellows. Those who are 30 percent overweight have a 42 percent greater mortality rate. High blood pressure, often the prelude to irreversible circulatory difficulties, is closely associated with excess body fat and, in many cases, drops markedly with a loss of weight. Obesity also seems to be a precondition or a predisposing condition for some forms of diabetes.

Studies have shown that fat people are at a disadvantage in the American business world. They are subject to a low-level, but pervasive kind of discrimination that translates into less job security, fewer promotions, and lower pay. Indeed certain executive placement agencies will not deal with a job hunter who is markedly overweight as a matter of policy. In other cultures and in other times fat people were considered sexually attractive. Titian's bevy of women were both obese (by contemporary standards) and intended to be erotically exciting. Hamlet was a kind of ideal Renaissance hero—lover, scholar, swordsman, thinker, soldier—and at one point in the play describes himself as "fat." The passage is dropped in modern productions because of the incongruity of a fat hero to twentieth century audiences. William Conrad, who has probably done more for the image of fat people in his former TV series *Cannon* than anyone else since President Taft, is careful not to overstep the boundaries. His interest in the girls on the show is best described as fatherly.

The great majority of people who are fat are so for one reason—caloric input exceeds output. The body is a kind of very sophisticated heat engine which burns food instead of coal or gasoline. Surplus fuel is stored in the form of fat and is used to power the muscles. To lose weight, one must reduce fuel consumption or increase muscular output.

The average American takes in 3500 calories a day and burns only 2600 of these calories. The rest turn to fat. Exercise, particularly those exercises which engage the major muscle systems, can result in a weight loss. Jogging, swimming, and cycling are three of the best. Cycling has unique advantages.

CONDITIONING METHODS

The bicycle is first of all a vehicle with utilitarian purposes. It can be used for commuting, touring, and running errands as well as a calorie burner. The machine and the exercise it entails tend to become integrated into one's life. There is positive reinforcement, as the learning psychologists say, between these utilitarian rides and training sessions. One senses in a very tangible and practical way improvements in physical conditioning. Swimming and jogging tend to remain isolated from the other activities of life.

Swimming and jogging are basically repetitious exercises involving laps on a closed circuit. In theory, at least, one could jog anywhere. In practice, most joggers pick a course and stay with it because they sense that decisions and variations of the routine would compromise the program. This syndrome does not apply to bicyclists. One feels free to ride anywhere, trusting to the watch and cyclometer to keep tabs on the energy expended.

Bicycling is more oriented toward group activity than most other forms of non-competitive exercise. One has time and leisure to talk with other cyclists on the road, and the mutual dependence upon the machine encourages dependence upon each other's skills and abilities. Most people prefer group physical endeavor and are more successful training in a group than they would be by themselves.

Bicycling burns calories at a surprising rate. Tests conducted by the American Medical Association on a respiration calorimeter indicate that maintaining a 13 mph speed over flat ground consumes 660 calories an hour. Consumption increases sharply with velocity. A touring cyclist can burn 6000 calories a day, equivalent to nearly two pounds of body fat.

THE PSYCHOLOGY OF HEALTH

Exercise has certain psychological effects as well. While these effects are difficult to document—we are, after all, dealing with states of mind and not measurable qualities such as oxygen consumption rates—they are well known. The ancients were very much aware of the mind-body connection. Greek folk wisdom identified a healthy body with a healthy mind and vice versa. Plato discussed the brutalizing effects of a one-sided education in athletics. He had been an Olympic champion in his youth and had first hand knowledge of the subject.

The military has been very much aware of the need to physically condition men in order to make them brave. Some of Emperor Hadrian's edicts concerning the indulgent life enjoyed by garrison troops on the Rhine say as much. Marine D. I.'s seem to have the same opinion and insist that a recruit is not a Marine until he had, among other things, done 3000 pushups. As everyone who has gone through basic training knows, the psychological results are profound. But until recently there has been little objective research in the area.

A.C. Werner and Edward G. Cottheil compared athletes at West Point with other cadets and found the athletes to be more sophisticated, dominate, sociable, self-sufficient, and tough-minded. Thomas K. Cureton and William Heusner studied Olympic medalists and perceived a similar pattern. The conclusions of a third study by Walter Kroll, Gordon Cooper, et al, tended to collaborate the other two in very broad outline.

A.H. Ismail and L.E. Trachtman took part in an experiment at Purdue that is of interest to anyone who would like to get into condition. The results were published in *Psychology Today* (March, 1973) under the title "Jogging the Imagination."

Sixty middle-aged men—college professors, administrators, counselors, and the like—all associated with the University and all having sedentary jobs volunteered for the program. Careful physical examinations were given before and during the course of the program. Fat metabolism processes, cholesterol levels, blood-serum acidity, and other data were charted and recorded. The men met three times a week for 1 1/2 hours and were run hard. At the start only a few could run 1/4 mile. Ten months later these same men were running three and even five miles. The authors' describe the training as "grueling."

The usual physical benefits of systematic exercise were realized—the men grew thinner and, from a cardiovascular point of view, healthier. But the psychological changes were profound. The experimenters identified these changes with the aid of Raymond Cattell's 16 Personality Factor Test. The test rates 16 personality traits on a ten-point scale. The traits are fixed with opposing pairs of adjectives, e.g., "tough minded—sensitive," "self-assured—guilt prone,""expedient—conscientious."

Two subgroups were formed, one containing the most physically fit and the other the least fit. Initially the high-fitness group had high scores in the areas of self-assurance and imagination. By the end of the program the least fit had increased their scores on imagination and were more self-sufficient (insofar as a trait reflects an actual quality) than the high-fitness group. Before long the experimenters were able to analyze the scores on four personality traits and determine with good accuracy the man's physical condition! The most important determinate was the degree of self-assurance. Those who had generous amounts of this trait would tend to do well in terms of exercise heart rate, maximal oxygen intake, and other objective criteria of physical condition. The next most important determinant was imaginativeness. Persons with high scores on this trait tended to be physically fit as well as enthusiatic about ideas, absorbed in inner constructs, and, alas, accident prone. In addition, the high-fitness group scored high in emotional stability, which seems to be the most critical factor in the study. Lack of emotional stability is associated, to one degree or another, with various personality disorders although in itself it is not a sign of disorder. The low-fitness group did not do so well initially in terms of this trait. But by the time the conditioning program had finished, the low-fitness group scored as well as the high-fitness group.

One disconcerting aspect of the experiment was that as the low fitness group became physically fit, their level of guilt increased. The researchers suspect that this is because the group recognized that they were still far from top condition, or that the time taken for the exercise regimen reduced their work accomplishments. It could be supposed that the high-fitness group had long before adjusted to the need for exercise time.

HOW TO GET STARTED

Before one undertakes a physical fitness program it is only common sense to have a thorough physical examination. Older people or people who suspect that they might have a coronary irregularity should go to a specialist for an ECG under stress, and other sophisticated tests.

But mere age is no barrier. One of the most convincing proofs of this is Ed "Foxy Grandpa" Delano, the 70-year-old bicycle racer from Vacaville, California. He set a record at the Asti 100 in 1972, covering 107 miles in six hours in the rain. His average speed approached that of men 20 years younger. For four straight years he has earned gold medals at the Senior Olympics.

Whatever your program, whether it is part of a group effort, or based on Aerobics or one of the other published plans or simply a resolution to cycle so many miles a week, it should be consistent with your fitness. The secret of exercise is not to drive yourself to exhaustion or to frustration with impossible goals. Work at the program systematically, only increasing distance or average speed as you are sure you can handle it. Three times a week is a good minimum, but the exercise days should be spaced out evenly. Try to work for at least 45 minutes during each period.

The big difficulty is sticking to a program. It helps to train with a group, but if that is not possible, at least keep a record of your mileage and times. The record itself becomes a kind of structural imperative to get you out of the house on those wintry evenings. And keep after it. Exercise can save your life.

4

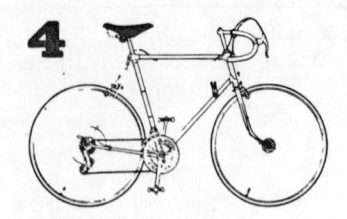

Touring

Touring by bicycle is not everyone's cup of tea, and certainly not for those who measure their progress in miles traveled per day. On a bike tour the journey itself is the greater part of the goal. Perhaps these feelings are best summed up in a letter to the author from Mr. Ed Arszman, Coordinator for Zero Automobile Growth. While stressing that ZAG is not, per se, a bicycle organization, Ed has this to say about two-wheelers:

> The bicycle is after all an *experience-oriented* vehicle. Pedaling it gives one a sense of the energy costs involved in movement...and a very intimate *feel* of the terrain, the place one is passing through. We bicycle because bicycling, more than any other mode of transit, gives us a true and very genuine sense of movement...a sense of actually moving.

Add to this the awareness of nature, the sense of self-sufficiency and accomplishment in breaking free of internal combustion and most of the other niceties of civilization, the honest fatigue of a body well used, and we have some sense of what touring is about.

TOURING BIKES

Almost any bike can serve as a tourer. After all, Thomas Stevens rode 3700 miles across the United States on an ordinary in 1884. And at least one intrepid gentleman is reported to be doing the same on a unicycle. Until very recently, Europeans toured on three-speed utility bikes.

The Raleigh International shown in Fig. 4-1 is a good example of a basic, though somewhat light, touring machine.

Fig. 4-1. The Raleigh DL-170 International. A good lightweight tourer with 531 frame and fork, Weinmann center-pull brakes, Simplex derailleur, Campagnolo cotterless crank and hubs, Silca pump, and a Brooks saddle.

A tourer should have a wheelbase in the 42-in. range for ride, stability, and for the carrying space. A ten-speed derailleur with intelligent ratios is almost a must. Some tourists have gone to 12-speed or 15-speed sets. The extra plate or chainwheel spreads the range and, with the proper jiggling, can narrow the spread between gears for easier shifting. Unless the bike is really loaded, it will not be necessary to replace the wheels with heavier spokes or go to a cross-4 pattern. Accessories such as dynamo kits should have their brackets brazed on, rather than bolted. Use a pencil-tip flame and allow the frame to cool at its own rate in order to normalize the stresses. It is wise to treat fasteners with Loctite or the equivalent. These anaerobic adhesives are sometimes called chemical locknuts. A few drops on the thread holds the fastener securely, but not so tight that disassembly is impossible. Fenders should be fitted, unless you expect to do much back-country work—gumbo mud packs itself between the fenders and tires. Good-quality alloy rims are quite adequate and, in the very long run, may outlive steel which tends to rust at the crimps and fatigue at the spoke holes.

WHAT TO CARRY

The amount and kind of gear you need depends upon the length of the tour and upon what arrangements you make for

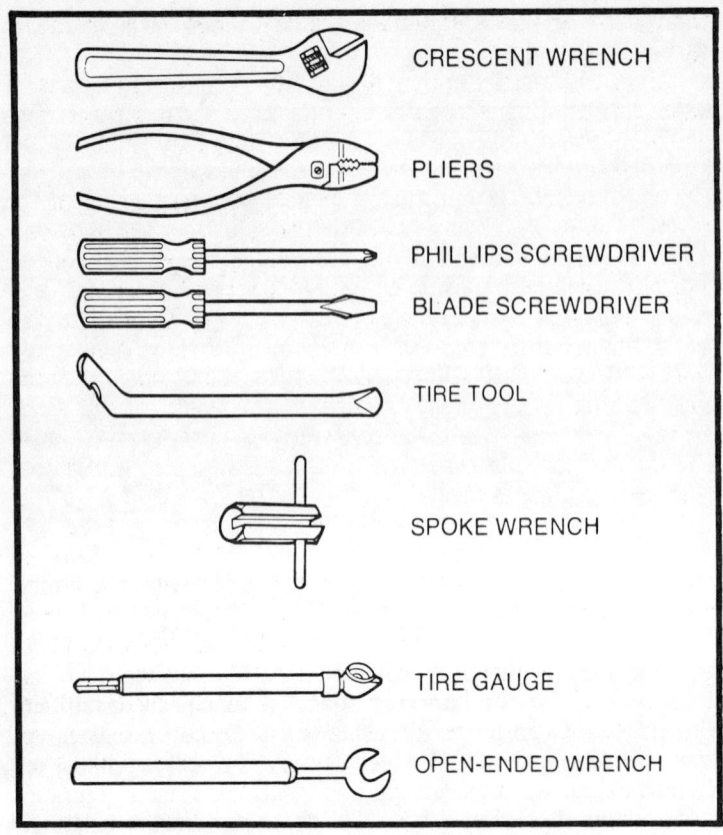

Fig. 4-2. A collection of tools for the cyclist. (Courtesy Mossberg)

eating and sleeping. But some equipment is essential for any tour. Your horse comes first and most specifically his shoes. Carry a spare tube (or several tubulars, tied in a figure eight behind the seat), two valve cores, tube-repair kit with fresh rubber cement, and the requisite tools. Some clinchers can be worked on and off the rim by hand, saving a few ounces in tools. Next in priority are control cables—usually the inner wires are enough—taped motorcycle fashion along the top tube. Night riding, not recommended, but sometimes necessary, means that you should carry a spare head and tail lamp bulbs. Some headlamp nacelles have dummy sockets for additional bulbs; if not it is a simple matter to tape the spares behind the reflector or to purchase a set of handlebar plugs with a recess for carrying extra bulbs. Nuts and bolts, selected to accommodate your bike, are a good investment as are several chain links. Three-speed people should carry spare indicator chain (Sturmey-Archer) or indicator lever

(Shimano). Spokes and nipples are best taped to the frame or carried in the pump.

Plus the tools mentioned you will need are tire tools, a blade and Phillips screwdrivers, pliers, a spoke wrench, tire gauge, appropriately sized open-ended wrenches (the stamped kind are the lightest and the handiest), backed up by a small Cresent wrench. In addition, you will need a rivet extractor even for bikes which have master-linked chains. The extractor and spare links will enable you to repair a broken chain on the side of the road. The insurance value is worth the weight.

An ounce or two of oil should be carried, primarily for use on the chain before each day's ride and after rain. Tool supply houses stock small squirt cans with capped spouts. Some cyclists manage to carry a tube of mechanic's soap since almost any repair entails greasy hands. This product, sold under various names in auto parts stores, is waterless, stainless, and wipes clean.

Another item which is worth its weight in portage is a flashlight. If space is a premium—and it always is on a tour of any length—the light can be mounted in a handlebar clamp and double as an emergency head lamp. By far the best type is one of the Coast Guard-approved waterproof types, although any flashlight, even a tiny penlight, is better than none.

You will also need a toothbrush, toothpaste, sun tan lotion, first aid kit, extra shirt, a change of underwear, and socks as well as miscellaneous toilet articles. And, if you are like most cyclists, a good supply of high-energy snacks.

Various carrying bags are available, from miniscale behind-the-seat pouches to woodsmen's back packs. Most experienced riders prefer the additional weight and sail effect to be on the back wheel and choose nylon pannier bags of the general type shown in Fig. 4-3. Smaller loads can be fit into a handlebar bag. The one pictured in Fig. 4-4 can be mounted to the bars or behind the seat. As a last resort you can get additional capacity with a frame mounted bag.

There is an art to packing. Frequently used bulky items, such as sleeping bags and shelters, should be on top. Emergency gear—first aid kits, wet weather togs, tools, maps and the like—should be readily accessible. All other items can be safely secured below, segregrated in individual baggies.

PLANNING

After you have determined your destination, the two most important factors are the routing and the weather. Road maps, available from tourist bureaus and oil companies, give an overall picture of the distances and major roads, but should

Fig. 4-3. Bike panniers. (Courtesy Gerry, a division of Outdoor Sports Industries)

be supplemented by more detailed, smaller scale maps. See Fig. 4-5 for a real trip.

The U.S. Geological Survey National Topographical Map Series is the best. As the title indicates, these quadrangles show the topography—the rise and fall of the terrain. This information is vital to a cyclist, particularly one who may be packing 35 pounds of gear. The most detailed is the 1:24,000 scale series. Limited in area to something on the average of 50 square miles, these quadrangles show every trail, stream, and outhouse. The 1:62,500 scale is the best choice for route planning. One inch equals slightly less than four miles. Each sheet covers an area of 5000-8000 square miles. The 1:1,000,000 series is for transcontinental voyagers. Further information can be had from the USGS, Washington, DC 20242. National Forests are mapped by the U.S. Coast and Geodetic Survey, Dept. of Commerce, Washington, DC. Information on touring Canada is available from the Canadian Government Travel Bureau, Ottawa, Canada K1A0H6.

In addition, you might look into the *North American Bike Atlas* which can be purchased from American Youth Hostels, 20 West 17th St., New York, NY 10011.

Other maps are available from state highway departments and from county and municipal governments. Privately printed maps showing points of historical and local interest are sometimes stocked by bookstores or can be purchased through the Chamber of Commerce.

The best time of the year to tour North America is in the fall. Guidebooks include basic information on climatic conditions. The most complete source is compiled by the National Oceanic and Atmospheric Administration. NOAA Climatological Data is available in large metropolitan libraries.

BIKEWAYS

Parts of the California Aqueduct Bikeway are open. When finished this bikeway will be the longest in the world—a 20-foot

Fig. 4-4. Bar or seat-mounted bag. (Courtesy Gerry, a division of Outdoor Sports Industries)

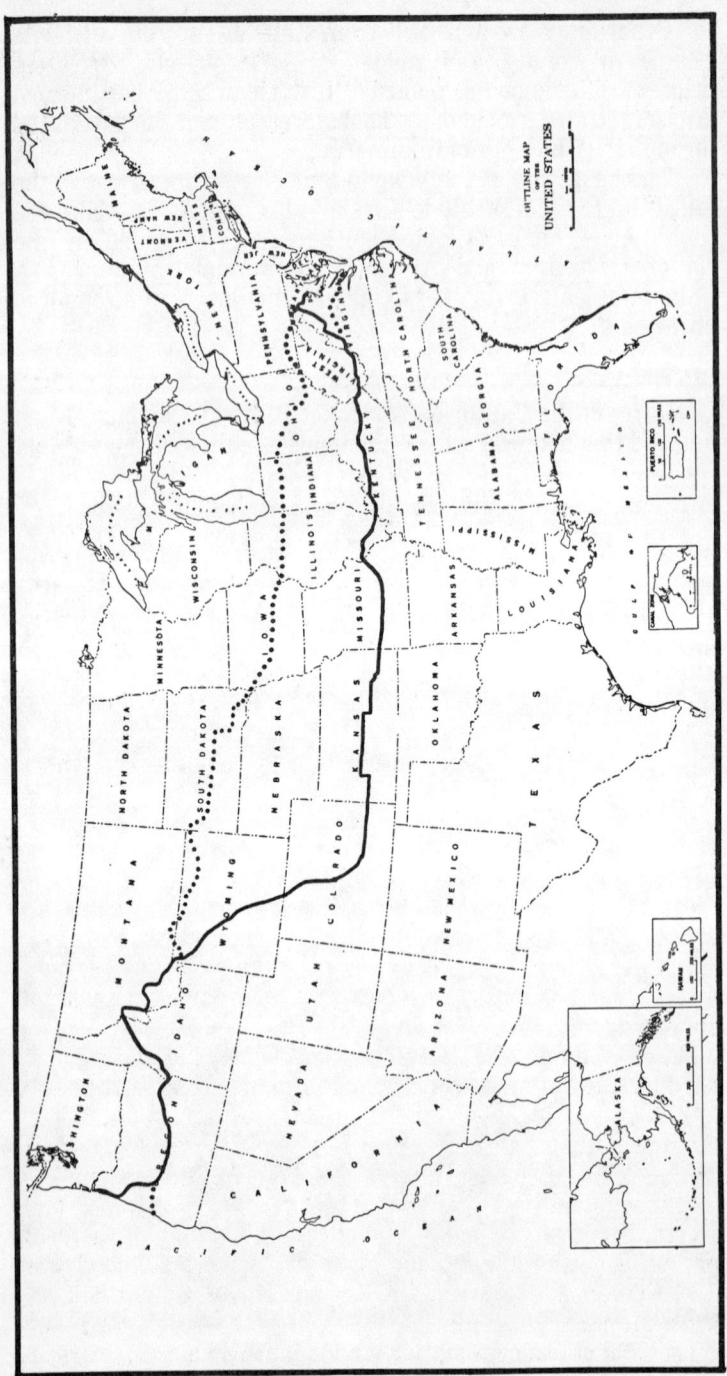

Fig. 4-5. Trans-America trail. The dotted lines show the northern alternative route, which is scheduled to open in 1978

wide swath of smooth asphalt stretching 444 miles up through the center of the state. An ingenious system of gates makes the bikeway secure from motorized vehicles. The route goes through some of the most scenic parts of California from the San Luis dam in the southern desert to the Bethany Reservoir in the north. Every few miles there are shaded rest stops with water and toilet facilities.

The Ohio bikeway from Mt. Gilead to McConnelsville will be open by the time this book is in print. Nearly all of the 100-mile route is isolated from auto traffic. The Chesapeake & Ohio Canal towpath is open to bikes and, while not up to modern roadbuilding standards, is a wonderful way to travel from Washington, DC to Cumberland, MD. The stone-paved road is flanked by camping and recreational facilities.

The ultimate trip is the 3700 Trans-America Bike Trail from Oregon to Virginia (Fig. 4-5). It has been chosen with a view toward negotiability and with emplasis upon our heritage. The route parallels or crosses many of the trails whose memory rings in history—the Continental Divide Trail, the Santa Fe Trail, the Chisholm Trail, the Trail of Tears—and lingers at places that have helped to form the national character. You will cross the Tetons, cycle over the Great Divide at Togwotee Pass, see the fabled Shenandoah Valley, and ride through the B & O tunnel that John Henry helped to build. Seventy-six days out of Fort Stephens, Oregon—terminus of the Lewis and Clark Expedition—trans-American cyclists will arrive in Jamestown, Virginia, the site of the first English colony in the New World. An alternate route follows the Shenandoah Valley, and along the banks of the Potomac to end in Washington, DC.

Individuals or organizations can take part. The whole trail can be negotiated or you may choose segments of it, including a number of loop trails. The first of these to be scouted is a 400-mile circuit around the Selway-Bitterroot Wilderness in Idaho and Montana.

Costs are nominal. A full-service tour including food and overnight accommodations will be approximately $400. Accommodations include campgrounds, floor space in public and private buildings, and, in some locations, "home hostels." A number of families have opened their homes to the cyclists.

Bikecentennial is nothing if not thorough. Leaders and assistants will be trained in first aid, safety, minor mechanical repairs, group problems, and logistics. However, the cyclists will be independent during the day and travel at their leisure, either alone or in groups. Trails will be thoroughly scouted beforehand and accomodations made far in advance.

Bikecentennial Inc., is a nonprofit organization, created to celebrate the founding of the nation and the introduction of bicycling to this country 100 years later. For it was in 1876 in Philadelphia, the site of America's first centennial celebration, that a display of English bikes caught the fancy of Colonel Pope. He went on to found the American bicycle industry. The word "Bikecentennial" was coined by June Simple, a member of the Hemistour Alaska to Argentina bicycle expedition. Her husband, Greg, had suggested a coast-to-coast tour earlier. The first serious discussion of the idea was at a stop in Chocolate, Mexico. Discussion continued on the ride the next day. Purely by accident—or omen—the only cyclometer in the group read 1776 that evening. Dan Burden was taken ill with hepatitis and had to leave the tour. Upon his recovery, he and his wife Lys began the tremendous task of organizing, publicizing, and finding support for Bikecentennial. They were fantastically successful—Bikecentennial was endorsed by the American Revolution Bicentennial Administration, received plaudits from the Secretary of Transportation, Claude S. Brinegar, was officially sanctioned by the League of American Wheelmen, and has been raised to an affiliate status by the board of directors for American Youth Hostels.

While the kickoff data was the summer of '76, Bikecentennial is an ongoing concept and has plans which include activities through 1987 and beyond. For further information, write:

>Bikecentennial
>P.O. Box 1034
>Missoula, Montana 59801

Over 300 bikeways totaling some 4800 miles exist today. Most are newly created in response to the boom in two-wheelers. Oregon, a state which never really forgot the first boom, can boast bikeways built almost a century ago. Some of the more enterprising state authorities are purchasing abandoned railway rights-of-way and converting them to biketrails. In Pennsylvania, Dr. Maurice K. Goddard, Secretary of the Department of Enviromental Resources, arranged the purchase of 25 miles of Penn Central roadbed north of Harrisburg. The trail, soon to be revamped, runs through the heart of the Allegheny Mountains. Wisconsin has used the same strategy to piece together parts of the Sugar River running south of Madison. The trail is eight feet wide (for machine grading) and gravelled with limestone.

But, by the nature of things, most tourists will have to share the road with autos and trucks. The latter are particularly dangerous; the bow wave generated by these monsters has been known to literally blow a cyclist off the road. If at all possible, choose a secondary road, one that is relatively free of high-speed traffic and with side shoulders. Farm-to-market roads are excellent, although somewhat indirect. There has been some litigation about the right of bicyclists to use the interstate highway net. If you want to do this—and it is very hazardous—at present you are confined to the western states. Whether it's legal or not, western state troopers generally ignore cyclists. This is not true elsewhere, and particularly not true in the northeast.

A cyclist in top physical form can do 200 miles a day. But that is head-down, heavy, and hard grinding and not what most tourists would consider recreation. Anything between 35 and 50 miles a day is certainly adequate and will leave you time and leisure to see the country.

SLEEPING ACCOMMODATIONS

Motels look awfully good after a day in the saddle. In the cities its always wise to pick a motel on the far side of town. This way, you will miss the heavy traffic going into the city the next morning. If you are sure of your schedule—if you know the terrain and your limitations—you can wire ahead for motel reservations. Otherwise accommodations are problematic after five or six P.M.

American Youth Hostels are much less expensive than motels, but are few and far between once you leave the coastal regions. To stay in one you will have to have a pass and a sleeping sack. The sack is a simple affair stitched up out of a bedsheet and is merely an indoor sleeping bag. No bedding is provided. Hostels provide male and female dorms and are run on the principle that everyone should pitch in and do a few chores.

Camping is a special kind of activity that is expensive in first investment and must be learned. When you decide to sleep out you are almost committed to the idea of cooking, which means a stove, utensils, and packaged food. A bike is up to these loads if the equipment is chosen; with an eye to lightness and compactness.

The first consideration is getting a good night's sleep. After riding all day your muscles will be sore, your arms will ache, and you may have collected a bruise or two. Insomnia is a luxury you can't affort. Professional woodsmen, accepting the necessity of a good night's sleep, are positively fussy about their bedding.

In order to sleep well, you need to be warm, dry, and level. The sleeping bag is a device to keep you warm. Bags come in a bewildering variety from homemade affairs cobbled up out of Army blankets to full mummy bags. The latter are tapered from 36 inches or so at the shoulders to 23 inches at the feet. Once inside, the sleeper closes the hood, and there he lies, snug as King Tut. These bags are a favorite of cycle campers because they are light (a good one weighs no more than three or four pounds) and warm. However, the confinement takes a bit of getting used to and if you have any latent tendencies toward claustrophobia, they will become apparent the first night on the ground.

Besides choosing the style of bag, you will need to determine the kind of insulation. Kapok is the cheapest and bulkiest material, and by no means the most insulative. The next step up is wool which gives moderate weather protection and is quite durable. It will not mat with use like kopok. Synthetic fibers, Dacron and the others, are more expensive than wool but take up less space and are machine washable. Cyclists on a budget usually settle for a good Dacron bag with a synthetic and cotton cover. The very best insulation is eider down. Whatever bag you choose, purchase it from a reliable dealer. Only a few states require that the type of insulation be labeled. In most states you must take the dealer's word for it.

You will also need some barrier between the bag and the ground. An air mattress is by far the best choice and worth the weight to anyone who plans to spend more than an occasional night out. The tufted type is the best bet, particularly if the tubes are heavily reinforced.

A tent is necessary. While the average precipitation is quite low in most areas of the United States from July to September, no part of the country is immune from occasional showers. You can, on a short trip, chance the weather with a fly (such as a 7 by 10-ft piece of nylon) rigged as a lean-to, but modern developments in tents make this almost obsolete, current designs accommodate two medium-sized people, weigh less than four pounds, and fold into a package that you can carry in your coat pocket. The lightest balloon cotton is heavy compared to some of the synthetics. Fiberglass and aluminum structural members have taken the place of poles and guy lines.

Cooking Out

You will need to pack your own fuel, since firewood is scarce and not to be used casually. Alcohol stoves are popular with some campers, particularly those ingenious stoves which have a cover that doubles as a cooking pot. Sterno is the most primitive form of the alcohol stove. Sterno (solidified alcohol) is packed in five ounce tins and the "stove" is a bracket which slips over the can. There is no control of the flame (other than to hold the pot off the bracket) and fuel consumption is fairly high.

Various types of gasoline stoves are available, the most practical of which are pressurized by heat. The warmth of your hands is enough to trigger the cycle. However, gasoline is messy and dangerous to store and to handle.

Propane stoves are, at least in their domestic form, heavy and require a large cylinder of fuel. The French Bleuet, widely used in Europe and available here, is fueled by small cannisters, not unlike—but not interchangeable—with those used to recharge cigarette lighters.

Stoves, utensils, and the other camping gear you will need are available from speciality shops and mail order houses. Speciality shops stock high-quality goods, much of it representing the latest in technology. Mail-order houses offer a wide range of less-exotic items. Three well respected houses are:

L.L. Bean Inc. Freeport, ME 04032

Gerry Mountain Sports, P.O. Box 910,
831 Pearl St., Boulder, CO 80302

Herter's, Route 1, Waseca, MN 56032

Preflight Inspection

Check the bike over carefully and give particular attention to bearings, spokes, and chain. Replace the tires and control cables as a matter of course and go for a few shakedown rides. Once on the road you do not want to be working on your bike, doing things that should have been done in the garage.

A shakedown ride should tell you about the condition of the engine. If you are new to cycling or out-of-shape, some sort of preparatory physical program would be a good idea. True, a few days on the road will bring you up to par, but those days can be filled with aches, pains, and a feeling of inadequacy unless you are in some kind of condition to begin with. A bike tour should be a joyful experience, a melding of body and machine. It shouldn't be a kind of mini-Camp Lejeune. Jogging is a fast and relatively easy way to improve your lung capacity and circulation. Ultimately our efficiency as heat engines depends upon how much and how well we use oxygen. Some really serious tourists do a bit of weight lifting, concentrating on the legs and calves, before going on the road. Like jogging, weight lifting is a fast way to a very specific end, which in this case is physical strength. But the ultimate form of training is simply riding your bike.

What to Wear

Cycling shorts, chamois-lined to prevent chafing, are a good bet for temperate climates. In extreme heat situations long, loose trousers help protect you from the sun and reduce liquid loss. The latter can be a very critical factor in parts of the U.S. Blue jeans are tough and give some protection from pavement burns, but the heavy seams soon make themselves felt. A cotton tee or tank shirt is always a good bet and can be worn under a nylon windbreaker in the mornings and during the heat of the day. Cycling gloves, particularly those made of heavy leather, are important as is some sort of head gear. Ideally you should wear a helmet, but any sort of cover is better than nothing.

Fig. 4-6. Wet weather gear. (Courtesy The Jacobs Corporation)

Cycling shoes for summer wear feature perforated uppers and ventilated soles. Steel inserts make them comfortable on rat-trap pedals and flexible uppers allow ankling. In a pinch you can get by with bowling shoes.

Rain is always a hassle and it means a steady shower of muddy water along the shoulder of a highway as the cars and semis roll by. A poncho may seem like a good idea, but really isn't. The thing billows and flaps and usually ends up in the chainwheel. A rain suit of the kind illustrated in Fig. 4-6 is ideal. Pack it high and easily accessible.

Cold weather touring seems to be getting popular. It requires a special ensemble and some knowledge of the effects of cold and chill factors. Basically, you need an outer layer of a fine woven synthetic to block the wind. The under layers depend upon the temperatures encountered, but should be arranged in multiples. In other words, do not depend upon a super-heavy triple bear and wolverine furred coat. It will be too hot much of the time—a cyclist can easily burn 6000 calories a day and more in adverse weather—and difficult to launder. The basic windbreaker can be supplemented as needed with a sweat shirt, a sweater, and a thermal undershirt. On really cold days you will need heavy trousers and longjohns. Gloves are a better choice than mittens in anything but the most extreme climates. The gloves should incorporate flares to cover the jacket cuffs. Welder's gloves are hardly elegant, but they do the job.

5

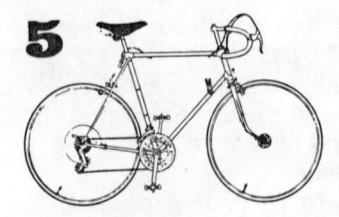

Buying a Bike

The bicycle manufacturing industry consists of hundreds of small, generally family-controlled firms and a handful of corporate giants typified by Raleigh in England and Schwinn in the United States. Brakes, wheels, crank assemblies, and other proprietary components are purchases from independent suppliers such as Bendix, Huret, Maeda, Campologno, and Weismann. In almost all instances, bicycles are assembled products with the parent firm responsible for little more than the frame. Schwinn is almost unique in that it franchises retail outlets; other makes are sold in lots to a distributor and resold in one or two tiers. Custom-built and low-production machines are sold through mail order houses, retail outlets, or directly from the factory. Replacement parts are distributed in parallel with the bicycles. The parts situation is eased somewhat by the interchangeability of many components (e.g., spokes, bearings, rims) but is made somewhat complicated by the inch-pound and the various national metric standards. In addition, there is product differentiation between the component manufacturers in the parts themselves and in the special tools required to disassemble and assemble them.

BICYCLE TECHNOLOGY

In broad outline, bicycle technology draws from that great burst of creativity which ended with the First World War. All of the major features of the contemporary bicycle were developed in that period and have undergone only marginal improvements since. We still do not have adequate brakes, and are still handicapped by primitive lighting systems. The more sophisticated bicycles require constant adjustment and tinkering to stay "in tune." Technological improvements have been few and far between. For instance, only recently have aftermarket accessory builders supplied sealed bearings. This particular development was characteristic of automobiles from the first.

Why is this so? In retrospect, at least, it appears that the structure of the industry is inherently against change. Small, low-capital input firms are rarely innovative, and the larger bicycle manufacturers seem more concerned with rationalizing production than in basic research. What technological development there is has been inspired by racing. As useful as racing is to "improve the breed," the lessons learned on the track do not apply directly to consumer products. The requirements essential to competition are alien to the utilitarian requirements of the average rider. The durability of a racing machine is only of significance in terms of a particular contest, and even then the rules may be relaxed (as they are in the Tour of France) to allow a rider to substitute mounts. Severe maintenance requirements are acceptable as well as high unit costs.

The situation is slowly changing for the better. The bicycle boom has introduced the sport to masses of people who have the preconceived notion that a bicycle should perform at least as well as an automatic dishwasher. Buyers are beginning to expect (and get) some sort of warranty against failure. Shimano has a long-standing company policy of keeping 10 percent of its home labor force employed in research. Another good omen is the way in which Yamaha used motorcycle technology in its motocross bike. While this is a special-purpose machine with limited appeal, the effectiveness of the Yamaha effort is apparent. Another plus is governmental regulation. The impending standards have forced the manufacturers into some notion of safety and durability. On the federal level these standards are generally functional rather than descriptive...that is, levels of performance are set, but how they are met is entirely a matter of manufacturer's choice.

Another problem is the unevenness of workmanship and materials. Quality control ranges from excellent in prestige machines like the Schwinn Paramount or the Cinelli Supercorsa to abysmal among some of the cheaper bikes. Until very recently bicycle manufacturers have enjoyed a seller's market—the problem was production and not quality.

Anything with two wheels and ten speeds sold as fast as it could be built. Consequently, prices skyrocketed and quality tumbled.

Major component builders produce similar items under the same name that vary widely in the quality of materials and finish. For example, the Shimano Eagle derailleur is hardly of the quality of the Sun Tour. And while the Campagnolo Nuovo Record is the acme of derailleur quality the Valentino is substandard.

The market has softened and there is some evidence that manufacturers are paying more attention to quality, although it is still possible to purchase a barely workable bike at a fairly high price. Quality tends to be worse on those bikes which are in sudden demand. Recently there has been a run on the 20-inch frame with ten speeds. Also motocross bikes and parts are almost unobtainable for retailers who misjudged the popularity of these machines and did not order early.

WARRANTIES

Few imported bikes carry an express, written warranty. Exceptions are Raleigh, Peugeot, and Browning. However, this may not mean that the customer is totally without recourse. Many states have adopted the Universal Commercial Code which gives the salesman's verbal promises legal validity, and many jurisdictions have accepted the broad principle that a product carries an implied warranty to perform in a manner commensurate with its intended use.

Manufacturers warranties generally cover the frame and components, but not the tires. Browning warranties the components to be free of defects in workmanship and materials for one year and the frame for ten years. Coverage by Columbia, Murray Ohio, and Huffy varies with the model. Usually the frame is warranted for one year and the components for six months, however AMF covers both for one year.

Schwinn offers the most generous warranty of any manufacturer. Schwinn-built and Schwinn-approved frames and components are warranted to be free of defects in materials and workmanship forever! In addition the customer is entitled to a free 30-day check-up and adjustment. However there will be a dealer labor charge to replace defective components after the 30-day period, and labor will be charged for frame replacement after one year.

The large retail houses have their own policy, independent of the manufacturer. Sears will repair the frame for the life of the machine and replace or repair components for the first six months. Montgomery Ward policy is variable but, like all such businesses, they depend upon satisfied customers. Federated Stores is generally quite liberal in their product support.

However, no warranty is completely inclusive. The customer has the responsibility to care for his machine, operate it within its design limits, and make repairs and adjustments promptly. Written warranties carry the disclaimer that "this warranty is in lieu of all others real or implied." This disclaimer does *not* have the force of law and cannot abrogate the provisions of the Uniform Code, but it does tend to limit the manufacturers' and dealers' responsibilities to those provisions stated in the warranty.

WHERE TO BUY

If the initial price is your only concern, the best place to purchase a bicycle is at a department store or discount house. Savings are even more dramatic if you wait until the off-season or if you purchase a discontinued line. Well established department stores—as opposed to most discount houses—have generous return policies and will refund your money if you are not satisfied.

But there are disadvantages. Mass marketeers must have volume to stay in business and volume is usually opposed to the concept of real quality. You may get more for your money at one of these outlets, but you will not get top quality. Merchandise is purchased by lot. The store may buy 50,000 bicycles from one distributor or may have overseas buyers dealing directly with the manufacturers. This approach cuts unit costs, but does not have the continuity of contract sales. Spare parts may be difficult to find and the store's mechanics tend to lose interest in bikes which have been replaced by another model. Nor can the salesperson be expected to know much about bicycles and trained mechanics are scarce.

Assembly of a 10-speed is a rather demanding task requiring some two to three hours and at least a short test ride. The assembly of cheap bikes can be more critical than for the expensive models which have more forgiving components. Bicycle repair is a skilled trade that takes years to master. In many instances, department store bike mechanics are primarily assemblers and small engine mechanics. No one else in the store has anywhere near the skills needed to cope with two-wheelers. This lack of skill is reflected in shoddy work and long waits for parts. A really good bike mechanic knows that he can substitute certain parts that are available locally. Service difficulties are compounded by the sometimes careless construction of mass market bikes and by the refusal of many legitimate bike shops to service department-store purchases. One study has shown that an $80 ten-speed bike costs the owner $50 in repairs during the first year of ownership.

Costs, at least initially, are higher in a bicycle shop, and the policy on returns may not be as lenient as with the chain stores. Dealers usually pay more for their merchandise and enjoy a higher markup. A $275 bike wholesales at between $175 and $185, and although distributors try to enforce a price structure, dealers have been known to charge a premium for machines currently in demand. However, most bike shops are heavily involved in service, and consensus is that the service department should at least pay the overhead. This means that the dealer tries to purchase bikes which are repairable and which are supported by readily available spares.

The training of the mechanics is important. Most shops want their mechanics to be generalists and proficient in all aspects of the trade. A few, as epitomized by Sea Schwinn in Costa Mesa, CA, have adopted the methods of automobile dealerships. One mechanic specializes in assembly, another in fine tuning, and two more devote their time to bench work. The better shops have at least one master mechanic who may be the foreman or the owner. Chuck Sink of Sink's Bicycle World is a good example of an owner who learned the trade before many of his customers were born. Another is W.C. Chipley. Mr. Chipley operates Chipley's Hardware and Bicycle in Charlotte and writes a column on bike maintenance and collecting for *The Charlotte News*.

Whether the emphasis is on mechanical excellence, competitive sports, touring, or on bicycles as a principal or alternate means of transportation, the better shops manage to develop an empathy with their customers. This kind of empathy is lacking in department stores and discount houses where the relationship is defined by the cash nexus.

WHICH BRANDS

If you're new to the sport, the best advice is to purchase name brands. You may pay a premium for a Peugeot, Raleigh, Schwinn, Jeunet, or Mercier, but a few dollars is well spent in terms of peace of mind. However you should remember that the name itself is not always an absolute guarantee of quality. Many of these firms produce inexpensive lines as well as their more prestigious models.

It is generally felt that cheap Italian ten-speeds are to be avoided in favor of French or English models. The writer will concur with this one, if only because most inexpensive English ten-speeds are built by Raleigh and because the French have a way of using components built in France which tends to improve the cost effectiveness of their lower-echelon machines. The Germans are said to have a blind spot in bike technology, which is all the more mysterious because of their excellent automobiles and luxury motorcycles. It is true that sport bicycling does not have the following in Germany that it enjoys in Belgium or France and that touring, at least for the older generation, is almost an English monopoly. Nor are German bikes well known outside of the Federal Republic. But the Steyr, (built by Puch) is a fine utility bike available with a fully lugged frame, hub transmission, and center-pull brakes. It is one of the most durable bikes on the market, designed for years of troublefree riding. Japanese machines are often described as derivatives of European models. There is a marked similarity in some of the components but no more so than between some continental makes. With careful shopping, Japanese bikes can be the best dollar values of all.

Speaking very broadly and excluding the top-of-the-line models, American manufacturers tend to excel in building the bikes with which they are most intimately acquainted. Honest single- and 3-speed middleweights are an American speciality. These bikes serve well in short-range commuting, paper routes, and factory and warehouse transport, and are almost always good values for the money. The bulk of domestic ten-speed production is intended for the teenage market. The bikes are heavy—sometimes heavier than the same company's three-speed models—but, at their best, are durable. In a number of instances some effort has been extended to make the derailleurs kid-proof. American sidewalk bikes are of variable quality; at worst they are toys, and dangerous toys. The better examples borrow from adult bike practice.

One should be very cautious when considering machines made in the Soviet Union, Czechoslovakia, Korea, Taiwan, Hong Kong, India, and Mexico. Most are intended for a relatively unsophisticated market. Parts availability and dealer support is problematic, although this certainly could improve for the better should these lines become popular here. At present their best recommendation is their low prices.

WHICH BIKE

Adult bikes (the industry considers anyone over 14 an adult) come in many styles and shapes. The major distinguishing marks are frame type, weight, and number of speeds. (See Fig. 5-1 for general nomenclature.)

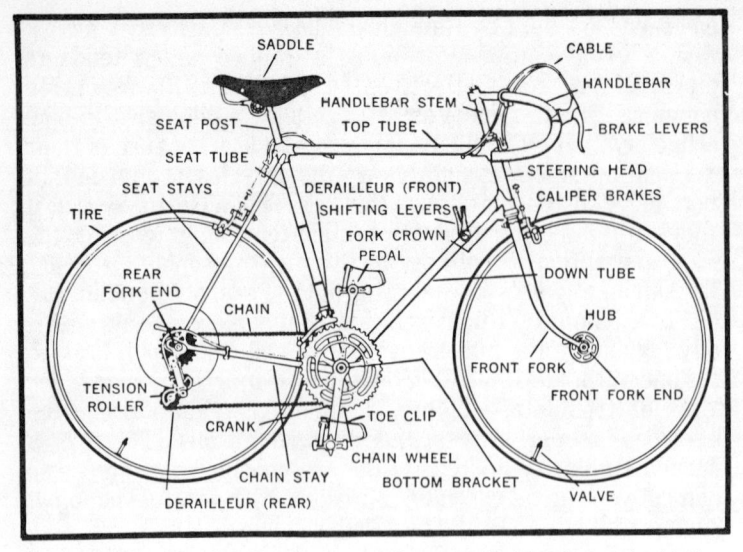

Fig. 5-1. Bicycle nomenclature. (Courtesy Raleigh Industries Ltd.)

The double diamond (sometimes called diamond and triangle) frame makes the most efficient use of the tubes since the loads are in compression or tension. Figure 5-2A illustrates a classic example of this frame type. Ladies' bikes traditionally have an open or dropped frame. The Browning five-speed is an example of the American varient of the ladies' frame. The upper tube is curved to increase the width of the stepover (Fig. 5-2B). The European version, as shown in Fig. 5-2C is slightly more strength efficient since it employs straight tubes. A few mixte frames have appeared in this country and offer the best rigidity attainable in the open-frame configuration (Fig. 5-2D). Open-framed bikes have crossed the continent, but these machines are not recommended for touring because of the lack of full triangulation. The American middleweight frame employs double or single top tubes with a slight convex bend, which accounts for the name *camelback* sometimes given these frames (Fig. 5-2E). The advantage of the middleweight is its near indestructability. These bikes are used for paper routes, warehouse work, and wherever weight is not a prime concern.

Folding bikes are characterized by a single large downtube which may be pressed steel or in the form of a flanged tube. Folding bikes are considered as marginal transportation.

The weight of a machine is a function of its frame design and the materials used. It is one of the most important parameters in bicycle design since it has a direct bearing on the machine performance and tractability, both on the road and during those clumsy moments when the bike has to be lifted and otherwise manhandled. Weight, or more exactly the absence of it, accounts for some of the paradoxes of bicycle design. As stated, the cost of the bike generally is a rough index to its weight. Light components are more expensive because of the more exotic materials used, and because of the care in construction needed to optimize strength. Expensive machines make do without side stands, splash guards, built-in dynamos, and other niceties which one might associate with comfortable travel. And the very expensive bikes tend to be more fragile than their heavier counterparts, since the designers have taken some license with strength-to-weight ratios. It is assumed that the owner of a 20-pound sports machine is knowledgeable enough to take care of it.

The number of speeds or gears is traditionally used as an index of bicycle quality and has been pegged more or less consistently (with some overlap) to the weight and cost of the machine. Single-speed models weigh in at 35 to 40 pounds, and good ones such as the Schwinn K series list for about $80. Three-speed hubs are usually offered as a ten-dollar or so extra for these bikes. Another group, typified by the Raleigh DL-22, are available only with 3-speed hubs and are a few pounds lighter and a few dollars costlier than those with coaster-brake ancestry.

At their lowest stage of evolution ten-speeds tip the scales at 35 pounds and can be purchased for $80 or so. As the weight is progressively reduced, the price goes up. The Itoh

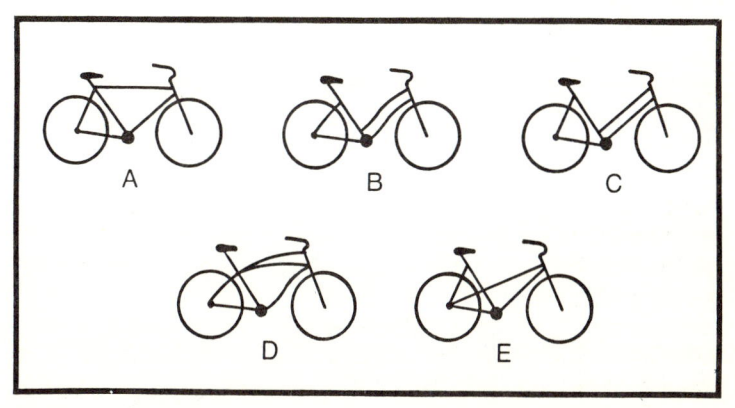

Fig. 5-2. Frame types. (A) double-diamond frame, (B) American-style open frame, (C) European-style open frame, (D) mixte frame, and (E) the American camelback.

Roadracer is pegged at a little more than $200 and weighs 22 pounds. The Zeus Competition can be had for $300 and weighs a pound less than the Itoh. Twelve and 15-speed bikes are, for the most part, high-quality touring machines and are light for their class.

The weight—price relationship is instructive in broad outline, but it cannot be used as the sole criterion. At the extremes, the contrast between sport bikes and mass-produced clunkers is obvious. But in the middle ground the relationship between weight and mechanical excellence grows blurred. Weight is, after all, a static quality. A bicycle's dynamics are determined by forces generated by the rider's body, the road, and the machine itself. Many of the larger and more conservative manufacturers trade off weight for reliability. Extreme weight consciousness can be, technologically speaking, a dead end. The surest (and cheapest) way to reduce weight is for the rider himself to lose weight. As far as the machine is concerned it makes little difference whether the poundage is in thick-walled tubing or adipose tissue.

Another mark of the serious bicycle is the riding position. The upright position is demanded with American middleweights, children's bikes on the "Chopper" pattern, and on English three-speed tourers (a misnomer if there ever was one). It feels natural and looks dignified. While perfectly adequate for toddling through the neighborhood, the upright position is grossly inefficient. In the first place it puts the leg muscles at a mechanical disadvantage. When one needs these most powerful muscles, one instinctively goes into a racer's crouch. Notice how you lean forward and tuck your feet under when you rise from a chair. Along with power, leaning forward also gives flexibility. One's center of gravity is lower and slight movements of the shoulders shift mass in the horizontal plane. Moving bicycles are steered primarily by weight shifts. Transferring some of the weight of the torso to the front wheel through the forearms improves the tractability of the machine. Tires are loaded more evenly and the mass of the rider tends to be centralized in the mid-section, which is the state engineers call a low polar moment of inerta. The result is more predictable handling in wet conditions and through high-speed curves. Another advantage is that leaning forward reduces the frontal area or sail effect. Cheating the wind means longer and less tiring rides.

Underslung bars allow the rider to change hand positions at will. For coasting and distance riding the hands are positioned on the straight sections (Fig. 5-3A). When power is

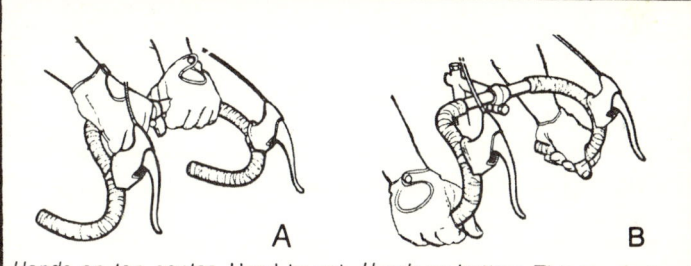

Hands on top center. Used to get greater power from back muscles for hill climbing.

Hands on bottom. This streamlined body position reduces wind resistance.

Fig. 5-3. Hand positions. Normally, the hands are positioned near the brake levers. (Courtesy Raleigh Industries Ltd.)

needed, the hands drop to the curve, anchoring the body against the reaction from the leg and torso muscles (Fig. 5-3B).

The upright position is not particularly healthful, either. The lower vertebrae are particularly vulnerable to damage in this position since they are compressed anvil-like, by the weight of the torso and arms. Experiments with snowmobiles have shown that a small dropoff can generate tremendous g-forces, several magnitudes greater than those experienced by aircraft pilots during ejection. The forward leaning position separates and frees the vertebrae, reducing the loads. And the forward-leaning position transfers weight from the chest to the arms, allowing deeper and easier breathing. And breathing is, of course, the prime function that allows the human body to convert heat into mechanical energy, via oxygen intake

Finally, it should also be remembered that the upright position requires a sprung saddle. The comfort of these devices is illusory and purchased at the cost of propulsive efficiency. The springs which absorb and dissipate road shocks also act in the same manner against the thrust of the leg muscles.

COMPONENTS

The level of excellence of the individual components should be reflected in the price of the machine. In recent years this has not always been so. The confusion engendered by the unprecedented demand of the late '60s and early '70s encouraged shoddy workmanship and dubious advertising claims. As long as it's a seller's market, there can be no guarantee that you automatically get what you pay for. To paraphrase a famous U.S. senator, the bicycle business is not a charitable enterprise.

Frames
The frame is the fundamental component which, more than the effect of all other components combined, determines the character of the machine.

Frame Materials. Cheap bikes are made from seamed steel tubing, resistance welded at the joints. This grade of high-carbon steel is similar to that used in garden furniture and has a yield (tensile) strength of some 40,000 pounds per square inch. This will produce a permanent deformation in the tubing. In order to build adequate strength and rigidity into the structure, heavy wall thicknesses are required which give the frame a muleish character, although it is considered acceptable for sidewalk bikes. The seam can often be detected under the paint.

Seamless tubing is normally made with superior (low-carbon) steel. Yield strength is in the neighborhood of 60,000 pounds per square inch. Most bicycles are constructed of this material and it is obviously adequate for the average rider. In better bikes low-carbon steel is alloyed with minute amounts of chrome or chrome and molybdenum. Chrome-moly tubing is described as *aircraft quality* since it finds wide use in airframes, and is found on several Japanese bikes and the Schwinn Sports Tourer among others. This steel is sometimes known as 4130—its Society of Automotive Engineers classification number. While it is a superior product, it is not as light nor as "live" as manganese molybdenum.

Manganese molybdenum is an alloy of high-carbon steel which has a yield strength of 90,000 pounds per square inch cold and 80,000 pounds per square inch after having been subject to brazing temperatures. It is resilient and has a superior resistance to fatigue. Reynolds 531 (the numbers refer to its chemical composition) is by far the most famous and available brand, although other firms produce a comparable product. Columbus tubing is used in many Italian bikes, including at least two models from Bianchi. Falk tubing is found on the Frejus and Legano bikes; and Day and Day on the better Japanese products.

The use of quality steels reduces the weight of the frame without adversely affecting its rigidity or durability. This weight reduction comes about because of the lighter gauges specified and not because of any significant weight difference between the various alloys. Further weight reductions can be had by butting the tubing. The ends are butted or made thicker than the midsection by reducing the inside diameter. Either or both ends may be butted. In the case of the latter the tubing is described as *double butted*; otherwise the term is *single butted* or, on some ad copy, simply *butted*. A double-butted Reynolds top tube typically is 0.022 inch thick in the middle and 0.032 inch at the ends. Dimensional accuracy is held to 0.003 inch. Manganese-moly tubes may be straight-gauge, single- or double-butted. American 4130 is straight-gauge, while the Japanese variety is sometimes butted.

Butting puts more metal at the joints where stress is most severe and where heat damage from brazing or silver soldering is concentrated. Besides the weight saved in not making the center sections any stronger than they need be, the frame recovers more quickly from stress, increasing the rider's sense of control.

A word of caution about exotic frame tubing. On a given bike only the seat tube, down tube, and top tube may be of top quality. The rear stays and forks may be of a lesser grade, although only the most expert rider would sense this. There's even a saying in the industry that there are more Reynolds decals than tubes.

Steel is not the only frame material. Plastic has been used in frames made by the now-defunct Original Plastic Bicycle Co. While I have not been able to examine one of these bikes or find any reliable information about them, experience with plastics would raise questions about fatigue resistance.

Aluminum bikes are built by several manufacturers and offer some weight saving over steel. The only objection to these frames is the feeling of "deadness" which seems to be a characteristic of this metal. It is not as springy as steel. Titanium frames are quite practical, but because of the expense of the metal and the difficulty of machining it, they remain extremely expensive. The latest development is a spin-off from the space program. Magnamite-graphite frames are made with fibers of graphite for strength. These frames are exceedingly light (the frame of the Mossberg X-1001 series weighs 3.10 pounds), have excellent fatigue resistance and give the "live" ride of the best steel. Figure 5-4 illustrates a track bike built on this frame.

The test results are interesting. The hanger bracket deflection test is illustrated in Fig. 5-5. A pedal load was applied three inches outward from the center of the hanger bracket to simulate the point of load exerted by the rider's foot on the pedal. The load was applied off-vertical in order to

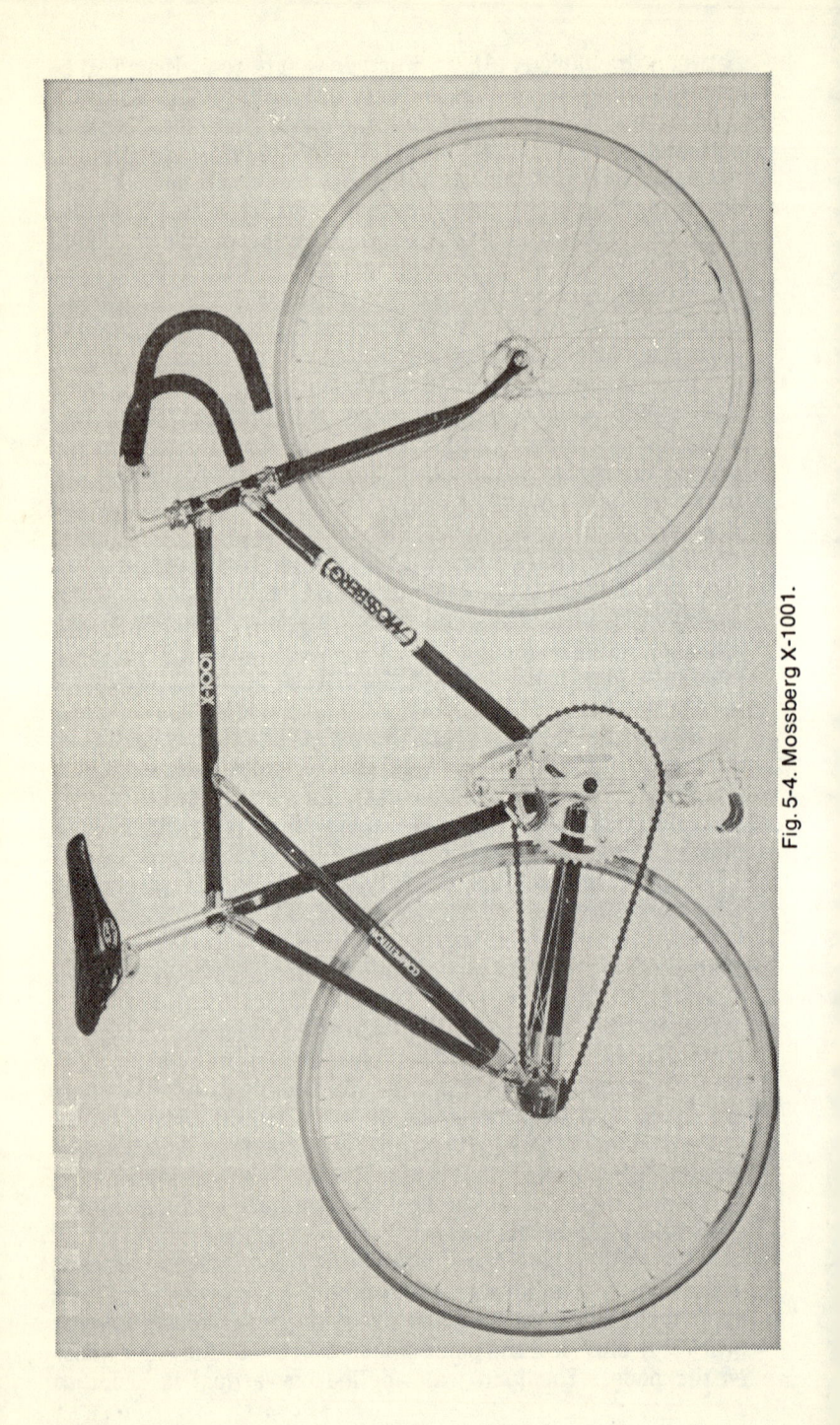

Fig. 5-4. Mossberg X-1001.

compensate for the direction of force being transmitted through the rider's skeletal system. The accompanying chart summarizes the results. In another test (Fig. 5-6) a 390-pound load was applied straight down at a point seven inches from the center of the hanger bracket to simulate the rotational load applied by the rider's foot upon the pedal, with the pedal at a 90-degree angle. The load represents a total torsional force of 2730 pounds (390 pounds × 7 inches) upon the frame. The purpose was to measure frame deflection or the torsional flex of the frame away from the centerline.

A third test (Fig. 5-7) measured horizontal deflection. The frame was anchored at three points and a 48.5-pound load applied downward at the steering head. The results are given in the figure.

Frame Construction. The joints where the tubes meet are the most critical areas of the frame: failure is most likely to occur here. The tubes may open at the joint or shear a half-inch or so behind it from the effects of heat used in the bonding process.

The tubes are joined by welding or brazing. Children's bikes and a few very low-priced ten-speeds are welded. The process uses an electric arc and is often almost entirely automatic. There are several disadvantages in welding.

Frame Construction	Lbs. of Applied Pedal Load			
	200	600	900	1,100
	Frame Deflection			
Mossberg Magnamite graphite	.053	.167	.298	.379*
Titanium	.056	.239	Failure	
Steel	.054	.214	Failure	

*Mossberg Magnamite-graphite frame experienced failure only under load of 1,145 lbs.

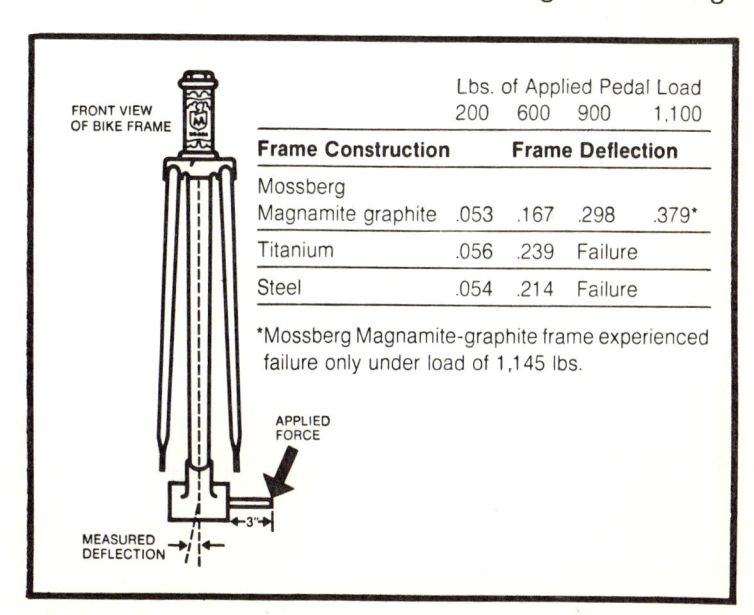

Fig. 5-5. Hanger-bracket deflection to failure, in inches. (Courtesy Mossberg)

Frame Construction	Frame Deflection
Mossberg Magnamite graphite	.0977 inch
Titanium	.1399 inch
Steel	.1014 inch

Results: Frame deflection of Mossberg Magnamite graphite was 43.19% less than titanium; 3.79% less than steel.

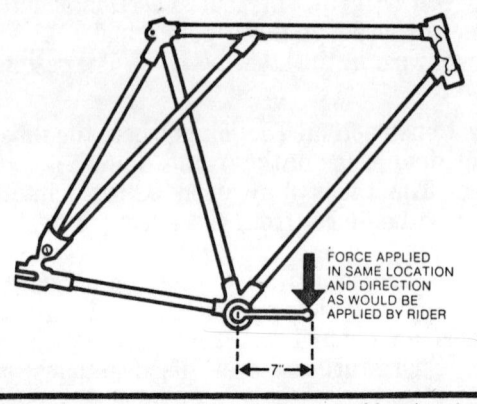

Fig. 5-6. Frame deflection. (Courtesy Mossberg)

Frame Construction	Frame Deflection
Mossberg Magnamite Graphite	.436 inch
Titanium	.770 inch
Steel	.512 inch

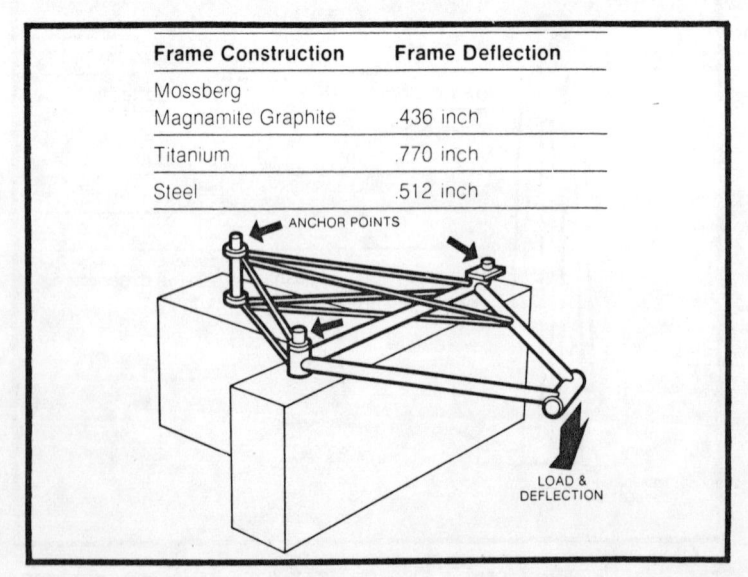

Fig. 5-7. Horizontal deflection under a 48.5 pound load. (Courtesy Mossberg)

Heavy-gauge tubing must be used and, even then, the effect of heat on material adjacent to the weld is bad. Care must be taken in adjusting the arc for penetration, and the surfaces of both tubes must be puddled and a filler rod melted into the puddle of liquid metal. Trikes and sidewalk bikes, probably because of the light gauges used, seem particularly vulnerable to poor penetration.

Most brazing is done with a relatively soft alloy of copper and zinc. The joint is heated with an oxy-acetylene torch and the brass allowed to flow into the joint. So long as the surface is clean and the tubes are in close proximity to each other, brazing makes a strong and durable bond. It is less damaging to the tubes since the joints need only be heated to the melting point of the filler.

Silver brazing or silver soldering, as the process is sometimes called, is preferred by a minority of custom frame builders. Silver is easy to work and also produces a good bond without the necessity of high temperatures. But it is less forgiving than brass and quite expensive.

Brazed joints may be finished by a lug, which is a pressed steel sleeve, spanning the tubes (Fig. 5-8). While most riders find lugs attractive, the purpose is to distribute stress over and through the joint to the widest possible area. The alternative is to employ a filleted joint as done by Schwinn and DBS. The fillet gives a rounded appearance to the joint and may detract from the esthetics of the frame. Since a slightly heavier tube section is needed with fillets the weight saved by eliminating

Fig. 5-8. Lugged frame construction. (Courtesy Ware's Cycles)

Fig. 5-9. Lugless frame construction. (Courtesy Ware's Cycles)

lugs is mostly illusory. However, filleted joints are quite strong and in destruction tests have outperformed equivalent lugged joints.

Welded bicycles have no lugs or fillets. Hence, the saying that lugless frames are a sign of inferiority. If *lugless* means *resistance welded*, one must agree (Fig. 5-9).

The time you spend scrutinizing the joints on a bicycle is time well spent. Lugs may hide shabby work as well as be a sign of master craftsmanship. The tubes should meet. Gaps and obvious fills weaken the joint and may signal early failure. The lugs themselves should be finished without parting lines or tool marks. Look carefully at the edges of the lugs. Unless smoothed and filleted into the tube diameter (a mark of some exceedingly well-built machines), the edges should be proud and sharp. There should be little or no evidence of cleanup work with a file to remove spilled brass. The lug pattern is optional. Really elaborate cutaways resembling floral growths and the like may be visually interesting, but require a lot of expensive handwork.

The fork ideally should be of high quality steel, drawn and butted. The headset—the bearings and races—is extremely critical. Looseness or a slight hesitation will ruin the responsiveness of the bike and may even make it dangerous. The practice of using nylon bushings in headsets for children's bikes is inexcusable. As far as it is known, all adult bikes use some sort of antifriction bearing here. Uncaged ball bearings are superior to the caged variety, although they are a little more of a hassle when the fork has to be dropped for repair or repacking. The cones should be tapered to offer a wide track for the balls. Straight-cut cones are a mark of a poorly designed bike and soon indent, taking the edge off responsiveness.

Frame Fit. Adult frame sizes vary from about 16 inches to 27.5 inches. Larger sizes are available from the smaller concerns on special order. While several fitting systems are in vogue, the basic rule is that you should purchase the largest frame that you can comfortably straddle with your feet flat on the ground. There should be 1.5 to 2 inches of clearance between the top tube and crotch (Fig. 5-10). For most people the frame should be at least 12 inches smaller than inseam length measured to the heel of the shoe. Raleigh dealers have a machine to determine (or at least to standardize) fits. Custom builders have their own formulas which take into account the intended use of the machine. Tourists generally fare better with a slightly larger-than-average frame because of the more upright riding position. Track racers prefer a smaller package for reduced frontal area.

Frame size is almost universally measured from the centerline of the bottom bracket to the point where the seat stem enters the seat tube. For convenience, the measurement is taken along the length of the seat tube and not vertically as one might suppose. A few custom builders measure from the center of the bottom bracket to the centerline of the top tube at the point it joins the seat tube. These frames are about half an inch larger than the specification would indicate.

Wheels

Alloy rims are light, corrosion resistant, and have adequate strength for most riders and riding conditions. Aluminum, however, is inferior to steel in terms of strength and the quality engineers call *notch resistance*. Steel is

Fig. 5-10. Frame fit is important. (Courtesy Mossberg)

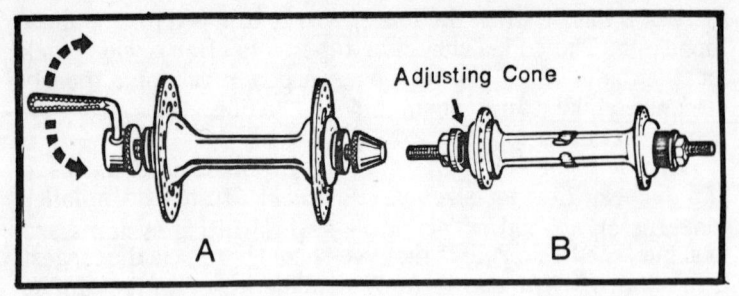

Fig. 5-11. Quick-release hubs. (A) large-frame hub, (B) standard small-flange variety. (Courtesy Raleigh Industries Ltd.)

preferred for touring and knockabout riding. Spokes are made from stainless or medium carbon steel which may be rendered corrosion-resistant by chrome plating or by galvanizing. Chrome plating produces an attractive, if somewhat gaudy wheel, but may weaken the spokes unless it is followed by heat treating. And the quality of chrome, or more particularly, the depth of the initial copper flash, determines the spoke's resistance to oxidation. Galvanized spokes are somewhat drab in appearance and give only marginal protection. In all, the best choice is stainless steel. The loss in yield strength can be compensated for by increasing the number of spokes, going to a heavier gauge, or by the spoke pattern (see Chapter 12 for further details). Flanges are available in several diameters described as large (60 + mm) or small (30 mm). Large-flange hubs give additional stiffness to the wheel and are generally favored on premium bikes as are quick release hubs (Fig. 5-11). Wing nuts are adequate for the front wheels but should not be used on the rear. Standard wheel diameters are 26 and 27 inches and should offer no difficulties unless you are very short or very tall.

Tires

Tires come in two basic constructions. The *clincher tire* is held to the rim by means of air pressure. It is heavy, but has the advantages of good puncture resistance, excellent wearing qualities, and good air retention. Gumwalls, a fairly recent development, have lower rolling resistance than the older compounds and are worth the small extra charge. *Tubulars,* or *sew-up,* tires are intended for racing bicycles, and are secured to the rim by cement (Fig. 5-12B). They give a far superior ride than the heavier clinchers with less pedal effort. On the other hand, sew-ups are prone to road damage. Flats are easy to change, at least for the initiated, but the drill requires some practice to master. Another characteristic is that these tires are designed to seep air and must be inflated before use. More than a few hardy souls have crossed the nation on sew-ups, with a supply of spares folded behind saddle, accepting the periodic inconveniences as a small enough price to pay for the pedaling and handling benefits. Tubular and clincher rims have different profiles; unless you are willing to invest in a second set of wheels, select the type of tire when you purchase the bike.

Saddles

Mattress saddles are supported on springs and are intended for upright riding. As explained previously, these saddles waste energy and should not be considered for serious riding. Racing saddles are unsprung and quite narrow to allow thigh movement. Some acclimatization is required, but you will eventually find these saddles practical. Of course, ride harshness is also a function of frame stiffness and wheel construction. A compromise is the loop spring saddle such as the Brooks B-72 Tourist. A single loop of heavy wire absorbs the worst bumps without diverting too much muscle power.

Saddles may be covered with heavy leather or with a synthetic such as nylon. Leather requires care. It must be broken in with diligent applications of neats'-foot oil and much riding but the break-in period can be reduced with ministrations from a ball-peen hammer. Saddle soap is used as a preservative. Nylon may not have the feel of leather, but it requires no break-in, is cooler, and does not have to be protected from the weather. Unica and Brooks are recognized as two of the leading saddle makers.

Handlebars and Headstems

These components should be of light alloy on any bike which has claim to quality. Dropped bars are described by

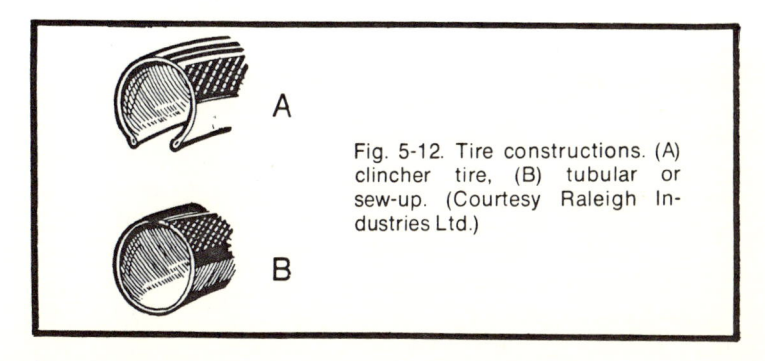

Fig. 5-12. Tire constructions. (A) clincher tire, (B) tubular or sew-up. (Courtesy Raleigh Industries Ltd.)

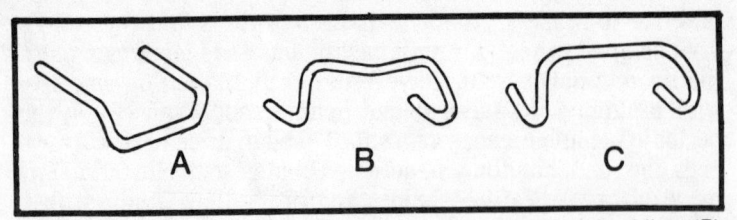

Fig. 5-13. Handlebars. (A) conventional steerhorn for upright riding, (B) Radonneur bars (note the V-shaped horizontal), and (C) the popular Maes bar.

their shape. There are three basic handlebar styles: conventional, Randonneur, and Maes (Fig. 5-13). The conventional bars are identified by the upsweep of the tubes as they leave the stem. Radonneur bars are popular in racing, and are fairly comfortable for touring, since there is room on the horizontals to rest your hands. Radonneur bars do not, however, enjoy the popularity of the Maes. Maes bars are the best all-around choice for touring and general knockabout riding. People with short arms may find the Radonneur with its backsweep to their liking.

Good names in stems are GB, Cinelli, and Pivo. Cinelli offers an adjustable stem which moves the handlebar outboard of the steering head for hard-to-fit anatomies. Because of its construction the stem is made of steel and somewhat heavy.

Cranks and Cranksets

The crank on inexpensive American bikes is a single-piece steel forging. It is heavy and imprecise, but quite strong. Medium-quality machines secure the cranks to axle with pins. Better bikes employ the cotterless form of construction for superior stress dissipation. These various crank assemblies are illustrated in Chapter 11.

Pedals

Because of their racing heritage top-line are usually fitted with integral toe straps as shown on the Mossburg in Fig. 5-4. Toe straps (also called clips) are for the experienced rider and should not be used until you have developed enough skill to undo them while riding. They should be left open in traffic. Whether fitted with straps or not, all quality bikes feature alloy "rat trap" pedals. The cleats hold the pedal against your shoe for best leverage, particularly in hilly country. The serrations may be blunt for comfort or quite sharp for a sure grip. In any event, you cannot expect to ride very far in tennis shoes. Rubber pedals are not as comfortable as they look and have a relatively short life-span under adult use.

Gears

Three-speed planetary gears are adequate for light travel on smooth streets and are, of course, a marked improvement over single-speed coaster brakes. Major repairs are rare but can be complicated. Fortunately most difficulties can be traced to cable stretch and adjusted outside of the mechanism without disassembly. Five-speed derailleurs are almost as troublesome as the ten-speeds and seem to be a bad trade-off between limited ratios and mechanical bothers. Most of these transmissions are found on bikes intended for American adolescents. Ten-speed derailleurs are the norm for adult bikes. Tourists find 12 or even 15 speeds advantageous, although the latter are generally a bit finicky about staying in adjustment.

The Campagnolo Nuovo Record is generally conceded to be the best and is standard on bikes in the $300–$500 range. Bikes costing a hundred dollars less may be fitted with one of the lesser Campys such as the GT or Valentino. In this case it would be wise to specify a Sun Tour or the excellent Huret Jubilee.

In the $100 to 200 range you should expect a good Shimano, Huret (either the Allvit or Luxe), or the heavy but rugged Simplex Prestige. These derailleurs do not have the reputation as being the best and are not finished to the standards demanded by the connoisseur. But they are perfectly workable mechanisms. The same cannot be said of the cheapest ten-speeds; derailleurs on these bikes are made of steel stampings, are crude, and are mechanically unreliable. Shifting is stubborn and maintenance costs are high.

Brakes

Besides coaster brakes, there are drum brakes, which in this country are limited to tandems and a few delivery cycles. Rim brakes are either side pulls or center pulls. Side-pull brakes have enjoyed a renaissance in popularity in spite of the fact that most are hard to adjust and to keep in adjustment. One exception is the Campagnolo side pull for tubular-tire rims. It is expensive—retailing at more than many ten-speed bikes cost—but the action is unparalleled. These brakes are fitted to such machines as the Fiorelli Sprint No. 1 and the Swedish Crescent. A few top-line or near top-line bikes employ Universal side pulls, although most builders prefer center pulls from Campagnolo, Weinmann, Mafac, or Universal.

Rear wheel rim brakes are the bane of the mass-marketed ten-speed. It is almost usual to find that the brake fails to generate any stopping power, refuses to open fully, or jams full on. The difficulty may be in the caliper mechanism itself or in the actuating cable. The cable should be long enough to arc widely at the handlebars and at the seat tube, and should be made of quality material to transmit braking force without stretch. Some cyclists replace even quality cables with those designed for motorcycles. The slight weight penalty is accepted for freedom from stretch and progressive action incurred.

Another problem is that some very inexpensive caliper mechanisms are cast in light alloy to imitate racing practice. The alloy used is the type dismissed as "pot metal" and has only a remote similarity to dural. Under tension, the brake arm deflects. This deflection can be so severe that the whole mechanism shifts and jams the caliper blocks between the rim and seat stays, locking the wheel into a skid.

Brake levers may be hooded with a rubberoid shield over the mechanism and may feature a quick-release mechanism. Campagnolo quick-releases are at the caliper blocks, the advantage being that the wheel can be removed without upsetting the brake adjustment.

APPEARANCE

The overall appearance of the bike may be important in itself; to many riders is it almost the sole basis of choice. From a more utilitarian standpoint the finish gives clues to the maker's attitude toward his products. You may reasonably conclude that a bike with paint runs, rough cast parts, and dull chrome is lacking in subsurface qualities as well. However, super finish is expensive and can become an end in itself. Atala bikes have been known for their cobbly appearance which belies their mechanical superiority.

The paint should be baked-on enamel, liberally applied. Bikes are subject to weathering and particularly to chipping. Epoxy is a good paint, in most aspects superior to enamel. As far as I can tell no manufacturer yet employs epoxy, although you could custom order it from one of the more innovative builders. Chrome is expensive and is usually limited to the lower extremities. The Fuji Newest is an all-chrome bike with a coat of paint to disguise its uniqueness from the unaware. Of course, the ultimate finish is raw titanium, but that is another subject.

BEFORE YOU BUY

Check the bike's reputation with experienced riders. No one knows everything about bikes, but if you talk to a number of people you will get a pretty good idea of the standing of the various makes. Enthusiast magazines feature road tests which are sometimes informative, but are rarely objective. Much better information can be had from Consumers' Reports and other consumer-oriented magazines. Unfortunately the range of bikes tested is quite narrow.

Ask the dealer for permission to take a test spin. Even the finest components may not jell into a pleasing mix. All mechanical adjustments should be correct on the floor demonstrator. Should the rims wobble or the brakes be erratic, you can assume that the design of the bike is faulty or that the dealer doesn't know or care about service—only sales.

6

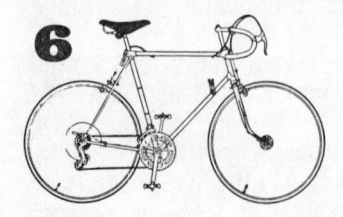

Bike Safety

Bicycles have been described as the "most benign of machines." And they are, especially when compared to other means of transportation. However, bicycles are not by any stretch of the imagination safe. They are inherently unstable, have poor acceleration, are for the most part fitted with brakes that deteriorate when wet. Bumps in the road must be absorbed by the frame and rider rather than being dampened by a suspension mechanism as in the case of motorcycles and autos.

At best estimate there are about one million injury-producing accidents a year involving bicycles. Approximately 372,000 of these accidents require hospital treatment. The most serious type involves auto-cyclist collision and accounts for some 38,000 hospital admissions per annum. Eleven hundred of these result in death to the cyclist. Not surprisingly, the government has placed bicycles at the top of its "most dangerous products" list.

The number of accidents roughly parallels the growth of the sport. In the last decade the accident figure has increased by some 220 percent. The Surveillance Systems Bureau of the Product Safety Commission is monitoring emergency room admissions in 119 hospitals spotted around the coutry in an attempt to identify the immediate cause of bike accidents. The data is still very incomplete, but it seems to indicate that the largest single factor is rider error.

Mistakes become more frequent and the results are more serious when bicycle and auto traffic are mixed. Unfortunately, some mixing of these incompatible vehicles is inevitable. Even sidewalk bikes enter auto space as they cross driveways. And the federal government, while willing to open bike trails, certainly is not going to build a complete bike road network.

RIDING DEFENSIVELY

A cyclist must ride defensively since the mastodons with which he shares the road are part-blind, sometimes indifferent, and outweigh him by a factor of 30 or more. The Bicycle Institute of America has developed a set of basic rules for cyclists:

- Obey all traffic regulations. A bicycle is a road vehicle and is subject to the rules which govern powered traffic. Do not run a stop light because of the difficulty in downshifting a derailleur.
- Ride with the traffic over against the right lane. Riding with traffic will reduce the frequency of accidents and their severity as well as keep you out of trouble with pedestrians.
- Always ride single file in a group. The width of your vehicle cluster is more critical then its length in most traffic situations.
- Ride in a straight line. Motorists must be able to predict your position and are unprepared for the maneuverability of bicycles.
- Ride alertly. You are subject to attack from every direction except the vertical. Motorists can turn in front of you, shoulder you into a line of parked cars, overtake you from the rear, or open doors as you whiz by. New cars with their high seatbacks are the worst offenders in the last regard. Use your ears as well as your eyes. You can hear a car approaching before it jiggles into sight in your mirror.
- Ride courteously, giving pedestrians a wide berth. Do not ride on sidewalks unless city ordinance allows it.
- Ride with all the control the machine can give you. This means regular inspection and maintenance, packages secured and ballasted low on the centerline and no passengers. Do not hitch tows from other vehicles.

Bicycles are very responsive to small irregularities in the road surface. The tire adhesion area is small and high inflation pressures coupled with unsprung wheels makes road contact precarious. Watch out for loose gravel, oil spills, and potholes.

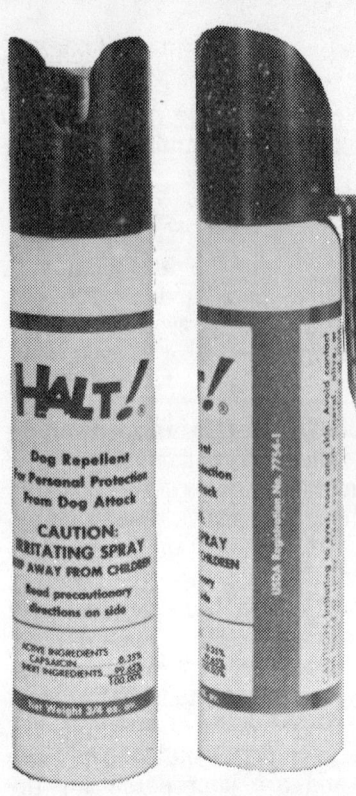

Fig. 6-1. Dog repellent. (Courtesy Action Accessories)

Railroad crossings and the few trolley tracks which survive are particularly vicious. Should the rails cross the roadway at an angle you are almsot sure to lose control; and even head-on, the chances of denting a rim are good. Perhaps the worst surface hazard is the expanded steel gridwork found on bridges. These grids may extend for six feet or more on either approach to the bridge and deny all control. Once your wheels become imprisoned in the mesh remaining upright becomes a problem. Dismount near the curb and walk the bike over.

All of these hazards become more dangerous in wet weather. Rain can disguise the potholes, lubricate the loose gravel, and give steel the sheen of ice. And moisture cuts rim-brake effectiveness by 75% or more.

Dogs are another problem. There is something very lonely about confronting a snarling German Shepherd who is programmed to hunt and has a better power-to-weight ratio than you do. Unless he is a very aggressive animal and has appropriated the whole neighborhood, the dog attacks because you have violated his territorial instinct which extends for less than a hundred feet around his home. But once triggered it seems that a hunting instinct takes over and he may chase you for blocks. A can of repellent is handy to have at this time (Fig. 6-1). If worse comes to worse, dismount and try to keep the bike between you and the animal. If at all possible, take cover behind something solid. Once line of sight contact is broken, most dogs forget what they are about.

REFLEXES

Ultimately bicycle safety is a matter of trained reflexes. Recognizing this, the Bicycle Institute of America has developed a series of exercises designed to improve rider response. These exercises form the nucleus of a training program for schools and adult riders.

The series begins with the group coasting 40 feet or more on one pedal. Riders mount on the left side, leaving the left foot trailing and with both hands on the bars. The maneuver is repeated on the right side. Once all riders have gained proficiency in this, lessons are given in proper mounting. One pedal should be 45 degrees from the horizontal. When starting, riders push off with one foot, apply pressure to the pedal with the other, while easing into the seat. A variation is to look back as if the exercise were taking place on a city street. Next the group learns how to stay within a 4 inch wide painted strip which extends for 100 feet. After this skill is mastered, the riders are instructed to remove one hand at a time from the bars, make gear changes, look over their shoulders for approaching traffic, and make hand signals.

The exercises progressively become more demanding. A figure-8 track is marked out on a 9 foot radius (Fig. 6-2) and the riders are expected to keep their front wheels within 6 inches of the line at steadily increased speeds. This exercise teaches confidence in making turns.

The next phase involves braking. First a line is used as a marker (Fig. 6-3). The riders have about a 60-foot run at the line and approach at normal speed. With practice the front wheel can be stopped within three inches of the line. The purpose is to give a sense of the relationship between speed and braking force. The emergency-stop test is a bit more rigorous since it involves boards placed across the pavement. Riders should come to a stop with the tire just in front of the obstacle. Neither wheel should skid. Speeds are increased until each rider has mastered the technique of a controlled emergency stop.

The next excercise is deceptively simple. Weighted cans or fist-sized stones are placed several inches on either side of a painted strip. The strip is about six inches wide and the

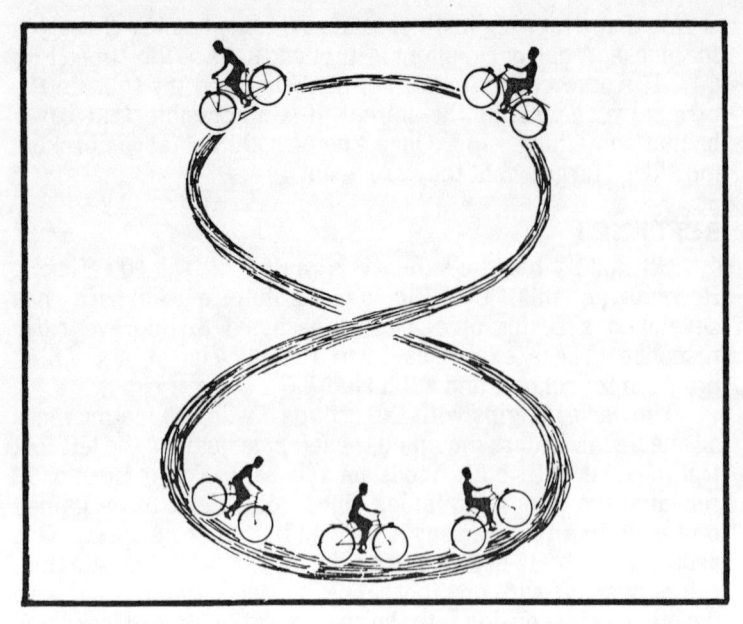

Fig. 6-2. Figure-8 exercise. (Courtesy Bicycle Institute of America)

obstacles are staggered every six feet. The rider merely must stay on the strip. However, if he does the natural thing and looks at the obstacles, he will unconsciously veer into them. The only way to stay out of trouble is to concentrate on the

Fig. 6-3. Braking test, first phase. (Courtesy Bicycle Institute of America)

strip. This exercise demonstrates the complex relationship between eye and muscular response and is invaluable training for riding on pockmarked city streets like those in Washington, DC.

Other drills involve massed side-by-side starts, short radius turns, and direction changes on command. Side-by-side riding gets one accustomed to moving objects on the flanks and should make the experience of urban traffic less traumatic. The short (five foot) radius turn is a coordination builder and a convenient skill. Riders must keep both feet on the pedals, stay within the painted strip, and use brakes with discretion. Changing direction on visual cue involves three bikes in a triangular formation. On a hand signal from any rider, the group swings sharply to the left or right. Positions rotate; the point requires most alertness. Speeds increase with demonstrated skill, although it has been found necessary to warn riders beforehand that turns are made by leaning and looking into the direction of turn. Keeping ones eyes on the signal man invites a spill (an easier variant is shown in Fig. 6-4). Turning on audio command is done in individual exercises (Fig. 6-5). An instructor flanks the rider's path and gives a whistle or horn signal just as he passes. The signal is followed by a sharp *Right, Left*, or *Ahead*, in best Fort Benning tradition. The rider has one bicycle length to respond.

The most realistic (and in unsupervised hands, the most dangerous) of these exercises is the open-door test. It can get hairy. The group to be tested passes a row of cars parked at the curb. Instructors are placed in the cars and open the doors at random. The cyclists must swerve or brake as required.

Fig. 6-4. Swerving on visual command. (Courtesy Bicycle Institute of America)

Fig. 6-5. Swerving on verbal command. (Courtesy Bicycle Institute of America)

For obvious reasons this exercise must begin at very low speeds. It is held under traffic conditions and the cyclists must be conditioned by the previous drills to listen for approaching cars. The instructors must open the doors only wide enough to obtain the desired effect. Cyclists are taught to watch for shoulder movements which telegraph that the door is about to swing open.

A safer method is to use cardboard cartons of about the size of car doors. The instructors are positioned between parked cars and thrust the cartons into the riders' path.

THE BICYCLE

Even with the best habits and surest reflexes, your control over your machine is only as good as its innate responsiveness. Wheel and particularly frame design are the major

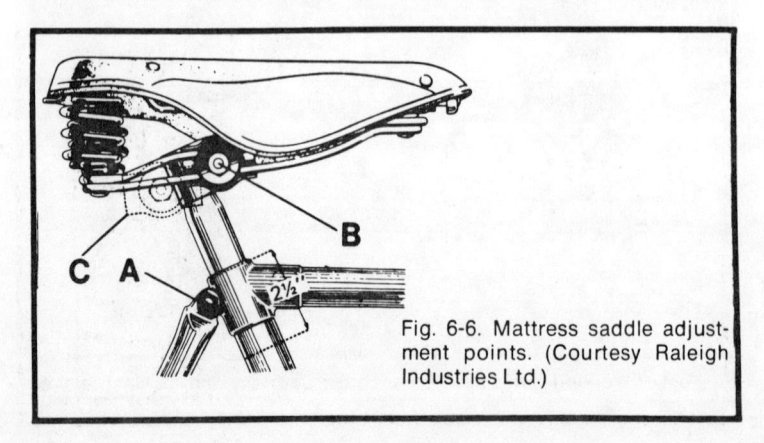

Fig. 6-6. Mattress saddle adjustment points. (Courtesy Raleigh Industries Ltd.)

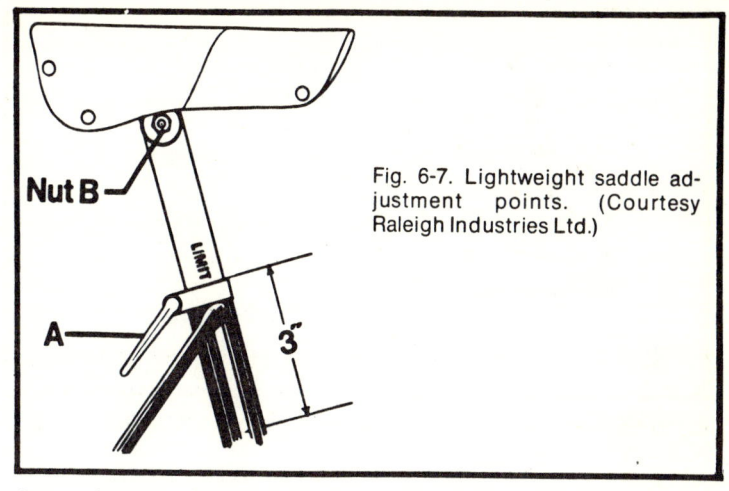

Fig. 6-7. Lightweight saddle adjustment points. (Courtesy Raleigh Industries Ltd.)

determinates of how well the machine obeys your muscular commands. As a practical matter, responsiveness is given determined on the drawing board, although you can make some experiments with tire tread patterns and, within limits, inflation pressures.

The Saddle

The saddle should be secure and adjusted to fit. Adjust vertically by loosening the seat lug (the nut in Fig. 6-6A or quick-release lever in 6-7A). Your knee should be slightly bent at the downward limit of pedal travel. Some riders make this adjustment by placing the heel on the pedal (see Figs. 6-7through 6-10 for saddle positioning). If the leg is straight, the correct bend will result when the ball of the foot is positioned

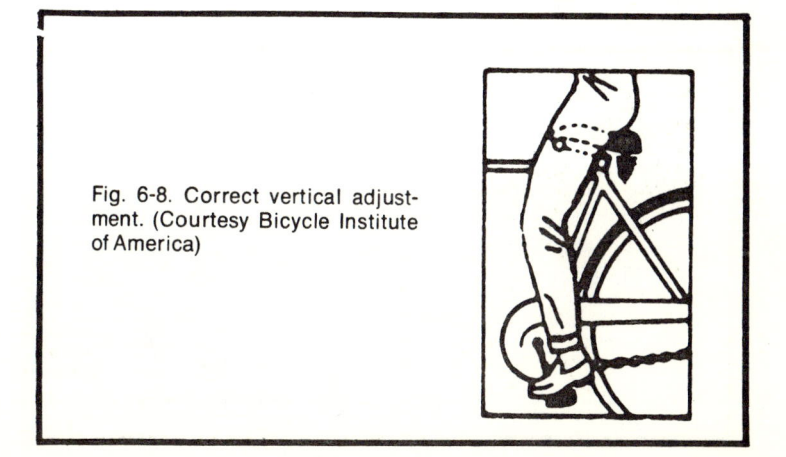

Fig. 6-8. Correct vertical adjustment. (Courtesy Bicycle Institute of America)

101

Fig. 6-9. Saddle too far to the rear. (Courtesy Bicycle Institute of America)

over the pedal. The saddle pillar should remain 2 1/2 to 3 inches within the frame. Extending it further will cause severe mechanical stress and can be hazardous. Quick-release levers are somewhat fragile, and no tools should be needed or used to gain leverage. The square-head nut can be repositioned in the frame so that the lever tightens with a downward movement.

The nut in Figs. 6-6B and 6-7B controls the tilt of the saddle. One or two nuts may be present. Most riders prefer a slight upward tilt of the nose for security during braking. Fore-and-aft adjustment is also made at B. The clamp, as shown by the dotted lines in Fig. 6-6C is reversed for mattress saddles. As a rule of thumb, this adjustment is correct when the nose of the saddle extends 2—2 1/2 inches forward as a vertical line drawn through the bottom bracket axis. Individual riders have their own preferences which are usually based on good anatomical reasons. Tighten all adjustments securely and ride several miles to check the adjustment.

Handlebars

Loosen the expander bolt A in Fig. 6-11 several turns and rap it sharply downward. This will free the expander and allow the stem to move. Prestige stems employ recessed head

Fig. 6-10. Saddle too far forward. (Courtesy Bicycle Institute of America)

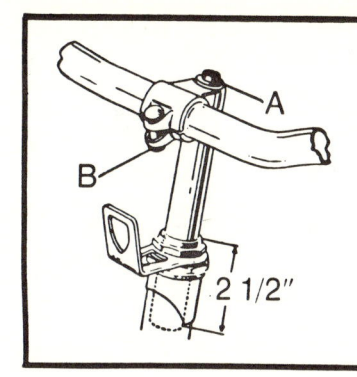

Fig. 6-11. Handlebar and stem adjustment. (Courtesy Raleigh Industries Ltd.)

expander bolts which offer one less protrusion and are stronger than the capscrew types. Other bikes may have quick-release levers as shown in Fig. 6-12. Raise or lower the bars until they are comfortable. The stem must remain buried at least 2 1/2 inches in the head tube for adequate strength. Some bikes have a restrictor which fixes this dimension.

The angle is set by loosening bolt B in Fig. 6-11 and rotating the bars. Incidentally, handlebars can wear out if the bolt is not securely tightened. A few slips and the knurling goes, making it impossible to tighten the bars.

The reach or the overhang of the stem varies with make and model. It has a great deal to do with control since the reach helps to determine how much of the rider's weight is supported on the front wheel. If you find that you are cramped by the bars or that you lean forward excessively, substitute a stem with a different reach. Some riders may find an adjustable stem, such as the Cinelli No. 2, a good investment. The handlebar is held in a clamp which can be moved forward and back.

Frame

Inspect the frame for trueness at regular intervals. This precaution is more important with sophisticated frames than with the heavy, seamed tube variety. This should be done

Fig. 6-12. Quick-release stem. (Courtesy Raleigh Industries Ltd.)

QUICK RELEASE LEVER

103

before investing heavily in a bike of doubtful parentage. A quick way to check is to ride the bike "hands off"—general misalignments will betray themselves as a tendency to pull to either side. Shimmy or a "rubbery" feel to what was once a taut bike means structural failure at the frame joints or wheels. In some instances, especially when laquer is used, frame parting may first show itself as hairline cracks in the paint at the joints. If you can't see anything wrong, but the bike just doesn't feel right, take it into a bike shop. They'll have the necessary tools and knowledge to determine if the bike is tight and aligned.

Brakes

The bike should come to a smooth, progressive stop with all braking wheels sharing the braking chores. Adjustment and other maintenance procedures are detailed in Chapter 7. Other than routine compensation for wear, the most critical problem is the control cables which must be kept lubricated and free of binds. If a single strand is broken, replace the inner cable since the remaining strands will soon fail.

Some bikes have lamentable rim brakes. (These can come even from old-line factories which should care enough about their reputations not to allow this sort of product out the door.) The problem shows up in the proportioning of braking forces between the front and rear wheels. It is possible to lift the rear wheel in a panic stop, converting the bicycle into a unicycle, or, at the other extreme the rear wheel may lock up of its own accord. The latter difficulty is caused by flexible calipers which bend under braking forces. The blocks wedge between the rim and seat stays, locking the wheel into a skid as noted in Chapter 5. Replace the whole assembly with a quality brake.

Too much braking on the front wheel can be caused by insufficient pressure on the rear blocks or by too much friction on the front blocks. Flexible calipers are usually the cause of poor rear brake performance. Rather than going to compress the calipers, the cable merely bends the actuating arm. Excessive friction on the front blocks can be cured by going to a different pattern and/or block composition. The cobbled European pattern is usually less efficient than the smooth American block. For really fine tuning you can adjust tire pressure. Within limits defined by bounce on uneven surfaces, the harder a tire is, the more braking power it generates (on dry pavement).

Wheels

With the wheel off the pavement, test for wobble by spinning the wheel and holding a piece of chalk or a Magic

Marker near the rim. Note the pattern of marks. Also, tap each spoke lightly with a small wrench. A tight spoke will give a high frequency "ting" as it is struck. All of the spokes should play the same tune. Egg-shaped wheels can be seen when tracking behind the bike, although thorough inspection requires that the cover be removed.

The wheel should spin freely without noise or hesitation. Dirt in the bearings will make a crackling sound while dried grease will reduce the free spin time. With the axle nuts tight, there should be just a hair of side play. You may not be able to see the play, but you should feel it as you alternately press and pull on the wheel.

The inflation pressure is usually marked on the sidewall and varies from 100 pounds per square inch for racing tubulars to 35 pounds per square inch for sidewalk tires. At any rate, the tire should not bulge with your weight upon it. Using the corner station to fill tires is easier than using a hand pump, but it is disconcertingly easy to overfill a bicycle tire so be careful.

Bottom Bracket and Crank

The crank should be disassembled and the bearings cleaned and greased at least once a season. Sealed bearings, available for the crank and for the wheels, eliminate this messy chore but are expensive. They are economical if you have your work done at a shop. The crank should turn easily without lateral or more than a touch of endplay and it should be silent. A crunching sound means that there is sand in the bearings.

The pedals should be lubricated and inspected for wear. All of your energy is transmitted through the pedals. If toe-straps are used—a great energy conserver, although somewhat intimidating for beginners in traffic—they must be secure.

Transmissions

Bicycle transmissions, whether of the derailleur, planetary, or coaster-brake variety are prone to sudden slippage. The problem may be one of maladjustment, stiff chain links, bent sprockets, or parts failure. Obviously such a situation must be corrected before the bike is ridden. Even a single slip (if we forget for a moment about derailleurs which will slip and make purchase in the normal course of a sloppy shift) means the bike should be grounded. It is axiomatic that if a machine fails once, it will fail again.

Accessories

Forty-nine states require a head lamp and a red reflector at the rear. Seven states insist that this equipment be fitted to

CHECK YOUR BIKE FOR SAFE OPERATION

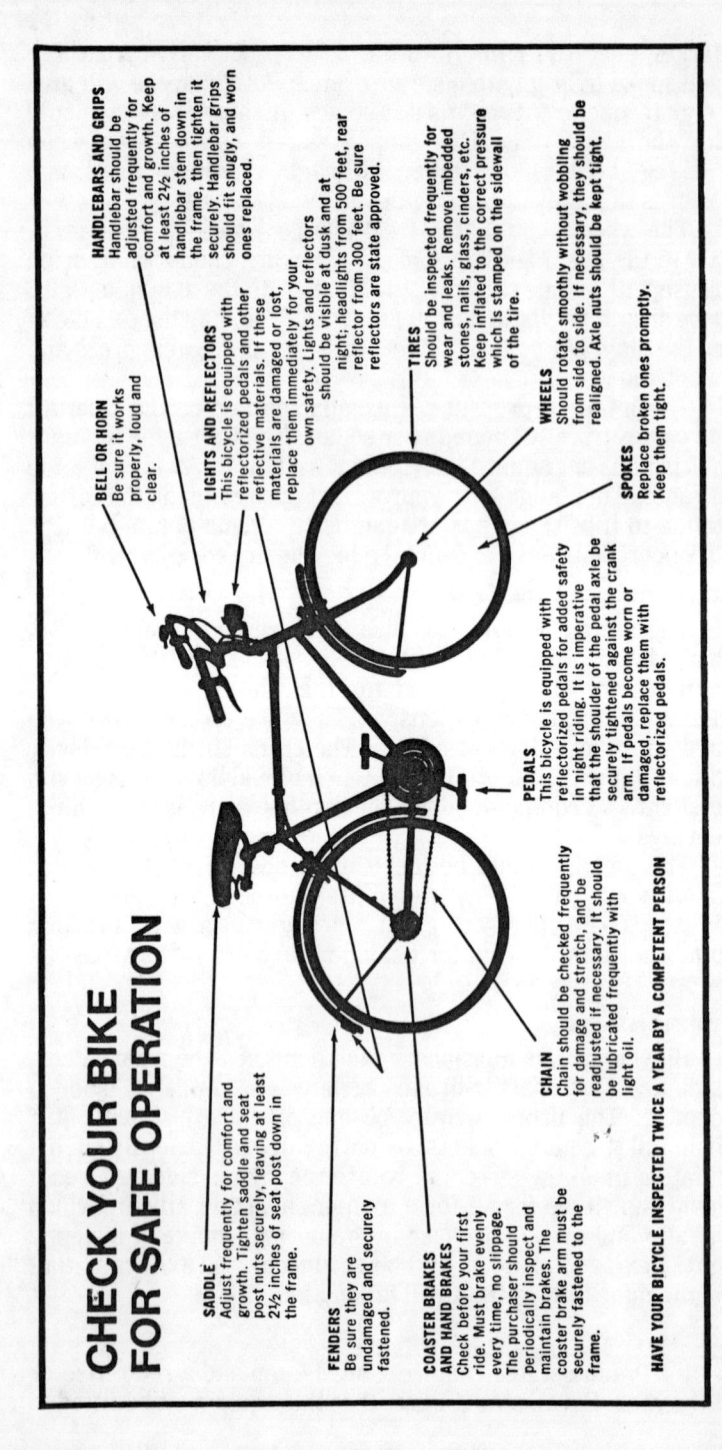

SADDLE
Adjust frequently for comfort and growth. Tighten saddle and seat post nuts securely, leaving at least 2½ inches of seat post down in the frame.

FENDERS
Be sure they are undamaged and securely fastened.

COASTER BRAKES AND HAND BRAKES
Check before your first ride. Must brake evenly every time, no slippage. The purchaser should periodically inspect and maintain brakes. The coaster brake arm must be securely fastened to the frame.

CHAIN
Chain should be checked frequently for damage and stretch, and be readjusted if necessary. It should be lubricated frequently with light oil.

PEDALS
This bicycle is equipped with reflectorized pedals for added safety in night riding. It is imperative that the shoulder of the pedal axle be securely tightened against the crank arm. If pedals become worn or damaged, replace them with reflectorized pedals.

HANDLEBARS AND GRIPS
Handlebar should be adjusted frequently for comfort and growth. Keep at least 2½ inches of handlebar stem down in the frame, then tighten it securely. Handlebar grips should fit snugly, and worn ones replaced.

BELL OR HORN
Be sure it works properly, loud and clear.

LIGHTS AND REFLECTORS
This bicycle is equipped with reflectorized pedals and other reflective materials. If these materials are damaged or lost, replace them immediately for your own safety. Lights and reflectors should be visible at dusk and at night; headlights from 500 feet, rear reflector from 300 feet. Be sure reflectors are state approved.

TIRES
Should be inspected frequently for wear and leaks. Remove imbedded stones, nails, glass, cinders, etc. Keep inflated to the correct pressure which is stamped on the sidewall of the tire.

WHEELS
Should rotate smoothly without wobbling from side to side. If necessary, they should be realigned. Axle nuts should be kept tight.

SPOKES
Replace broken ones promptly. Keep them tight.

HAVE YOUR BICYCLE INSPECTED TWICE A YEAR BY A COMPETENT PERSON

Fig. 6-13. Safety checkpoints. (Courtesy Bicycle Institute of America)

all bikes used on public roads; the other 42 are only concerned with night operation. The diameter of reflectors and the intensity of the lamp varies between states as does enforcement. Three states—New York, Rhode Island, and Nebraska—require reflective tires.

The Consumer Product Safety Commission, acting under the authority of the Consumer Products Safety Act of 1972, has promulgated a set of safety standards which would apply to most bicycles in interstate commerce. In response to a barrage of complaints by industry spokemen, the implementation date was extended from January 1 to May 1, 1975 and then extended again. The only machine to escape proposed regulation are bikes made to the customer's order and track machines. These proposals, now in legal limbo, are nevertheless instructive since they represent the first scientific approach to bicycle safety.

Lamps

Consumer Product Safety Commission believes that reflectors are of more benefit than lights for night visibility. No one, I hasten to add, suggests that you ride blind. The difficulty with lights is reliability. Lamp filaments shake themselves to pieces with disconcerting regularity, batteries run down and may not be replaced, and designers have been unable as yet to solve the problem of generating current while the bike is stationary. Raleigh's combination battery and generator set is a step in the right direction (the battery automatically comes "on line" when generator output drops), but it alone is hardly the definitive solution. You should at least have a tail lamp when riding at night. A generator-driven lamp is preferable for extended use, although urban residents would do well to invest in a battery rig. One of the best generator sets is the French Soubitez (Fig. 6-14) which delivers three watts to a single headlamp bulb. A tail lamp can be wired in parallel if both bulbs do not together draw more than three watts. Be wary of generator sets made in the Orient. All clip-on generators are hard on paint since the generator must be grounded to the frame or fork, but the Hong Kong specials peel square inches of paint as they slip and spin on their mountings. Nor, once tied down, are these generators reliable. Switch contacts are exposed in the lamp fairing and oxidize about as quickly as the reflector tarnishes.

Battery-powered lamps come in a number of reputable varieties from lanterns to arm lamps. The latter have Janus-faced lenses with a red filter on the rear. All of these lamps employ dry cell batteries of the carbon or alkaline type.

As of yet, no manufacturer has devised a bike light using rechargeable nickel cadmium cells.

Reflectors

While no reflector is as visible from a distance as the feeblest tail lamp, a reflector does function well beyond the throw of automobile headlights. Assuming that they are designed correctly and mounted securely, reflectors require no maintenance (other than cleaning) for the life of the machine.

The Bicycle Institute of America concurs with this reasoning. Since July 1, 1973, domestic manufacturers have met the BMA/6 visibility standard which requires ten reflectors of various colors. The federal standards would add spoke or sidewall reflectors—the choice is up to the consumer. Pedal and spoke mounting has a great advantage since these reflectors move relative to the bicycle and should quicken the motorist's recognition.

But not any reflector will do. CPSC regulations are spelled out with great specificity: reflectors must develop high intensity values, be heat and cold resistant, and be able to withstand the impact of a 1/2 inch steel ball dropped from the height of 30 inches. In addition, reflectors are immersed in water in a container pressurized to 2 1/2 pounds/square inch for 15 minutes. Leakage between the lens elements will be shown as a drop in performance.

Older bikes should be updated to CPSC standards because 80 percent of auto/bike accidents occur at dusk or after sundown. A number of American and foreign firms make reflectors to meet these standards, but, as of this writing, they are not so marked. The best bet is to attempt to purchase

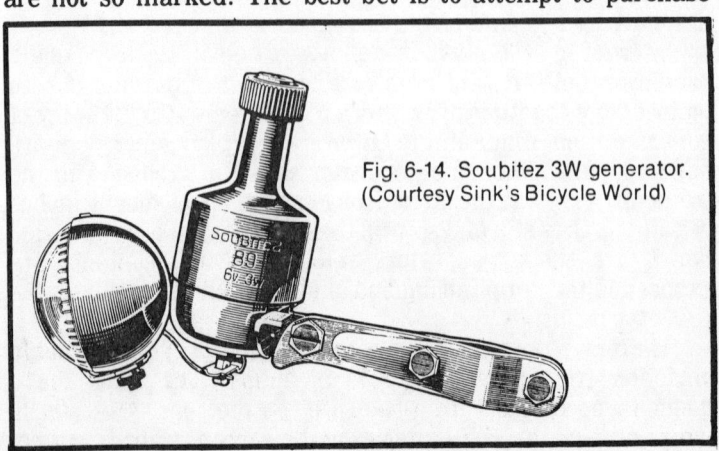

Fig. 6-14. Soubitez 3W generator. (Courtesy Sink's Bicycle World)

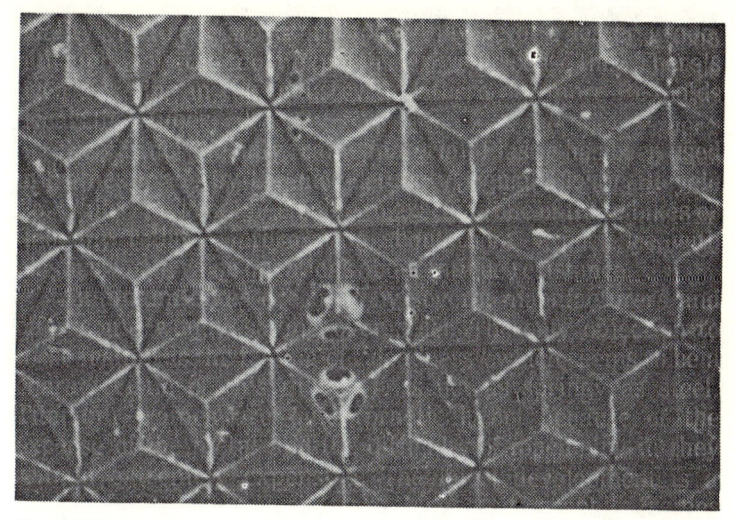

Fig. 6-15. Micro-photograph of Reflexite. (Courtesy Rowland Development Corp.)

factory originals, identical to those on the current production bikes. Additional reflectors are by no means a case of overkill.

The Rowland Development Corp. markets a new reflective material called Reflexite. Although based on the familiar four-corner prism (Fig. 6-15) it is several times more efficient than competing products. Reflexite will respond to auto headlights up to 600 feet away and continue to function with 90 percent efficiency when covered with a film of water. This material is not currently available as bicycle hardware, but can be purchased as adhesive Hot Dots or strips for attachment to clothes as well as frame parts (Fig. 6-16).

Flags

Fluorescent flags are primarily daylight warning devices. Most flags are mounted vertically on a six or seven foot fiberglass pole. These flags are especially useful in the jagged hills of Appalachia where a bicycle can disappear in thirty feet. Dobi offers a clearance flag (Fig. 6-17) for flat country to be mounted horizontally on the passing side to help motorists judge the distance between themselves and the bike. The flag is suspended on a coil spring and is retractable when not in use. Some cyclists object to flags, believing them to be another useless appurtenance to compromise the functional beauty of the bicycle. Esthetically they may be right, but from the point of view of safety, flags make sense and add only a few ounces of drag.

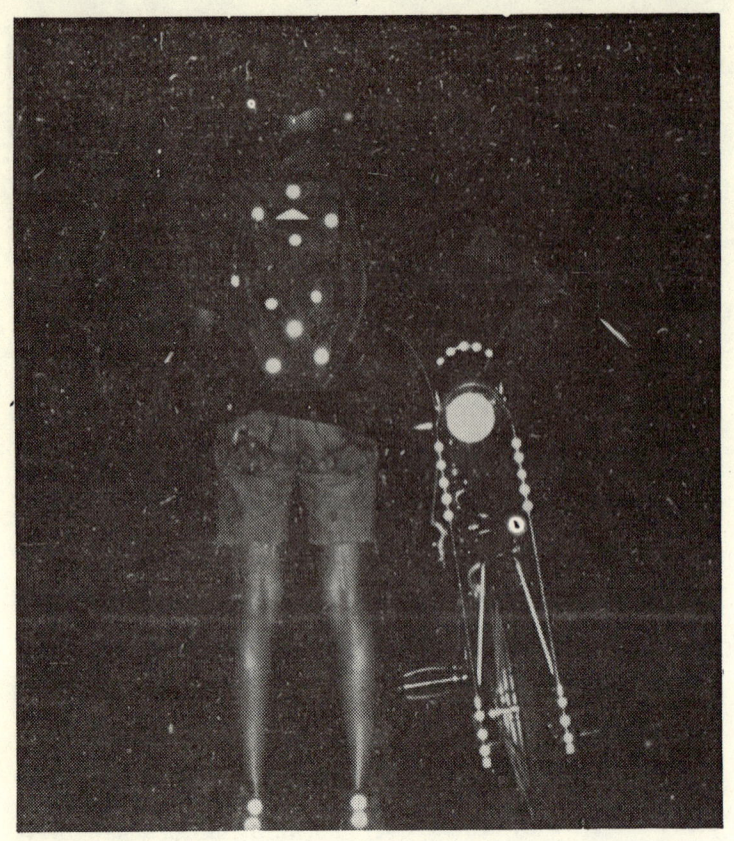

Fig. 6-16. Reflexite at night. (Courtesy Rowland Development Corp.)

HELMETS

Helmets are also subject to heated dispute. Those who wear them can quote statistics showing that head injuries are not common, but when they do occur are by far the most lethal. The wind-in-the-hair crowd counters with vaque but serious objections—helmets are pretentious, Walter Mittyish, and another step away from simplicity of man and bike. Sometimes one hears the extreme view that helmets are a modern vulgarity on part with power-driven pencil sharpeners and electric golf carts. This argument overlooks that high hats, particularly the silk hat which has since become known as the opera hat, were designed as primitive crash helmets. Made fashionable by fox hunters, these hats were part of the uniform of early cyclists.

As far as I can determine, no one has done much research of bicycle helmets. Motorcycle helmets are too heavy and hot and may actually increase the chances of collision with autos because of impaired hearing. Track helmets are light but skeletal and leave one feeling a bit naked. Nor do these helmets protect the base of the skull. Helmets designed for mountain climbing are a good choice, as are hockey helmets. White is the best color in terms of visibility and heat reflection. If you decide to paint your helmet, check with the manufacturer. Polycarbonate shells do not tolerate paint very well and may lose a great deal of impact strength in the process. The same caution applies to decals. Nor should the integrity of the structure be compromised by holes for visors or motorcycle style handlebar locks.

BIKE SECURITY

Bicycle theft is a fact of life in metropolitian areas and is spreading to suburbia and rural communities as well. The yearly toll for the state of New Jersey is about 23,000 bikes worth some $1.3 million; California residents lose some 100,000 bikes a year. In some localities it is estimated that a full 20 percent of the bike population is stolen each year.

What can be done about it? Or more specifically, how can you secure your bike? There are several types of bicycle thieves each with a characteristic *modus operandi*. The casual thief saunters about the streets looking for an unlocked machine. A dog chain is enough to discourage him since he wants no part of bolt cutters or other incriminating appliances. He has been known to drop a bicycle and run if the owner had the foresight to park it in high gear. Another category can be

Fig. 6-17. Clearance flag from Dobi.

described as bicycle muggers. Operating in gangs in the larger cities, these gentlemen lurk on bike trails and appropriate cycles by force.

The most proficient thieves look for an unattended bicycle and are not deterred by chains, cables, and Gothic padlocks. Bolt cutters are their stock-in-trade; most operate out of pickup trucks or vans so the strategem of removing the front wheel will merely leave you with a souvenir of your departed bicycle. Generally these professionals steal from open parking spaces since they do not want to face a burglary rap. Some, however, are not so discriminating and will break into a garage or dwelling to obtain an expensive bike.

In the last analysis bike security is a matter of probabilities. Absolute security eludes us here as in other areas of life. But there are ways to deter theft, at least theft by less determined individuals. Park your bike in a well-lighted, well-trafficked place. Secure the frame—not the wheels—with a chilled chain or a cable. Neither of these will defeat a cutter, but will make the job harder. Some cables have soft inner strands which must be gnawed through, rather than snapped. Chains are heavy and we all know a connoisseur with an 18 pound bike and a 20 pound chain. Unfortunately large diameter chains mean security. It is many times more difficult to cut a 3/8 inch chain than a 1/4 inch one. Further security can be had by suspending the bike from an overhead, denying the thief the leverage he would have by placing one handle of the cutter on the ground and leaning on it. The weak link is often the lock. Do not use warded padlocks which can be picked by dexterous six-year olds. These locks can be usually identified by their stamped, double-bitted keys. Tumbler locks are much more secure and the better ones bar both ends of the shackle. A cheap, single-bitted lock can be shocked open with a hammer and length of 2×4. Consumer's Union recommends the Corbin 2883A, Hurd 716, and Yale 850 among others. Some cyclists swear by the legendary Kryptonite lock. Made of 1 1/2 inch stainless steel, this lock was tested by Boston's Association for Bicycle Commuting in a very direct fashion. A bike, minus front wheel, was secured to a street sign in Greenwich Village. The Kryptonite lock withstood two weeks of assault by Village residents.

Wherever possible keep your bike by your side. You may not be able to take it into a restaurant, but you can usually park it where you can keep an eye on it while eating. And while bicycles may not be the ultimate in office decor, there is almost always a large closet or storeroom available. At home bring the bike inside, out of the garage.

Rim Brakes

The Consumer Product Safety Commission's test standards for bicycle brakes were published in January 1976 and deserve careful scrutiny, since they are the best introduction to the dynamics of bicycle braking that we have.

Two-wheel brakes—a category which means rim brakes in practice—were to be subject to several performance tests. The loading test required a force of 100 foot-pounds to be applied to the hand levers ten times in succession. No visible damage was to result and clearances between the brake blocks, and wheel rims were to remain within specification. (Lever distortion and cable stretch would immediately show as an increase in the pad-to-wheel clearance.) Another test was to place a 150 pound weight on the seat and apply 100 foot-pounds to the control levels. The bike was to be rocked back and forth over dry pavement for a distance of three inches. Brake blocks and levers were to remain in place and functional.

The dynamic test required that the bike be halted within 15 feet from a speed no greater than 15 mph with an applied torque of 40 foot-pounds on the levers. The rider would weigh 150 pounds.

CPSC standards made no provision for wet testing. Rim brakes are exposed to the weather and can suffer a dramatic loss of stopping power in the rain or in a heavy fog. At their most efficient these brakes can generate a force of 1 g or better as the tire treads act as a kind of cogwheel on the pavement. In the wet stopping power may only be 0.15 g. All

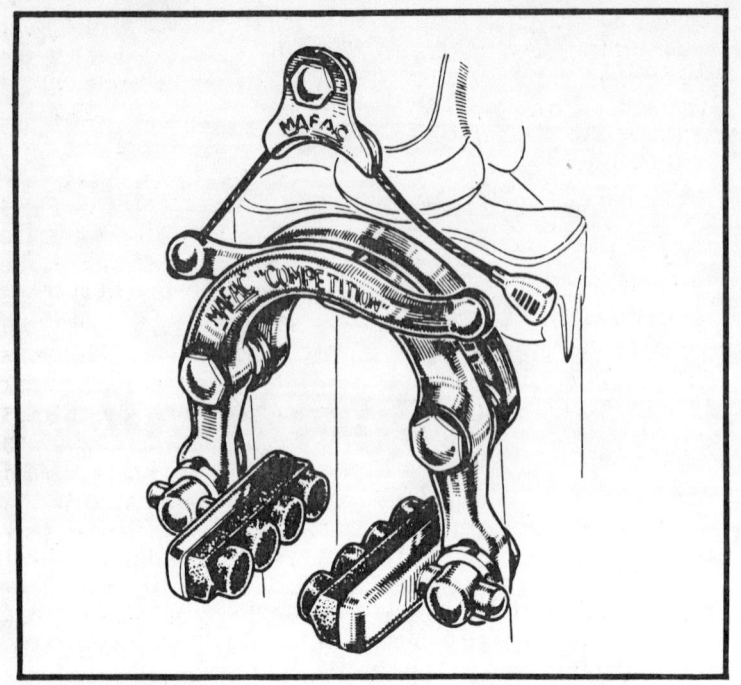

Fig. 7-1. Mafac Competition center-pull brake. (Courtesy Ware's)

vehicles suffer this effect to some extent, but rim brakes are particularly susceptible because of their exposure.

However, this same open construction enables the brakes to cool. In downhill runs the cooling effect is important. Coaster brakes, enclosed in a weather-proof and essentially air-tight housing, have been known to literally weld themselves together in severe use.

SIDE PULL VS CENTER PULL

Side-pull calipers route the control cable to one arm, usually the left. As the inner element of the cable is retracted it pulls the right caliper arm and brake block (or shoe) toward the rim. At the same time an equal and opposite force is exerted on the cable sheath which, pressing downward, forces the left arm toward the rim. Center-pull brakes do away with this push-pull action and operate by lifting a bridge (the triangular part at the top of the drawing in Fig. 7-1) and a transverse cable. The ends of the cable are anchored at the caliper arms.

Side-pulls (shown in Fig. 7-2) are favored today, perhaps because Campanolo has bet its reputation on this configuration. At their best, these brakes are somewhat lighter than center-pulls and are used widely in competition. On the other hand, side-pulls can be frustrating to adjust, especially if you stray from top-line models. The difficulty is that the calipers stubbornly remain off-center when released.

Center-pulls are favored by many of the more conservative riders. Traditionally center-pulls have been a mark of quality and continue to be more expensive than the cookie-cutter side-pulls found on department-store bikes. The self-centering action of the bridge and transverse cable keeps them honest in the adjustment department, although advantages in other areas are questionable. Side-pulls approach the rim almost perpendicularly. Center-pulls attack the rim from an angle of 15 degrees or so. Whether or not this improves brake performance is debatable, but the angle does cause the blocks to move up toward the tire as they wear. And as you can see by comparing the length of the brake arms on either side of the pivot points (shown in Fig. 7-3) the side-pull gives very little mechanical advantage. The multiplication of hand force is almost entirely limited to the brake lever. This means that these brakes take more force to operate, but require less lever movement than center-pulls which have gobs of mechanical advantage due to the low pivots.

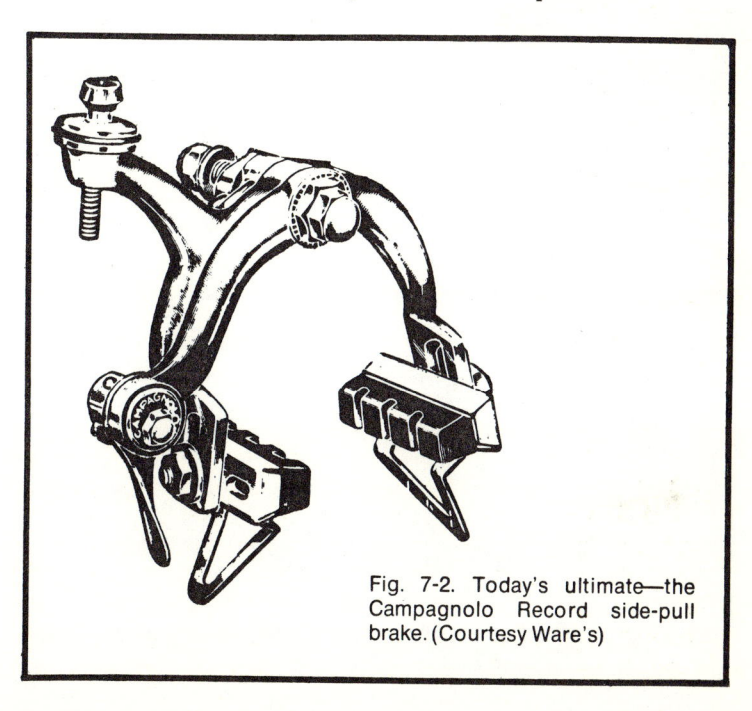

Fig. 7-2. Today's ultimate—the Campagnolo Record side-pull brake. (Courtesy Ware's)

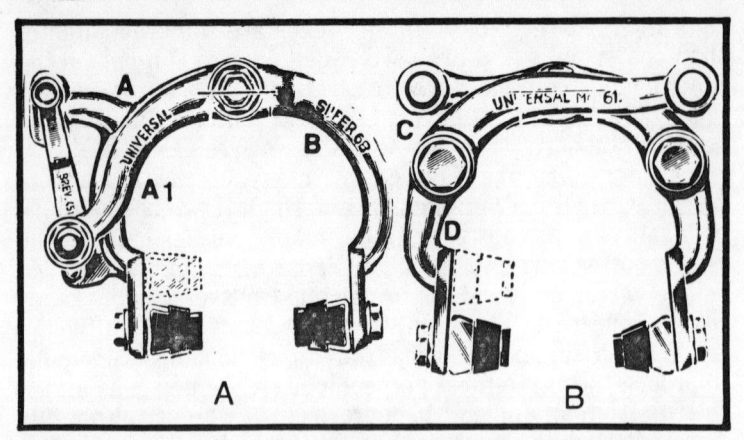

Fig. 7-3. Universal side-pull (A) and center-pull (B). Note the difference in the length on both sides of the pivot. The mechanical advantage of the side-pull is the average of A and A1 divided by B. The mechanical advantage of the center-pull is C divided by D. (Courtesy Sink's Bicycle World)

ADJUSTMENT

The brake blocks should be within 1/8 inch of the rims in the released position. Gross adjustments are made by loosening the anchor bolts, squeezing the calipers together, and pulling the inner element down with a pair of pliers. Fine adjustments are made by loosening the locknut A in Fig. 7-4 and turning the barrel adjuster B. Backing the adjustor off will bring the shoes together. Do not back it so far out that the threads disappear in the bracket; some thread must show for mechanical strength.

The brake blocks should be parallel to the rim and may not come into contact with the tire sidewalls. If possible the blocks should be centered in the groove to forestall difficulties as the

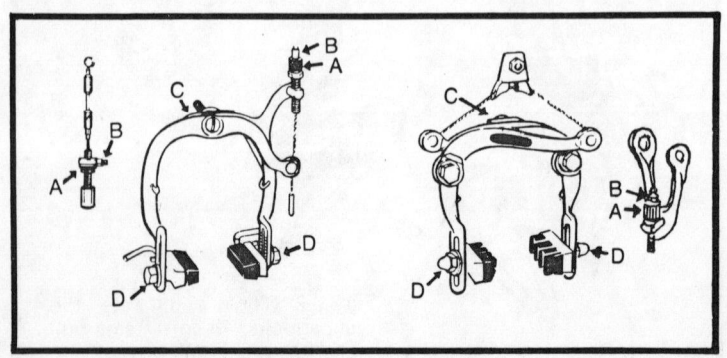

Fig 7-4. Major adjustment points on side- and center-pull brakes. (Courtesy Raleigh Industries Ltd.)

116

blocks wear. Loosen the capnuts D in Fig. 7-4 and set the blocks as required. These adjustments will go easier with a "third hand" (Fig. 7-5).

In addition, the blocks must be equidistant from the rim in the released position. The problem rarely develops in center-pull designs, but is not unusual with side-pulls.

It may be possible to loosen the pivot bolt or stud and reposition the caliper as needed. If this does not help matters, the brake will have to be disassembled. Figure 7-6 is an exploded drawing of the popular Shimano Tourney with a parts list for front and rear applications. This brake is typical of most side-pulls.

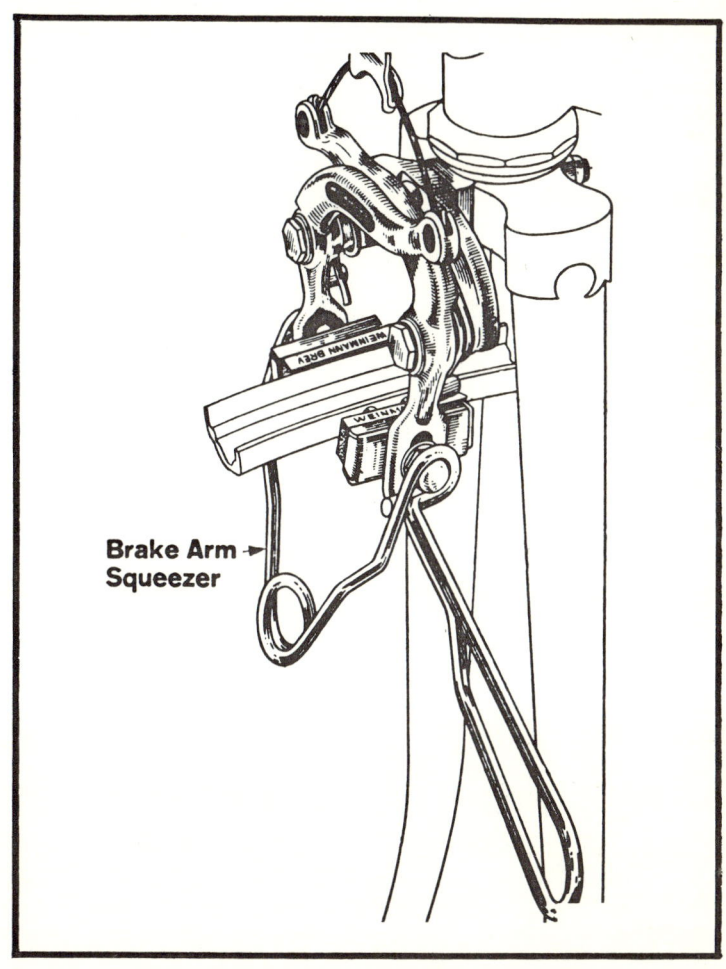

Fig. 7-5. Third hand. (Courtesy Action Accessories)

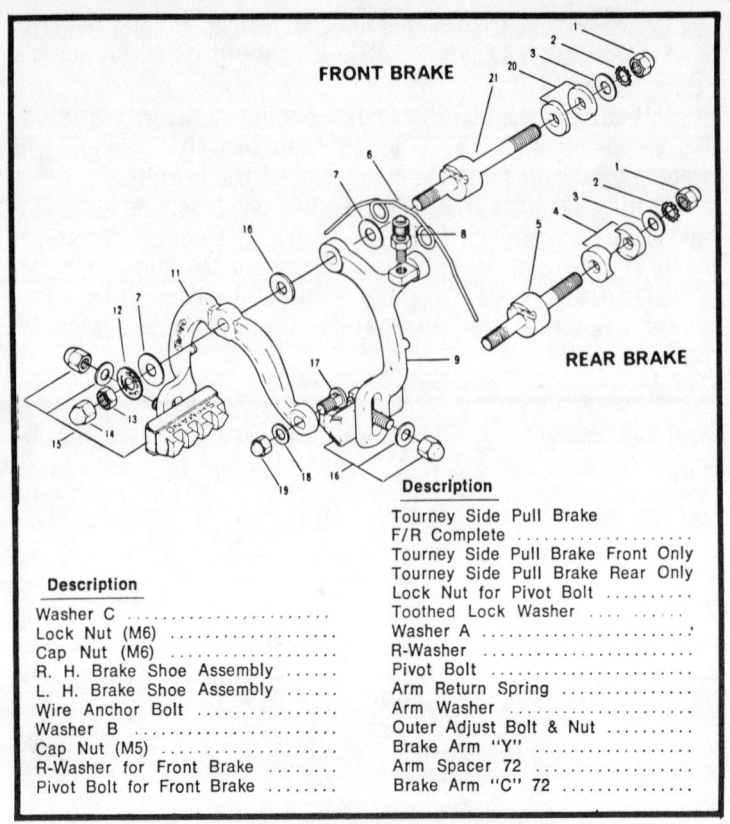

Fig. 7-6. Shimano Tourney side-pull brake. (Courtesy Browning)

Description

- Washer C
- Lock Nut (M6)
- Cap Nut (M6)
- R. H. Brake Shoe Assembly
- L. H. Brake Shoe Assembly
- Wire Anchor Bolt
- Washer B
- Cap Nut (M5)
- R-Washer for Front Brake
- Pivot Bolt for Front Brake

Description

- Tourney Side Pull Brake F/R Complete
- Tourney Side Pull Brake Front Only
- Tourney Side Pull Brake Rear Only
- Lock Nut for Pivot Bolt
- Toothed Lock Washer
- Washer A
- R-Washer
- Pivot Bolt
- Arm Return Spring
- Arm Washer
- Outer Adjust Bolt & Nut
- Brake Arm "Y"
- Arm Spacer 72
- Brake Arm "C" 72

An off-center condition will result if:

- the pivot bolt is turned so that its slot is not parallel to the ground. The pivot bolt (Nos. 5 and 21) is the reaction member for the spring (No. 6) which acts on it through the slot milled across the large diameter of the bolt
- the spring is bent or warped
- the pivots are rusty, dirty, or binding. You can check the pivots by working the arms by hand
- the caliper arms interfere with each other. The adjustment for this is at the locknut nut (No. 13) and the capnut (No. 15). To remove loosen the locknut 1/2 turn to bring it out of contact with the capnut; remove the capnut; and remove the locknut

Other calipers may not be identical to the Shimano pictured here and it is important that you get the parts sequence correct. Make note of the parts as you remove them or, if worse comes to worst, use the other brake as an assembly guide. The central stack of washers and spacers on the pivot bolt goes like this:

- capnut
- locknut (snugged against it for security)
- washer, usually with the brand name
- spacer (thicker than a washer)
- brake arm
- second spacer (often thicker than the first)
- second brake arm
- spacer
- spring

Handle the spring with care since it is quite powerful and may catapult into the air or bite your fingers. Bike mechanics favor duck bill pliers for this job. Clean and inspect the parts, lubricate with light grease, and assemble. Note which side the Y-shaped arm was on and remember that each arm is flanked by a spacer.

Another reason for failure to self-center is a slipped pivot bolt. Loosen the capnut on the far side of the pivot, away from the brake arms. It will usually be secured by the capnut and locknut arrangement shown in the drawing of the Shimano.

Center the brake blocks by hand (with the pivot loose the whole assembly will rotate) and, holding them in position, retighten the pivot nut. This technique works if the pivot and slot are integral as shown here; unfortunately not all brakes have this feature. Raleigh and Phillips units have a smooth-faced pivot. The slotted member is the forward one of the radius washers (Nos. 4 and 20). Radius washers are called that because they are arced to mate with the frame tube. Merely turning the pivot bolt has no effect on the washer or the spring.

If the brake arm spring exerts an uneven force, the best advice is to replace the spring. Barring that, you can sometimes make a satisfactory repair by bending the spring. With a large bar or a screwdriver, press down on the high point of the spring's curve on the side opposed to the malpositioned arm. Use caution.

Another possible cause of failure is that the levers are touching each other, either because of accident or because one of the spacers was left out. You will be able to see the levers touch and wear marks, if the condition has persisted for any length of time. Assuming that the parts are in place, determine which is bent (the damage will usually be confined to the

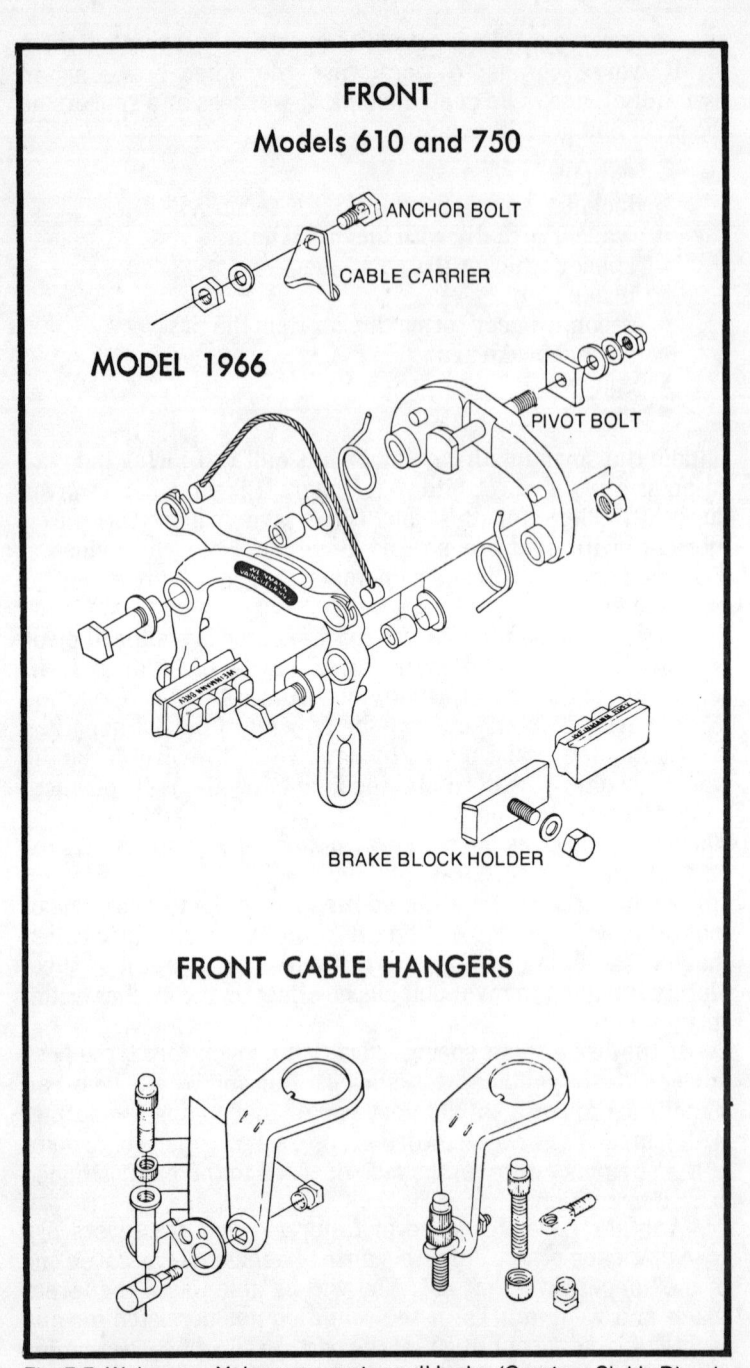

Fig. 7-7. Weinmann Vainqueur center-pull brake. (Courtesy Sink's Bicycle World)

forward-facing lever), disassemble, and straighten the lever in a vise. Bend it carefully and do not overshoot the mark. Repeated flexing will snap the lever. On-the-bike repairs can be done with a screwdriver if you are cavalier enough. Insert the tip of a large screwdriver at the point on the levers where they rub, and pry against the direction of the bend. The brake assembly is somewhat spindly and you will have to pry further than you anticipate.

Of course, bending a safety-related part such as a brake arm is something which must be done at your own discretion. The arm may be weakened and fail.

Center-pull brakes usually return to rest without complaint. But problems can develop with any of them. Disconnect the cable at the bridge anchor bolt (Fig. 7-7) and work both ends of the assembly—the hand lever and the caliper—by hand.

The caliper assembly can be rotated a few degrees on the pivot bolt. Loosen the capnut a few turns, grasp the brake arms, and arc the assembly as needed. Frozen pivots are another possibility, particularly on a bike that has been exposed to the weather. If penetrating oil and much working of the brake arms does not free them, the caliper will have to be disassembled.

Remove the transverse cable by loosening the anchor nut on the cable hanger or by squeezing the brake arms with a third-hand tool. Once the blocks are against the rim, the transverse cable should slip out of its mounts on the ends of each brake arm. The Weinmann Vainquer is typical of many in that the cable ends fit into a hole and slot arrangement. While this method of attachment cannot be faulted, it is possible to butcher the cable when removing and installing it. Do not crimp or force the cable into the slots. It should fall into place with just a touch of direction. Some mechanics use a bicycle tire iron as a guide. The cable is hooked over the slot in the tool. Other brake styles, such as the Mafac pictured in Fig. 7-8, secure the cable ends on hooks.

Carefully remove the pivot bolt and catch the nut and lockwasher. Now with the caution bred of pinched fingers, remove the brake springs or spring. Use pliers. You will note that the Weinmann has two springs and that they are not interchangeable. The bent end is up. The Mafac has a single spring with the coils facing forward. These remarks do not apply to all makes and models, but they do point out the need for close observation if the brake is to be assembled correctly.

Clean the pivots with solvent and remove rust with steel wool. Inspect the pivots for wear or bending. In some cases

Fig. 7-8. Macfac Racer. (Courtesy Browning)

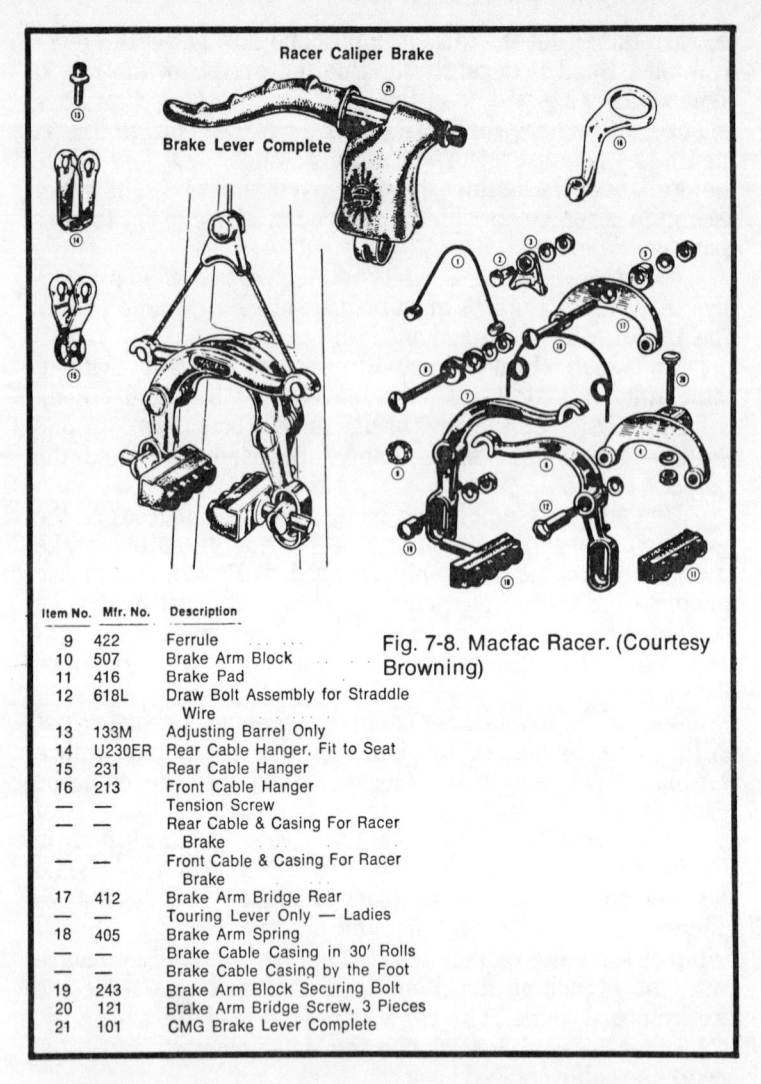

Item No.	Mfr. No.	Description
9	422	Ferrule
10	507	Brake Arm Block
11	416	Brake Pad
12	618L	Draw Bolt Assembly for Straddle Wire
13	133M	Adjusting Barrel Only
14	U230ER	Rear Cable Hanger, Fit to Seat
15	231	Rear Cable Hanger
16	213	Front Cable Hanger
—	—	Tension Screw
—	—	Rear Cable & Casing For Racer Brake
—	—	Front Cable & Casing For Racer Brake
17	412	Brake Arm Bridge Rear
—	—	Touring Lever Only — Ladies
18	405	Brake Arm Spring
—	—	Brake Cable Casing in 30' Rolls
—	—	Brake Cable Casing by the Foot
19	243	Brake Arm Block Securing Bolt
20	121	Brake Arm Bridge Screw, 3 Pieces
21	101	CMG Brake Lever Complete

you might be able to purchase new pivots locally, although your best bet is through one of the mail-order supply houses.

Lubricate the mechanism at the wear points and assemble. A screwdriver blade can be used to shoehorn the spring into place.

BRAKE BLOCKS

The brake blocks should be parallel to the rim and, under application, meet with it and not the tire sidewall. Should this happen the tire will fail quickly and dramatically. Two types of block are available. The most popular has a threaded stud which secures it to the brake lever. The Weinmann shown in Fig. 7-7 employs this type of block. The only caution is that excessive force will strip the threads on the stud. The Mafac in Fig. 7-8 uses blocks held by friction bolts. The advantage of this arrangment is that the blocks can be adjusted for angle to conform with the rim and lever geometry. The blocks and rim should be parallel at the point of contact.

The blocks should contact the rim along their whole length, although some riders claim that a few degrees of toe-in gives more reliable performance in the wet. Toe-in can, in some cases at least, reduce or eliminate brake squeal. The best way to obtain toe-in is to file the forward edge of the brake blocks where the blocks come into contact with the rim. Applying the brakes will seat the blocks on this new profile.

Note: End caps on the block holders must point forward. The drawing in Fig. 7-7 is as viewed from the front of the bike and shows the brake-block holder with its closed end forward. The end not visible is open to allow replacement of the blocks. If the holders are installed backwards the blocks will work loose under braking.

The matter of brake proportioning is subject to dispute. It is generally agreed that the front brake should reach lockup only under heavy force, if at all. The rear brake should lock early, but not be so touchy that it burns flat spots on the tire bottom with the slightest flinch of the hand lever.

Bad proportioning is usually the result of cable stretch and arm deformation. Some brake arms can be seen to bend as the shoe makes contact with the rim. Experimentation with different brake blocks (always in pairs) is sometimes worthwhile. European blocks tend to be hard and have a lower coefficient of friction than the softer American blocks.

BRAKE LEVERS

Brake levers may incorporate a quick-release for the cable in the form of a pushbutton, although Campagnolo and other quality brands often incorporate the release at the arm (Fig. 7-2). Middle-quality bikes sometimes incorporate an extension lever running across the handlebars. In theory the extension is a safety feature since the brakes are easily accessible from all hand positions. Purists consider such gadgetry effeminate—on par with 32T freewheel plates—but many riders feel more secure with them. The most significant advance in levers is surely the Raleigh self-adjusting unit. It features a ratchet which automatically (and audibly) compensates for block wear and cable stretch as the lever is

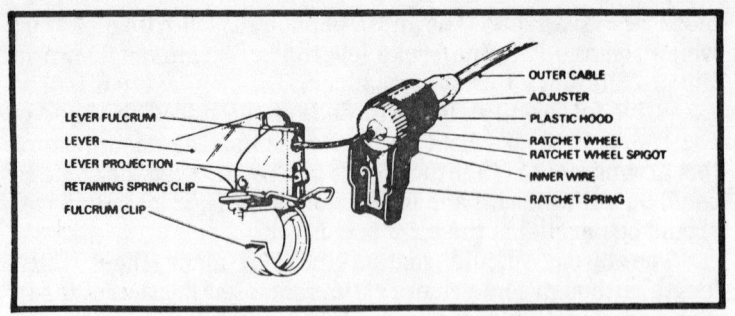

Fig. 7-9. Raleigh self-adjusting brake arm. (Courtesy Raleigh Industries Ltd.)

depressed. It works very well and should make routine brake adjustments obsolete.

This mechanism is shown in Fig. 7-9. Rotation of the serrated ratchet wheel is counter-clockwise on the right-hand lever and clockwise on the left-hand one. Should the brakes be too tight, the ratchet can be turned by hand, a click or so to loosen, without dismounting.

Figure 7-10 illustrates a more conventional design in exploded view. This Weinmann lever features a rubber hood and long-wearing nylon bushings.

CABLES

Control cables should be frequently inspected for any irregularity which would affect braking action. As mentioned several times in the course of this book, a single broken or crimped strand will cause the others to fail. Replace with best-quality cables from a reputable dealer or bike supply house. Do not skimp on these vital parts. Lubricate periodically with light oil.

To remove a cable for replacement or thorough lubrication, loosen the lower end at the brake. Working from below the lever, push the "pear" out of the the lever.

Some few cyclists replace factory brake cables with motorcycle cables, which are heavier, sturdier, and reasonably immune to stretch. Depending upon your bike and whether the rear cable has an interrupted housing, the job can be quite simple or can involve poring over motorcycle parts catalogues and frame bracket substitutions or modifications. If you opt for this course, be sure to specify 1×9 inner cable. It is a single wound strand consisting of nine individual wires. Another type, known as 7×7 is made up of seven strands of seven wires each. Each strand is wound separately and all are then wound together, making a very flexible but relatively weak cable. Brass ball and barrel ends are soldered into place with acid flux, and preferably by dipping the cable end into molten solder.

STIRRUP BRAKES

Stirrup brakes, favorite stoppers of the British constabulary, are popular wherever bikes have become a means of daily transport. Though rare in this country, stirrup brakes have much to recommend them. Actuation by rod rather than cables involves a weight penalty, but is compensated for by almost zero maintenance. Rods do not wear out.

The adjustment drill varies in some particulars from that for conventional rim brakes, but the purpose of the exercise—to bring the blocks within close proximity of the rim—is the same. Figure 7-11 shows the critical linkages. A number of rear stirrup brakes have a second adjustment point under the bottom bracket. It is a conventional barrel with lockwasher arrangement.

Begin with the front wheel. Raise the stirrup until the blocks almost touch the rim. Steady lever B and brake arm C. Loosen nut A. The stirrup rod should move upward to compensate for the movement of the blocks toward the rim.

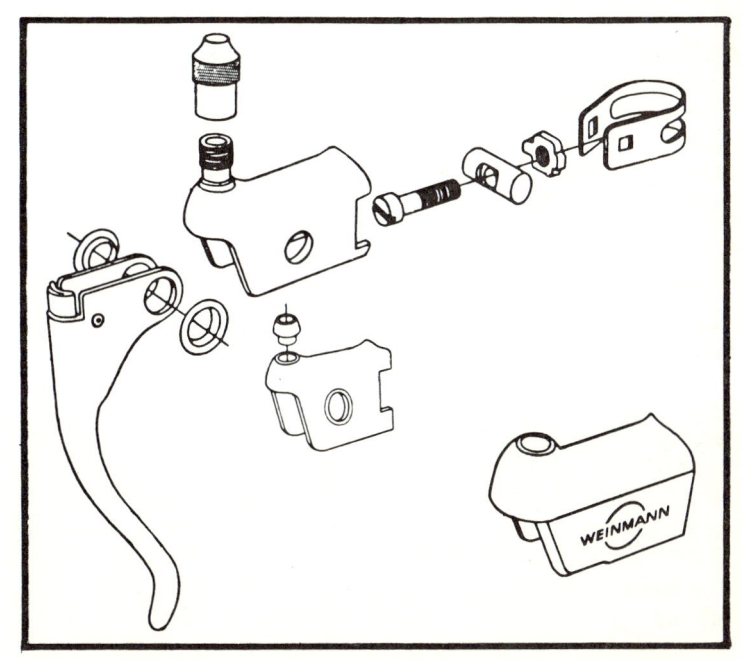

Fig. 7-10. Brake lever in exploded view. (Courtesy Sink's Bicycle World)

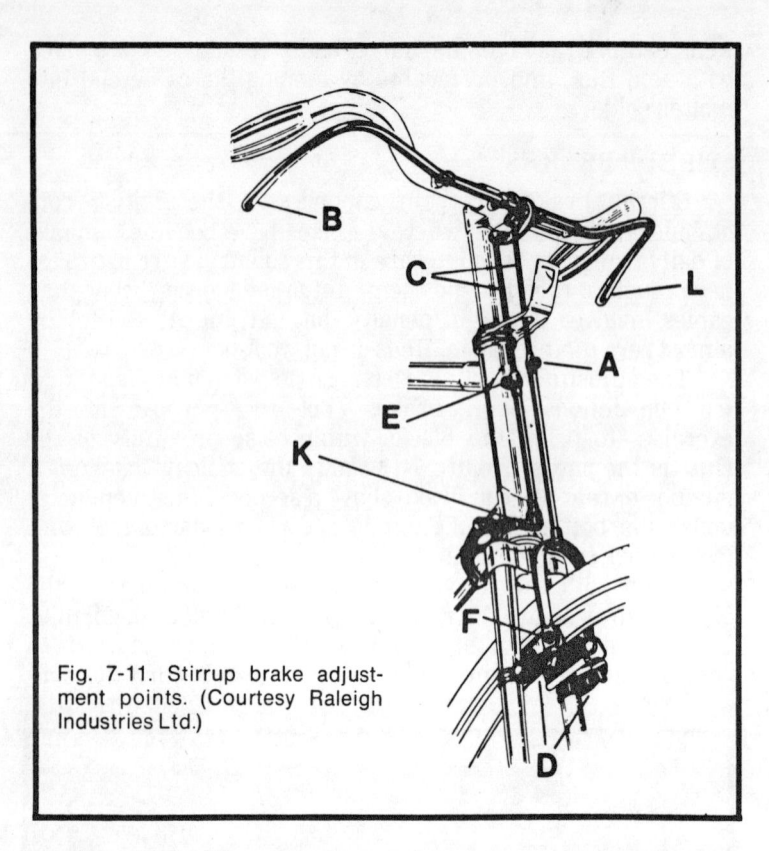

Fig. 7-11. Stirrup brake adjustment points. (Courtesy Raleigh Industries Ltd.)

Holding everything together, tighten nut A. With the control lever depressed, loosen nuts F and retighten. This last operation aligns the blocks with the rim.

The rear brake takes a bit more doing. The major adjustment is at rod nut E. Loosen and apply pressure on bellcrank K to bring the rear shoes adjacent to the rim. Hold lever L and rod C with your third and fourth hands. Tighten nut E to lock the blocks into position. As you did for the front, loosen the securing nuts on the blocks and hold the control lever down. The blocks will align themselves with the rim. Tighten the nuts.

Derailleur Transmissions

The secret of effortless cycling is to pick a comfortable cadence and hold it. Most people pedal best and longest at a cadence of 60 to 75 crank revolutions a minute. Because a bicycle is under varying load—during acceleration and coasting, up and down hills, with following winds and bucking headwinds—some sort of multispeed transmission is necessary.

The derailleur has evolved as the most popular type of bike transmission because of its light weight, relative simplicity, and the flexibility it offers in choice of ratios. Derailleurs are available in five, ten, twelve, fifteen, and eighteen-speed variants with a few hand-built experimental units having as many as thirty-six speeds. Ten-speeds seems the best compromise for the usual cyclist.

GEAR RATIO

The gear ratio is determined by the number of teeth (corresponding to the diameter) of the large chainwheel, the number of teeth of the rear sprocket, and the wheel size. The length of the pedal cranks has an effect on pedal effort, but is ignored in gearing calculations.

The formula for gear ratio is:

$$\text{Gear ratio} = \frac{\text{chainwheel teeth}}{\text{sprocket teeth}} \times \text{wheel diameter}$$

For example, the popular 48-tooth chainwheel, 20-tooth sprocket combination on a 27-inch wheel gives us a gear of 64.8 inches. A ratio chart is included in Table 8-1 for the 27-inch wheel size.

In addition to the number of speeds available, derailleurs are rated by their capacity or range. The Sun Tour Skitter is a general purpose design intended for the teen-age market. The sprocket cluster at the rear ranges from 14 teeth to 28 teeth for a 14-tooth difference. The front chainwheels are 36 teeth and 50 teeth giving the same 14-tooth variation. The total capacity of the transmission is therefore 28 teeth or the sum of the differences between front and rear sprockets.

Expensive bicycles are usually intended for people in very good physical form. The gearing tends to be high and with a narrow range. Typically these bikes have a 49×55 chainwheel set and a 14, 15, 16, 17, and 18 tooth cluster. A much better choice for the average rider—particularly one who contemplates doing much touring—would be something on the order of 14, 17, 20, 24, and 30 tooth cluster coupled to a 40×49 tooth chainwheel.

Consideration should be given to gear spacing. It should be as evenly divided as possible to prevent flat spots in acceleration and should be spaced far apart enough to justify all 10 or 15 speeds. Otherwise, combinations will give you essentially the same gear twice. Extreme variations in tooth size strain the derailleur and chain, although this problem is eased with one of the large-capacity units. Some successful large-capacity designs are the Huret Jubilee 2253, the Shamano Crane GS , and the heavy, but strong, Sun Tour GT . The just-announced Campagnolo Rally has an extreme range—it will handle a rear spread of 13 to 36 teeth and 54 to 36 teeth at the front. It shifts with the willingness of a close-ratio racing transmission.

A wide-capacity derailleur differs from the conventional sort in several particulars. The cage is usually lengthened to match the greater diameter of the low-gear sprocket. And the arc of travel may be increased to accommodate the surplus of chain on the small or high-gear sprocket. In addition, the geometry of the bicycle and the chain also has something to do with it. A loose, worn-in chain is more tolerant than a new chain. The length and angle of the chain stay may be critical since this helps to fix the angle of attack of the chain as it is derailled. Sometimes it helps to pull the rear wheel back as far as it will go in the dropouts.

SHIFTING

There is an art to painless gear changing:

- Shift when moving forward. Do not force the mechanism when stopped and be particularly careful not to shift while backpedaling. The best that can happen is that the chain will throw. In city traffic, anticipate the lights.
- Reduce the pressure on the pedals when shifting. Continue to turn the crank, but allow the chain to develop slack so it can be jockied over the sprocket or chainwheel.
- Make shifts positively. Lingering between ratios will convert your derailleur into the proverbial "coffee grinder" as the chain saws between sprockets. Some of the Japanese designs make shifting easier with detents on the levers for positive engagement. Others have to be learned by feel.
- Learn the shift pattern. The gear combinations on ten- and fifteen-speed bikes are not a simple arithmetic progression.

NOMENCLATURE

Basic derailleur parts are shown in Fig. 8-1. A is the freewheel mechanism upon which is mounted the sprocket or plate cluster. The freewheel ratchets so that the wheel may turn faster than the pedals for coasting. B is the rear changer or rear derailleur. It consists of a spring-loaded cage, the jockey roller C and the tension roller D. The function of these parts will be described in a moment. For now it is enough to say that these two rollers lift the chain and place it on adjacent plates. The front changer or derailleur is shown at E and the chainwheel at F.

FREEWHEELS

The sprocket cluster consists of three, four, five, or six sprockets, or plates, secured to the freewheel body and driving the wheel through ratchets. Figures 8-2 and 8-3 illustrate typical freewheel clusters. The cluster is always assembled with the smaller or higher geared plates to the outside.

While six-speed clusters are desirable for mountainous terrain and touring with baggage, the addition of the extra plate has not been without difficulties. In many instances the derailleur mechanism is stressed beyond comfortable limits in the lowest gear. Frequent adjustments may be necessary. The

Table 8-1. Gear Ratio Chart
(Courtesy Sink's Bicycle World)

Chain Wheel Wheel Size	24th 27in.	26th 27in	28th 27in	30th 27in	32th 27in	34th 27in	36th 27in	38th 27in	40th 27in	42th 27in	44th 27in
sprocket size											
12	54.1	58.5	63.0	67.5	72.0	76.5	81.1	85.5	90.0	94.5	99.0
13	49.8	54.0	58.1	62.3	66.4	70.6	74.7	78.9	83.1	87.2	91.4
14	46.2	50.1	54.0	57.8	61.7	65.5	69.5	73.3	77.1	81.0	84.9
15	43.2	46.8	50.4	57.6	61.1	64.8	68.4	72.0	75.6	79.2	79.2
16	40.5	43.7	47.2	50.6	54.0	57.2	60.9	64.1	67.5	70.9	74.3
17	38.1	41.2	44.4	47.6	50.8	54.0	57.2	60.3	63.5	66.7	69.9
18	36.0	39.0	42.0	45.0	48.0	51.0	54.0	57.0	60.0	63.0	66.0
19	34.1	36.8	39.7	42.6	45.5	48.2	51.1	54.0	56.8	59.7	62.5
19	32.4	35.1	37.8	40.5	43.2	45.9	48.7	51.3	54.0	56.7	59.4
21	30.8	33.4	36.0	38.6	41.1	43.7	46.4	48.9	51.4	54.0	56.5
22	29.4	31.9	34.3	36.8	39.2	41.6	44.2	46.6	49.1	51.5	54.0
23	28.1	30.5	32.8	35.2	37.5	39.9	42.4	44.6	47.0	49.3	51.6
24	27.0	29.2	31.5	33.7	36.0	38.2	40.5	42.8	45.0	47.3	49.5
25	25.9	28.0	30.2	32.4	34.6	36.7	38.9	41.0	43.2	45.4	47.5
26	24.9	27.0	29.0	31.2	33.2	35.3	37.4	39.5	41.5	43.6	45.7
28	23.1	25.0	27.0	28.9	30.8	32.8	34.8	36.6	38.6	40.5	42.4
30	21.6	23.4	25.2	27.0	28.8	30.6	32.4	34.2	36.0	37.8	39.6
32	20.3	20.3	23.6	25.3	27.0	28.7	30.4	32.1	33.8	35.4	37.1
34	19.1	19.6	22.2	23.8	25.4	27.0	28.6	30.2	31.8	33.4	34.9

Chain Wheel / Wheel Size	45th 27in	46th	47th	48th	49th	50th	52th	53th	54th	55th	56th
sprocket size 12	101.2	103.5	105.7	108.0	110.2	112.3	117.0	119.3	121.5	123.7	126.0
13	93.4	95.5	97.6	99.7	101.8	103.9	108.0	110.0	112.1	114.2	116.3
14	86.7	88.7	90.6	92.6	94.5	96.4	100.3	102.2	104.1	106.0	108.0
15	80.9	82.8	84.6	86.4	88.2	90.0	93.6	95.4	97.2	99.0	100.8
16	76.0	77.6	79.3	81.0	82.7	84.4	87.8	89.4	91.1	92.8	94.5
17	71.5	73.1	74.6	76.2	77.8	79.4	82.6	84.1	85.7	87.3	88.9
18	67.5	69.0	70.5	72.0	73.5	75.0	78.0	79.5	81.0	82.5	84.0
19	64.0	65.4	66.8	68.2	69.6	71.1	73.9	75.3	76.7	78.1	79.5
20	60.8	62.1	63.4	64.8	66.2	67.5	70.2	71.5	72.9	74.5	75.6
21	57.9	59.1	60.4	61.7	63.0	64.3	66.9	68.1	69.4	70.7	72.0
22	55.2	56.5	57.6	58.9	60.1	61.4	63.8	65.0	66.2	67.5	68.7
23	52.8	54.0	55.2	56.3	57.5	58.7	61.0	62.2	63.6	64.5	65.7
24	50.7	51.8	52.9	54.0	55.1	56.3	58.5	59.6	60.7	61.8	63.0
25	48.6	49.7	50.8	51.8	52.9	54.0	56.2	57.2	58.3	59.4	60.4
26	46.7	47.8	48.8	49.9	50.9	51.9	54.0	55.0	56.0	57.1	58.1
28	43.4	44.4	45.3	46.3	47.2	48.2	50.1	51.1	52.0	53.0	54.0
30	40.5	41.4	42.3	43.2	44.1	45.0	46.8	47.7	48.6	49.5	50.4
32	38.0	38.8	39.7	40.5	41.3	42.2	43.9	44.7	45.6	46.4	47.3
34	35.7	36.5	37.3	38.1	38.9	39.7	41.3	42.1	42.9	42.9	44.5

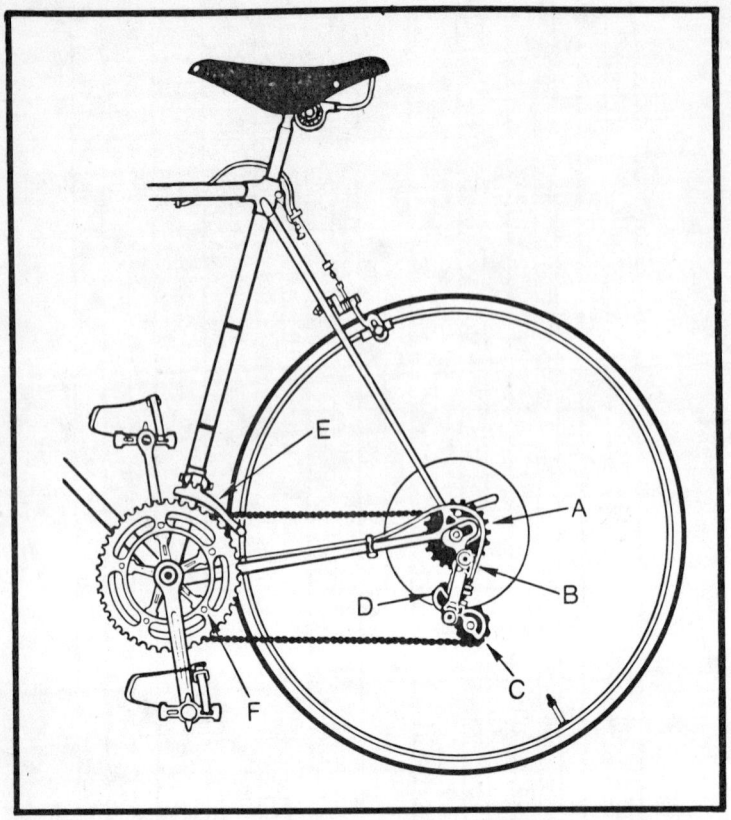

Fig. 8-1. Derailleur transmission. (A) freewheel, (B) rear changer, (C) jockey roller, (D) tension roller, (E) front changer, (F) chain wheels. (Courtesy Raleigh Industries Ltd.)

rear wheel may have to be dished (offset) more to allow space for the extra cog and, while this usually does not lead to problems, it does weaken the wheel. A more serious objection is that the extra cog requires that the cluster be assembled with overhang. That is, the freewheel body is shorter than the width of the stacked plates. While some five-speed units have the outboard cog overhung and threaded to the next plate, rather than directly to the hub, this procedure is not recommended, especially if the plates are made of light alloy.

The typical cluster is made of steel which can, depending upon the alloy and heat-treatment, give long and faithful service. Racing and sports tourer machines are fitted with aluminum plates with titanium rumored to be present as an alloy in at least one. The durability of aluminum is subject to dispute—most riders have good results with it, although there

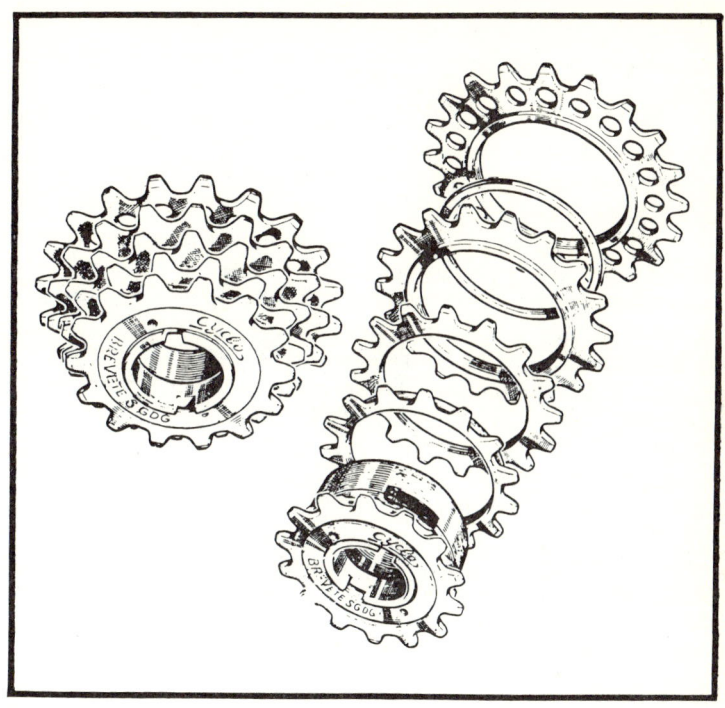

Fig. 8-2. The Cycle freewheel. (Courtesy Sink's Bicycle World)

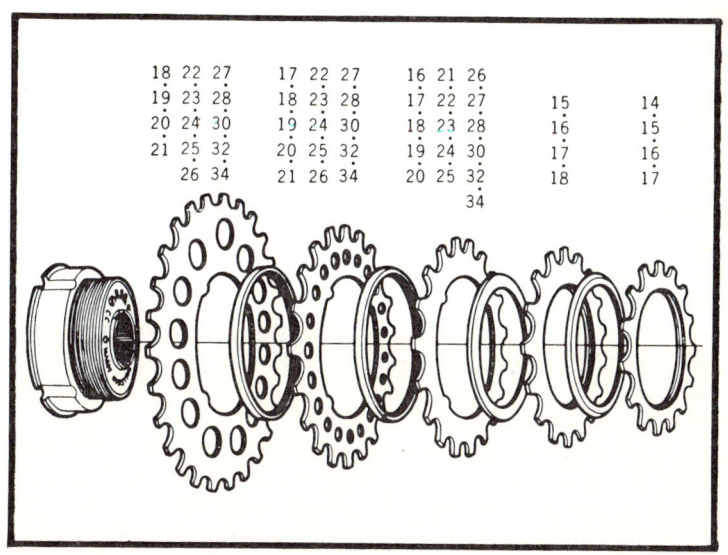

18 22 27	17 22 27	16 21 26		
19 23 28	18 23 28	17 22 27	15	14
20 24 30	19 24 30	18 23 28	16	15
21 25 32	20 25 32	19 24 30	17	16
26 34	21 26 34	20 25 32	18	17
		34		

Fig. 8-3. SunTour 8.8.8 freewheel. The numbers give the sprocket tooth options. (Courtesy Sink's Bicycle World)

have been reports of early failure. Aluminum compacts and develops surface hardness as it is used, which should make these sprockets more durable than a simple hardness comparison with steel would indicate. Anodization also is used to increase the surface hardness and to give a selling point—with this process the metal can be tinted. Currently gold is the "in" color.

It is convenient to be able to remove the plates without dismantling the entire mechanism. And it is more than convenient to be able to replace the plates individually. The French Cyclo, shown in Fig. 8-2, has its outboard plate integral with the freewheel body. The outer two plates are integral on Cyclo six-plate clusters. These are the plates which, being smaller, wear most rapidly. Detachable sprockets can be replaced fairly economically and encourage experimentation with different ratios.

The freewheel threads into the hub. National thread standards vary and it is not always possible to interchange parts. The English standard is used on French bikes for export to this country as well as on British machines. The thread size is 1.370 in. × 24. The first figure is the diameter and the second is the number of threads per inch (tpi). The Italian standard is 35 mm × 24 tpi and the French national is 34.7 mm × 1 thread per millimeter. Since the diameters are close and 25.4 mm equals 1 inch, you might suppose that these parts would marry. They will, but the threads will be damaged because of the dimensional differences and because of the differences in thread profiles.

The sprockets should be replaced if they show obvious wear. As the teeth wear the chain rides higher on the teeth, ultimately giving them a hooked profile. Unless you have a cluster with very soft plates, it is advisable to replace the chain as well. Failure to do so will rapidly wear the new sprockets and may give rise to shifting difficulties.

CLUSTER REMOVAL AND DISASSEMBLY

Take the rear wheel out of the frame and mount it in a vise with the freewheel mechanism upright. Cover the jaws of the vise with lead or copper facings (in a pinch you can use strips of hardwood) to protect the axle threads. The freewheel is held by a locknut and positioned by a spacer. Remove the locknut (counterclockwise) and the spacer. The spacer may be threaded or it may merely slip over the axle.

The next step is to separate the freewheel from the hub. A special tool is required. Atom, Normandy, and Shimano freewheels are splined; most of the others have a pair of

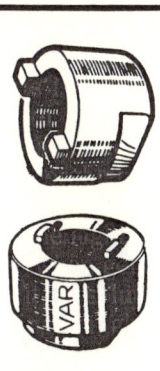

Fig. 8-4. Freewheel removal tools. Top; Cyclo, Regina: middle; Atom, Maillard, Milremo: bottom; Atom, Sprint. (Courtesy Sink's Bicycle World)

notches milled on the outboard end for tool purchase. Freewheel extractors are available from Sink's and other mail order houses and are stocked by some of the larger bike shops. Cost is between two and five dollars. Figure 8-4 illustrates three varieties. Some interchange between tools and hubs is possible, especially with European freewheels.

Index the tool with the splines or slots, run the axle nut down to seat the extractor and back the nut off about half a turn. This is to allow room for the freewheel to unthread. Holding the wheel securely, turn the tool with a wrench. You might have to give the wrench a sharp hammer blow to break the threads loose or it may be necessary to hold the extractor in a vise and turn the wheel. Remove the tool and turn the freewheel off of the hub by hand.

Mount the hub vertically in the vise holding it by the largest sprocket. With a chain wrench rotate the outboard sprocket counterclockwise to unthread it from the freewheel body. You can make up a wrench from a length of discarded bike chain and a piece of strap iron or you can purchase one. Figure 8-5 shows a chain wrench used in concert with a professional sprocket holding tool.

Remove the spacer ring with a knife blade and place it on the bench for later assembly. The spacer rings are not necessarily identical and must be replaced as they were originally assembled. The second sprocket is threaded on most designs. Remove it with the chain wrench. Late model (after 1968) freewheels may have the inboard sprocket splined as

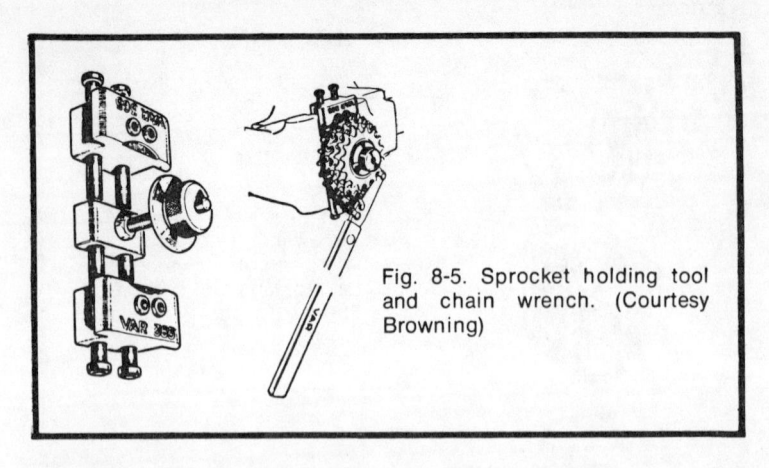

Fig. 8-5. Sprocket holding tool and chain wrench. (Courtesy Browning)

shown in Fig. 8-3. Freewheels such as the Cyclo secure all sprockets by means of threads (Fig. 8-2). You may run into a freewheel with left-hand threads on the inboard pair of sprockets. Many of the earlier models were built on this pattern.

Clean the sprockets and spacers in solvent and dry with a lint-free rag or paper towels. Inspect the sprockets carefully. Bent teeth can be straightened by placing the sprocket in a vise with the affected tooth just showing above the jaws. Bend with a Crescent wrench. Small burrs can be filed smooth.

Assemble the sprockets and spacers on the hub. Each sprocket should be equidistant from its fellows. If not, the spacers have been confused or the sprocket shoulders have been reversed. Oil the threads and tighten each sprocket with a chain wrench.

Before threading the assembly onto the hub it is always a good idea to inspect the ratchet mechanism. On some bikes you can see the ratchet pivots. For the others one should disassemble the hub or, if not that, at least listen to the sound the pawls make as they trip over the teeth. The clicks should come in pairs—one, two...one, two.... Skipping a beat means that grease has hardened or that the spring has failed.

Oil the hub threads and carefully guide the freewheel over them. Turn hand-tight. Riding the bike will tighten the freewheel body the rest of the way.

FREEWHEEL BODY OVERHAUL

Figure 8-6 is a cutaway view of a typical freewheel body. The inner and outer shells are separated by two rows of 0.125 inch ball bearings. Shims establish end clearance for the bearings. The assembly is held together by a threaded cone.

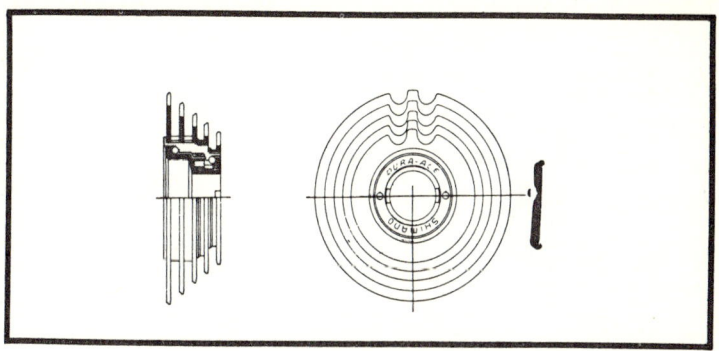

Fig. 8-6. Dura-ace freewheel.

With the proper tool (a pin wrench) or the improper ones (a hammer and punch), turn the cone clockwise to loosen. It traditionally has a left-hand thread. Once the cone is free, remove the washer-shaped dust cover. Use a screwdriver or a knife blade to pry it off. It should pop off without suffering permanent deformation.

The bearings are uncaged and easy to lose. If one is lost you have to replace the whole set on that side since a new bearing is microscopically larger than the others and will take most of the stress. Clean the parts in solvent, dry, and inspect:

- the shells with particular attention to the threads
- the bearings for dull spots, pits, or other surface irregularities
- the bearing races for galling or brinneling
- the pawls for wear or chipping. These tiny parts (Fig. 8-7) are as important as any component on the bike and transmit as much as 500 km-cm of torque

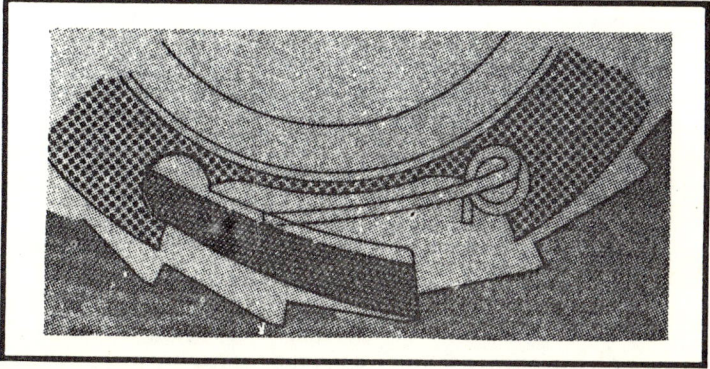

Fig. 8-7. Pawl and ratchet assembly. (Courtesy Shimano Industrial Co. Ltd.)

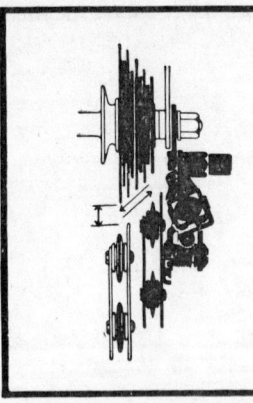

Fig. 8-8. Derailleur lateral movement. (Courtesy Maeda Industries, Ltd.)

Replace the spring as a matter of course. Assemble with a light, water-resistant grease such as available from Schwinn dealers. Imbed the bearings in grease to hold them to the races during assembly. Depress the pawls and slip the outer freewheel body home over them. Turn the freewheel body over, being careful to keep the parts squeezed together so the bearings stay put. Grease both sides of each shim and install. Lay a bead of grease on the race and place the bearings in it. If your count is right you will have a full race without room for an additional ball.

Thread the race down by turning it counterclockwise. Secure it with a pin wrench; the spacers make the adjustment. Test your work. The freewheel should turn counterclockwise with an accompaniment from the pawls. It should lock when you turn it clockwise. If there is more than a smidgeon of side play, remove the race and add another shim. If the bearings are tight, remove a shim. Various thicknesses of shims are available from dealers. Do not use hardware-quality washers.

REAR CHANGERS AND CONTROL LEVERS

The rear changer or as it is more often called, the rear derailleur, has two functions. It nudges the chain from one sprocket onto another while holding chain tension constant. To derail the chain, it moves laterally and at the same time pivots to compensate for different sprocket sizes. The mechanism is not complicated in concept, but the execution demands a certain precision. Small misadjustments, dirt and grime, and lack of lubrication can defeat it. See Figs. 8-8 and 8-9.

Control Levers

The derailleur mechanism cannot be discussed apart from the control levers and cable. Pulling back on the right-hand lever causes the rear changer to move against its spring, jockeying the chain over the large sprockets on the freewheel. Pushing forward releases tension on the spring and the changer shifts into a higher gear. Figure 8-10 illustrates the various control-lever mounting options and the next drawing shows a typical cable route from (in this case, handlebar) levers to changers.

Troubleshooting

Difficulties in shifting can often be traced to the cables. Frayed, kinked, or splayed inner cables will respond tardily if at all to control lever inputs. By the same token, a cable with a collapsed or gnawed outer casing will also be reluctant to move. A fretted outer casing can sometimes be cut and trimmed. Nick the wire coils with a triangular file. Now gripping the cut end with pliers, twist against the lay of the coils. The break will be clean, without burrs. The outer casing is the reaction member of the pair—should its ends be dog-eared, the casing will tend to telescope upon itself, rather than transfer motion to the changers. Replace the cable if you have any doubt about its integrity.

The cables must be lubricated along their full length and particularly where the inner element leaves and enters the casing. The best way to do this is by removing the inner element and applying a coat of Lubriplate. However, the control levers should not be lubricated. These levers are friction-devices and lubricant will encourage phantom shifts.

The derailleur pivots in an arc, fore-and-aft, to compensate for the different sized sprockets. If it did not pivot, the chain would be tight on the large (low-gear) sprocket and loose on the small (high-gear) plate. The pivot may be located high on the cage arcing the whole unit, or it may be located low, at or near the jockey roller. It is spring-loaded.

Lateral movement, or the stroke, of the mechanism is achieved by a pantograph mechanism. Figure 8-8 illustrates the action of the Sun Tour. The geometry of the Maeda design is such that the cage remains equidistant from the sprockets, a feature which is said to make shifting easier.

Rear changers are mounted to the rear wheel dropout either on the rear hanger (the more expensive option) or by means of a bracket which slips over the rear axle. So the changer remains in place when the wheel is removed, the bracket is bolted to a threaded hole. Figure 8-9A is an exploded view of the Simplex Criterium. (Figures 8-9B and 8-9C show the Huret Albrit and the Sun Tour VT.) As packaged the simplex derailleur is intended for mounting on a hanger

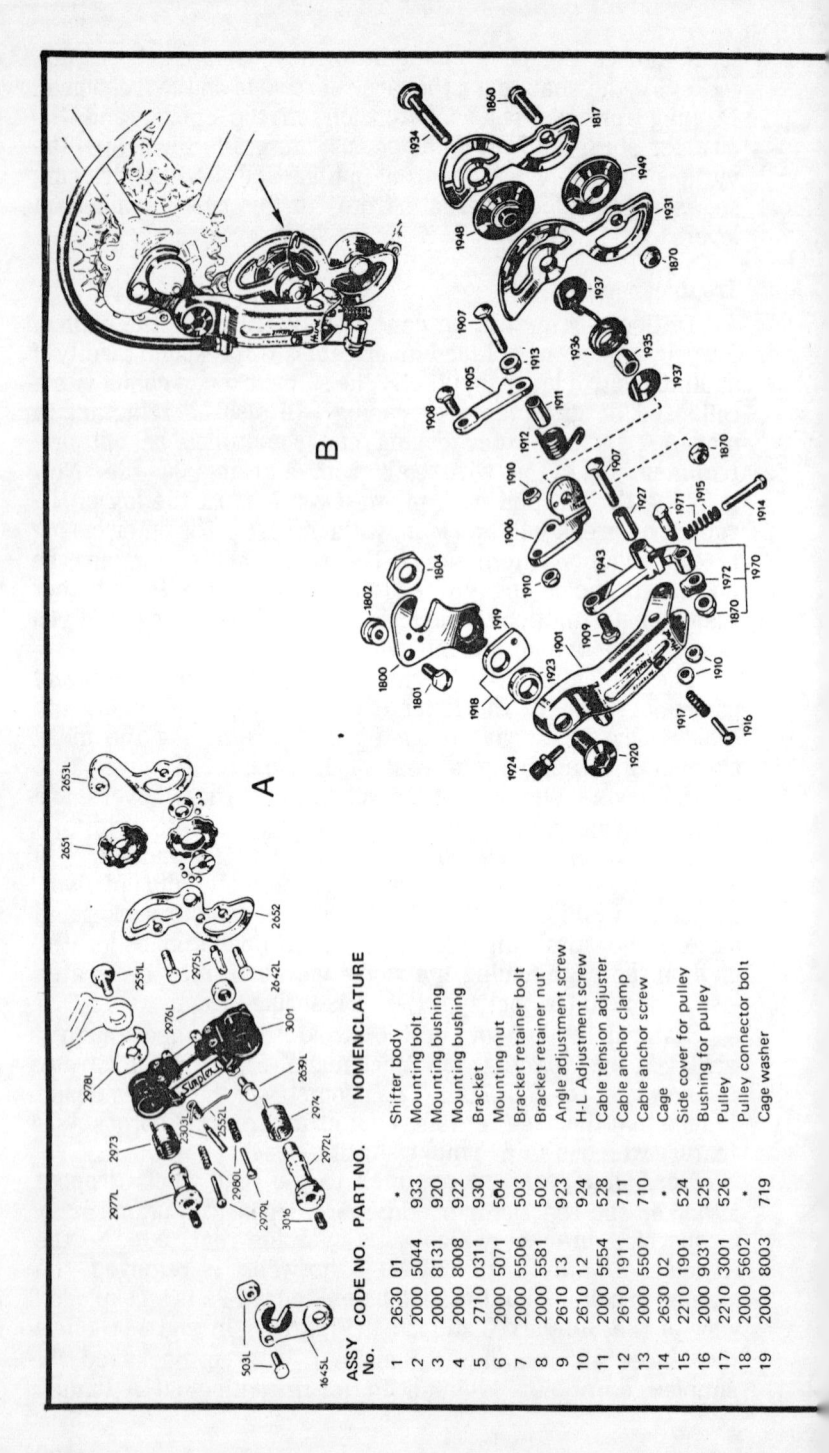

ASSY. No.	CODE NO.	PART NO.	NOMENCLATURE
1	2630 01	*	Shifter body
2	2000 5044	933	Mounting bolt
3	2000 8131	920	Mounting bushing
4	2000 8008	922	Mounting bushing
5	2710 0311	930	Bracket
6	2000 5071	504	Mounting nut
7	2000 5506	503	Bracket retainer bolt
8	2000 5581	502	Bracket retainer nut
9	2610 13	923	Angle adjustment screw
10	2610 12	924	H-L Adjustment screw
11	2000 5554	528	Cable tension adjuster
12	2610 1911	711	Cable anchor clamp
13	2000 5507	710	Cable anchor screw
14	2630 02	*	Cage
15	2210 1901	524	Side cover for pulley
16	2000 9031	525	Bushing for pulley
17	2210 3001	526	Pulley
18	2000 5602	*	Pulley connector bolt
19	2000 8003	719	Cage washer

140

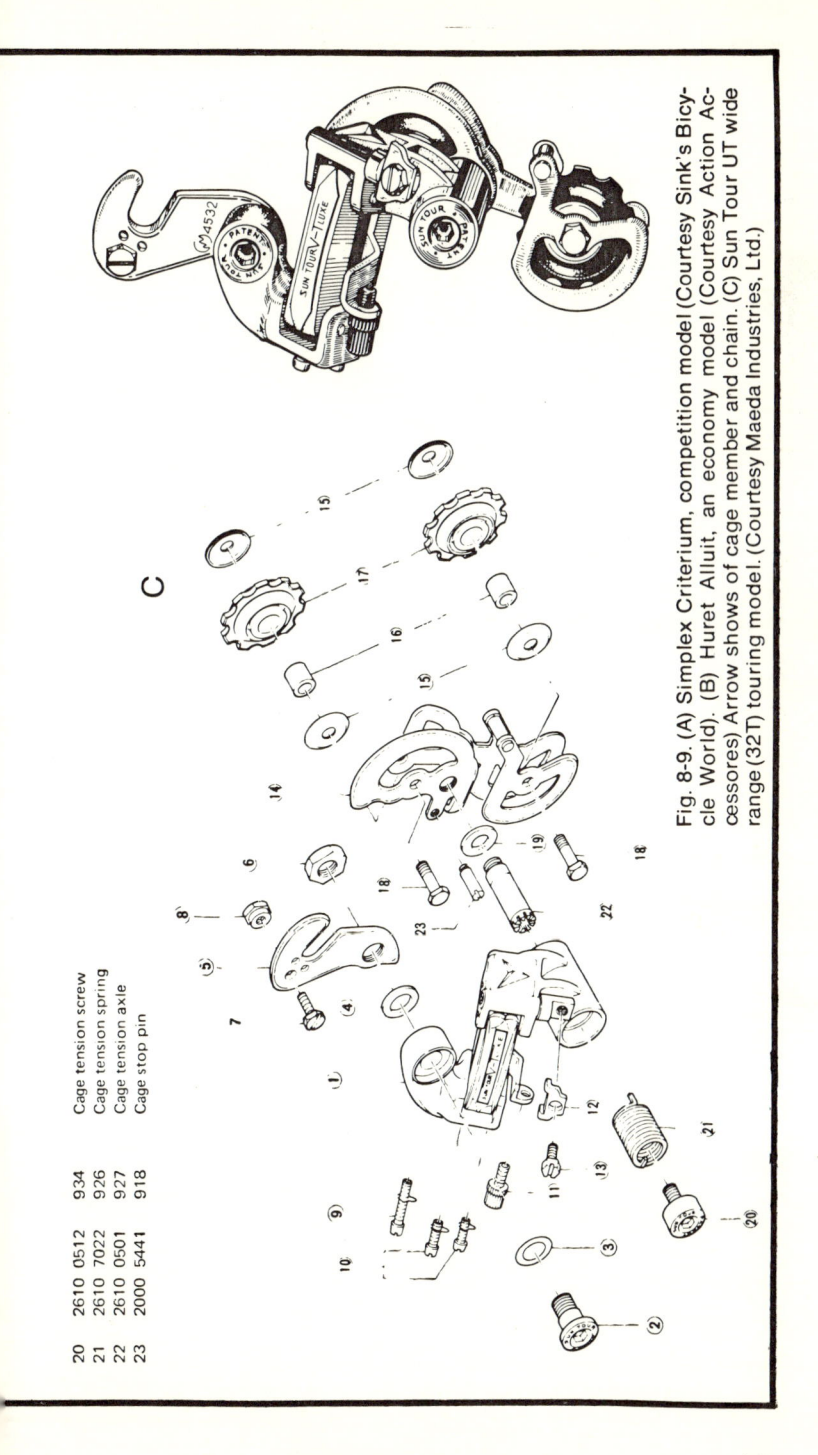

Fig. 8-9. (A) Simplex Criterium, competition model (Courtesy Sink's Bicycle World). (B) Huret Alluit, an economy model (Courtesy Action Accessores) Arrow shows of cage member and chain. (C) Sun Tour UT wide range (32T) touring model. (Courtesy Maeda Industries, Ltd.)

20	2610 0512	934	Cage tension screw
21	2610 7022	926	Cage tension spring
22	2610 0501	927	Cage tension axle
23	2000 5441	918	Cage stop pin

141

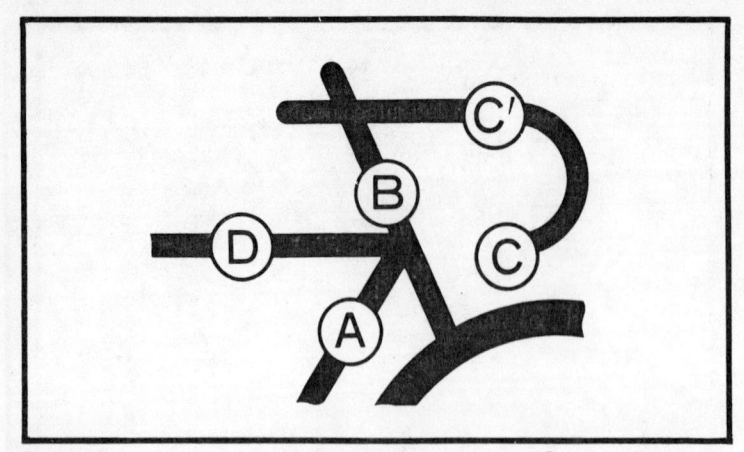

Fig. 8-10. Letters indicate lever mounting positions. (Courtesy Maeda Industries, Ltd.)

(shown at the top center of the drawing). One can, however, purchase a bracket (shown on the left as part number 1645L) to accommodate the mechanism to the general run of bicycles. Campy and most other derailleurs are fixed by a ten mm bolt. Figures 8-10 and 8-11 show lever mounting positions and cable routing.

After long use or exposure to weather the levers will benefit from disassembly and cleaning. Figure 8-12 illustrates Sun Tour DLW and SLW breakdown. Work with one at a time.

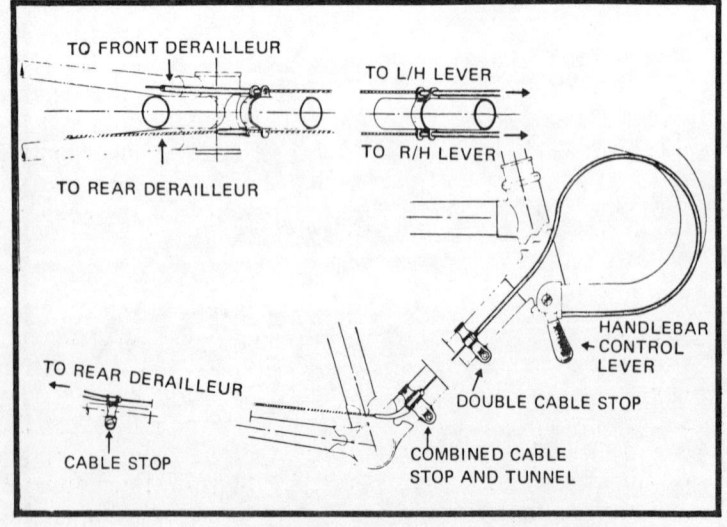

Fig. 8-11. Cable routing. (Courtesy Maeda Industries, Ltd.)

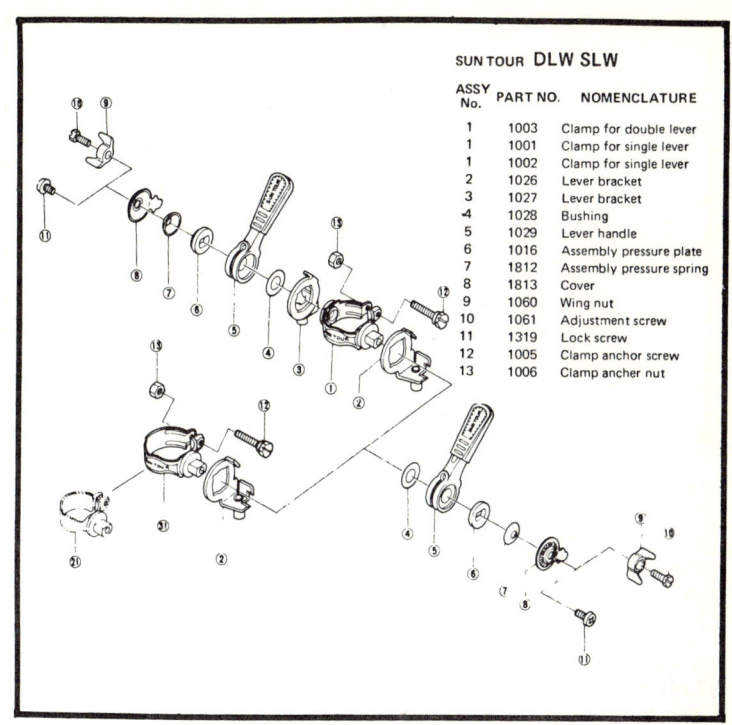

ASSY No.	PART NO.	NOMENCLATURE
1	1003	Clamp for double lever
1	1001	Clamp for single lever
1	1002	Clamp for single lever
2	1026	Lever bracket
3	1027	Lever bracket
4	1028	Bushing
5	1029	Lever handle
6	1016	Assembly pressure plate
7	1812	Assembly pressure spring
8	1813	Cover
9	1060	Wing nut
10	1061	Adjustment screw
11	1319	Lock screw
12	1005	Clamp anchor screw
13	1006	Clamp anchor nut

Fig. 8-12. Sun Tour DLW and SLW in exploded view. (Courtesy Maeda Industries, Ltd.)

Note carefully the sequence of washers and spacers which, of course, varies from make to make. If you lose count, carefully disassemble the other lever and use it as a model. The wing nut (part No. 9) determines the degree of friction. It should be tightened so that the lever stays put, but does not move so reluctantly that shifting becomes difficult. Other control levers employ a screw rather than a wing nut. The friction screw may be under a cowling as in the case of the Schwinn Sting-Ray and other bikes with a Detroit decor.

CABLE ADJUSTMENTS

Cables stretch with use and require periodic retensioning. Small adjustments are made at the threaded end of the outer casing which is located at the rear and front changer. The outer casing threads into a fixture and is secured by a locknut (Fig. 8-13). The drill is to turn the bike over or, more conveniently, raise the rear wheel. The adjustment barrel should have approximately 1/8 inch of thread showing on the through side of the fixture to establish that the threads have a

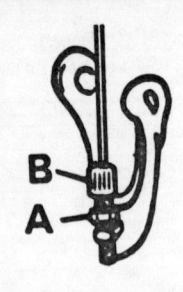

Fig. 8-13. Locknut A and adjustment barrel B that are typical of derailleur brakes. (Courtesy Raleigh Industries Ltd.)

good bite and to enable you to make quick roadside adjustments. Less than 1/8 inch will limit the range of adjustment. To obtain this, turn the barrel clockwise until it is centered in the fitting. Now loosen the anchor bolt and nut which secures the inner cable element to the changer and pull on the cable with a pair of pliers. Holding tension on it, retighten the anchor bolt and nut.

At this point we have plenty of thread on our adjustment barrel and we can go on to make the routine adjustment.

Turn the pedal crank and move the control lever forward to the limit of its travel. The derailleur should shift into high. The control cable should be a bit slack in high gear since there is no point in straining it at this, its limit of travel. Slack can be obtained by turning the adjustment barrel clockwise, threading it inward and increasing the effective length of the inner element. For gross adjustments you can retract the inner element out of the anchor bolt a hair. Check the adjustment several times by shifting to low and back to high.

Failure to shift to the large low-gear sprocket can mean too much slack in the cable since the control lever only has a relatively small arc of travel. If this travel is absorbed in slack, the changer will move to some intermediate gear at the limit of lever travel.

REAR CHANGER ADJUSTMENTS

Most derailleur adjustments involve the rear changer since it is the last in the series of power-transmission components and by far the most complex. Support your bike in a stand or, lacking that, turn it over on the saddle and handlebars. Protect these components from scuff damage.

Sprocket Alignment

A line drawn through the middle sprocket on five-speed changers should pass through the center of the chainwheel; on

15-speed changers it should pass through the middle chainwheel; and on ten-speeds it should fall between the paired chainwheels (Fig. 8-14). Unless these parts are aligned the chain will flex excessively costing energy and accelerating wear on the side links. In extreme cases the sprockets may be so far out of true that the chain refuses to shift to one end of the range.

Two possibilities exist: the sprocket cluster or the chainwheels are out of true. The sprocket cluster can be moved outboard by disassembling it as described previously and adding a machined and heat-treated spacer. It may be necessary to include a washer between the outboard (small) plate and the right-hand dropout to force the chainstays apart for plate clearance.

It is not practical to move the sprocket cluster in the other direction (i.e., inboard).

Tracking

Tracking difficulties are usually caused by accident or by the practice of laying the bike down on its right side. Derailleurs are quite vulnerable to bending damage. The first sign of difficulty may be a refusal of the chain to stay on the front chain wheel when the pedals are reversed. This phenomenon may be accompanied by grinding noises when pedaling and the inner walls of the changer cage may show erosion from chain contact.

The jockey wheel should track down the center of the chain rollers. Bend the derailleur cage as needed. Use a large Crescent wrench for leverage and make the adjustment in a clean movement; missing the mark and readjusting may fatigue the cage, particularly if it is light alloy. Because of the differences in the way rear changers are articulated, it is difficult to generalize about the pressure point. Changers which are reminiscent of an old-fashioned extending telephone

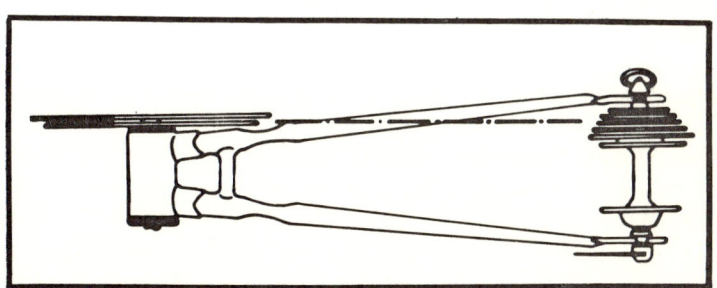

Fig. 8-14. Sprocket and hub bottom bracket alignment. (Courtesy Raleigh Industries, Ltd.)

> **Campagnolo or (Zeus)**   **Simplex**   **Huret**
>
> Screw "A" limits the outward movement of the gear unit
> Screw "B" limits the inward movement of the gear unit
> Screw "C" is the cable clamp bolt

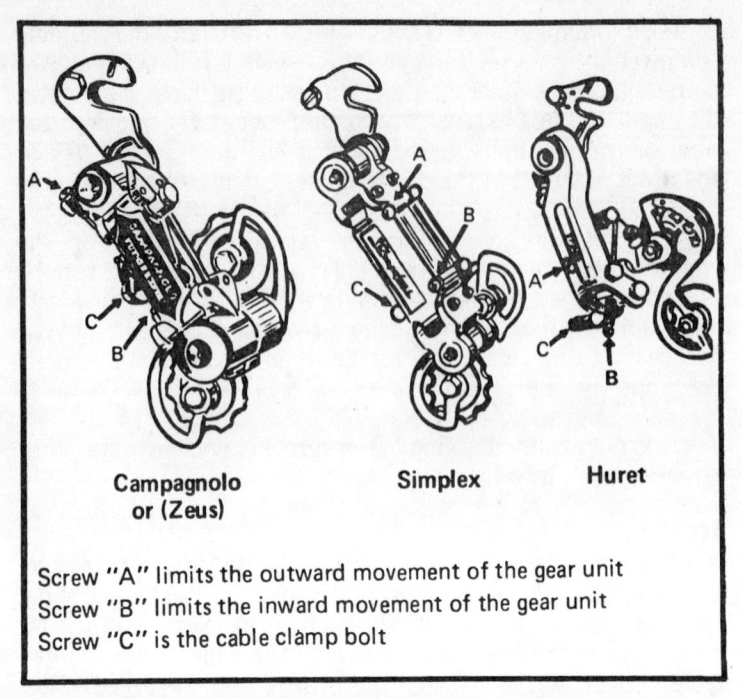

Fig. 8-15. Rear changer adjustments. (Courtesy Raleigh Ltd.)

(e.g., the Huret) should be bent at the jockey axle. Campagnolo-pattern changers are rectangular affairs, pivoting high. Apply pressure at the box on the Campagnolo logo. In either case the point is to bend the structural members of the assembly together and not individually.

Stroke Adjustments

The stroke adjustments control the limit of travel at either end of the range. We will assume that the cable is adjusted correctly and the chain and sprockets are in good condition. Figure 8-15 shows the adjustment points for three popular derailleurs. Should yours vary from those illustrated, distinguish between the high and low gear adjustment screws by observing the action of the changer.

The low-gear range screw limits the inboard movement of the cage. If the cage moves too far inboard it will deposit the chain between the largest sprocket and the spokes. And if the cage is constrained by the low-gear adjustment screw it will refuse to bring the chain far enough inboard to catch low gear. In most cases a small adjustment will do the trick. Be cautious, especially when retracting the screw.

The high-gear screw limits the outboard range. Too much will throw the chain off the smallest sprocket and too little will rob you of the highest gear.

Suppose you have made these adjustments, checked the cable tension (a trifle loose when the changer is in the lowest gear) and the derailleur still refuses to perform over its full range. What then? The chances are that it is dirty and needs cleaning and relubrication. Rather than take the unit apart for this very routine bit of maintenance, clean it with a product such as Ashland Chemical's Chain and Derailleur Clean. Lubricate with light oil.

Chain Tension

New chains should be cut with the same number of links as the original. If you switch sprockets or rear derailleurs you should consult your dealer as to the exact chain length. He will have a chart or the requisite experience to give you an exact answer. While you should have a half-inch of slack with the chain on the largest sprockets, front and rear, the angle of the derailleur varies with make and may vary with sprocket diameter. For example Sun Tour GT and Honor rear derailleurs are normally mounted perpendicular to the ground. But the maker suggests that if a low gear sprocket of 30, 32, or 34 teeth is installed, the cage should tilt back ten degrees (Fig. 8-16). The reason is to assure full chain wrap over the large sprocket. Simplex suggests that the chain be drawn tight over the two largest sprockets and the cage pulled

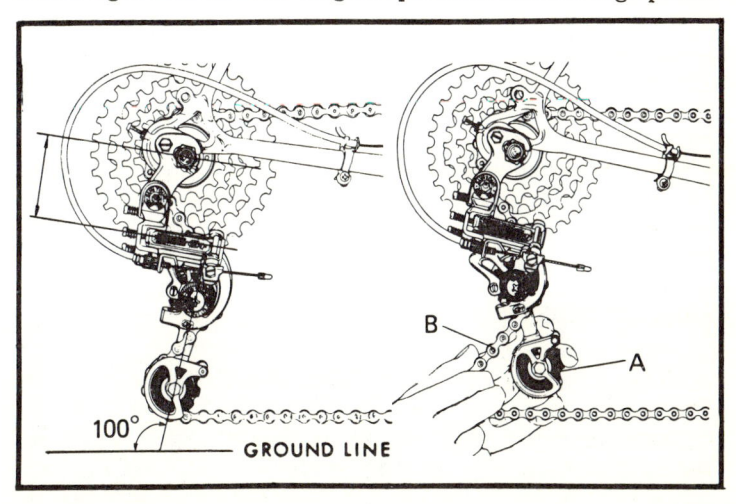

Fig. 8-16. Sun Tour GT and Honor adjustment with large (30, 32, or 34T) plates. (Courtesy Maeda Industries, Ltd.)

full forward. Add three links and you are in business. The outer loop of the cage should arc tangentially with the chain as shown by the arrow in Fig. 8-9B on the Huret. This part helps guide the chain.

In addition the derailleur spring must be adjusted or if necessary replaced to obtain proper running tension. Too little will evidence itself as chain flop and slippage in high gear; too much will accelerate wear and rider fatigue. Apply just enough tension to keep the chain honest.

Initial adjustment should be okay for a long time. The only reason to vary it is to take into account chain stretch and loss of tension of the spring. Derailleurs almost always have some provision for adjustment. One end of the spring is secured and the other end can be rotated to tighten the spring coils. The adjustable end may terminate in a row of holes or may be fitted into a threaded fastener. As the fastener is tightened the spring winds. Many of these fasteners have a dust cap covering the head to keep amateurs at their distance. The cap is removed with a knife blade or the edge of a small screwdriver.

In general terms—subject to the proviso that tension is a necessary evil and should be as minimal as possible—1/2 to 1 turn preload on the fastener is enough. If the changer has a row of holes to secure the spring end, use the adjacent one and test.

Some typical mechanisms are the recessed or Allen head bolt used on the Sun Tour and Simplex (Fig. 8-9A part No. 2972L and Fig. 8-9C part No. 20). The end of the Huret spring is bent in the shape of a hook, shown near the arrow in Fig. 8-8B. The hook fits over hooks on the cage. The Campagnolo is adjusted by removing the jockey cage axle to free the chain from the cage. You will find three holes (two on the Nuovo Record) on the inner cage giving alternate mounting positions for the spring end. Originally the spring is in the most forward one. As it weakens with age, move it an increment at a time to the rear.

CHAIN JUMPS

Chain jump can be a frustrating problem. Look for the obvious first—misalignment, inadequate tension, a bent sprocket—and go from there. Wear makes the sprocket teeth take the form of a hook. This hook, if pronounced enough, can throw the chain. For an immediate fix, try filing the tooth contour back to something approximating the original, but sooner or later the sprocket and chain should be replaced. A stiff link may also be the culprit.

OVERHAUL

With luck the replacement parts you need will be available in your locality or by mail order. Do not count on being able to find major castings or some of the odds and ends for European derailleurs. The wearing parts are usually in stock.

With the rear wheel off the ground, put the chain on the smallest sprocket. Remove the chain from the front sprocket. Be sure to work on a clean floor or put a cloth under the changer to catch small parts during teardown. Better still, detach the changer and mount it in a vise. The changer is secured by the axle nuts or quick releases and by a small bolt. The chain may be removed by opening a link or at the derailleur cage. Designs vary. The Sun Tour GT and Honor feature an open construction which allows the chain to slither free once the wheel is removed (Fig. 8-16). Others are disconnected by removing the tension roller (at the bottom of the cage) and pin. Be alert for falling parts. Most current tension rollers run on plain (one-piece) bearings. Side-thrust is established by shims which must be assembled in the reverse sequence of removal. Figure 8-9C parts Nos. 15, 16, 17, and 18 are typical of late practice. Other designs employ loose balls on the tension roller as does in the Simplex Criterium in Fig. 8-9A. Huret and other cantilever type changers are best disassembled off the bike. The point of attack is the pivot bolt shown as an Allen-head screw (part No. 1920) in Fig. 8-9B. It is wise to disarm the spring first so that you do not have to be concerned about getting mousetrapped.

Clean all parts, inspect for wear, and remove rust accumulations with a wire brush or steel wool. Lubricate with oil and assemble.

FRONT CHANGERS

Front changers are simpler than the rear and generally less troublesome. Two styles are available. The parallelogram type is preferred by discriminating (and affluent) riders. It is recognized by the presence of two adjusting screws to control the stroke (Fig. 8-17A and B). The pole type is mechanically simpler, but can be something of a hassle to adjust. Figure 8-17C illustrates a Simplex Prestige pole type changer. As is usual with bicycle components, the more expensive types are cast in light alloy.

Traditionally you pull back on the left shift lever to make the chain climb on a larger chainwheel. Some Japanese designs work in the reverse: the spring pushes the chain on the larger chainwheel while the lever must be pushed forward to order the chain on the smaller ring.

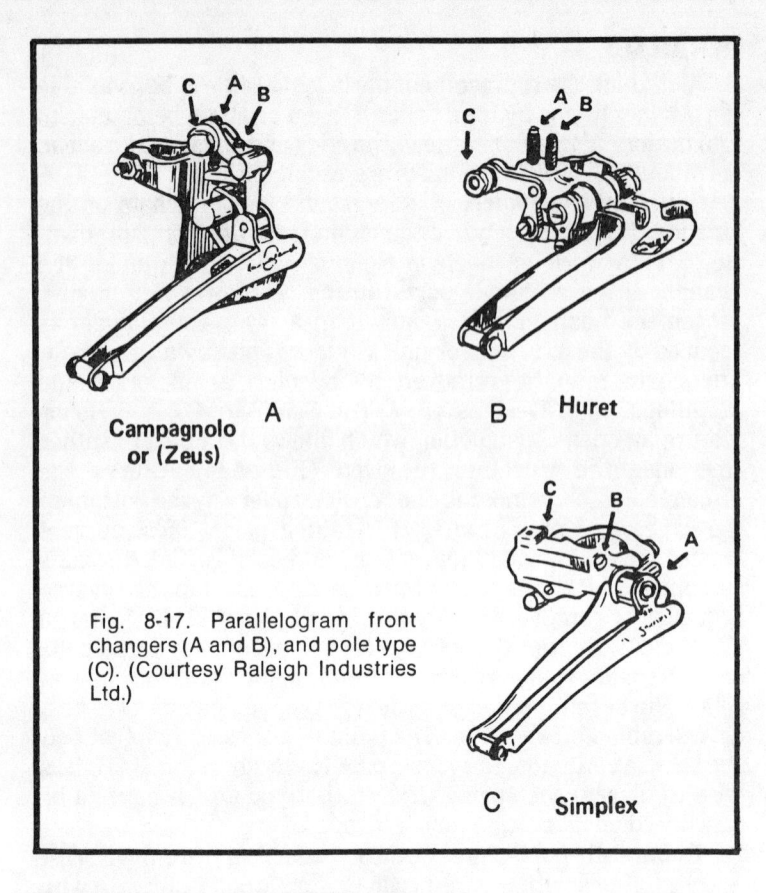

Fig. 8-17. Parallelogram front changers (A and B), and pole type (C). (Courtesy Raleigh Industries Ltd.)

A Campagnolo or (Zeus)
B Huret
C Simplex

Troubleshooting and Adjustment

The mechanism must be kept reasonably clean and well lubricated to insure consistent response. Adjustment involves the position of the front changer on the frame, the stroke, the position of the chain guide relative to the chain, and cable tension. The drill is confused by Sun Tour's idiosyncratic spring-loading. The instructions given referring to the position of the left-hand control lever should be reversed for Sun Tour front changers.

With the rear wheel supported off the ground, move both control levers full forward and pedal to shift chain onto the two smallest sprockets. The front changer control cable should be taut. If it has slack, loosen the anchor bolt or screw (shown in the drawings in Fig. 8-17 as C) and with a pair of pliers pull the cable tight. Without releasing tension on the cable, secure the anchor. If you have a parallelogram changer such as illustrated in Fig. 8-17 A and B, the low-gear adjustment is at screw A. Turn until the chain guide just misses the inside member of the guide. For pole-type changers consult Fig. 8-17C. The inboard or low gear adjustment is made at screw B. Adjust until the guide just clears the chain.

Next, move both control levers full back to put the chain on the outer or high-gear sprockets. Adjust screw B on parallelogram derailleurs so the chain is just off contact with the outer member of the guide. The screw B is adjusted again on pole-type derailleurs. You will end up splitting the difference between the low-gear and high-gear guide clearance.

The guide has adjustments distinct from the stroke. The vertical adjustment—how deeply the guide shrouds the chain on the largest chain wheel—is determined by the position of the whole mechanism on the seat tube. Loosen the bolt or bolts and move the guide up or down so that it clears the chain by 1/32 inch or so. Figure 8-18 illustrates the Sun Tour adjustment; the lower edge of the guide should clear the top of the large chain wheel teeth by one mm (0.039 inch). The radial adjustment is correct with the guide parallel to the chain. To vary it rotate the whole mechanism around the seat tube. Further adjustment is possible on many; others must be carefully bent. The screw A in Fig. 8-17C is known as the pole screw. It may be loosened to rotate the guide on the pole, raising or lowering the roller at the aft end of the guide. The curve of the guide sideplates should conform as closely as possible with the curve of the large chainwheel. Two other adjustments are possible, but not recommended unless needed. Forward tip of the inner guide member can be bent

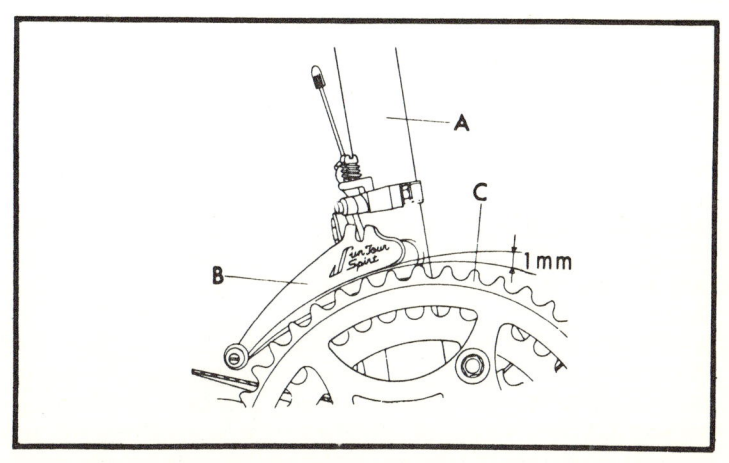

Fig. 8-18. Sun Tour guide clearance. (Courtesy Maeda Industries, Ltd.)

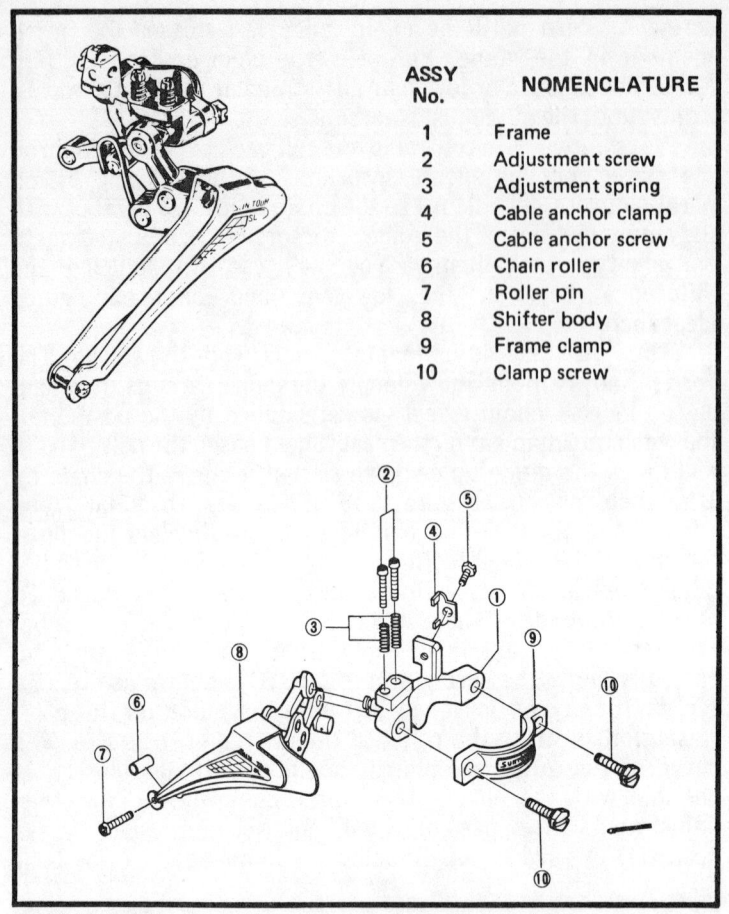

ASSY No.	NOMENCLATURE
1	Frame
2	Adjustment screw
3	Adjustment spring
4	Cable anchor clamp
5	Cable anchor screw
6	Chain roller
7	Roller pin
8	Shifter body
9	Frame clamp
10	Clamp screw

Fig. 8-19. Sun Tour parallelogram-type front changer. (Courtesy Maeda Industries, Ltd.)

outward, toward the chain to give some improvement in shifting. Naturally, you do not bend it so far that it is in constant contact with the chain. The outer tip of the outer member can be bent inward a very small amount to cure chronic chain throw. No guarantees, but sometimes this works.

Overhaul

Figure 8-19 illustrates a Sun Tour front changer. The links, which make up the parallelogram, are riveted into place. Consequently the chain guide, spring, and links are integral and should not be disturbed. Failure of any of these parts means that you must purchase another shifter body assembly.

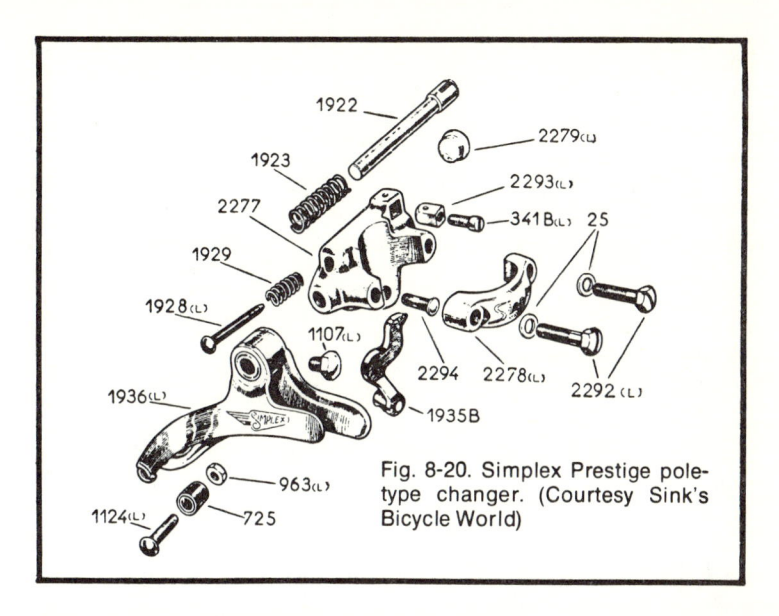

Fig. 8-20. Simplex Prestige pole-type changer. (Courtesy Sink's Bicycle World)

Figure 8-20 is a breakdown of the Simplex Prestige shifter. Small, nonwearing parts, such as the dust cap (part No. 2279), are normally not in inventory. Begin disassembly by removing the roller pin which has a standard right-hand thread and roller. This will free the chain from the guide. Disconnect the cable and mark the position of the bracket on the seat tube for later reference. Remove the changer from the bike and carry out further disassembly on a clean bench. Lay the parts out as they come off. Clean them in solvent and inspect. The chain guide and roller are the most vulnerable components, and suffer accelerated wear if misadjusted.

DERAILLEUR CHAINS

Nearly all derailleur bikes are fitted with a 1/2 × 3/32 inch chain. The first figure refers to the center-to-center distance between the rollers and is known as the pitch. The second figure is the width of the chain as measured between the inside plates (see Fig. 8-21). This chain replaced the 1/2 × 1/8 inch chain with the introduction of the five-sprocket cluster during the immediate postwar years, although the narrower chain is still used on three and four plate racing free wheels.

Occasionally you may encounter a hub transmission which has been converted to a derailleur. If the conversion involves the addition of a rear changer to an existing hub transmission—e.g., a Cyclo changer mounted in tandem with a Sturmey-Archer three-speed hub—the chain size will be

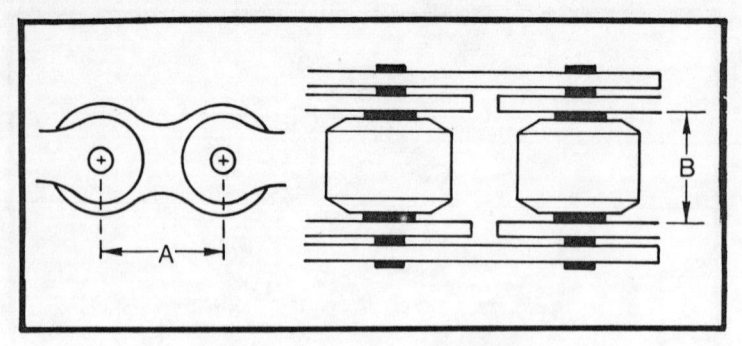

Fig. 8-21. Chain (A) pitch and (B) width.

unaltered. In this case it would be 1/2 × 1/8 inches. Only a few links need to be added to allow for the additional range of the plate cluster. Three-speed Cyclo's can develop a problem at the dropouts if the frame is not splayed by the addition of two 1/8 inch washers between the inner sides of the dropouts and the hub. But if the conversion was more ambitious and involved a substitution of a changer and wheel, chances are that the mechanic who did the job used a 1/2 inch × 3.3 mm chain. This chain will mate on the free wheel and on the original chainwheel.

In addition, you should be aware that not all bicycle chains of the same nominal size will interchange. Sedis, for example, does not seem to translate well.

Although master links are supplied with many replacement chains, these detachable links should not be used with derailleur transmissions. Purchase a rivet extractor such as the one in Fig. 8-22. Center the point of the extractor over a rivet. Turn the handle just far enough to force the rivet clear of the sideplate. Do the same for the other rivet on that sideplate. Reverse the procedure to install.

Chain Maintenance

The most important maintenance is to keep the chain well oiled. There are differences of opinion about the proper lubricants—some prefer the new foaming types which may contain low-friction, high-pressure metallic elements and soaps, others settle for an oil can. In any event the kind of lubricant is less important than the frequency of lubrication. Besides extending the life of the chain and reducing pedal effort, a film of oil will prevent rust—the archenemy of chains. Once the bearings surfaces become pitted the chain is useless.

Routine oiling simply involves squirting, spraying, or brushing light oil over the surface of the chain while it is in place. Wipe off the excess and allow the chain to drip dry before riding. If the chain is dirty it can be cleaned in place with solvent and a brush. Try not to splash any on the tires. A more convenient way is to use one of the aerosol preparations sold for this purpose in bike shops.

Serious cleaning (inside of the roller and pin) requires that the chain be removed and soaked in solvent. Dry and lubricate. Some authorities like to lubricate a dismounted chain by dipping it in 90-weight transmission oil. The oil resists washout and is viscous enough to stay on the chain.

After exposure to rain or snow moisture can be neutralized by an application of WD-40 or equivalent product. However do not make the mistake of many mechanics and use these light oils in lieu of a full-bodied lubricant. As useful as WD-40 and its brethren are as moisture inhibitors, penetrating oils, and rust looseners, they are not first class lubricants.

Chain Stretch

Chains do not stretch in the sense that the plates elongate However the bearing surfaces do wear and the cumulative effect is called stretch. While industrial chains can tolerate a 2 percent stretch before renewal, the uneven operation of a derailleur makes more severe demands on bike chains. As a rule the chain should be replaced if 12 links or 6 inches of chain measures 6 1/32 inches. You can check this by bracing the front wheel and having someone put pressure on the pedals. A less "scientific" method is to shift to the two largest sprockets. If the chain droops and the wheel is backed fully into the dropouts and gear changer tension is correct, you can be reasonably certain that the chain is stretched beyond tolerance. Of course, an immediate repair can be made by removing links.

Excessive stretch causes the chain to climb over the sprockets, eventually wearing them into hooks. When this occurs sprockets and chain must be replaced. But stretch is also present as side-clearance between the plates and roller ends. Some play is desirable since the derailleur demands a

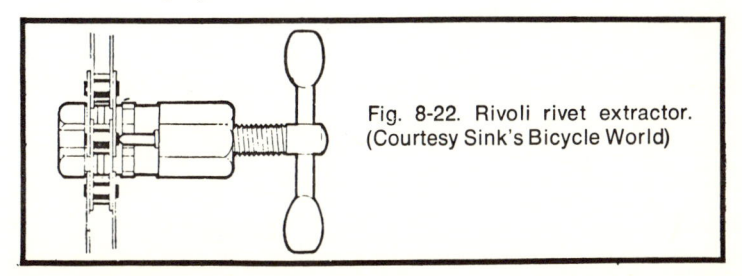

Fig. 8-22. Rivoli rivet extractor. (Courtesy Sink's Bicycle World)

certain flexibility for smooth shifting. But too much will cause the chain to jump the sprockets.

Stiff links also cause chain jump, but that can be identified by the regularity of the phenomenon. A completely worn-out chain will jump at random, while a stiff link will jump when it shifts onto another sprocket. With the rear wheel clear off the ground, observe the action of the chain. Mark, as best you can, the segment that jumps with chalk or soft crayon. If the marks cluster you can be sure that the trouble is localized and almost as certain that a stiff link is to blame. Remove the chain and work the affected links side to side by hand. Soak in penetrating oil. The nice thing about the Rivoli tool (Fig. 8-22) is that it includes a chain spreader to cope with tight links. With the chain on the spreader slot a quarter turn of the handle will force the plates further apart. Of course, if the side plates are bent no amount of spreading will help.

Crank and Hub Transmissions

Several new transmissions have been introduced here and abroad. One group shifts automatically by means of torque demand or rpm. Perhaps the simplest of these is the two-speed unit built in prototype form by Fichtel & Sachs of Schweinfurt. This firm is known primarily for its anti-friction bearings, automotive transmissions and clutches, small engines, and is the only large-scale manufacturer of Wankel-patent engines for industrial purposes. The transmission employs a pair of weights which swing outward and shift into second gear at road speeds of approximately 17 kmh (see Fig. 9-1.)

AUTO-TORQ

A more radical automatic (one which offers an infinite variety of speeds within its range) is offered by BE Industries. It consists of two pulleys or sheaves mounted above the bottom bracket. The lower sheave is free to arc along slots cut into its mount (Fig. 9-2). As you can see in Fig. 9-3, the sheaves are connected by a V-belt. Power goes out the upper or fixed sheave.

The Auto-Torq, as BE has dubbed this device, has some interesting characteristics. In the first place it is not entirely positive; there is some slippage. Secondly a weight penalty on the order of 1.4 pounds can be expected over a ten-speed derailleur. These characteristics would seem to send this transmission the way of the sprung fork, but the situation is not so simple.

In the first place a small amount of slip seems to be less critical than one would assume: it may be tolerated in a device

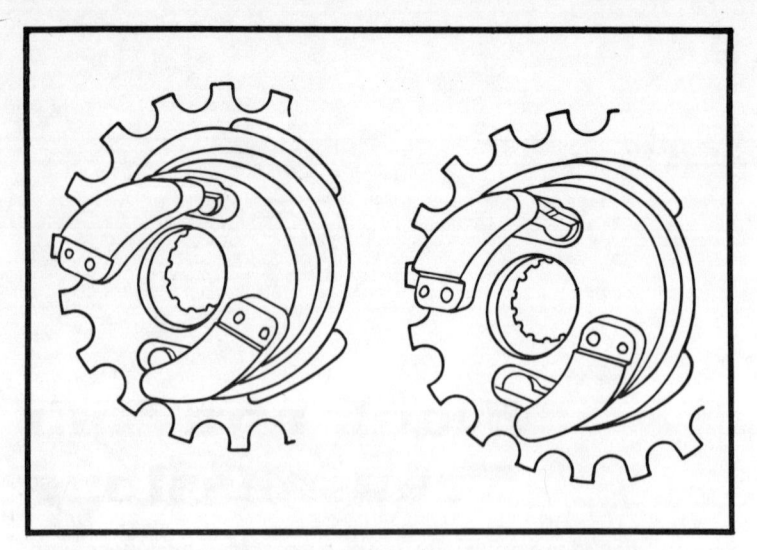

Fig. 9-1. Fitchel & Sachs centrifugally-operated transmission.

which reduces strain. On a flat, indoor track any slip would result in muscular activity which appears only as heat in the transmission—not as forward motion. Obviously, such a transmission would be inappropriate for this sort of use. On the other hand, most riders are subject to the effects of terrain and

Fig. 9-2. Auto Torq prototype. (Courtesy BE Industries)

Fig. 9-3. Sheave and belt arrangement. (Courtesy BE Industries)

wind. If, instead of a smooth, sheltered track, we consider an irregular road bed subject to gusting headwinds, the situation becomes quite different.

The rider will not downshift his derailleur for each gust or surface irregularity. Instead, he will demand more from his leg muscles. The level of physical strain can be plotted on a curve which will look something like the graph shown in Fig. 9-4. The broken line represents more or less ideal conditions leading up to a downshift. The dotted line portrays the fluctuations in strain caused by surface and wind irregularities. The Auto Torq is represented by the solid line. While the automatic requires slightly more effort over the long run, the level of strain is smooth and predictable as the transmission shifts to accommodate.

How this affects athletic performance is a subject which requires further study. But the experience of long-distance runners, oarsmen, mountain-climbers and others whose business it is to get the most out of the human engine over long periods, indicates that strain should be taken in steady and small doses. This is exactly what the automatic transmission does.

Test riders have confirmed that they experience less fatigue and have a better average performance with such a transmission.

The weight penalty over a good derailleur is significant in competition, but again it is not as significant as the bare

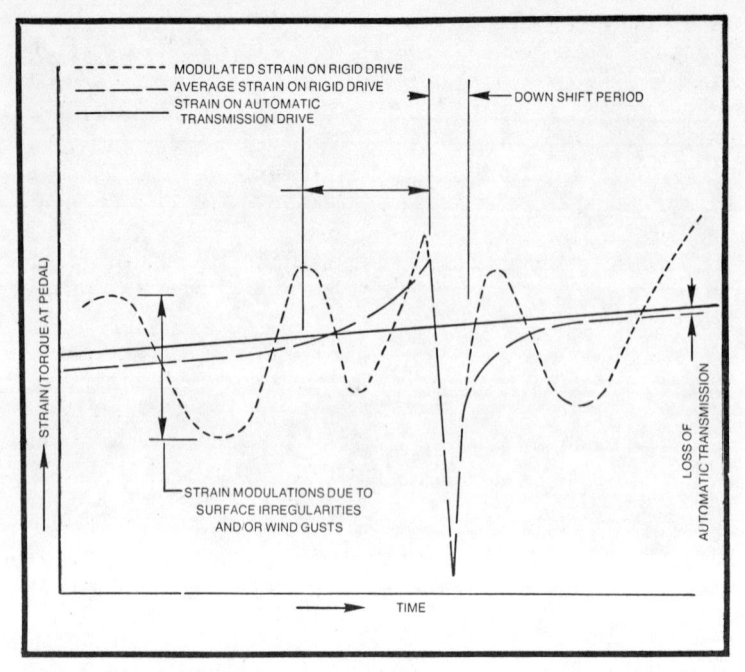

Fig. 9-4. Comparison of typical strain patterns on a manual shift bike and one equipped with an automatic transmission. (Courtesy BE Industries)

figures would indicate. A bicycle equipped with one of these transmissions should weigh 2 percent more than one with a conventional drive. Assuming that the bike weighs 35 pounds (a good average figure for middle-priced touring machines) and a 165 pound rider, the efficiency loss is only some 0.25 percent. This is because aerodynamic losses are much greater than wheel bearing and tire losses at competitive speeds.

Another advantage is that this type of transmission is relatively free of maintenance hassles. Unlike the derailleur with its double handful of parts, many of which clash and clunk, the torque-responsive element consists of a spring and ramp. The belts will eventually wear out, but should easily outlast the tires. The technology, proved on small motorcycles, snowmobiles, and in the Dutch DAF automobile, is well understood in a design sense and can be easily taught to mechanics.

The strain, as measured on the pedals, is a variable factor. Changing sheave diameter and spring tension can limit it for the infirm or elderly. One chooses between the level of input and forward velocity.

Operating Principles

Two principles are involved. The first is present in all V-belt drives and is illustrated in Fig. 9-5. Under torque demand, i.e., when the going gets rough, the belt wraps more tightly on the drive sheave and tends to be flung outward on the driven sheave. The effective diameters of the two sheaves have changed in favor of torque multiplication. But in itself this effect is marginal.

Significant torque multiplication occurs mechanically. The drive sheave is split into two halves. These two parts are held together by a spring and ramp arrangement similar to the drawing in Fig. 9-6. Normally the spring holds the halves together, squeezing the belt and forcing it to ride high on the groove. This condition, illustrated in Fig. 9-7A, represents a 1:1 ratio and is the equivalent of high gear. Under load movable sheave rotates a few degrees and cams open against spring tension. The groove widens and the belt snuggles down as far as it can go. The effective diameter of the drive sheave becomes smaller, giving a 3:1 ratio or an approximation thereof (Fig. 9-7B). (This device is still in development and the production ratios have not been fixed.) Torque multiplication—the tradeoff between speed and strain—is a function of the sheave ratio.

This device is a "stepless" transmission. Between the extremes of drive pulley diameter the ratios are infinitely variable in response to varying torque demands.

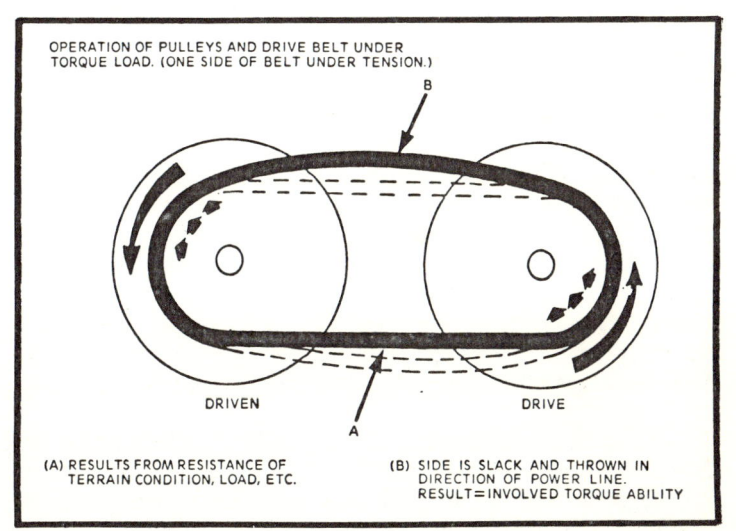

Fig. 9-5. A V-belt automatically responds to lead. (Courtesy Bombardier, Ltd.)

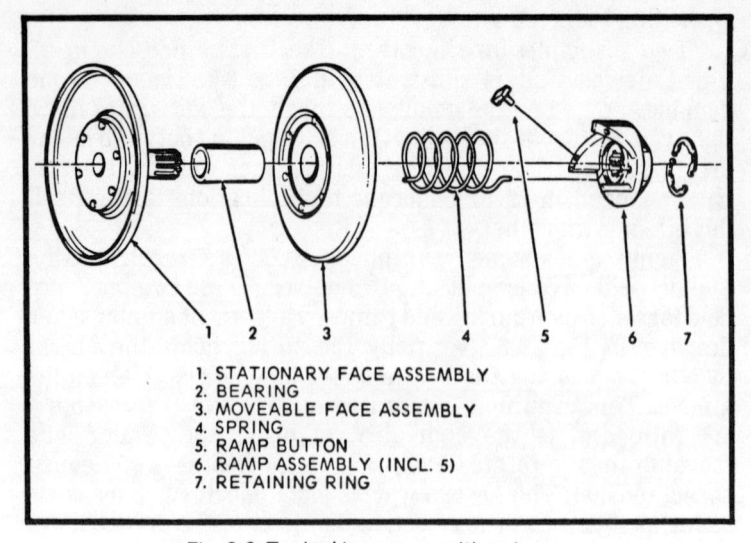

Fig. 9-6. Typical torque-sensitive sheave.

1. STATIONARY FACE ASSEMBLY
2. BEARING
3. MOVEABLE FACE ASSEMBLY
4. SPRING
5. RAMP BUTTON
6. RAMP ASSEMBLY (INCL. 5)
7. RETAINING RING

Overall ratios can be stretched by incorporating an additional transmission in the rear wheel hub. Some frictional losses are inevitable with such a scheme, but extended range might well be worthwhile for tourists. BE Industries has suggested the incorporation of a two-speed automatic on the Bendix pattern or one of the three-speed planetary sets.

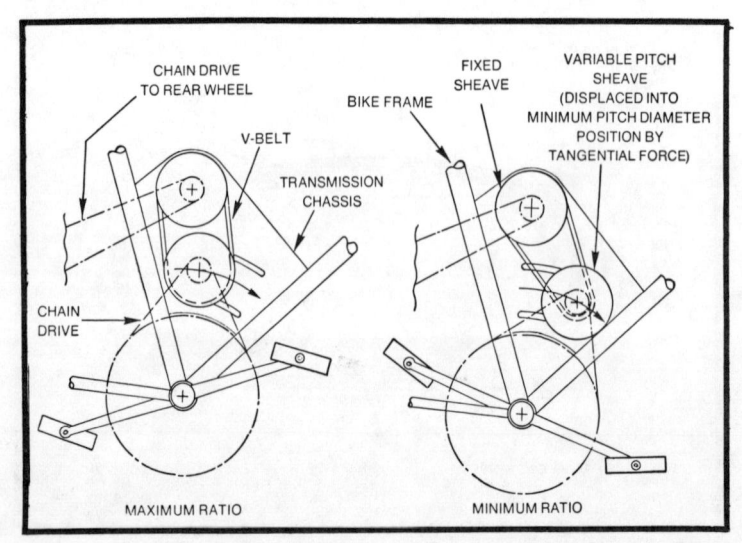

Fig. 9-7. Automatic torque converter bicycle transmisson. (Courtesy BE Industries)

DANA THREE SPEED

Another new transmission has been developed by the Dana Corporation as an aftermarket accessory, primarily for American bikes (Fig. 9-8). It is a three-speed planetary transmission and is distinguished from Sturmey-Archer, Shamano, and other designs by being mounted on the bottom bracket. The shift cables work in opposition for positive shifts, instead of the more usual arrangement which employs a single cable working against a spring. In addition, the Dana transmission automatically downshifts during braking. This feature is the equivalent of a power booster since reverse torque acting on the pedals is multiplied by the lower gear.

The transmission is in production and shows all the signs of careful engineering and development which are marks of Dana products. While other approaches promise more, their promise is as yet theoretical. The Dana unit can be purchased over the counter for fitting to any bike with a 2 1/4 inch bottom bracket.

Installation

Installation offers no particular problem so long as the hanger has an internal diameter of 2 1/4 inch. Break the chain, remove the original crank set, and install the extended crank axle and bearing assembly which is supplied with the kit (Fig. 9-9). The new axle is supplied with a fixed cone. The original bearings, adjustable cone, locknut, dust cover, and washer are retained. Schwinn, Monarch, and CCM bikes require a new

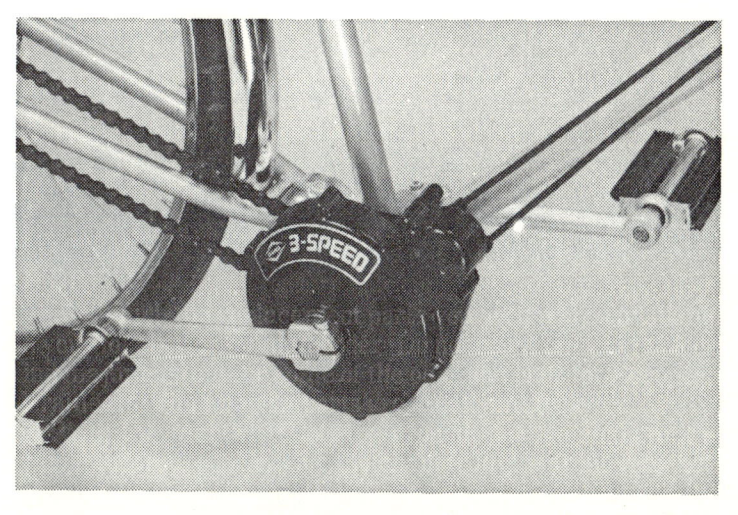

Fig. 9-8. Dana three-speed transmission.

Fig. 9-9. Axle extended.

cone and locknut purchased to fit the 24 TPI Dana axle. These parts are available from Schwinn as Nos. 56054 and 56057. Wald supplies similar parts in kit form as Nos. 244 or 1940. Naturally, the bearings and adjustable cone should be replaced if worn or pitted. Lubricate with light grease and install, setting the bearing clearance as indicated in Chapter 11.

A plastic washer is placed over the right or protruding end of the axle. The large diameter is next to the cone. Discard the washer on Columbia bikes and use the original dust cover. Lubricate the end of the axle.

Install the transmission case, mounting the reaction arm on the down tube (Fig. 9-10). If the mounting bracket is too small, remove the plastic tube. Assemble the cranks to the axle, flat side out. The right-hand crank has the letter R stamped on the pedal end. If the crank will not install flush with the end of the shaft—to within 1/16 inch—remove the transmission case and check the position of the plastic washer (or dust cover). The cranks are secured by a 1/4 inch × 1 inch cap screw, a variant of the cottered-crank principle. These screws must be tight. Secure the pedals, remembering that the left pedal has a left-hand thread. Turn it counterclockwise to tighten.

The control cables should not be disconnected from the transmission or from the twist grip assembly. Nor should any attempt be made to shift the transmission until the twist grip is

Fig. 9-10. Transmission case installed.

secured to the handlebars. Remove either handlegrip and loosen the two screws on the twist grip just enough to slip the assembly over the handlebar end. These screws must take a bite on a straight section of bar; if the assembly is too close to the stem, pull it back until you can tighten the screws.

Shift into second gear. Unscrew the adjustment fittings equally to remove cable slack and to align the No. 2 mark with the indicator (Fig. 9-11). Tighten the locknuts.

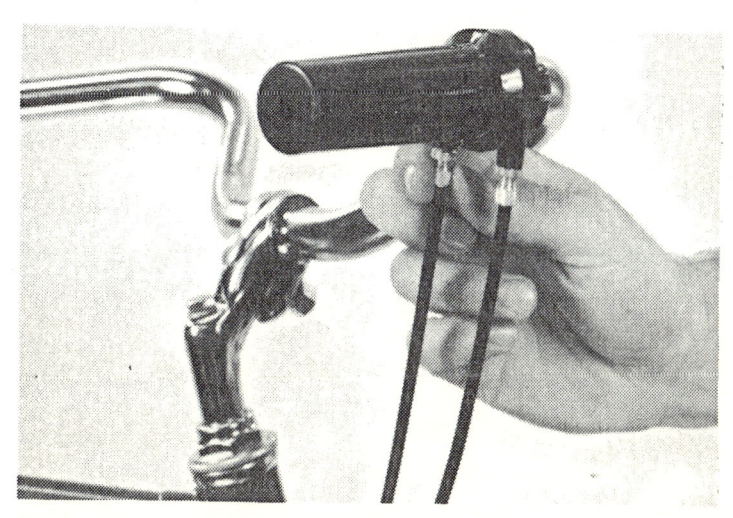

Fig. 9-11. Adjusting cables. There should be minimal free play in second speed.

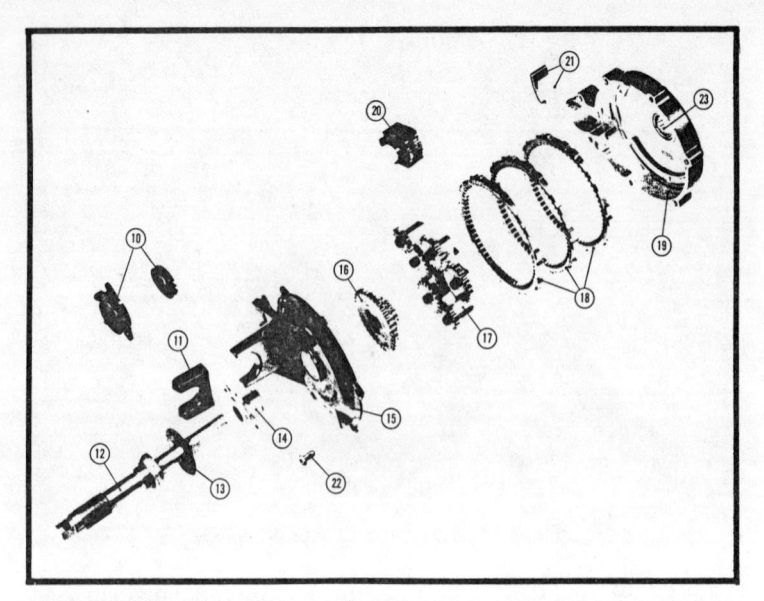

Fig. 9-12. Transmission in exploded view. The nomenclature is in the text. (Courtesy Dana Corp.)

All that remains is the chain. These transmissions are intended for 1/2 inch chain of the type almost universal on American bicycles. The only problem you might encounter is if you have a very old bike with "every other link" 1 inch chain. The rear sprocket will have to be replaced. Derailleur chain requires a break-in period to adjust to this transmission, but should settle down after a few hundred revolutions.

Run the chain over the sprockets, marking how much chain will have to be removed. Use a rivet extractor, although if necessary you can break the chain with the help of a small punch. The chain should have 1/2 inch free play with the rear wheel near the inner limit of travel in the dropouts.

Teardown

Figure 9-12 is an exploded view of the transmission. Detach the crank arms and reaction member. Remove the transmission from the bike together with the twist grip, cables intact. Remove the sprocket (No. 14), the cover screws (No. 22), and shifter cover (No. 10). Now the cables can be disengaged. Next take off the kickdown parts (No. 21), central sun gear (No. 16), planet-gear cage (No. 17), ring gears (No. 18), and the shifter assembly (No. 20).

The shifter assembly and the planet-gear cage should not be further disturbed. In the event of a malfunction, replace these components as complete assemblies. Clean all metal parts with solvent and inspect for damage. Look for chipped teeth, scored or worn bearing surfaces, galling against the case, and other irregularities. Coat the parts with Lubriplate 5555 or the equivalent light grease.

The shifter is the most critical part. Before final assembly, install it in the bulge on the housing and check its action on the ring gears. Turn the axle with a wrench and work the mechanism. The shifter should respond with a definite snap as its pawl engages.

Install the ring gears (No. 18), preferably in their original positions to minimize wear. These gears are, however, interchangeable. Insert the planet-gear cage (No. 17) into the ring gears by rotating the cage. Install the sun gear (No. 16). This job will go easier if the axle (No. 12) is used as an alignment tool. Install the kickdown parts (No. 21). The spring must be in place.

Next replace the cover. Use the axle to align the parts. The mounting screws are secured at this time—except for those two which hold the external shifter parts (No. 10). Torque the others in a criss-cross fashion to 70 inch-pounds.

Place the pulley (shown with its cover at No. 10) over the shifter shaft. Attach the cables to the pulley, being careful that the ends do not slip out of their grooves. With the transmission "belly up" on the bench, that is, with the cover and shaft up, the cables should be parallel when the twist grip is in an upright position. Should you cross the cables, no great harm will be done. The quadrant will indicate 3rd gear with the transmission in first gear. Tighten the two remaining screws, those which hold the exernal shifter parts, to 20 inch-pounds. Install the drive sprocket and mount the unit on the bike.

Cable and Twist Grip Replacement

To replace the twist grip or control cables remove the shifter cover (No. 10). Note the lay of the cables and detach the cable ends from the pulley. Remove the two screws holding the twist grip in place on the handlebars. The grip will come apart and the cables may be removed.

To assemble begin by threading the adjusting ferrules completely into the twist grip clamp. This is to provide thread for later adjustment. Attach the top clamp half, leaving the screws loose enough to slip the twist-grip assembly over the handlebars. Install the cables on the transmission pulley, observing the correct placement. After the grip is secured on the handlebars, adjust the cable slack by turning the adjustment ferrules counterclockwise. There should be

Table 9-1. Dana Transmission Troubleshooting Chart

SYMPTOM	REPAIR STEPS
Twist grip has mushy feel and/or excessive free play. Transmission "locks up" when shifting Transmission will not shift into 1st and/or 3rd gear. Clicking noise when pedalling in 1st and/or 3rd gear.	Adjust cables. Free play should be minimized. Make sure cable ends are correctly positioned in pulley. Replace cables.
Transmission shifts too hard.	Make sure twist grip turns free on handle bar—not binding on curved section of handle bars. Adjust cables. Replace shifter assembly.
Transmission has forward neutral.	Replace shifter assembly.
Transmission braking mode inoperative.	Kickdown parts out of position.
Transmission has excessive drag.	Mainshaft bearing adjustment may be too tight. Plastic dust cover may be binding. Transmission cover alignment must be checked. Loosen cover bolts—rotate shaft—retighten bolts.

minimal free play with the transmission in second gear and the handlebars in their normal (straight ahead) position.

Troubleshooting

This transmission is as yet unfamiliar to many mechanics, and as always with a new technology, troubleshooting is difficult. The chart shown in Table 9-1, prepared from information provided by the Dana Corporation, should help.

PLANETARY TRANSMISSIONS

Planetary hub transmissions continue to have a solid, if unspectacular share of the market. In addition to bicycle applications, these versatile gear trains are found in automotive transmissions (in conjunction with a fluidic torque converter for automatic gear changes) and surprising number of industrial uses. The advantage of this arrangement is that the gears are always in mesh; changing is effected by braking and releasing the transmission members.

Figure 9-13 shows a generic planetary transmission. The shape of the cage and the number of gears varies with particular applications, but the relationship of the parts is the same as shown here. There are three members. The sun gear is central, the planet gears revolve around it. You can understand the derivation of the term "planetary" in context of these gear sets. The planetary gears are mounted in a cage or carrier. The whole assembly turns at the same time the planets revolve. This double motion accounts for the term *epicentric* which is also used to describe these transmissions. (Interestingly enough, this is the motion of the planets, spinning around the earth and at the same time turning on their axes, postulated by medieval astronomers.) The sun gear and cage assembly make up the first two members; the third is the internal, or ring, gear.

As mentioned earlier, gear changes are made by braking and applying power to the various elements. A number of possibilities exist (two of which give reversed outputs) but bicycle-hub transmissions confine themselves to three.

These conditions are shown in Fig. 9-14. In second gear the sun gear is fixed to the axle which is, of course, stationary and the cage is clutched in to the hub. Power goes in through the sprocket to the cage and hence to the wheel hub. The planets spin idly on the sun gear and the drive ratio is 1:1.

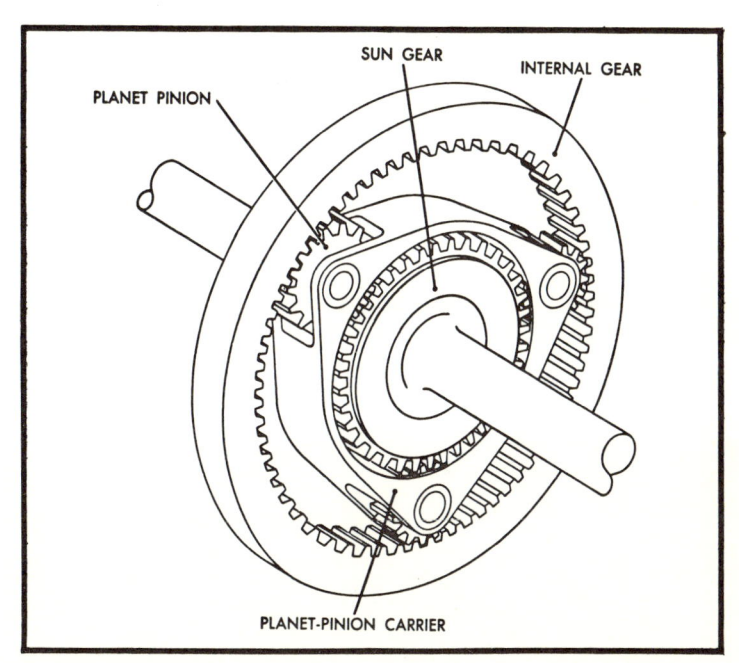

Fig. 9-13. Planetary transmission—major components less clutch.

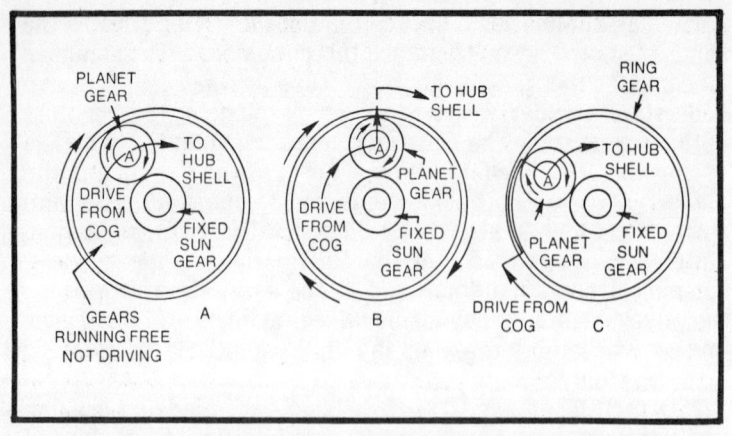

Fig. 9-14. Planetary gear operation. (A) second or normal gear, (B) third or high gear, (C) first or low gear.

In Fig. 9-14B the transmission is in high gear. Drive from the sprocket goes in through the planet spindles, of which one is shown in the drawing. The cage is driven. Again the planets rotate merrily around the central and fixed sun gear. But this time power is taken off at the ring gear which is clutched to the wheel hub. Power goes in to the center of the planet gears and leaves at their edges. *A speed multiplication is effected because the edges of the gears turn faster than the spindles.* Consequently the wheel turns more rpm than the sprocket.

Figure 9-14C illustrates low gear. In this case we lose the speed advantage but gain in torque. The ring gear is connected to the sprocket and turns with it. As it does the planets rotate on their spindles and the planet cage, connected to the spindles, rotates. Power to the wheel hub is taken off at the cage. *The cage turns slower than the ring gear because spindles rotate slower than the gear edges.*

To recapitulate:

- Second (normal) gear: Power goes in through the sprocket to the planet-gear cage and directly to the wheel hub. There is no torque or speed multiplication.
- High gear: Power goes into the sprocket to the planet-gear cage. The cage, mounted to the planets at their spindles, turns more slowly than the edges of the gears. Power is taken off at the ring gear which enjoys a speed advantage because it is driven by the planet-gear edges.
- Low gear: Power goes into the sprocket and to the ring gear. The planet gear spindles turn more slowly

than the gear edges, rotating the cage at this reduced speed. Power goes out through the cage to the hub.

STURMEY-ARCHER

The Sturmey-Archer was the first successful hub transmission and has been with us since the closing days of Victoria's reign. Some would say that it is still the best of the bunch. Generally these transmissions are used in conjunction with rim brakes, although coaster-brake and hub-brake versions have been produced. The latter configuration is popular in Europe.

Five-speed hubs are available, but the three-speed type remains standard. Until a few years ago, medium and close-ratio gear sets were available for the three-speed, but have been discontinued. Apparently the sporting segment of the market has abandoned hub transmissions, although there is much to be said for them in spite of the weight and efficiency limitations. The current wide-ratio hub offers a speed multiplication of 33 percent in overdrive, and a reduction of 29 percent in low.

Trigger Changers

Three control mechanisms are offered. The traditional control is in the form of a trigger, mounted on the right handlebar. Figure 9-15 illustrates this homely but reliable device.

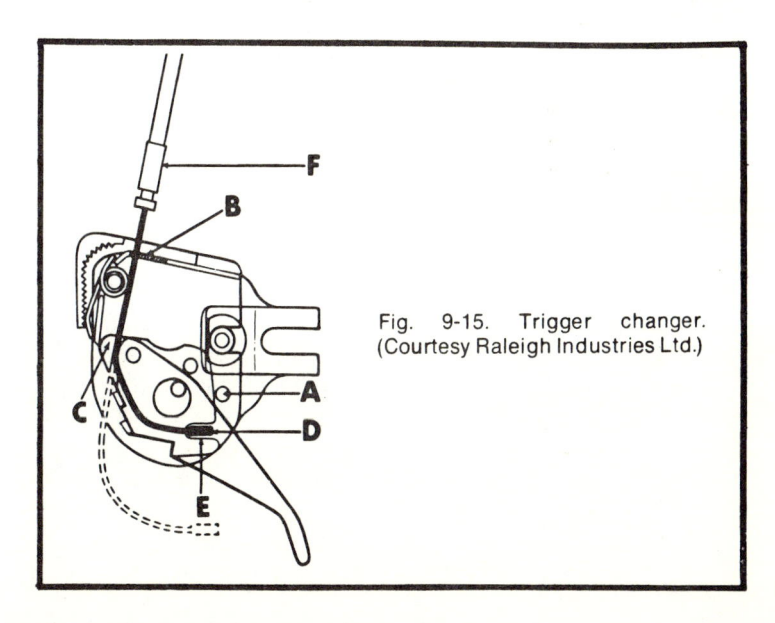

Fig. 9-15. Trigger changer. (Courtesy Raleigh Industries Ltd.)

Rust is the great enemy. Rather than attempt to make the mechanism waterproof—which would have been a difficult and expensive undertaking—Sturmey-Archer engineers opted to provide drain slots. Water will not accumulate and a good rain will flush the mechanism. But it must be kept oiled. Repairs, even if parts could be cannibalized, are not practical.

It is not necessary to remove the control from the handlebar in most instances. Remove the inner wire from the indicator chain at the hub. Loosen the knurled locknut and unthread the barrel-shaped socket. Remove the outer casing from the fulcrum clip located near the dropouts. Tug on the cable ferrule (Fig. 9-14, F) to detach it from the slot B. Pull the lever to the low gear position, right up against the stop A. Push the inner wire through the mechanism and pry up on the nipple D. Pull wire out between the ratchet and pawl C and through the slotted hole B.

Control cables are supplied in several lengths. A few inches of excess is not critical since you can move the fulcrum clip at the lower end toward the handlebars to compensate. If the replacement cable is still too long you should purchase the correct length or, if parts are hard to come by, cut the cable at the lower end and install an adjustable sleeve. Bike shops generally stock these parts.

Note: Plastic ferrules are subject to deterioration and will crumple the outer casing. Purchase a new plastic or, preferably, a metal ferrule to go with the new cable.

Twist-Grip Changers

Twist-grip changers have become popular in recent years as a sales gimmick (Fig. 9-16). Unfortunately these changers are prone to failure and spoil what is otherwise a "bulletproof" transmission. Repairs of a more serious nature than cable changing are not advised. Instead, replace the unit with a trigger changer.

The Sturmey-Archer twist grip features an automatic (or nearly automatic) adjustment. Remove large amounts of slack at the fulcrum clip (mounted on the right-hand chain stay). Loosen the pinch screw and slide the bracket along the chain stay. Moving it towards the handlebars tightens the cable. Once the slack is removed, tighten the pinch screw and turn the twist grip past No. 1 gear. The transmission should be adjusted correctly and indexed to the shift quadrant. However, the twist grip is limited in range. Once past this range and you will have to partially dismantle it to reset the cable.

To do this remove the twist grip from the handlebar. Loosen the twin mounting screws a few turns and slide it off.

Next take out the screws. The grip will part. Inside you will find a 3/16 inch ball bearing and a spring. The ball and spring are part of the detent mechanism which hold the transmission into the selected gear.

Coat the ball and spring with grease to keep them in place. Fit the cable end into the slot of the operating sleeve, and fit the inner wire into the slot of the gear-locating spring. Position the spring over the operating sleeve. At the same time be sure the ball is in the elongated hole of the sleeve and that the spring is fully depressed into its boss.

Hold the ball and spring down with your thumb and with one last look to be certain that the parts are mated, slip the top half of the casing over the operating sleeve. Several attempts and the digital dexterity of the proverbial London pickpocket may be required. The spring must compress into its groove. If it hangs up it will be ruined when you make the first shift. Hold the two casings together and run the clamp screws part way down. Slide the twist grip over the handlebar and tighten securely and evenly.

Sportshift Changers

The Sportshift is sometimes fitted to British versions of the high-rise bicycle. If the twist grip is intended to give the

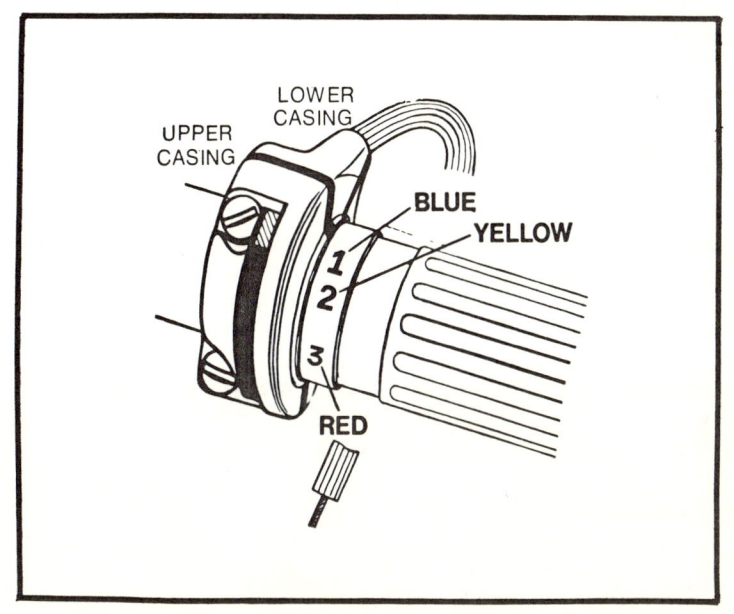

Fig. 9-16. Twist grip changer. (Courtesy Raleigh Industries Ltd.)

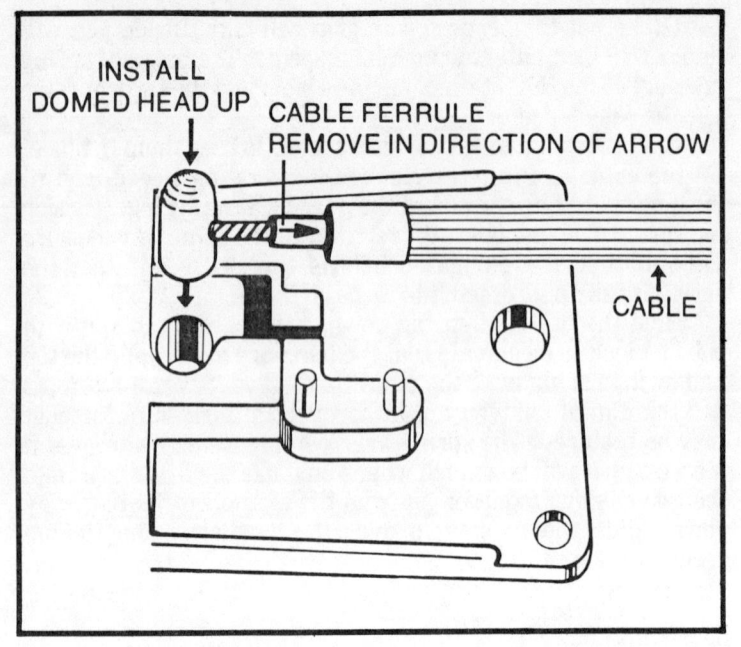

Fig. 9-17. Sportshift cable routing. (Courtesy Raleigh Industries Ltd.)

appearance of a motorcycle, the Sportshift and its progeny imitates the Hurst shifter. It is another item which is not, in the true sense of the word, repairable. However, the cable can be replaced.

To replace the cable, remove the Sportshift from the bicycle and detach the cable from the indicator chain at the hub. Remove the forward screw from the mounting plate; unscrew the lever knob and push the lever full forward. Remove the plastic cover. With a knife or small screwdriver, pry the cable ferrule free from its mounting slot. Some models have an indicator plate secured by pegs. The plate is made of plastic and must be gently freed and swung to the right to gain access to the cable ferrule.

Working from the underside of the mounting plate, disengage the cable end from the recess. When installing a new cable, the domed end of the barrel is up as shown in Fig. 9-17.

STURMEY-ARCHER HUBS

These hubs will occasionally need lubrication and bearing adjustment. The routine teardown, inspection, and repacking which is characteristic of other bicycle components is not recommended or necessary for the Sturmey-Archer. Its

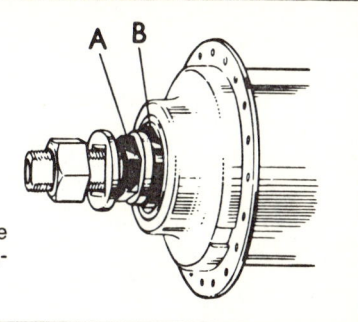

Fig. 9-18. Sturmey-Archer cone adjustment. (Courtesy Raleigh Industries Ltd.)

mechanism is entirely too complex for casual exploration. Lubricate frequently with Sturmey-Archer oil applied through the nipple in the center of the hub. Household lubricants, expecially the type that combines vegetable and mineral oils, will jam the mechanism. The bearings are adjusted at the left side (Fig. 9-18). The right side cone positions the hub on the axle and should not be disturbed. Loosen the locknut A in Fig. 9-18 and adjust the cone B. Finger tight and no more than a half turn counterclockwise will usually suffice. Remember to leave just a trace of surplus slack to account for axle buckling when the axle nuts are torqued.

Cable slack is common in these hubs and will result in the loss of one or two speeds. Large adjustments—as when replacing the cable with one that doesn't quite fit—are made at the fulcrum bracket mentioned previously. Small adjustments are made at the indicator chain. Put the shifter in No. 2 position. Loosen the locknut (No. 2 in Fig. 9-19) and turn the

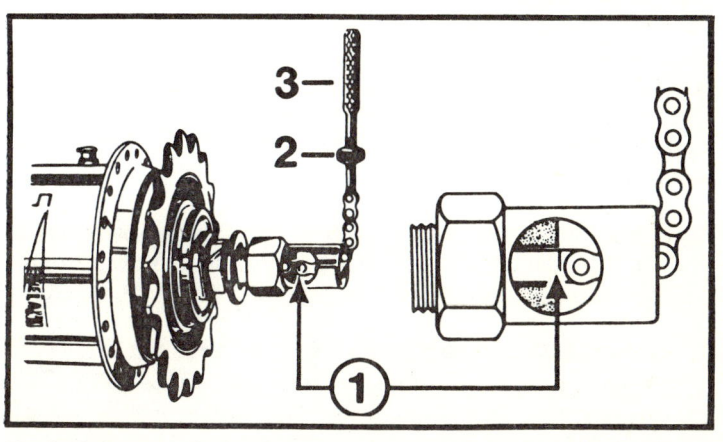

Fig. 9-19. Sturmey-Archer indicator rod adjustment. (Courtesy Raleigh Industries Ltd.)

cable barrel (No. 3) to move the shift rod in and out of the hub. The transmission is correctly adjusted when the flat at the end of the rod is even with the axle end as shown in the inset.

Eventually the chain will wear or be pinched against the nut end as the bike gets knocked about. Replacement is simple: unthread the cable barrel from the chain and unthread the chain from the rod. Install a new chain and tighten snugly by hand. Don't overdo it. The threads in the axle key will strip and you will find yourself taking the hub apart.

AW3 Hub

Figure 9-20 is an exploded view of the AW3 wide-ratio hub. It is by far the most popular of the Sturmey-Archer models and has been built by the millions. Begin by checking the obvious which, in this case, is the gear adjustment. The indicator may not be accurate if someone has dismantled the hub. Experiment with different indicator-rod positions before consigning the hub to perdition.

- No low gear: Assuming that the indicator-rod adjustment is correct, three faults can cause this condition. The low-gear pawls (Fig. 9-18, No. 15) may be assembled upside down so that they skid rather than engage; the thrust ring (No. 37) may not be mated with the axle key (No. 34); or the axle spring may be the incorrect part for this hub.
- Slipping low gear: This condition is dangerous both to the rider and the transmission and must be corrected. It can be caused by faulty adjustment of the right-hand cone (thus upsetting the indexing between the indicator rod and nut), a binding indicator chain, or a binding cable. Extreme wear on the cruciform clutch (No. 21) will also cause this symptom.
- Slipping second gear: Since second is direct drive expect that the ring-gear pawls (No. 23) are worn or that the pawl springs (No. 24) have given up the ghost.
- Slipping third gear: This condition is rarely encountered. Dirt between the clutch sleeve (No. 20) and the axle can bind the parts and defeat the clutch spring (No. 39). The spring may tire with age and fail to move the clutch sleeve. The pinion pins (No. 19) may be excessively worn as may the clutch (No. 21).
- Self-induced shifting between low and second: This disconcerting malfunction is usually traceable to worn gear ring pawls (No. 23) or failed springs (No. 24).

- Reluctant shifting: Check the cables first with attention to the alignment of the guide pulley (if fitted). Check the indicator chain for binding links. Douse the hub with SA oil. A twisted clutch spring (No. 39) or a bent axle may also cause or contribute to this problem.
- Dragging hub: This is a bearing or an alignment problem. Check the cone clearance, lubricate, and keep in mind the possibility that someone may have packed an extra ball in the ball cup (No. 26). There are supposed to be 24 balls here. Check the chain stay alignment. Rust or a coating of castor bean varnish (a residue of a much-touted household lubricant) can also bind the mechanism.

Teardown: Commence work from the left side. With the wheel on a bench, remove the left-hand locknut noting the sequence of spacers. Remove the adjustable cone. Now, from the right with a spanner or hammer and brass punch, remove the ball ring (No. 25). If a spoke is marked with a piece of string or adhesive tape this signals the thread start position for assembly. The Sturmey-Archer logo on one ball-ring detents should align with the marked spoke.

Should you wish to remove the sprocket, pry off the circlip with a screwdriver. Protect your eyes. Note the spacer arrangement and the lay of the sprocket dish. Some sprockets are mounted with the concavity in; others are reversed, depending upon application. In any event there must always be two 1/16 inch spring washers (No. 30) present. A 22-tooth sprocket is available as well as sprockets between 16 and 20 teeth.

Remove the pawl pins (No. 16), the pawls (No. 23), and the pawl springs (No. 24). The long end of the pawls point outward. Replace the springs as a matter of course.

Most repairs can be effected at this point, without further teardown. If necessary you can mount the axle in a vise, gripping it at the central (unthreaded) portion, and remove the right-hand cone. Note the position of washers at the locknut. Remove the clutch spring cap (No. 40), the clutch spring (No. 39), the thrust ring (No. 37), and unscrew the indicator rod (Nos. 35 or 36) from the axle key (No. 34). The key will drop out of the slot in the axle. The flat side of the key is to the right. The plane cage (No. 17) comes off next. Remove the planet gears (No. 18) and their pinion pins (No. 19).

If the left-hand ball cup shows evidence of scoring, it can be removed with a pair of tape-wrapped waterpump pliers. Normally the ball cup is left in place. It has a left-hand

178

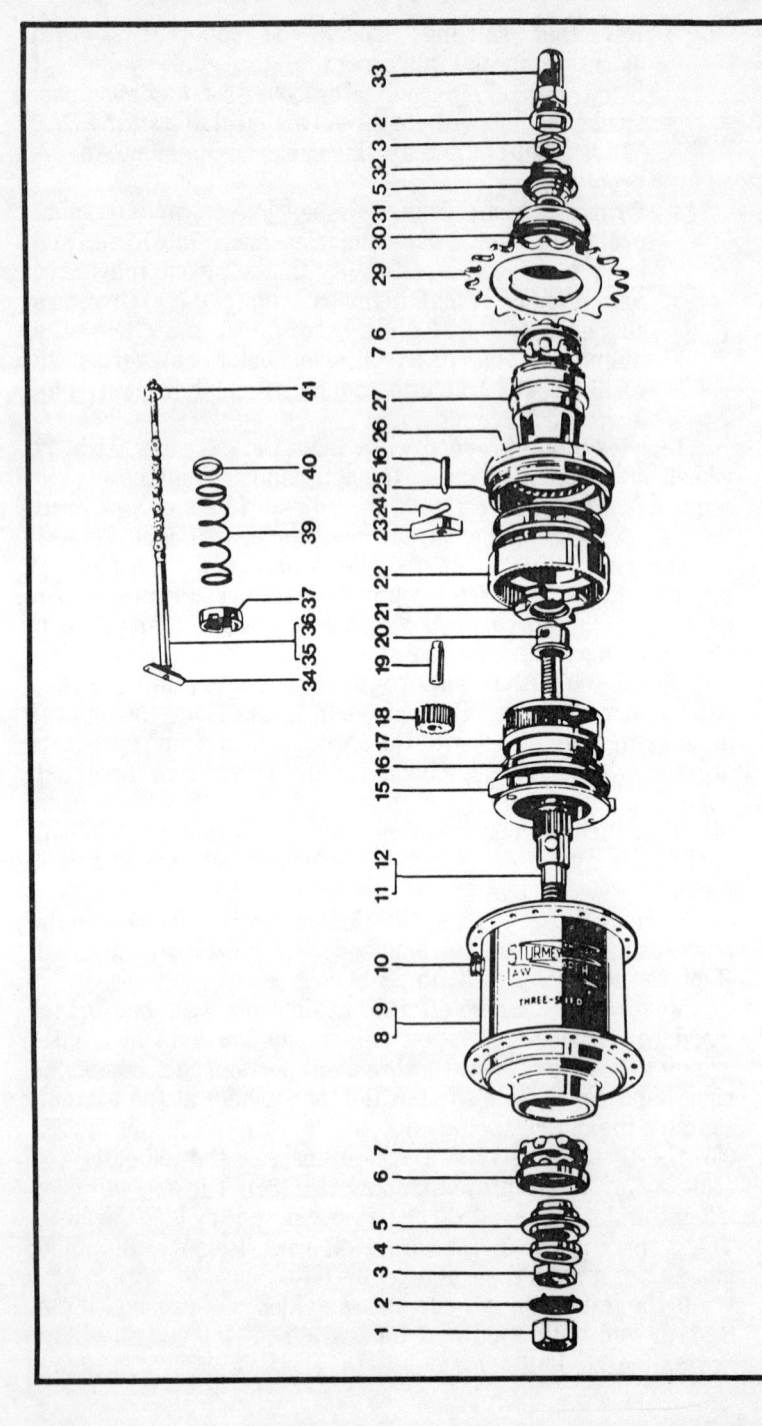

ITEM	PART NO.	Description
1	HMN 128	L.H. Axle Nut
2	HMW 145	Axle Lock Washer
3	HMN 132	Lock Nut
4	HMW 129	Axle Washer, ⅛" (3.2 m.m.) thick
5	HSA 101	Cone with Dust Cap
6	HSA 102	Outer Dust Cap
7	HSA 103	Ball Cage (with Ball Bearings)
8	HSA 104	Shell – 40 hole – and Ball Cup Combined
9	HSA 105	Shell – 36 hole – and Ball Cup Combined
10	HSA 106	Lubricator (Plastic)
11	HSA 107	Axle – 5¾" (146 m.m.)
12	HSA 108	Axle – 6¼" (159 m.m.)
15	HSA 111	Low-Gear Pawl
16	HSA 112	Pawl Pin
17	HSA 113	Planet Cage
18	HSA 115	Planet Pinion
19	HSA 114	Pinion Pin
20	HSA 116	Clutch Sleeve
21	HSA 117	Clutch
22	HSA 118	Gear Ring

ITEM	PART NO.	Description
23	HSA 119	Gear Ring Pawl
24	HSA 120	Pawl Spring
25	HSA 121	R.H. Ball Ring
26	HSA 122	Inner Dust Cap
27	HSA 123	Driver
29	HSL 716 / HSL 720 / HSL 722	Sprocket, 16-20 plus 22T
30	HMW 127	Sprocket Spacing Washer (2 off)
31	HSL 721	Sprocket Circlip
32	HMW 147	Cone Lockwasher
33	HMN 129	R.H. Axle Nut
34	HSA 124	Axle Key
35	HSA 125	Indicator Coupling – 5¾" (146 m.m.) Axle
36	HSA 126	Indicator Coupling – 6¼" (159 m.m.) Axle
37	HSA 127	Thrust Ring
39	HSA 128	Clutch Spring
40	HSA 129	Clutch Spring Cap
41	HMN 134	Indicator Coupling Connection Lock Nut

Fig. 9-20. An AW 3 hub. (Courtesy Action Accessories)

thread—turn clockwise to loosen. Replacement cups are sometimes hard to come by and you may have to purchase a hub and cap as a unit.

Inspection. Clean all parts in solvent and dry with compressed air (regulated at 30 psi or less for safety) or with dry, lintless cloth. Pay particular attention to the condition of the six bearing races. Wear points are the pawls, pinion pins, gear-ring splines, and clutch tips. Do not attempt to dress these parts with a file. Once wear begins it is progressive and rapid. Check the axle for bends at the center (slotted) section and replace the nasty little pawl springs. If the outer dust cap has been remove, press on a new one.

Assembly. Thread the left-hand ball cup on the hub by turning it counterclockwise. Do not apply so much pressure on the pliers that the cup distorts. The left-hand thread will tighten itself in use.

The pawls and pawl springs require care in assembly, since there are several ways to put them together wrong. Only one way will work. Place the ring gear, teeth down, on the bench. The pawls are positioned as indicated in the exploded view—the curved surface is inboard and the squared-off end pointing up and away from the axle. The spring loops are over the pinholes. The pawl pins hold the springs in position. The long end of the spring is compressed against the gear ring; the curved end is under the pawl, pivoting it upward. Insert the pawl pins through the springs and pawls with the flat side to the right. If assembled correctly the pawls will snap to attention and the pins will be flush with the carrier.

Apply a bit of grease to the dust caps. Grease goes into the recesses of the right-hand ball ring (No. 25), the driver (No. 27), and the left-hand (outer) dust cap (No. 6). These are the only places grease should be used on the AW transmission.

Fit the planet cage (No. 17) over the axle. It helps if you position the axle in a vise with the slot for the axle key up. Install the pinion gears (No. 18) and pinion pins (No. 19). The turned-down ends of the pinion pins extend out of the cage to make engagement with the clutch. Next, slide the clutch sleeve (No. 20) over the axle. The flange is down. Insert the axle key (No. 34), flat side up, with needlenose pliers. The key slides in the slot in the center of axle. Thread the indicator rod (No. 35 or 36) into the key. The thrust ring (No. 37) and washer (if fitted) go on next. The flats on the axle key index with the slots on the thrust washer. Place the gear ring (No. 22) and planet cage (No. 17) over the axle as an assembly. Now install the right-hand ball ring (No. 25). If the balls have been disturbed, count them to make sure that all 24 are there. Insert the driver

(No. 27) and the caged bearing set (No. 7). Thread the right-hand cone on to the shaft finger tight and back off no more than a half turn.

The transmission is half assembled. Carefully remove the axle and assembled parts stack from the vise and turn it over so the left-hand end of the axle is up.

The planet cage pawls offer an opportunity for frustration. They, like the low-gear pawls, have a definite lay on their pinions and are spring-loaded. The correct position is reasonably clear from the appearance of part No. 15 in the drawing. Identify the driving edge. It must mate with serrations on the gear ring (No. 22). Insert a pawl pin (No. 16) through the outside flange and approximately halfway through a pawl. With tweezers and great patience, position the loop of the spring under the pawl and concentric with the pin hole. As before, the spring loops are anchor points and ride over the pawl pins. The hooked end of the spring is below the pawls, raising them into engagement. The straight end bears against the flange. If you have done the work correctly, the pawls will be extended into the driving position.

Pour an ounce of Sturmey-Archer oil into the planet cage and over the bearings and insert the whole assembly into the hub. Things will stay together better if you support the wheel in the horizontal and slip the parts stack in from below. Install the dust cap (No. 26). If your hub is marked as indicated under Teardown, note the position of the telltale. Align the manufacturer's mark on the cap detent with this mark and thread. Tighten with a punch and hammer. Install the left-hand cone and adjust the bearings for a trace of play. Place the sprocket over the driver, noting which side is dished and the sequence of spacers. Snap it in place with the circlip (No. 31). Put the wheel back into the dropouts, adjust the chain (approximately 1/2 inch between the centers of the chain wheel and sprocket) and adjust the indicator rod.

S5 Five Speed

The Sturmey-Archer S5 hub is by all odds the most sophisticated hub available today, and may well represent the crest of development of the basic design. The ratios are impressive, although somewhat demanding:

- First gear: 33.3% speed reduction
- Second gear: 22.1% speed reduction
- Third gear: direct drive
- Fourth gear: 26.6% speed increase
- Fifth gear: 50% speed increase

Table 9-2. Sturmey-Archer 5-Speed Gear Ratio Table (Courtesy Raleigh Industries Ltd.)

NUMBER OF TEETH		26" WHEEL					27" WHEEL					28" WHEEL				
CHAINWHEEL	SPROCKET	1 SUPER LOW	2 LOW	3 NOR-MAL	4 HIGH	5 SUPER HIGH	1 SUPER LOW	2 LOW	3 NOR-MAL	4 HIGH	5 SUPER HIGH	1 SUPER LOW	2 LOW	3 NOR-MAL	4 HIGH	5 SUPER HIGH
40	14	49.5	58.7	74.3	94.1	111.5	51.4	61.0	77.1	97.7	115.7	53.3	63.2	80.0	101.3	120.0
	15	46.2	54.7	69.3	87.7	104.0	48.0	56.9	72.0	91.2	108.0	49.8	59.0	74.7	94.6	112.1
	16	43.3	51.3	65.0	82.3	97.5	45.0	53.3	67.5	85.4	101.3	46.7	55.3	70.0	88.6	105.0
	17	40.8	48.3	61.2	77.5	91.8	42.3	50.2	63.5	80.4	95.3	43.9	52.1	65.9	83.4	98.9
	18	38.5	45.7	57.8	73.2	86.7	40.0	47.4	60.0	76.0	90.0	41.5	49.1	62.2	78.7	93.3
	19	36.5	43.2	54.7	69.2	82.1	37.9	44.9	56.8	71.9	85.2	39.3	46.5	58.9	74.6	88.4
	20	34.7	41.1	52.0	65.8	78.0	36.0	42.7	54.0	68.4	81.0	37.3	44.2	56.0	70.9	84.0
	22	31.5	37.4	47.3	59.9	71.0	32.7	38.8	49.1	62.2	73.7	33.9	40.2	50.9	64.4	76.4
44	14	54.4	64.5	81.7	103.5	122.6	56.5	66.1	84.9	107.5	127.4	58.6	69.5	88.0	111.4	132.0
	15	50.8	60.3	76.3	96.6	114.5	52.7	62.6	79.2	100.2	118.8	54.7	64.9	82.1	104.0	123.2
	16	47.7	56.5	71.5	90.5	107.3	49.5	58.6	74.2	93.9	111.3	51.3	60.8	77.0	97.5	115.5
	17	44.9	53.2	67.3	85.2	100.6	46.6	55.2	69.9	88.4	104.9	48.3	57.3	72.5	91.8	108.8
	18	42.4	50.2	63.6	80.5	95.4	44.0	52.1	66.0	83.5	99.0	45.6	54.0	68.4	86.6	102.6
	19	40.1	47.6	60.2	76.2	90.3	41.7	49.4	62.5	79.1	93.8	43.2	51.2	64.8	82.0	97.2
	20	38.1	45.2	57.2	72.4	85.8	39.6	46.9	59.4	75.2	89.1	41.1	48.6	61.6	78.0	92.4
	22	34.7	41.1	52.0	65.8	78.0	36.0	42.7	54.0	68.4	81.0	37.3	44.2	56.0	70.9	84.0
46	14	56.9	67.4	85.4	108.1	128.1	59.1	70.1	88.7	112.3	133.1	61.3	72.7	92.0	116.5	138.0
	15	53.1	63.0	79.7	100.9	119.6	55.1	65.4	82.8	104.8	124.2	57.2	67.9	85.9	208.7	238.9
	16	49.8	59.0	74.4	94.5	112.1	51.7	61.3	77.6	98.2	116.4	53.7	63.6	80.5	101.9	120.8
	17	46.9	55.5	70.3	89.0	105.5	48.7	57.7	73.0	92.4	109.5	50.5	59.9	75.8	95.9	113.7
	18	44.3	52.5	66.4	84.0	99.6	46.0	54.5	69.0	87.3	103.5	47.7	56.5	71.5	90.5	107.3
	19	41.9	49.7	62.9	79.6	94.4	43.6	51.7	65.4	82.8	98.1	45.2	53.6	67.8	85.8	101.7
	20	39.9	47.2	59.8	75.7	89.7	41.1	49.1	62.1	78.6	93.2	42.9	50.9	64.4	81.5	96.6
	22	36.3	43.1	54.5	69.0	81.8	37.7	44.6	56.5	71.5	84.6	39.1	46.3	58.6	74.2	87.9
48	14	59.3	70.4	89.1	112.8	133.7	61.7	73.1	92.6	117.2	139.0	64.0	75.8	96.0	121.5	144.0
	15	55.4	65.7	83.2	105.3	124.8	57.5	68.1	86.4	109.4	129.6	59.7	70.8	89.6	113.4	134.4
	16	52.0	61.6	78.0	98.7	117.0	54.0	64.0	81.0	102.5	121.5	56.0	66.4	84.0	106.3	126.0
	17	49.0	58.0	73.5	93.0	110.3	50.8	60.2	76.2	96.4	114.3	52.7	62.5	79.1	100.2	118.7
	18	46.2	54.7	69.3	87.7	104.0	48.0	56.9	72.0	91.1	108.0	49.8	59.0	74.7	94.6	112.1
	19	43.8	51.9	65.7	83.2	98.6	45.5	53.9	68.2	86.3	102.5	47.1	55.8	70.7	89.5	106.1
	20	41.6	49.3	62.4	79.0	93.6	43.2	51.2	64.8	82.0	97.2	44.8	53.1	67.2	85.0	100.8
	22	37.8	44.8	56.7	71.8	85.1	39.3	46.6	58.9	74.5	88.4	40.7	48.3	61.1	7.3	91.7

The usual Sturmey-Archer sprockets are offered—16 to 20 teeth and 22 teeth. Table 9-2 is a gear ratio table, showing the range of this transmission in three popular wheel sizes.

Structurally the S5 hub is an outgrowth of the AW3 and earlier designs. Parts which can be interchanged include the driver, caged bearing sets, gear ring, clutch, right-hand axle nut, and gear-indicator rod (6 1/4 inch axle). A double sun gear and matching pinions account for the additional speeds. These parts are shifted from the left and require their own shift lever.

Adjustment. The adjustable cone is on the left. Loosen the locknut and position the cone so that there is only a trace of side play at the rim. Tighten the locknut and recheck. The gear adjustment begins with the right-hand side (Fig. 9-21). With the right-hand control lever in the full forward position, screw the barrel (No. 3) about halfway down on the indicator coupling. Back off the locknut (No. 2). Now slide the fulcrum clip along the chain stay until there is no slack in the cable. With the right-hand control lever in the midposition, make the final adjustment at the barrel (No. 3). The shoulder of the indicator rod should be flush with the end of the axle as shown in the inset of Fig. 9-21. Tighten the locknut against the barrel. This is, of course, the same adjustment procedure used for the more familiar three speed.

The left-hand adjustment is something new for Sturmey-Archer fans. With both the right- and left-hand control levers full forward, insert the push rod into the axle. Thread the bellcrank, shown in Fig. 9-22 as No. 3, on the axle as

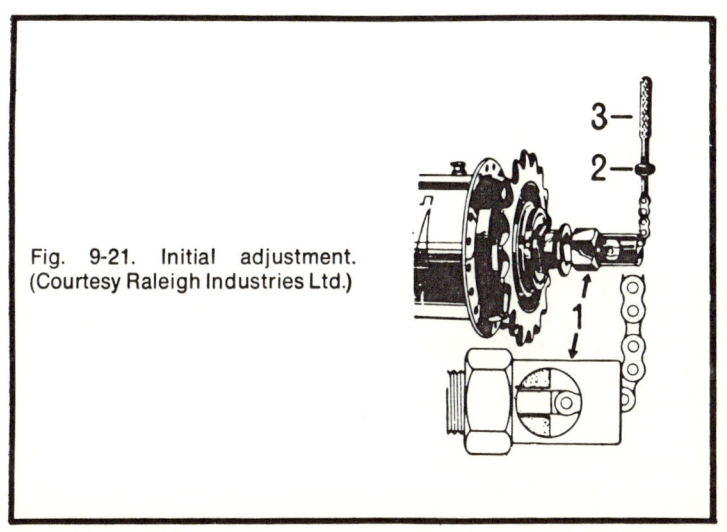

Fig. 9-21. Initial adjustment. (Courtesy Raleigh Industries Ltd.)

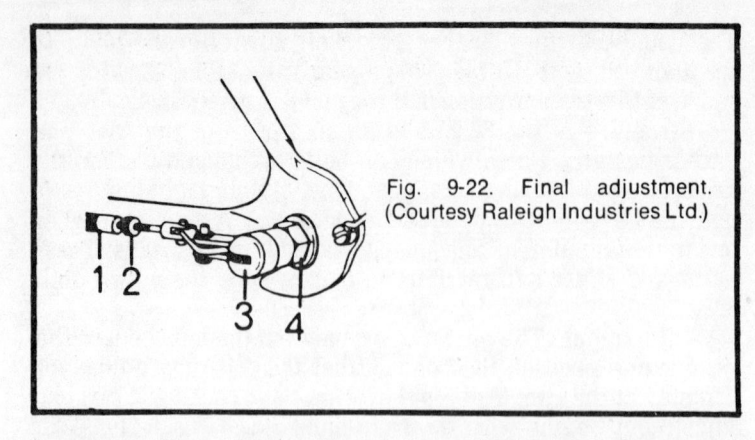

Fig. 9-22. Final adjustment. (Courtesy Raleigh Industries Ltd.)

far as it will go. Back off enough to align it with the control cable. Screw the barrel (No. 1) halfway down on the bellcrank arm. Leave the locknut (No. 2) loose. Slide the fulcrum clip along the chain stay to take up any slack in the control cable.

The next step is critical. With the wheel stationary, work the pedal cranks back and forth, while at the same time pulling the left-hand control lever back. You can feel the transmission engage at the pedals. Pull out the bellcrank arm with your fingers and adjust the barrel (No. 1) to take up slack in the cable. Tighten the locknut (No. 2) up against the barrel.

Late-model hubs have a visual telltale for the left-hand adjustment. The bellcrank has a circular hole in it and the pushrod is notched with a red band. The adjustment drill is the one already described; the window is merely an indication that the transmission is engaged. When the gears are meshed the red band should almost disappear into the axle.

Troubleshooting. As with any hub transmission, the major problem is maladjustment. Before assuming the worst, check the right-hand adjustment. With the gear-control lever in the No. 3 position, the end of the indicator rod should be dead level with the end of the axle. Reluctant shifting is usually caused by lack of oil. A teaspoon or so of Sturmey-Archer oil may be all that is required to put the bike back on the road. More serious complaints and appropriate remedies are outlined below:

- No first (super-low) gear: Suspect the left-hand control cable. Excessive slack will give this symptom. The same effect will be had if the low-gear pawls are improperly assembled. They may be upside down or reversed.
- First and second gears are there, but hard to find: Usually this is a control-cable problem. Check for

broken strands and lubricate generously. The low-gear spring may be fatigued, in which case it must be replaced. A bent axle key can produce the same erratic performance.
- Slips in first gear: The control cable is again the main suspect. It may be frayed or kinked. The low-gear spring can be bent or the pawl springs may be incorrectly installed. The latter will not occur unless the transmission has been opened, since it is highly unlikely that all pawl springs will fail.
- Shifts automatically between first and second, or first, second, and normal: This state of affairs would almost be humorous if you did not realize that you had a bit of work ahead of you in replacing the gear-ring pawls.
- Slips in first and second: Since two low-range gears are involved the control cable is not at fault. Check for a weak low-gear spring. Severely worn dog-ring teeth (Fig. 9-23, No. 34) may also cause or contribute to the problem. Generally, however, you will find that the dog-ring locknut (Fig. 9-23, No. 32) is loose.
- Slips in second and high gears: The left-hand control cable is too tight.
- Slips in third (normal) gear: The gear-ring splines or sliding clutch is worn. The best policy is to replace both of these parts.
- Slips in fourth and fifth gears: An incorrect right-hand cone adjustment can produce this symptom as well as a faulty clutch spring. Another possibility is wear on the planet cage dogs and clutch.
- Hub turns stiffly and may drag on pedals when free wheeling: First check the cone adjustment on both sides, then the chain stay ends for trueness. These parts should be parallel to each other. The planet pinion gears have timing marks which must be in register. Another possibility is that there are too many balls in the ball ring. The correct number is 24.
- No gears: This one is simple. The pawls are stuck. Lubricate with Sturmey-Archer oil.
- Reluctant gear change: More often than not, this is a matter of rusted, frayed, or dry control cables. Replace or lubricate as needed. Wear on the indicator chain link may also produce sluggish gear changes, at least for those gears that the chain causes to engage. A bent axle is another possibility, along with distorted axle spring.

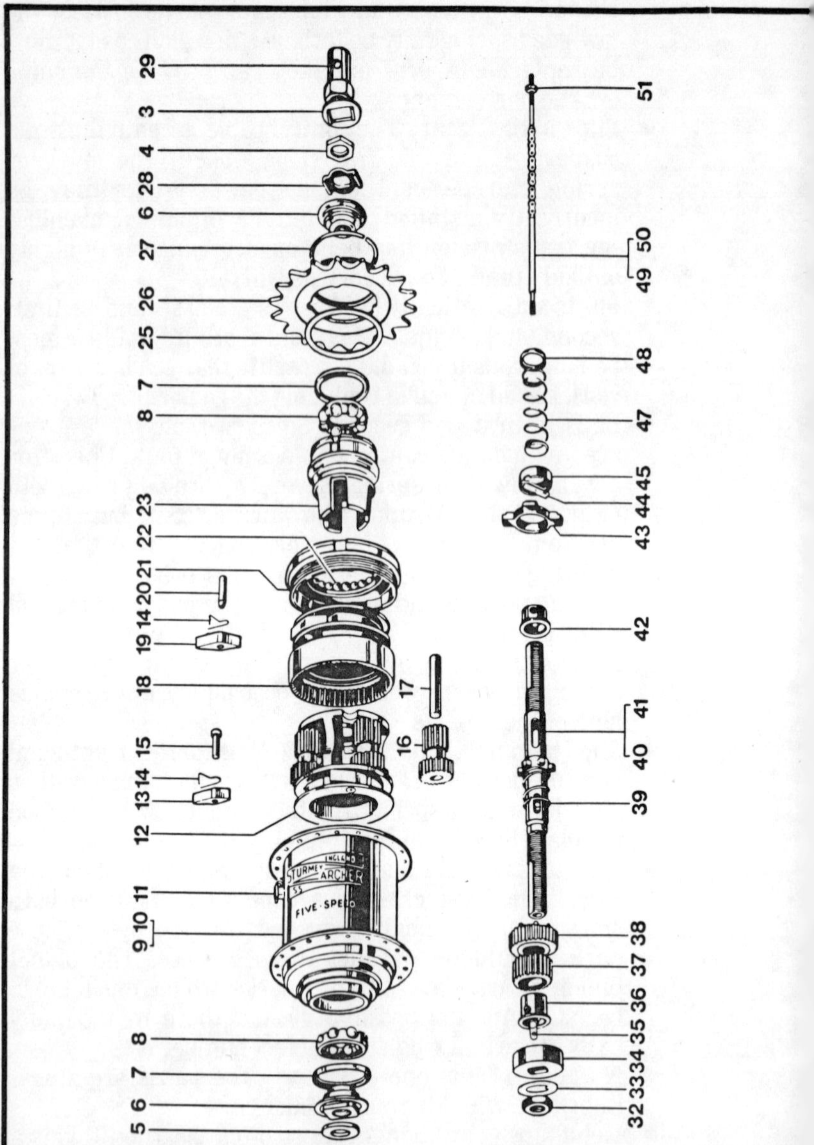
1
2
3
4
5
6
7
8
9 10
11
12
13
14
15
16
17
18
19
14
20
21
22
23
8
7
25
26
27
6
28
4
3
29
STURMEY ARCHER
ENGLAND
FIVE · SPEED
30 31
32
33
34
35
36
37
38
39
40 41
42
43
44
45
47
48
49 50
51

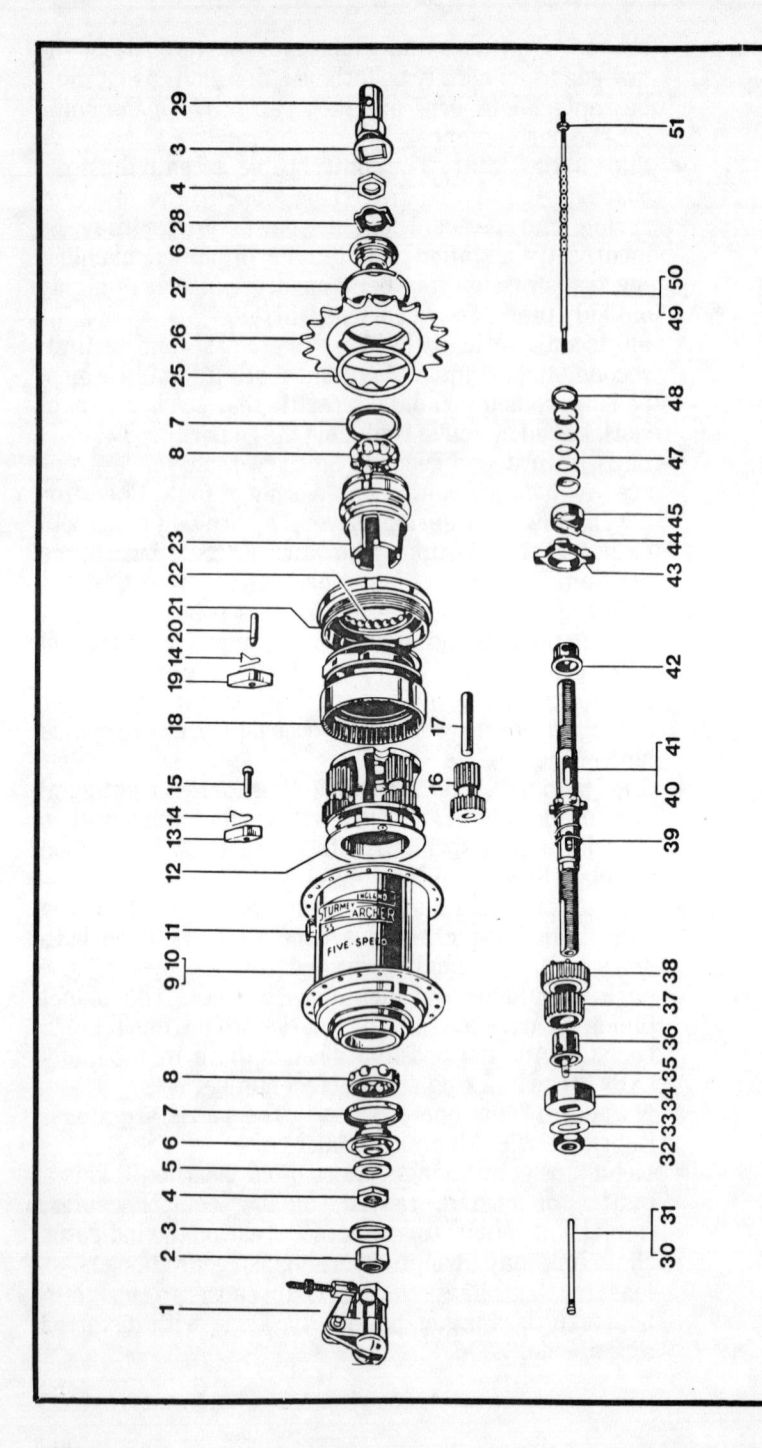

ITEM	PART NO.	Description
1	HSJ 679	Bellcrank (Steel)
2	HMN 128	Left-hand Axle Nut
3	HMW 145	Axle Washer
4	HMN 132	Locknut
5	HMW 129	Axle Spacing Washer ⅛" (3.2 m.m.)
6	HSA 101	Cone
7	HSA 102	Outer Dust Cap
8	HSA 103	Ball Cage
9	HSA 271	Shell – 40 hole – and Ball Cup Combined
10	HSA 270	Shell – 36 hole – and Ball Cup Combined
11	HSA 106	Lubricator (Plastic)
12	HSA 132	Planet Cage
13	HSA 111	Low Gear Pawl
14	HSA 120	Pawl Spring
15	HSA 133	Pawl Pin – Planet Cage
16	HSA 134	Planet Pinion
17	HSA 135	Pinion Pin
18	HSA 118	Gear Ring
19	HSA 119	Gear Ring Pawl
20	HSA 112	Pawl Pin – Gear Ring
21	HSA 121	Right-hand Ball Ring
22	HSA 122	Inner Dust Cap
23	HSA 123	Driver
25	HMW 127	Sprocket Spacing Washer
26	HSL 716-720	Sprocket – 16-20T
27	HSL 721	Sprocket Circlip

ITEM	PART NO.	Description
28	HMW 147	Cone Lockwasher
29	HMN 129	Right-hand Axle Nut
30	HSA 287	Gear Push Rod 6" Axle (152 mm)
31	HSA 288	Gear Push Rod 6¼" Axle (159 mm)
32	HMN 133	Locknut for Dog-Ring
33	HMW 149	Lockwasher for Dog-Ring
34	HSA 138	Dog-Ring
35	HSA 268	Low Gear Axle Key
36	HSA 140	Pinion Sleeve
37	HSA 141	Secondary Sun Pinion
38	HSA 269	Primary Sun Pinion
39	HSA 273	Low Gear Spring
40	HSA 274	Axle – 6" (152 mm)
41	HSA 145	Axle – 6¼" (159 mm)
42	HSA 116	Clutch Sleeve
43	HSA 117	Clutch
44	HSA 124	Axle Key
45	HSA 127	Thrust Ring
47	HSA 128	Clutch Spring
48	HSA 129	Spring Cap
49	HSA 126	Gear Indicator Rod Right-hand 6" Axle (152 mm)
50	HSA 126	Gear Indicator Rod Right-hand 6¼" Axle (159 mm)
51	HMN 134	Connector Locknut

Fig. 9-23. S5 transmission (Courtesy Raleigh Industries Ltd.)

Teardown. Figure 9-23 is an exploded view of the S5 hub and will be our reference picture. Start from the left-hand side. Remove the bellcrank (No. 1), the axle nut (No. 5), and cone (No. 6). The arrangement of washers shown in the drawing is typical, but not necessarily universal. Bikes with nonstandard dropout widths require different hub spacing. Make note of the spacer sequence.

Unscrew the right-hand ball ring (No. 21) from the hub or shell (No. 9) with a spanner wrench or a hammer and brass punch. It has a standard thread (counterclockwise to remove). It is suggested that the ball ring and hub be marked for proper assembly since the ring has a special two-start thread. (A two-start thread is an arrangement where the nut can start in one of two places on a 360° turn.) If assembled wrong, the wheel will have to be retrued.

Place the left-hand end of the axle in a vise gripping across the flats, and remove the right-hand axle nut (No. 29), washer (No. 3), locknut (No. 4), cone lockwasher (No. 28), and cone (No. 6). Lift off the clutch spring (No. 47) and the cap (No. 48). Next take out the driver (No. 23), the ball ring (No. 21), and the gear ring (No. 18). Remove the thrust ring (No. 45). Push the axle key (No. 44) out of its slot in the axle (noticing that the flats on the ends of the key align with slots in the thrust ring), remove the clutch sleeve (No. 42) and the sliding clutch (No. 43). The stepped side of the clutch arms face the sprocket.

Remove the pinion pins (No. 17), the pinion gears (No. 16), and the planet cage (No. 12). The low-gear pawl pins (No. 15) are riveted into place. If necessary they may be removed by filing the rivet's splayed end and driving the pins out with a small punch. The pawls and springs can then be removed.

The planet gears are secured by a locknut. Leave them in place unless the gears or related parts are damaged. Unscrew

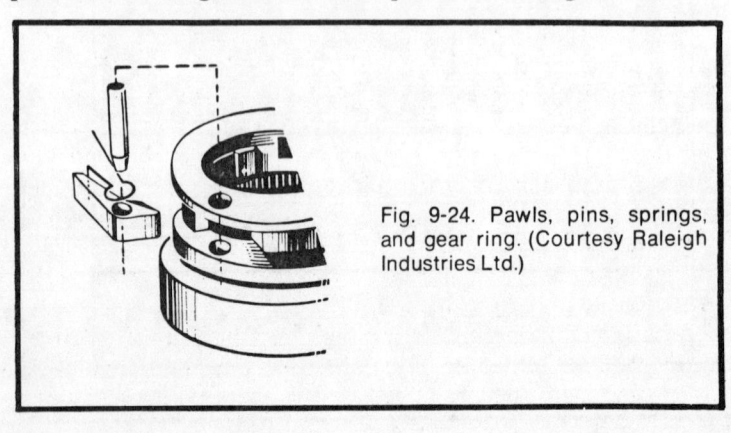

Fig. 9-24. Pawls, pins, springs, and gear ring. (Courtesy Raleigh Industries Ltd.)

the locknut (No. 32). Remove the lockwasher (No. 33) and the dog ring (No. 34). Push the planet pinions (Nos. 37 and 38) over the axle dogs and pull out the sleeve (No. 36) which you will find under the smaller sun gear. Push out the axle key (No. 35). Slide the sun gears, sleeve, and low-gear spring (No. 39) off the axle.

Inspection. After cleaning all parts in solvent, make the following checks:

- Slide the clutch up and down over the driver prongs. It should move freely.
- Count the loose balls at the right-hand ball ring. You should have 24 3/16-inch balls.
- Examine the gear ring for cracks, chipping, and wear on the teeth and internal spline.
- Check axle trueness by rolling it on a flat surface (a piece of plate glass is ideal) or by chucking it in a drill press or lathe. Examine the axle clogs for rounding off.
- Inspect all ball races pitting or excessive wear.
- Examine the sliding clutch for rounding off at the points of engagement.
- Examine the pinion teeth for breakage or excessive wear.
- Do the same for the planet-cage dogs.
- Look carefully for wear on the pawls and pawl ratchets.

Assembly. The S5 transmission consists of five subassemblies. Begin by fitting the ball cage (No. 8) in the left-hand ball cup (integral with the hub). The bearing should be placed as shown in the reference drawing. The recess in the outer dust cap (No. 7) should face outwards. If you fit a new bearing it is almost mandatory that you replace the dust cap as well.

Next fit the right-hand ball cage (No. 8 and interchangeable with the left-hand cage) to the driver (No. 23). The recess in the dust cap (No. 7) faces outwards. Again, if you replace the ball cage it is strongly recommended that you fit a new dust cap. If the sprocket has been removed from the driver fit the dust cap (No. 7) over the driver before the sprocket. The dust cap should be centered on the driver flange. Fit the sprocket, normally dished side in, and spacer(s) (No. 25) as originally assembled. Fit the circlip (No. 27); remember to protect your eyes.

Place 24 3/16-inch balls and the inner dust cap (No. 22) to the right-hand ball ring (No. 21). The dust cap should be positioned deep enough to locate the balls without binding them.

Fit the pawls, pins, and springs into the flange on the gear ring. To do this with minimum frustration, place the gear ring (No. 18) teeth down on the bench. Place a pawl spring (No. 14) on the side of a pawl so that the loop is over the pinhole and the hook of the spring is under the long nose of the pawl (No. 19). While holding a pawl pin (No. 20) ready in the left hand, grip the nose of a pawl and a foot of the spring between the thumb and forefinger of the right hand and slide the pawl—tail first—between the flanges of the gear ring. When the hole in the pawl and loop of the spring match the holes in the flanges, slide the pawl pin home, blunt end up. The relationship holding between these parts is shown in Fig. 9-24. Failure to install them correctly will mean another trip through the transmission.

Next fit the pawls, pins, and springs into the planet cage. Hold the planet cage (No. 12) in the left-hand with the flanges down. Position a pawl (No 13) between the flanges. If the pawl is at 12 o'clock, the flat surface should be to your right and the pinhole to the left of the holes in the flanges. Push a pawl pin (No. 15) through the hole of the inner flange and, with your left thumb over the pin head, hold it in contact with the side of the pawl. With your right hand take the hook of the pawl spring (No. 14) between thumb and forefinger and thread the straight leg under the pawl pin from the rear and pull the spring forward until the loop of the spring encircles the pawl pin. Now with a finger of the right hand, hold the foot of the spring under the nose of the pawl and advance the pawl until the hole in it aligns with the holes in the flanges. Push the pawl pin home.

All of this is simpler than the telling; with the pin in place the parts should be anchored between the flanges and lie as shown in Fig. 9-25.

Support the pin head on an anvil or piece of flat steel and peen the ends over lightly. Go easy with the hammer since the flanges must remain true and the pin head must not foul the pinion gears.

Smear grease on into the channels of the dust caps. The grease is a kind of dust trap and is not intended as lubrication.

Working from the left-hand side of the axle—identified by the shorter of the two slots—slide the low-gear spring (No. 39), the primary sun gear (No. 38), the secondary sun gear (No. 39), and the sleeve (No. 36) over the axle in that sequence. Slide the whole assembly down to engage the star-shaped axle dogs. Holding the sun gears in position, slide the secondary sun gear (No. 37) up far enough to expose the low-gear keyhole in the axle. Insert the low-gear key (No. 35) into the slot, centering it

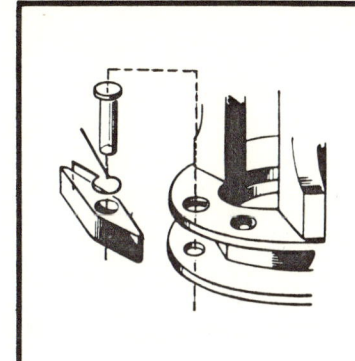

Fig. 9-25. Pawls, pins, springs, and planet cage. (Courtesy Raleigh Industries Ltd.)

as best as possible. Allow the sun gears to spring back and secure the key. Thread the gear pushrods (Nos. 30 and 31) into the low-gear key.

Fit the dog ring (No. 34) so that it engages the axle flats and secure with the washer (No. 33) and the locknut (No. 32). Tighten the nut with a wrench. Torque specifications are not given, but snug it securely, remembering that the axle is compromised by slots.

Hold the axle upright by the flats in a vise. Slide the planet cage (No. 12) over the end of the axle and fit the double pinion gears. It is very important that the marks on the pinions point outward as shown in the drawing in Fig. 9-26. Failure to time these gears correctly will result in drag during free wheeling and other unpleasantness. Check the action of the gears by meshing them with the gear ring (No. 18). The ring should turn easily without "hard spots." Set the ring gear aside for later assembly.

Next put the clutch sleeve (No. 42) into position. The flange is away from the sprocket. The clutch goes on after the sleeve and fits over the flange. It has a pair of milled slots which must engage with the flats on the axle key (No. 44). Now install the gear indicator rod (Nos. 49 or 50) threading it into the axle key. The key and clutch assembly must be able to slide back and forth smoothly and without protest.

Install the gear ring (No. 18), the right-hand ball ring (No. 21), the driver (No. 23), the clutch spring (No. 47), and the clutch-spring cap (No. 48) in that sequence. The right-hand ball ring should have 24 3/16 inch balls.

The right-hand cone (No. 6) is run up on the axle finger tight and backed off exactly one-half turn. This adjustment is critical since this cone positions the whole mechanism. Install

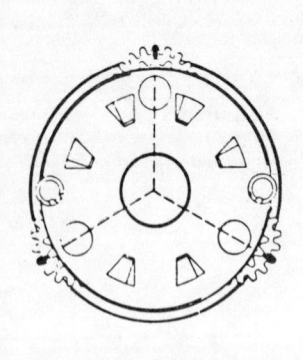

Fig. 9-26. Pinion gear timing marks. (Courtesy Raleigh Industries Ltd.)

the lockwasher (No. 28) and the locknut (No. 4). Tighten the locknut with a wrench. With the planet cage (No. 12) held upright, pour two teaspoonsful of Sturmey-Archer oil over the mechanism.

Insert the parts stack into the hub and tighten the right-hand bell ring (No. 21) finger tight. Check your register marks for alignment and tighten the ball ring securely with a hammer and soft punch. Finally run in the left-hand cone (No. 6) and adjust for a slight, almost imperceptible amount of side play. Install the washer (No. 5 and others which may not be shown on the drawing) and locknut (No. 4). Snug the locknut with a wrench and check the bearing clearance.

Install the wheel in the frame and fit the axle washers (No. 3) and axle nuts (Nos. 2 and 29). Adjust the bellcrank (No. 1) and gear indicator rod (Nos. 49 or 50) as outlined previously.

S2 Automatic

The Sturmey-Archer S2 is not unlike the Bendix family of automatic transmissions in that two speeds are offered by reversing the pedals. Closer examination shows, however, important differences in the hardware. The Bendix system depends upon tapered clutches and drive screws, while the Sturmey-Archer employs a cam and a floating sun gear. The S2 shares relatively few parts with other Sturmey-Archer designs. The sprockets are interchangeable across the range as are the caged bearings and miscellaneous hardware. Sprockets are offered in a progression from 13 to 20 teeth with an additional choice of a 22 tooth.

Normal gear is direct drive. On signal the transmission downshifts giving a 28.6 percent underdrive. While two speeds may not be the most exciting prospect for the touring rider, this transmission is adequate for its intended role; it provides a low gear for small-wheel and folding bicycles. Until the advent of the S2 most of these machines were fixed in direct drive.

Adjustment: Bearing adjustment is made at the left-hand cone. Loosen the locknut and turn the cone until the wheel has a trace of side-play at the rim. The right-hand cone is fixed at the factory. In the event of disassembly, the right-hand cone is run down finger tight on the axle (before the left-hand cone is fitted), and backed off exactly one half turn. Further rotation of the cone is prevented by a washer and locknut.

Teardown: Figure 9-27, an exploded view of the transmission, is our reference picture. Compared to most planetary gear trains, the S2 is quite simple. Remove the wheel from the frame and remove the axle nuts (No. 1) and the washers (No. 2). Next remove the left-hand locknut (No. 3), washer (No. 4), and cone (No. 5). Note the position and number of these washers for future reference.

Unthread the right-hand ball ring (No. 23) with a hammer and brass punch. It has a standard right-hand thread. Withdraw the gear unit. Hold the left-hand end of the axle in a vise (gripping the flats to protect the threads), and remove the right-hand locknut (No. 3), washers (Nos. 4 and 30), and the right-hand cone (No. 5). The sprocket (No. 28) comes off next along with the two 1/16 inch spacers (No. 27). The driver (No. 26) follows and the right-hand ball cage (No. 7). The gear-selector cam (No. 25) and the gear ring (No. 22) lift off.

The sun-pinion spring (No. 12) is pried off the sun pinion (No. 11) and the planet cage (No. 13) is removed as an assembly. Remove the sun pinion (No. 11) and the sun-pinion pin (No. 10) from the axle (No. 9).

It is always a good idea to replace the pawl springs (Nos. 18 and 20). Remove the pins (Nos. 16 and 21), pawls (Nos. 17 and 19), and springs from the planet cage and gear ring. Note that these ratcheting parts are not interchangeable between the cage and ring.

Assembly

Check:

- axle trueness
- gear teeth for wear or breakage
- bearing balls and races
- cam and gear ring for rounding off
- parts and ratchets for wear

194

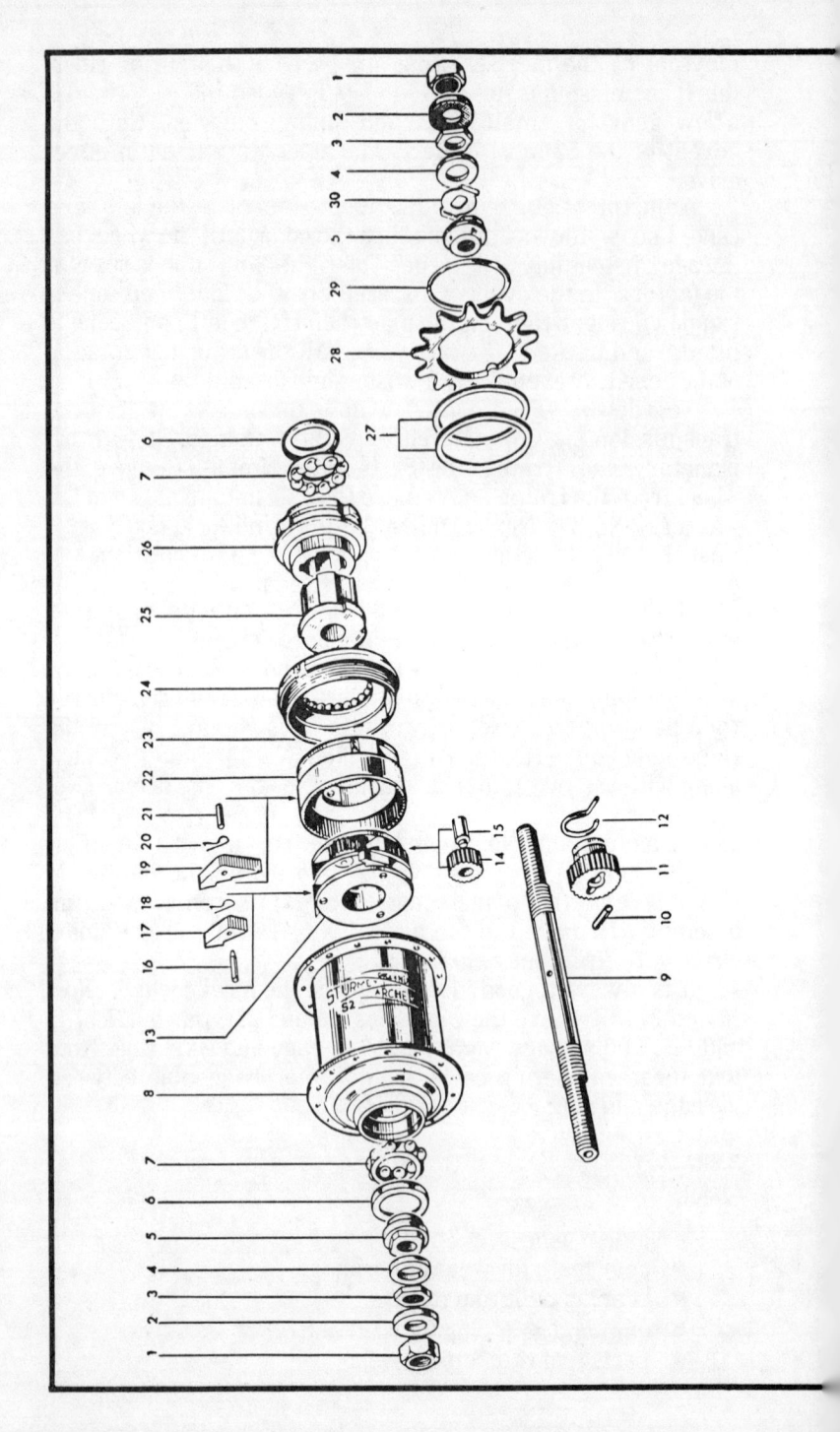

ITEM	PART NO.	DESCRIPTION
1	HMN 128	Axle Nut
2	HMW 124	Axle Washer
3	HMW 132	Locknut
4	HMW 129	Washer
5	HSA 257	Cone
6	HSA 241	Dustcap
7	HSA 103	Ball Cage with 8 ($\frac{1}{4}$" dia.) Bearings
8	HSA 259	Hub Shell with Ratchet Ring (36 hole)
	HSA 258	Hub Shell with Ratchet Ring (40 hole)
9	HSA 242	Axle $5\frac{3}{4}$" (146 m.m.)
	HSA 243	Axle $6\frac{1}{4}$" (159 m.m.)
10	HSA 244	Sun Pinion Pin
11	HSA 245	Sun Pinion
12	HSA 246	Sun Pinion Spring
13	HSA 247	Planet Cage
14	HSA 248	Planet Pinion
15	HSA 249	Planet Pinion Pin
16	HSA 112	Pawl Pin (Planet Cage)
17	HSA 250	Pawl (Planet Cage)
18	HSA 120	Pawl Spring (Planet Cage)
19	HSA 252	Gear Ring Pawl
20	HSA 253	Pawl Spring (Gear Ring)
21	HSA 254	Pawl Ring (Gear Ring)
22	HSA 251	Gear Ring
23	HSA 121	Ball Ring
24	HSA 122	Inner Dust Cover
25	HSA 256	Gear Selector Cam
26	HSA 255	Driver
27	HMW 127	Sprocket Washer $\frac{1}{16}$" (1.6 m.m.)
28	HSL 713-22	13T–22T Sprocket
29	HSL 721	Circlip
30	HMW 147	Cone Locking Washer

Fig. 9-27. Sturmey-Archer automatic transmission. (Courtesy Raleigh Industries Ltd.)

Fig. 9-28. Planet-cage pawl assembly. (Courtesy Raleigh Industries Ltd.)

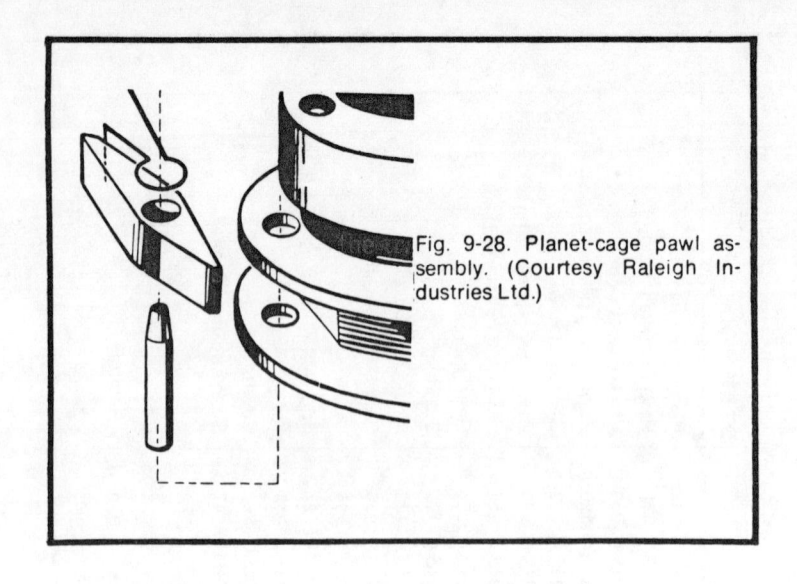

Clean all parts in solvent immediately prior to assembly, and douse with Sturmey-Archer oil. Place the left-hand end of the axle in a vise with the hole for the dowel pin toward the right-hand or sprocket side of the axle. Place the pinion pin (No. 10) into the slot and fit the sun gear (No. 11) on the axle, indexing the gear with the pinion pin. The planet cage (No. 13) is next. Position it on the axle and add the planet pinions (No. 14) and the pins (No. 15). The pins will only fit one way—the small diameter end away from the sprocket.

Now assemble the pawls (No. 17), springs (No. 18) and pawl pins (No. 16). The small end of the pins is pointed at the pinion gears. The relationship of these parts is shown in Fig. 9-28.

Fit the sun gear spring (No. 12) over the sun gear. Assemble the pawls (No. 19), pawl pins (No. 21), and springs (No. 20) into the gear ring (No. 22) as shown in Fig. 9-29. The tapered end of the pins goes into the wide flange of the gear ring. Place the gear ring over the axle, assuring yourself that the leg of the sun gear spring (No. 12) fits into the recess cut in the inside of the gear ring. The right-hand ball ring (No. 23) goes over the gear ring. It must have 24 ball bearings. Next install the gear selector cam (No. 25) inside the gear ring. Now assemble the driver (No. 26), right-hand ball cage (No. 76), dust cap (No. 6), sprocket (No. 28), spacing washers (No. 27) and circlip (No. 29). This subassembly is shown in Fig. 9-30 and again as a part of the whole in the exploded reference drawing. Alert readers will notice that the spacing washers

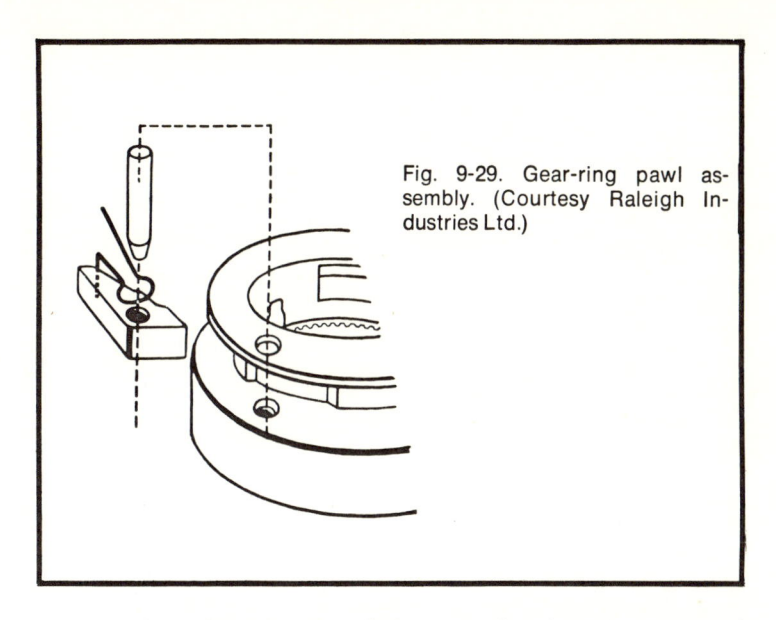

Fig. 9-29. Gear-ring pawl assembly. (Courtesy Raleigh Industries Ltd.)

are on the inboard side of the sprocket in Fig. 9-27 and sandwiched on either side of it in Fig. 9-30. Different bikes require different spacing for sprocket alignment. Once the parts are together, place the subassembly over the axle, mating the splines and grooves on the driver and gear selector cam.

Snug the right-hand cone (No. 5) with your fingers and back off a half turn. Secure it with the cone lockwasher (No. 30), the spacing washer (No. 4), and locknut (No. 3). Tighten

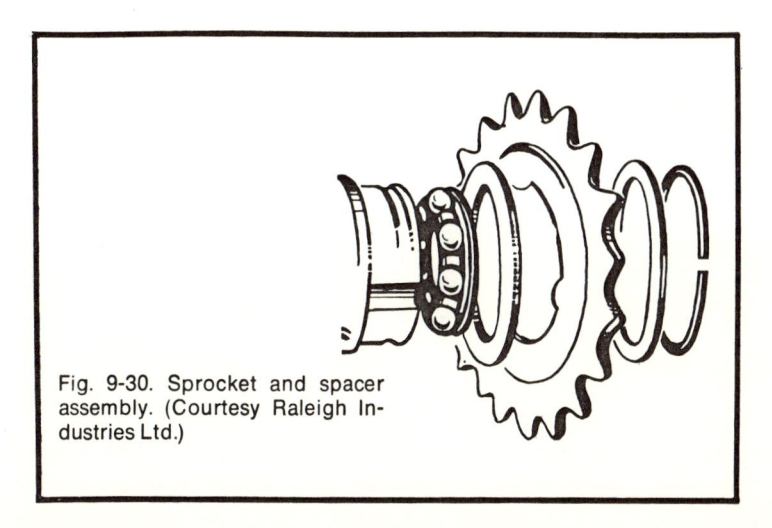

Fig. 9-30. Sprocket and spacer assembly. (Courtesy Raleigh Industries Ltd.)

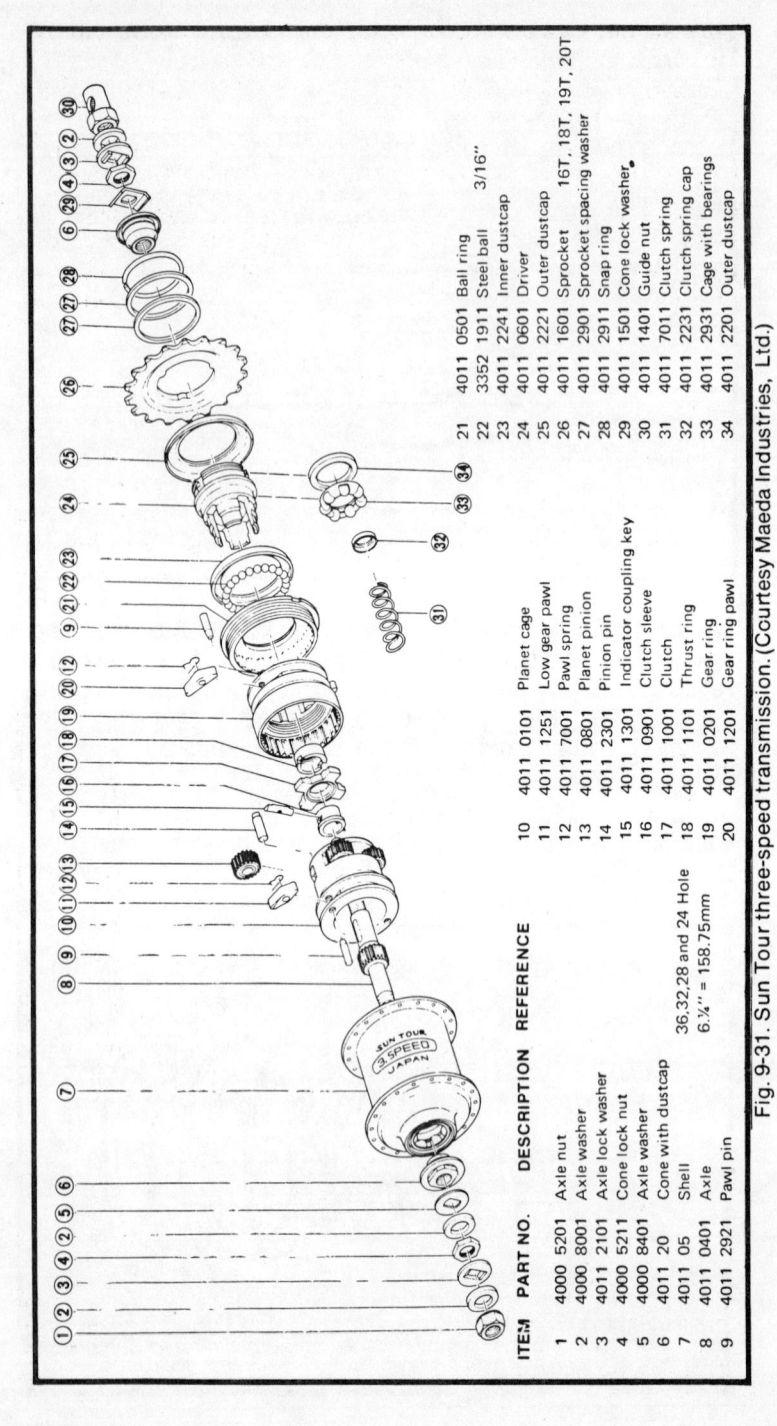

ITEM	PART NO.	DESCRIPTION	REFERENCE
1	4000 5201	Axle nut	
2	4000 8001	Axle washer	
3	4011 2101	Axle lock washer	
4	4000 5211	Cone lock nut	
5	4000 8401	Axle washer	
6	4011 20	Cone with dustcap	
7	4011 05	Shell	36,32,28 and 24 Hole
8	4011 0401	Axle	6¼" = 158.75mm
9	4011 2921	Pawl pin	
10	4011 0101	Planet cage	
11	4011 1251	Low gear pawl	
12	4011 7001	Pawl spring	
13	4011 0801	Planet pinion	
14	4011 2301	Pinion pin	
15	4011 1301	Indicator coupling key	
16	4011 0901	Clutch sleeve	
17	4011 1001	Clutch	
18	4011 1101	Thrust ring	
19	4011 0201	Gear ring	
20	4011 1201	Gear ring pawl	
21	4011 0501	Ball ring	
22	3352 1911	Steel ball	3/16"
23	4011 2241	Inner dustcap	
24	4011 0601	Driver	
25	4011 2221	Outer dustcap	
26	4011 1601	Sprocket	16T, 18T, 19T, 20T
27	4011 2901	Sprocket spacing washer	
28	4011 2911	Snap ring	
29	4011 1501	Cone lock washer	
30	4011 1401	Guide nut	
31	4011 7011	Clutch spring	
32	4011 2231	Clutch spring cap	
33	4011 2931	Cage with bearings	
34	4011 2201	Outer dustcap	

Fig. 9-31. Sun Tour three-speed transmission. (Courtesy Maeda Industries, Ltd.)

the locknut with a wrench. Install these parts into the hub (No. 8). Turn the axle backwards to allow the ball ring (No. 23) to be tightened completely. Finish the job with a hammer and a brass punch.

Fit the left-hand cone (No. 5) and adjust the bearings. There should be a trace of side-play at the rim and none at the hub. Tighten the locknut against the cone and check the bearing clearance. Replace the wheel in the frame checking that the slots in the dropouts hold the flats of the axle stationary. Should the axle revolve, shifting will be erratic. Special lockwashers are available if needed.

OTHER MAKES

Sturmey-Archer is the recognized leader in hub transmissions, although several firms built these transmissions (on the AW pattern). You will find identical units marketed under the names Hercules and Schwinn-Approved Steyr, Styer, and Sun Tour. The latter does not have parts interchangeable with the Sturmey-Archer. An exploded view is included here with the parts numbers (Fig. 9-31).

The Shimano 3.3.3. is a cable-shifted three-speed unit which has gained popularity in recent years. It is mechanically

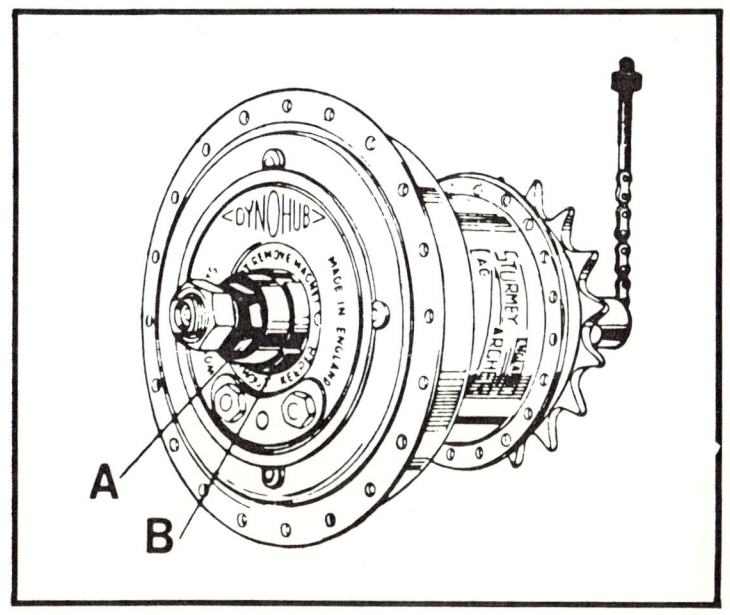

Fig. 9-32. Dynohub in tandem with a Sturmey-Archer three-speed. (Courtesy Raleigh Industries Ltd.)

199

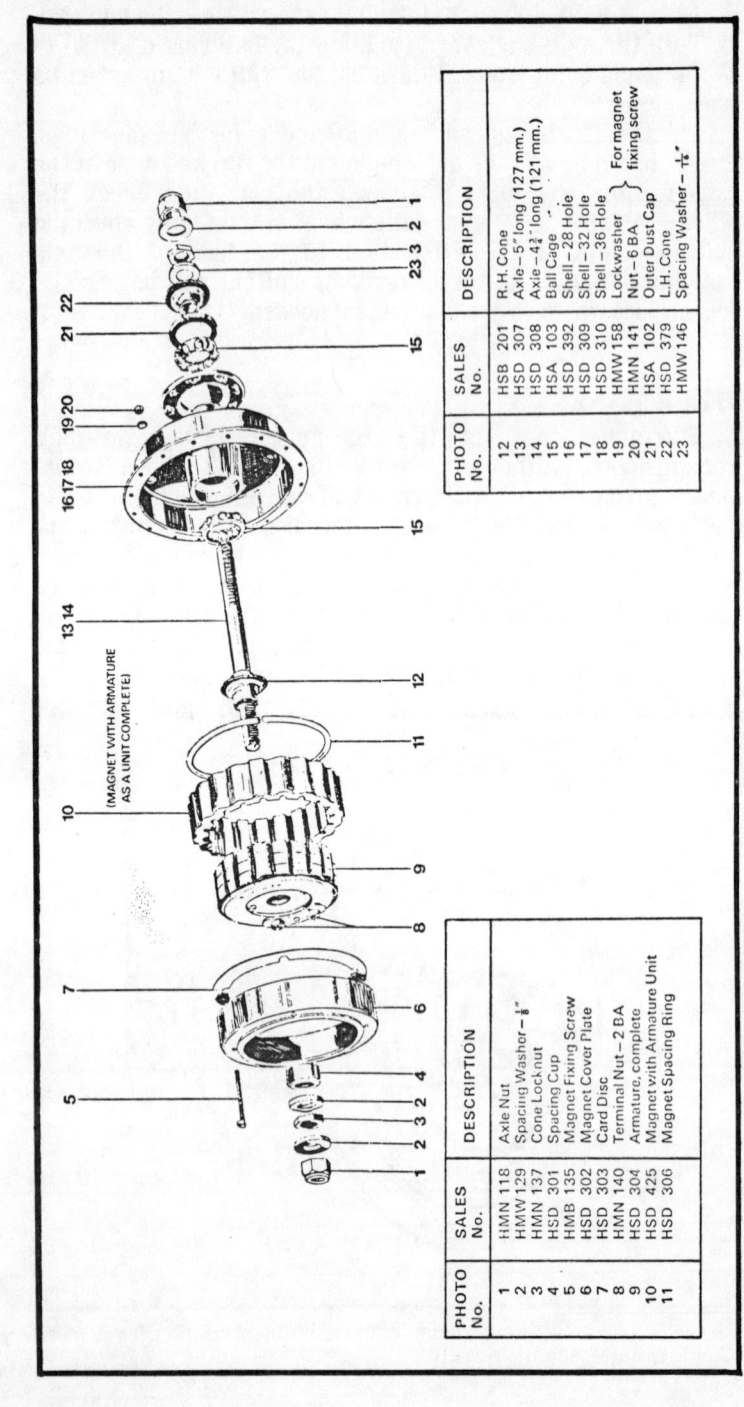

PHOTO No.	SALES No.	DESCRIPTION
1	HMN 118	Axle Nut
2	HMW 129	Spacing Washer – $\frac{1}{8}$"
3	HMN 137	Cone Locknut
4	HSD 301	Spacing Cup
5	HMB 135	Magnet Fixing Screw
6	HSD 302	Magnet Cover Plate
7	HSD 303	Card Disc
8	HMN 140	Terminal Nut – 2 BA
9	HSD 304	Armature, complete
10	HSD 425	Magnet with Armature Unit
11	HSD 306	Magnet Spacing Ring

PHOTO No.	SALES No.	DESCRIPTION
12	HSB 201	R.H. Cone
13	HSD 307	Axle – 5" long (127 mm.)
14	HSD 308	Axle – 4½" long (121 mm.)
15	HSA 103	Ball Cage
16	HSD 392	Shell – 28 Hole
17	HSD 309	Shell – 32 Hole
18	HSD 310	Shell – 36 Hole
19	HMW 158	Lockwasher — For magnet fixing screw
20	HMN 141	Nut – 6 BA — For magnet fixing screw
21	HSA 102	Outer Dust Cap
22	HSD 379	L.H. Cone
23	HMW 146	Spacing Washer – $\frac{1}{16}$"

Fig. 9-33. Dynohub alternator. (Courtesy Raleigh Industries Ltd.)

similar to the 3.3.3. with coaster brake discussed in the following chapter.

DYNOHUB

The Dynohub is a self-contained alternator (AC generator) mounted on the front wheel or on the left side of a Sturmey-Archer three-speed hub. Unlike the friction-driven generators it replaces, the Dynohub is a serious piece of engineering and is thoroughly repairable.

The bearings are adjusted from the left side (Fig. 9-32). Loosen the locknut A and with the proper C spanner (or less elegantly, the end of a sharp screwdriver) turn the slotted washer B to fix the clearance. It has a standard right-hand thread. There should be just a whiff of clearance with the axle nuts torqued. Indicator rod adjustment is the same as for the AW transmission.

Troubleshooting

The Dynohub, in spite of its formidable reputation, is mechanically (Fig. 9-33) and electrically (Fig. 9-34) simple. Troubleshooting offers no particular difficulty.

- Hub rubbing: Check bearing clearance since excessive end play will allow the armature to contact the field magnets. The space between the cover and the inner dust cap should be free of dirt and grit. Since some accumulation is inevitable, clean and pack with light grease. The disc between the magnet and cover plate (Fig. 9-33 No. 7) looks like a piece of Sturmey-Archer advertising, but it must be in place.
- Zero output: Check the wiring for continuity with an ohmmeter, paying particular attention to the lamp sockets. Other causes could be incorrect wiring or, in the worst case, a burned-out armature. Check the armature with a battery and hull as shown in Fig. 9-35. The bulb should light when connected as indicated by the solid lines. It should not light when grounded (dotted line).
- Erratic output: This means a poor connection. Check the wire ends, terminal nuts for tightness, and the sockets.
- Low output: Corrosion is the prime suspect. Go over the external connections with a penknife and scrape them clean. The inside surfaces of the sockets must be bright with no trace of rust or oxidation. The wrong bulbs will give the appearance of low output. The

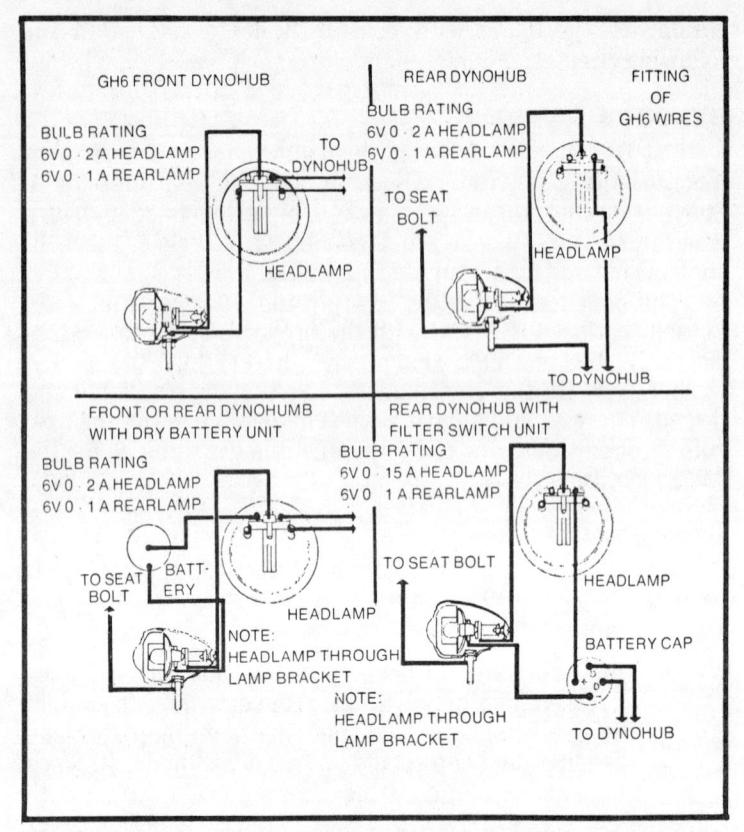

Fig. 9-34. Dynohub wiring diagrams. (Courtesy Raleigh Industries Ltd.)

headlamp requires a 6V, 0.2A bulb and a 6U, 0.15A with filter switch. The British bulb code M.E.S. is for the steel headlamp and a prefocused capless bulb is for the plastic rear lamp. The rear bulb is rated at 6V and 0.1A. Low output may also be caused by weak field magnets, although this condition would be unusual.

- Bulbs burn out: Some of this in inevitable and is due to mechanical shock. If the problem is chronic, suspect loose contacts in the wiring.
- Battery case corrodes: Dead batteries will eventually leak. Clean the interior of the case and the contact points.
- Batteries fail to switch in: Check the charge by substituting known-good batteries. Scrape the battery-circuit terminals and as a last resort replace the automatic switch, noting the connections.

Dynohub Teardown

Take the wheel out of the frame, remove the left-hand side locknut and spacers. The spacer stack is critical for chain alignment and must be reassembled in the original sequence.

Remove the four small nuts and lockwashers from the back side of the drum (Fig. 9-33, Nos. 19 and 20). Withdraw the screws from the front. You will find a 1/8 inch spacer plate (No. 7) on the outboard side of the magnet. Lift it off. Place the wheel over the bench, drum down, and rap lightly on the axle. The armature (No. 9) should drop along with the magnet (No. 10). Behind the magnet (between it and the drum) you will find another spacer (No. 11). Remove it.

NOTE: Do not separate the magnet from the armature. Interrupting the magnetic circuit will have adverse effects on the alternator output. If you must separate these components, first obtain a Sturmey-Archer keeper ring. Replacement magnets are supplied with keeper rings.

The left-hand cone and caged bearing can be left in place if undamaged. The dust cap is pressed on the cone and should be replaced with it as an assembly.

Assembly

After the nonelectrical parts have been cleaned in solvent, grease the left-hand bearing with Lubriplate 5555 or the equivalent and slip it over the axle, bearing cage outwards. Run the cone up. In the event the magnet and the armature have been parted, slide the armature into the magnet so that it displaces the keeper. The chamfer on the magnet and the terminal nuts on the keeper are on the outboard side. Adjust the cones for no perceptible play at the hub and slight play at the rim.

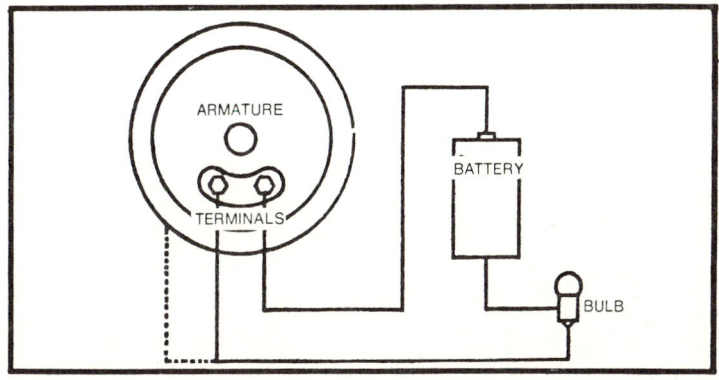

Fig. 9-35. Test connections. The lamp should light if connected as shown. It won't light with one lead grounded. (Courtesy Raleigh Industries Ltd.)

10

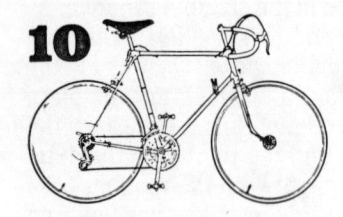

Hub Brakes

The story of hub brakes begins with the humble coaster brake. The coaster brake consists of a clutch to allow freewheeling and transmit power to the hub and a brake mechanism. Most surviving designs employ metallic shoes to stop the wheel and, hopefully, the bicycle. The shoes are moored to the left-hand chain stay by means of a reaction arm and band. Two types are used, the most popular of which is a pair of shoes that are cammed against the hub. The other approach is to arrange the braking surfaces as captive and rotating discs which are squeezed together by the action of the drive screw. Coaster brakes may be combined with a multispeed transmission or, as is more usually the case, drive the hub directly.

The United States is the home of the coaster brake and the scene of most of its development. Few continue in production, and many of the survivors are built under license in Asia, Europe, and Latin America.

One that didn't survive deserves special mention. The Morrow brake is remembered by the World War II generation as the most powerful and reliable brake of its day. It was an impressive mechanism, weighing a good 4 pounds and housed in an oversized hub. Drive was by the now-discarded "every-other-link" chain. The brake shoes on the earlier models were made of solid brass for good wear characteristics and heat conductivity. The shoes ran nearly the full length of the hub. Engagement was by a drive screw and the brake gave almost instantaneous action. If the Morrow had a weak spot it was the friction spring with the drive screw a close second.

For, in spite of the rugged appearance of this part, it chipped easily.

The Morrow was an anachronism with its machined and milled parts and could not compete with more modern designs. Contemporary brakes are hardly elegant in finish or conception. They are economical to build, employing castings and cold stampings wherever possible, and light because extraneous parts have been eliminated. And, in the final analysis, why would anyone want a Morrow when a Bendix, weighing only 2 1/2 pounds does the job as well.

BENDIX COASTER BRAKES

The Motor Components Division of Bendix has worked out some safety suggestions for their brakes. These suggestions may be applied with some modification to any coaster brake and should be read carefully:

- Clean the parts thoroughly for a careful visual inspection of the working surfaces.
- Bendix shoes have a wear telltale in the form of a groove on their friction surfaces. When this groove has disappeared, the shoes need replacement. It is always good practice to replace the shoes during any teardown: the shoes are subject to more wear than any other part of the brake.
- Inspect the brake arm clip for cracks or other signs of impending failure. This insignificant looking part is vital, since if it should fail the brake arm will be free to rotate. Some bikes have a safety feature in that the brake arm is blocked by the left-hand dropout, but one should not depend upon this.
- Check the square hole in the brake arm for signs of rounding out. Should the arm disengage from the shoes, the rider will be brakeless. Sachs brakes have a very good feature in that the brake arm is an interference fit with the shoe anchor. If it is loose, replace the arm or the arm and anchor.
- The condition of the bearings and cones is important. Replace these parts if you have any doubt whatsoever about their condition.
- Too tight a cone adjustment causes the wheel to drag and encourages early bearing failure; too loose an adjustment can cause the hub shell to crack and will pound the cones out.
- Bendix and most other manufacturers insist that the brake, bearings, and particularly the drive surfaces

be coated with a thick layer of light grease. Never attempt to restore the performance of a coaster brake by splashing a little kerosene into the mechanism. If the bike is operated in hilly country, specify high-temperature grease—coaster brakes get too hot to touch on downgrades. Lubriplate and other small refiners make this sort of light-viscosity and heat-resistant grease.

Models 70 and 70-J

The Models 70 and 70-J represent the current production, and are not fundamentally different from the earlier Red Band series (RB-2 and RB) and the Junior. Many parts are interchangeable and all brakes employ paired shoes. The difference between the 70 and 70-J is that the latter has been built around Model Junior inventories, while the Model 70 shares parts with the Red Band series. Figure 10-1 illustrates all Bendix brakes in exploded view and includes a complete parts interchange list.

Since parts may be loose in bins, these identification pointers will help you distinguish between current and past production:

- BB-502 Drive screw: The current part has an 0.03 inch by 0.015 inch groove at its largest diameter. The 1968 part had no groove.
- BB-510 Brake arm: The current part is stamped *70*. The last Red Band part was stamped *RB-2*.
- BB-532 Dust cap, arm side: This is now stamped *Bendix*. The RB-2 and Junior dust cap was slightly larger in diameter and had no identification marking.
- BB-533 Expander, anchor end: This critical part is identified by a 0.03 inch by 0.15 inch groove approximately 1/4 inch from the squared end. The RB-2 part does not carry this groove.
- BB-558 Dust cap, sprocket side: This is stamped *Bendix* in current (Model 70) production. The RB-2 and Junior cap resembles the BB-558, but is larger and has no marking.
- BB-610 Brake arm: This is stamped *70-J*. The comparable part on the 1968 Junior brake is stamped *Junior*.
- BB-615 Locknut: This part was used on the 1969 Junior brake models and was limited to those that had a gold dichromate finish. The comparable (BB-15) on the Model 70-J, the 1968 Junior, RB, and the RB-2 has a bright zinc finish.

- BB-633 Expander, anchor end: This has a 0.85 inch wide slot cut into the inclined surface. The similar 1968 Junior part does not.
- BB-659 Retarder: This is identified by the 0.85 inch slot cut into the drive-end expander.

Troubleshooting. Troubleshooting and overhaul procedures will be discussed with particular reference to the Model 70, but except for part numbers, all Bendix brakes are basically similar.

- Pedals slip in forward direction: This problem concerns the clutch. Usually it is caused by a weak retarder spring. Bend the retarder fingers inward slightly or, better, replace the spring. While listed as part of the retarder subassembly (BB-159) in Fig. 10-1, this part is available separately as BB-112. Another possibility is excessive wear on the tapered surfaces of the driving clutch (component part of BB-159 and not available otherwise) have worn. The worst case is that the hub itself has gone oversize.
- Pedals slip during braking: Insufficient retarder-spring pressure is probably the culprit, although it is not unknown for the dentils or grooves to strip out on the expander (No. BB-533) and the driving clutch (component of BB-159). Do not try to reform these mating surfaces since even the most careful repair will only be temporary. Replace the affected parts.
- Poor braking power: If the brake functions at all, the problem must be at the shoes and the inner diameter of the hub. These parts will develop a high gloss in surface which should be removed with coarse emery paper. All that is necessary is to roughen the surface. Clean the parts thoroughly to remove any abrasive particles and the fine grit which probably caused the problem in the first place.
- Brake fails to release on demand: Check the cone side play. There must be some play at the rim when the locknuts and axle nuts are drawn tight.
- Cracking or grinding noises: The chain is the prime suspect. An overly tight chain will groan and protest and one that is rusty or extremely dirty will do the same. Once rust has spread under the plates and rollers there is not much hope for the chain, although it may be worth the trouble to soak it in kerosene for a few days and try it. The same sort of grumbling may be heard if a new rear sprocket is run on an old chain.

MODEL 70

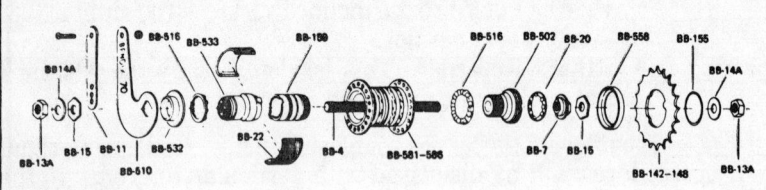

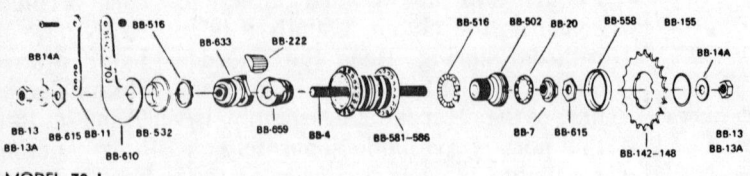

Parts: BB-13A, BB-15, BB-11, BB-532, BB-510, BB-516, BB-533, BB-22, BB-159, BB-4, BB-581–586, BB-516, BB-502, BB-20, BB-7, BB-15, BB-558, BB-142–148, BB-155, BB-14A, BB-13A, BB-14A

MODEL 70-J

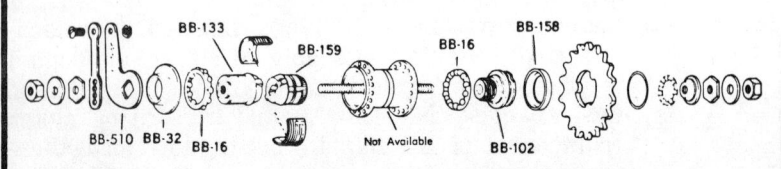

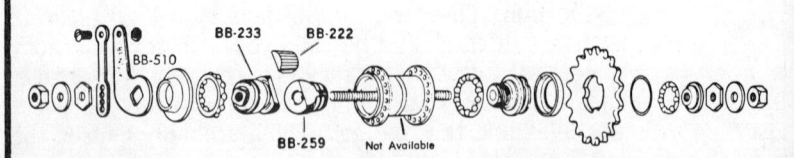

Parts: BB-14A, BB-13, BB-13A, BB-615, BB-11, BB-532, BB-510, BB-516, BB-633, BB-222, BB-059, BB-4, BB-581–586, BB-516, BB-502, BB-20, BB-7, BB-615, BB-558, BB-142–148, BB-155, BB-14A, BB-13, BB-13A

MODEL RB-2

Parts: BB-510, BB-32, BB-16, BB-133, BB-159, Not Available, BB-16, BB-102, BB-158

MODEL JUNIOR

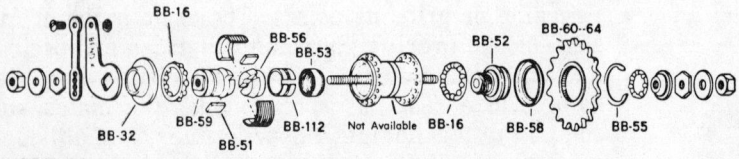

Parts: BB-510, BB-233, BB-222, BB-259, Not Available

MODEL RB

Parts: BB-32, BB-16, BB-59, BB-51, BB-56, BB-53, BB-112, Not Available, BB-16, BB-52, BB-58, BB-60–64, BB-55

SERVICE PARTS

Part No.	Description	Model 70	Model 70-J	RB-2	Junior	RB	Pcs. Per Pkg.	Wgt. Per Pkg. Oz.
BB-4	Axle, 6-5/8" long Standard Length	x	x	x	x	x	10	28
BB-7	Adjusting Cone	x	x	x	x	x	10	11
BB-11	Arm Clip Assembly, w/screw & nut	x	x	x	x	x	50	24
BB-13A	Axle Nut, 5/16" thick (2 required)	x	x	x	x	x	50	20
BB-14A	Axle Washer (2 required)	x	x	x	x	x	50	10
BB-15	Locknut (2 required)	x		x	x	x	50	20
BB-16	Retainer (10-1/4" balls) (2 required) No. 42			x	x	x	10	6
BB-20	Retainer (7-1/4" balls) No. 19	x	x	x	x	x	10	4
BB-22	Brake Shoes (2 required)	x		x			20	15
BB-32	Dust Cap, Arm Side			x	x	x	10	5
BB-36	Axle, 7-3/4" Extra Long			x	x	x	10	32
BB-43, 44, 45, 46, 47	Sprocket, Threaded, 14T-16T-18T-19T-20T x 1/8" x 1/2"	Original Bendix While They Last					10	24
BB-51	Brake Shoe Key (2 required)	No Longer Available				x		
BB-52	Driving Screw	No Longer Available				x		
BB-53	Driving Clutch - 3 start multiple thread					x	10	8
BB-55	Retaining Ring Sprocket	No Longer Available				x		
BB-56	Expander Drive End	No Longer Available				x		
BB-59	Expander, Anchor End	No Longer Available				x		
BB-60	Sprocket, Splined, 18T x 1/8" x 1/2"	No Longer Available				x		
BB-61	Sprocket, Splined, 19T x 1/8" x 1/2"	No Longer Available				x		
BB-62	Sprocket, Splined, 20T x 1/8" x 1/2"	No Longer Available				x		
BB-63	Sprocket, Splined, 10T x 3/16" x 1"					x	10	44
BB-64	Sprocket, Splined, 22T x 1/8" x 1/2"					x	10	40
BB-102	Driving Screw—6 start multiple thread			x	x		2	7
BB-112	Retarder Spring	x	x	x	x	x	10	4
BB-119	Trim Pack w/19T sprocket, 1-BB-11, 1-BB-155, 1-BB-158, 2-BB-14A, 2-BB-13A			x	x		10	48
BB-121	Repair Kit			x	x	x	1	24*
BB-133	Expander, Anchor End			x			5	22

*BB-121 available in 10-pak; weight is 15 lbs.

Part No.	Description	Model 70	Model 70-J	RB-2	Junior	RB	Pcs. Per Pkg.	Wgt. Per Pkg. Oz.
BB-142	Sprocket—3 Lug—15 Teeth 1/8" wide-1/2" pitch	x	x	x	x		10	15
BB-143	Sprocket—3 Lug—14 Teeth 1/8" wide-1/2" pitch	x	x	x	x		10	11
BB-144	Sprocket—3 Lug—16 Teeth 1/8" wide-1/2" pitch	x	x	x	x		10	18
BB-145	Sprocket—3 Lug—18 Teeth 1/8" wide-1/2" pitch	x	x	x	x		10	23
BB-146	Sprocket—3 Lug—19 Teeth 1/8" wide-1/2" pitch	x	x	x	x		10	27
BB-147	Sprocket—3 Lug—20 Teeth 1/8" wide-1/2" pitch	x	x	x	x		10	30
BB-148	Sprocket—3 Lug—22 Teeth 1/8" wide-1/2" pitch	x	x	x	x		10	40
BB-155	Retaining Ring Sprocket	x	x	x	x		10	2
BB-158	Dust Cap, Sprocket			x	x	x	10	3
BB-159	Retarder Sub Assembly (Consisting of Driving Clutch, Drive End Expander & Retarder Spring)	x		x			5	22
BB-222	Brake Shoe (1 required)		x		x		10	8
BB-233	Expander, Anchor End				x		5	23
BB-259	Retarder Sub Assembly (Consisting of Drinving Clutch, Drive End Expander & Retarder Spring)	Superseded by BB-659		x	x			
BB-500	Wrench Double end for cone & lock nut	x	x	x	x	x	2	12
BB-502	Drive Screw—6 start multiple thread	x	x				2	7
BB-510	Brake Arm, Stamped "70", for regular brake model (Knurled Hub)	x					10	26
BB-510A	Brake Arm, Offset-Tandem, Stamped "70"	x					10	26
BB-511	Preformed Arm Clip w/screw & nut	x	x	x	x		25	15
BB-516	Retainer (9-3/4" balls) (2 required)	x	x				10	6
BB-519	Trim Pack w/19T sprocket, 1-BB 11, 2-BB-13A, 2-BB-14A, 1-BB-558, 1-BB-155	x	x				10	48
BB-521	Repair Kit	x	x				1	24*
BB-532	Dust Cap, Arm Side	x	x				10	5
BB-533	Expander, Anchor End	x					5	22
BB-558	Dust Cap, Sprocket	x	x				10	3
BB-581	Hub Shell, 36°, .080 Ga.	x	x				1	13
BB-582	Hub Shell, 28°, .080 Ga.	x	x				1	13
BB-583	Hub Shell, 24°, .080 Ga.	x	x				1	13
BB-584	Hub Shell, 36°, .105 Ga.	x	x				1	13
BB-585	Hub Shell, 36°, .120 Ga.	x	x				1	13
BB-586	Hub Shell, 20°, .080 Ga.	x	x				1	13
BB-610	Brake Arm, Stamped "70-J", for junior brake model (Knurled Hub)		x				10	26
BB-633	Expander, Anchor End		x				5	23
BB-659	Retarder Sub Assembly		x				5	18

*BB-521 available in 10-pak; weight is 15 lbs.

Fig. 10-1. The Bendix coaster brake family. (Courtesy Bendix Bicycle & Ignition Components Division)

209

The best solution is to replace the chain, although you can muffle some of the protest by reversing the chain wheel. A bent axle can also be the problem. To check disassemble the brake and roll the axle on a flat surface. While the brake is apart, inspect the bearings and cones. Other possible faults are bent or distorted dust caps (BB-532 and BB-558). The distortion can be detected by noting the pattern of wear marks on the inner surfaces of the caps where they have come into rubbing contact with the hub. Check the manner in which the sprocket dust cap (BB-558) is assembled. It should be between the sprocket and shoulder of the drive screw (BB-502).

- Lost motion between forward hub engagement and braking: The usual reason is excessive slack at the cones. The arm-side bearing (BB-516) should be properly seated in the hub.
- Squealing when the brake is applied: A lubrication problem, often aided and abetted by dosing the brake with kerosene or gasoline. Such expedients give, as the patent-medicine commercials say, temporary relief. But within a few days brake performance is as bad or worse than ever. And wear on the brake shoes and hub accelerates. Disassemble the brake, remove all of the contaminated lubricant, and assemble using a good grade of light grease. If the brake shoes show signs of wear, replace them.

Dissassembly. Remove the wheel from the frame, observing the relationship between washers and other components to the rear fork. These brakes have been adapted to a fairly wide range of bikes by the use of spacer washers on either side of the dropouts. Remove both axle nuts and unfasten the brake arm from the arm clip, leaving the arm clip on the frame. Inspect this part carefully for cracking. Remove the chain at the chain wheel first and then from the rear sprocket. Clear the fender braces from the axle and pull the rear wheel from the frame.

The arm end of the axle should be clamped in a vise having copper inserts over the jaws to prevent thread damage. If you do not have sheet copper lying about, substitute hardwood. The axle locknut (BB-15) should then be removed as well as the adjusting cone (BB-7). Next comes the driving screw (BB-502), the cone bearing (BB-20) and the large bearing (BB-516). Remove the driving screw by turning it counterclockwise. Lift the wheel off the internals. The remainder of the drill is now quite obvious.

Assembly. Clean all parts, inspect and replace as needed. The arm-side bearing (BB-516) is assembled on the anchor expander (BB-533) with the balls toward the tapered surface. Less hassle results if you first thread the anchor expander on the axle, allowing about 1 1/8 inch of thread to show beyond the square on the expander. Grease the bearing, packing grease into every dent and hollow. Place it in the dust cap (BB-532) with the balls outward. Now, using the long portion of the axle as a handle, push the expander-axle subassembly through the bearing until it seats in the race (Fig. 10-2).

This bearing consists of 9 1/4-inch balls. Similar bearings are available at hardware stores and the like, but are not necessarily the correct replacement. If you have been reading this book through, you can appreciate that bicycle parts are only superficially standardized. Use only Bendix bearings.

Next assemble the brake arm (BB-510) and lock the parts into place with a locknut (BB-15). This assembly should then be mounted vertically in a vise with the arm down. The drive-end expander, retarder, and driving clutch subassembly (BB-159) are then placed on the axle.

Grease both expander surfaces and the shoes. Place them on the expander. The inside of the hub should also be greased. The word here is to use grease sparingly. All wear surfaces should be covered, but excessive grease will only clog the mechanism and run out over your spokes.

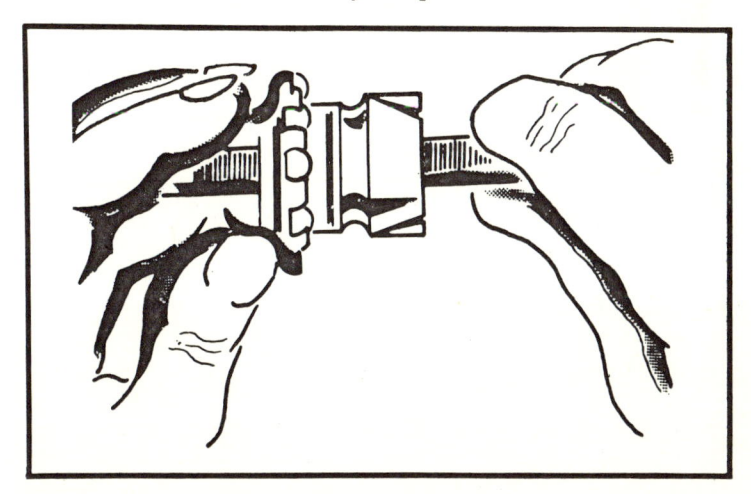

Fig. 10-2. Assembling the expander-axle assembly. (Courtesy Bendix Bicycle & Ignition Components Division)

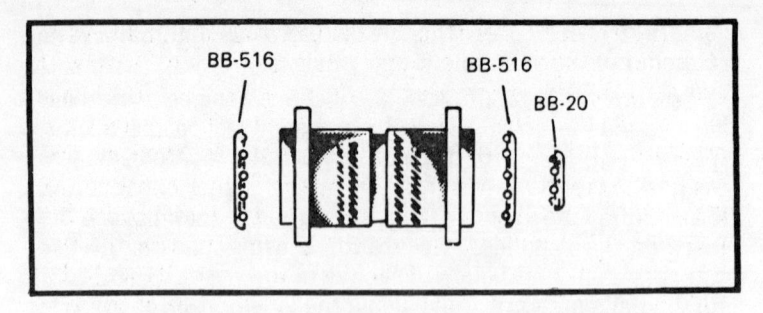

Fig. 10-3. Correct bearing assembly. (Courtesy Bendix Bicycle & Ignition Components Division)

Hold the brake shoes together with your fingers and place the hub over the entire assembly. Be sure the hub bearings are properly seated. The sprocket and bearing (BB-516) should then be installed with the balls toward the hub (Fig. 10-3).

Coat the threads on the driving screw (BB-502) with grease and screw it in place. Grease the adjusting cone bearing (BB-20) and place it in the driving screw with the balls toward the hub. The adjusting cone (BB-7) is run down on the axle and tightened finger tight against the bearing.

Back off the cone 1/4 turn. Hold that adjustment with a thin wrench and tighten the locknut with a second wrench. Bendix supplies these thin wrences under part No. BB-101. When you are finished there should be a slight amount of play at the wheel rim.

Place the sprocket-side dust cap (BB-558) over the driving screw. Index the three lugs on the sprocket to match the slots on the screw. Install the retaining ring (BB-155) in the groove next to the sprocket.

Position the wheel in the dropouts and fasten the clip. Ideally you should use a new clip each time the brake is disturbed. Use the chain stay as a form to bend the clip. Select the hole in the arm clip that hold the brake arm closest to the frame member. Do not tighten the screw and nut yet, since the rear wheel must be aligned parallel to the frame and the chain tension adjusted before this cap screw is finally snugged.

BENDIX AUTOMATIC TRANSMISSION-BRAKE COMBINATIONS

Bendix ceased production of all multispeed transmissions in 1970, and now concentrates its bicycle efforts on the Model 70 and 70-J coaster brake. However, there are still thousands of these transmissions in existence and the manufacturer informs me that many parts are still in stock.

There were three transmission-brake combinations. All offered two speeds and very reliable braking (within the context of any coaster brake). No external shift mechanism was used; the second speed was engaged by a slight back pressure on the pedals. Heavy pressure disengaged the drive and engaged the brake elements. The earliest model, identified by three red bands on the hub, employed discs or washers in the manner of the New Departure. The Red Band was built for four years until 1964. The Blue Band (3 blue bands) was similar in most particulars except that it employed brake shoes and featured a second-speed overdrive. The last of the transmissions was the Yellow Band with, (you guessed it) three yellow bands around the hub. It had the usual underdrive arrangement and shoe brakes.

BENDIX RED BAND TWO-SPEED

An exploded drawing is shown in Fig. 10-4 together with the parts nomenclature. There are two driving screws, one inside the other. The outside screw (AB-18 and 19, depending upon the number of sprocket teeth) is en bloc with the sprocket. It is the high-speed driving screw and the dominant one. The low-speed screw (AB-2) is connected to the first by a planetary gear set. Both have serrated clutches (AB-23 and AB-3 respectively) which attempt to engage tapers on the hub. The hub discriminates between drivers; the faster turning driver will take precedence over the more slowly turning one. When the sprocket is turned backwards, the high-speed clutch disengages, leaving the field to the low speed clutch. A kind of mechanical logic circuit signals the transmission to shift down. On a partial backpedal, the indexing spring (AB-26) indexes one space on the indexing sleeve which is integral to the high-speed screw. On alternate cycles small lugs or ears on the indexing spring prevent the high-speed clutch (AB-23) from moving toward the sprocket. Otherwise, slots in the high-speed clutch slide over the indexing spring and the clutch engages the hub, giving high gear. Full backpedaling causes the disc set (AB-22) to be compressed by the plate assembly (AB-6). Alternate discs are indexed to the hub with six lugs and turn with it. The remainder are splined to the cone-arm and disc support (AB-33) and prevented from turning by the brake arm (AB-10) which is secured to the chain stay.

Troubleshooting.

First check the cone adjustment. The wheel must have no more (or less) than a slight lateral play at the rim. Otherwise

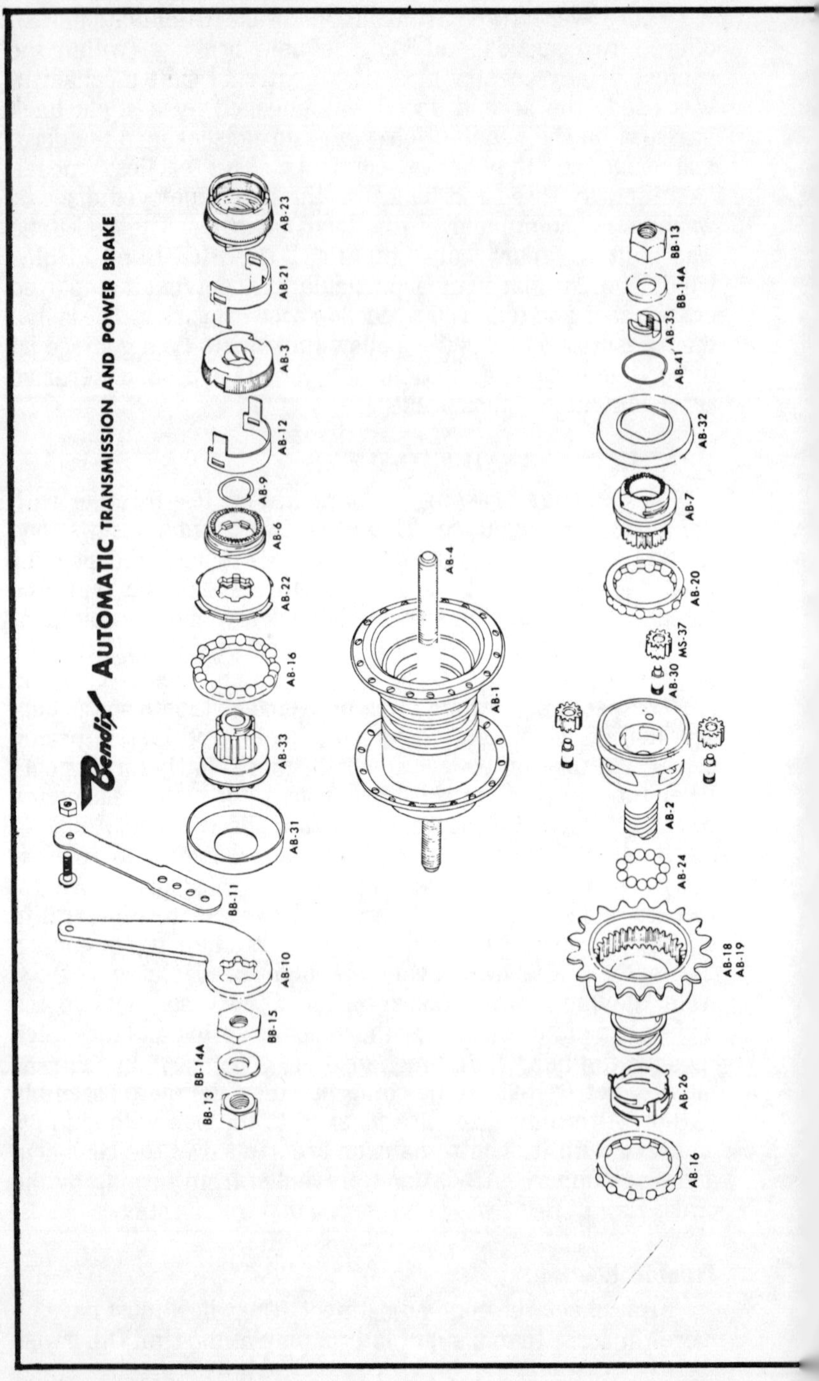

Bendix AUTOMATIC TRANSMISSION AND POWER BRAKE
BB-13
BB-14A
BB-15
AB-10
BB-11
AB-31
AB-33
AB-16
AB-22
AB-6
AB-9
AB-12
AB-3
AB-21
AB-23
AB-4
AB-1
AB-16
AB-26
AB-18
AB-19
AB-24
AB-2
AB-30
MS-37
AB-20
AB-7
AB-32
AB-41
AB-35
BB-14A
BB-13

ITEM	PART NO.	DESCRIPTION			
AB-1	482537	Hub Shell 36 Hole-13 Gauge	AB-20	482525	Retainer (12¼" Ball) Small, 1 Required
AB-1B	482556	Hub Shell 28 Hole-13 Gauge	AB-21	482521	Retarder Coupling, High Speed
AB-1C	482555	Hub Shell 36 Hole-11 Gauge	AB-22	482560	Brake Disc-Set (5 Brass, 5 Thin Steel—1 Thick Steel)
AB-1D	482563	Hub Shell 36 Hole-12 Gauge	AB-23	482561	Clutch—High Speed Assembly
AB-2	482544	Driving Screw—Low Speed	AB-24	909848	Ball (11¼" Loose) Packed 50 to Bag
AB-3	482523	Driving Clutch—Low Speed	AB-26	482535	Spring—Indexing
AB-4	482506	Axle 6⅜" Stamped "A"	AB-28	482542	Low Speed—Screw Assembly (Driver—Gears and Pins) Not Shown
AB-6	482557	Pressure Plate Assembly			
AB-7	482527	Adjusting Cone and Sun Gear	AB-30	482543	Pin, Planet Gear (3 Required)
AB-9	482518	Disc-Retaining Ring	AB-31	482519	Dust Cap—Arm Side
AB-10	482505	Brake Arm	AB-32	482528	Dust Cap—Sprocket Side
BB-11	*F-5614	Arm Clip Assembly (Clip, Screw and Nut)	AB-33	482508	Cone—Arm and Disc—Support
AB-12	482512	Retarder Coupling—Low Speed	AB-35	482541	Lock Nut, Adjusting Cone
BB-13	*F-5365	Axle Nut (2 Required)	MS-37	*477702	Planet Gear (3 Required)
BB-14A	*F-5643	Axle Washer (2 Required) 1/16"	AB-41	482529	Retaining Ring—Dust Cap
BB-15	*F-5760	Lock Nut, Arm Side (1 Required)	AB-45	482520	Clutch Pack Assembly—Not Shown
AB-16	*F-3291	Retainer (12¼" Balls) Large, 2 Required	AB-102	482545	Wrench Cone Adjusting Lock Nut
AB-18	482558	Sprocket, Driving Screw, High Speed with Sleeve Assembly (18T x ½" P x ⅛" W)	BB-106	*478438	Wrench, Axle—Lock Nut
AB-19	482559	Sprocket, Driving Screw, High Speed with Sleeve Assembly (19T x ½" P x ⅛" W)	AB-103	482562	Tool Disc Aligning

*Parts and Tools Interchangeable with Bendix Coaster Brake or Multi-Speed.

Fig. 10-4. Bendix Red Band brake and transmission.

operation of the transmission will be erratic. Adjustment is taken at the right side at the sun-gear cone (AB-7) which is secured by a lock nut. Special tools have been available from Bendix for this, but like spoke shaves, are of more antiquarian than practical interest. A pair of Channellocks will do the job.

If bearing adjustment does not solve the problem, dismount the wheel and remove the sun-gear cone, the caged bearing (AB-20), the low-speed drive screw (AB-2), the loose bearings (AB-24) and the high-speed drive screw and sprocket (AB-18 or AB-19). You should have 11 1/4 inch bearings. More or less may affect the operation of the transmission. Remove the rest of the parts.

Examine each for evidence of wear or breakage. As in all of these transmissions, the springs are supercritical. Check the bearings, cones, and the mating surfaces of the clutches.

It is necessary that the mechanism index properly. To check, place the parts over the axle as they would be in the hub and turn the sprocket. The first set of fingers—those on the brake-arm side—should enter the high-speed clutch (AB-23) and snag on the serrations without undue complaint. If they bend or flex, replace the index spring. Do not attempt to repair by filing or bending the fingers unless you have the only Bendix two-speed in the county. Turn the sprocket back and forth. With each backward and forward motion the indexing spring should move one space on the indexing sleeve which is part of the sprocket and screw. Small ears on the spring block the clutch every other cycle. These ears are subject to wear and sudden dissappearance.

Three conditions can prevent indexing:

- a worn, battered, or otherwise unserviceable index spring
- lack of engagement between the spring and the knurled interior of the high-speed clutch
- lack of engagement of the spring with the indexing sleeve

Lack of high-speed drive is simple. Assuming that the clutch engages the high-speed screw—that it is not blocked by broken threads or debris—the only possibility is wear at the clutch and hub interface. If either or both parts are worn, the clutch will ride out to the bearing race and stop. There should be between 1/16 and 1/32 inch clearance between the end of the clutch and the race.

The brake mechanism is power operated in the sense that it is driven by the torque-multiplying low-speed screw. The discs are necessarily few in number and take a beating even though they are made of brass and steel for wear resistance and heat dissipation. If they are rough, replace them. Test the mechanical action with the mechanism out of the hub, but fully assembled on the axle. About one inch of the axle should protrude from each end of the assembly. Tighten the arm locknut (BB-15) and the dust cap (AB-32) and adjust the sun-gear cone as if the assembly were to be fitted to the bike.

The beauty of this transmission is that you can see it work. Turn the sprocket full back and note if the disc pack is compressed. The low-speed pressure plate (AB-6) should move against the discs (AB-22). Failure to do so will deny braking and can be caused by:

- broken or foreign objects on the threads of the drive screws
- a weak high-speed retarder coupling (AB-21)

You should also keep in mind that the low-speed retarder coupling (AB-12) must generate more friction than the high-speed retarder spring (AB-21) for the transmission to behave properly.

Final Assembly

The Bendix requires liberal lubrication with light grease. Apply the grease during final assembly, paying particular attention to the bearings and stressed low-speed driving screw and that portion of the axle on which it rides. Start with the cone arm and disc support (AB-33). Thread it on to the axle until 1 1/8 inches of the axle protrudes. As shown in the exploded view, the short splines are on the outboard side. Now comes the caged bearing (AB-16). It is the larger bearing of the two and the balls face inward, toward the sprocket. The disc set (AB-22) is next and the sequence is important. Begin with a thin steel disc next to the cone arm. Alternately stack thick brass and steel discs. There are five brass and six steel discs. The last steel disc, a thick one, is toward the sprocket. Lubricate the steel discs by dipping them in a grease pot. Install the pressure plate (AB-6) and the internal lock ring (AB-9). The teeth of the disc are toward the sprocket.

Fit the low-speed retarder coupling (AB-12) over the pressure plate, indexing it to the lug on the plate. This coupling is distinguished from the high-speed coupling (AB-21) by its straight lugs. The high-speed coupling crimped at the ends. The low-speed lugs point toward the sprocket if you have assembled it correctly.

The high-speed coupling fits into the groove on the high-speed clutch (AB-23). Its lugs point toward the brake arm. Fit the low-speed clutch (AB-3) to the high-speed coupling. The lugs go into the slots and hook behind them. Now we have the high- and low-speed clutches held together by the high-speed retarder coupling. The tapered and serrated friction surfaces on the clutches should slant toward the sprocket side.

Slip the clutch assembly over the axle. Align all the ears on the discs so that the whole assembly will slip into the hub. There is a tool for this, but you can do it with patience and a little jiggling.

Assemble the indexing spring (AB-26) over the indexing sleeve on the sprocket and screw (AB-18 or 19). The small ears are toward the sprocket.

The planet gears (MS-37) secured by their pins (AB-30), go into the low-speed screw (AB-2). The big ends of the pins should be flush with the inboard edge of their mounting flange. Fix 11 balls (AB-24) with grease along the periphery of the internal ball race in the high-speed screw. Put the two screws together and check for free rotation. Place the second caged bearing (AB-16) on the race of the low-speed screw. Run the whole assembly into the hub by turning the sprocket. Bearing AB-20 is next, balls facing inward.

Thread the sun-gear cone (AB-7) over the axle. Rotate the sprocket to mesh the planet gears. Secure the dust cap (AB-32) to the sun gear cone with the lock ring (AB-41). Adjust the cone for just a trace of side play. Tighten the lock nut (AB-35) against it and, except for mounting the wheel, the job is finished.

BENDIX YELLOW AND BLUE BAND BRAKES

Both of these brakes are coupled to a two-speed transmission and both employ shoe brakes. The difference is that the Yellow Band gives direct and underdrive while the Blue Band gives direct and overdrive. Figure 10-5 shows the breakdown on the Yellow Band with parts nomenclature. Figure 10-6 does the same for the Blue Band and includes a list of Blue Band parts, not interchangeable with the underdrive model. Otherwise parts are identical for both. Repair procedures are nearly identical and can be discussed together.

Troubleshooting

The problems, symptoms, and causes that follow apply to both the Yellow Band and Blue Band brakes and transmissions.

- Refusal to shift: This problem can be traced to the indexing spring (AB-26). Make sure the perpendicular lugs on the spring are not bent or broken. The prongs

Part No.	Description
AB-7*	Adjusting Cone & Sun Gear
BB-11*	Arm Clip Ass'y (Clip, Screw & Nut)
BB-13A*	Axle Nut, 5/16" thick (2 required)
BB-14*	Axle Washer (2 required)
BB-15*	Locknut (1 required)
AB-16*	Retainer, Large (12-1/4" balls) (2 required) (Note: Do not use No. 68 Bearing in place of this special Retainer)
AB-20*	Retainer, Small (12 1/4" balls) (1 required)
AB-21*	Retarder Coupling, High Speed
AB-23*	Clutch, High Speed Assembly
AB-23A	Retarder Spring, High Speed Clutch
AB-24*	Ball, Chrome Steel (11-1/4" balls, Loose) Packed 50 only
AB-26*	Spring, Indexing
AB-30*	Pin, Planet Gear (3 required)
AB-32*	Dust Cap, Sprocket Side
AB-35*	Locknut, Adjusting Cone
AB-37*	Planet Gear (3 required)
AB-41*	Retaining Ring, Dust Cap
AB-302	Driving Screw, Low Speed
AB-303**	Driving Clutch, Low Speed
AB-304**	Axle, Dichromate Finish, 6 1/2" long
AB-306**	Expander, Drive End
AB-310	Brake Arm, Stamped "Model B"
AB-310A	Brake Arm, Offset Tandem
AB-312**	Retarder Spring, Clutch-Low Speed
AB-318	Sprocket-Driving Screw, High Speed, 18T
AB-319	Sprocket-Driving Screw, High Speed, 19T
AB-322**	Brake Shoe (4 required)
AB-328	Low Speed Screw Ass'y (Driver, Gears & Pins) (Not shown as Ass'y)
AB-331**	Dust Cap, Arm Side
AB-333**	Expander, Anchor End
AB-345**	Retarder Sub-Assembly (Low Speed Clutch, Drive End Expander & Retarder Spring,, Not Shown)
AB-102**	Wrench, Cone Adjusting Locknut (Not Shown)

* Interchangeable with all Automatic Brake Models.
** Interchangeable with Overdrive Automatic Brake Models

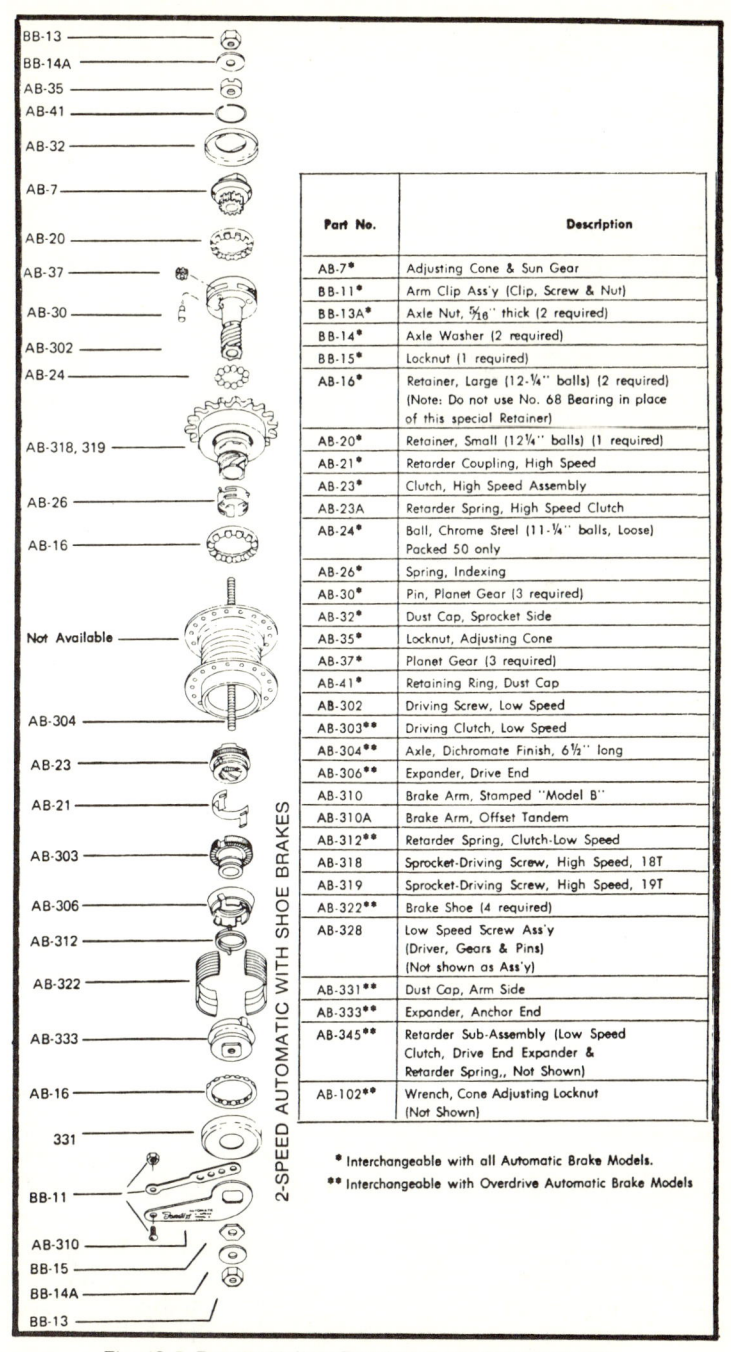

Fig. 10-5. Bendix Yellow Band brake and transmission.

that drag inside the clutch (AB-23) should have turned-up ends. Place the clutch (AB-23) on the driver with the indexing spring (AB-26) and rotate the assembly back and forth, noting that the indexing spring is shifting. As a general rule, you should replace both the spring and driver when you believe either is at fault. By all means replace the driver if the spring is worn or distorted.

- Slippage in drive: This one is a bit difficult. As a starter, put a sprocket wrench on the sprocket and shift through each gear, noting when slippage occurs. You can make the same test with the transmission disassembled by placing the sprocket driver (AB-318 or AB-319) with the indexing spring (AB-26) and bearing (AB-16) in the hub shell. Run the clutch (AB-23) on the driver. Put the transmission in direct drive and lean on the sprocket wrench. For overdrive (Blue Band) units both clutches and both drivers must be used. The remedy is to replace the slipping clutch (AB-23 or AB-303).

Another possibility is insufficient retarder spring pressure. The pressure should be greater on the retarder spring (AB-312) than on the retarder coupling (AB-21) on the clutch (AB-23). Run the clutch pack and expander on the driver (AB-318 or AB-319) with the indexing spring. Hold the driver in one hand and the expander (AB-306) by the other. Twist the expander into the drive position and note the retarder coupling on the clutch will turn while the retarder spring (AB-312) remains stationary. This is as it should be; if the spring (AB-312) rotates first the retarder coupling (AB-21) is weak and should be replaced.

- Pedals slip backwards during the braking mode: This is a safety related item and should be corrected with dispatch. The usual cause is insufficient retarder spring pressure. Replace the spring AB-312. Check the dentils on the driving clutch (AB-303) and driving end expander (AB-306) for alignment, wear, and compacted dirt which would keep them apart. Clean and replace parts AB-303 and/or AB-306 as necessary. Do not attempt to repair by reforming the dentils. It doesn't work.

- Poor or sluggish braking: Decayed braking performance can result from a high polish to the friction surface on the inside of the hub, usually developed simultaneously with the same mirrorlike polish on the brake shoes. Replace the brake shoes (AB-322); they are worn out. The hub is a bit expensive to replace and so most mechanics are content to roughen it with coarse (about 260 grit, wet or dry) emery paper. If you wish to apply power to the task, take a 1/8 to 1/4 inch steel rod, and split the end for an inch or so. Anchor one end of a strip of emery paper in the slot, and wrap it around the rod with the abrasive side outward. Mount the apparatus in an electric drill. Tear off the end of the strip as it dulls and glazes. Clean all parts thoroughly to remove every trace of grit.

- Brake is slow to release or drags when the bike is pedaled forward: As mystifying as this symptom sounds, the causes are simple and easy to correct. The most likely cause is an overly tight cone adjustment. The Bendix requires slight freeplay at the rim—after the axle nuts have been snugged down tight. This means, in effect, that the cones should be a hair loose before assembly. The axle will bow slightly as the axle nuts are secured. A permanently bent axle will also cause brake drag. If the cone adjustment is correct, the brake will have to be disassembled and the axle checked. Perhaps the best way to do this is to roll the axle on a flat surface such as a piece of plate glass or a machine-tool worktable. Chucking it up in a drill motor and checking for wobble is not accurate, since most drill-motor spindles are themselves bent.
- Cracking or grinding noises: Most of this sort of protest can be traced to the chain. Cleaning and relubrication may help, but if the chain is worn severely or rusted, the best bet is to replace it along with the sprockets. Another possibility is damage to the dust caps. Replace AB-32 and AB-331 if they are bent, multilated, or worn.
- Lost motion between forward and braking modes: One of the design features of the Bendix is its responsiveness between forward and stop. If you have to backpedal excessively, check the cone adjustment. Be certain that the arm-end bearing (AB-16) is properly seated in the hub. If the bearing is properly seated and the problem persists, replace the brake shoes (AB-322).
- Binding which may be accompanied by dentil noise: This is a hard one, but assuming that the cones have running clearance, it may be the result of warped dropouts. Check that the dropouts are parallel when the axle nuts are tightened. If the problem disappears

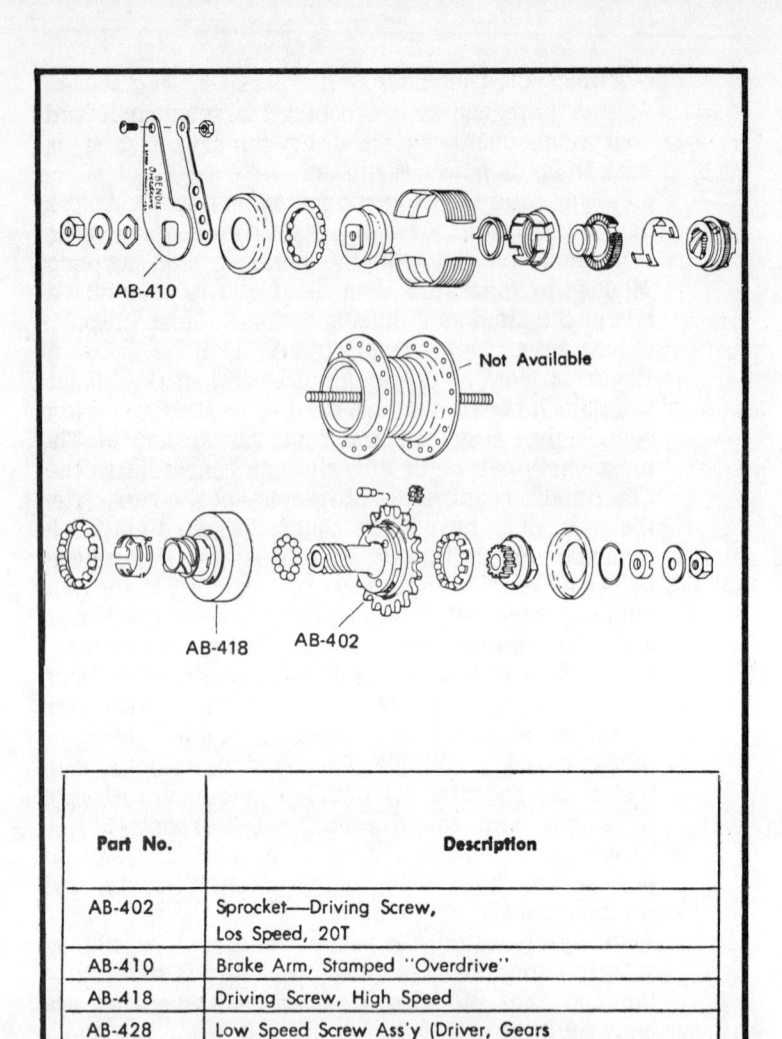

Part No.	Description
AB-402	Sprocket—Driving Screw, Los Speed, 20T
AB-410	Brake Arm, Stamped "Overdrive"
AB-418	Driving Screw, High Speed
AB-428	Low Speed Screw Ass'y (Driver, Gears & Pins) (Not shown as Ass'y)

Fig. 10-6. Bendix Blue Band brake and transmission. Parts called are not interchangeable with the Yellow Band.

when the axle nuts are loose, then the dropouts are obviously at fault. The best approach is to bend the dropouts with the help of a large Crescent wrench, an old-fashioned monkey wrench, or (if you do not care about tooth marks) with a pipe wrench. Bend cold. The same symptoms can be caused by a bent axle.

Overhaul—Yellow and Blue Band

This discussion is primarily concerned with the Blue Band (underdrive) model. Where appropriate, special reference is made to the Yellow Band (overdrive) model.

Put the transmission into low gear, so that the hub turns slower than the sprocket. This is a vital preliminary step: failure to engage low will result in damage to the coupling (AB-21). Clamp the brake-arm end of the axle in a soft-faced vise to prevent galling the threads, sprocket end upright. Remove the adjusting cone locknut (AB-35). Bendix makes a pair of wrenches for this operation. AB-102 fits the locknut while BB-100 holds the adjusting cone AB-7 stationary. Turn the sprocket clockwise by hand, unscrewing the cone which is integral with the sun gear. This part unthreads from the low-speed screw assembly. The latter is known in Bendix literature as AB-328 and consists of AB-302, AB-30 and AB- or MS-37. A bit confusing, but the separate assembly number simplifies inventories.

Blue Band (overdrive): Put the hub into direct drive so that the hub and sprocket turn together at the same speed. Otherwise, it is possible to damage the coupling (AB-21). Hold the sprocket stationary while unscrewing the sun gear and adjusting cone combination AB-7.

Back to the Yellow Band. Remove the small ball retainer (AB-20) from the low-speed driving screw assembly (AB-328). Remove both driving screw assemblies (AB-328 and AB-318) by turning the sprocket counterclockwise and lifting.

Blue Band (overdrive). Hold both driving screw assembles together while removing, to prevent a rain of loose ball bearings.

Yellow Band: Remove sprocket-side large ball retainer (AB-16) from the hub-shell. Carefully lift the hub shell up and away from the inner assembly, cupping your free hand around the bottom of the hub shell to hold the four brake shoes (AB-322). Remove the brake shoes, then the high-speed clutch and expander assembly consisting of AB-23, AB-21, AB-303, and AB-306. At this point the transmission is fairly well apart; all that remains is the three subassemblies.

Yellow and Blue Band Subassemblies

While you could organize these parts in another fashion, Bendix identifies three subassemblies—the brake arm, driver, and clutch expander.

Brake Arm. Clamp the long end of the axle in a soft-jawed vise and remove the locknut (BB-15). Lift off the brake arm

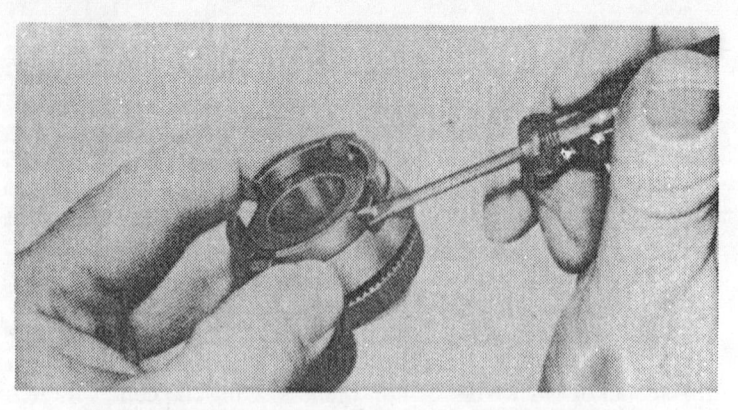

Fig. 10-7. Bendix retarder spring disassembly and assembly.

(AB-310) and the dust cap (AB-331). Unthread the anchor-end expander (AB-333) and retainer (AB-16). You can remove the bearing retainer by placing the expander flat on the bench and exerting even pressure around the circumference of the retainer. If this bearing needs replacement, be sure to specify the correct Bendix part. A No. 68 bearing won't work, even though it looks like it might.

Driver. Lift the low-speed driving screw (AB-328) from the high-speed sprocket screw (AB-318), being careful not to loose the uncaged balls (AB-24). There are supposed to be 11 of these balls. The planet gears, known variously as AB- or MS-37, are secured to pins AB-30. Press the pins out. Remove the indexing spring (AB-26) from the high-speed sprocket screw.

Clutch Expander. Unhook the end of the retarder coupling (AB-21) from the slots on the low-speed driving clutch (AB-303). Do the same for the retarder spring (AB-23A). Figure 10-7 shows how to separate the low-speed driving clutch (AB-303) and the drive-end expander (AB-306). The top side of the retarder spring (AB-312) is lifted with a small screwdriver and the spring peeled off.

Inspection. Clean all parts in solvent, replacing any that are worn or damaged. The troubleshooting guide a few pages back is a good index of possible failure. The Bendix transmission requires grease on all parts with two exceptions. The indexing spring (AB-26) and the high-speed clutch (ASB-23) shoud be oiled with a high grade motor oil. Be very generous with the grease on the axle and bore of the driving screws. Texaco Regal Starfak No. 2 gives good results.

Assembly. Assembly is not difficult if you follow the illustrations. Begin with the clutch expander. Use the low-speed driver for support and thread on the low-speed

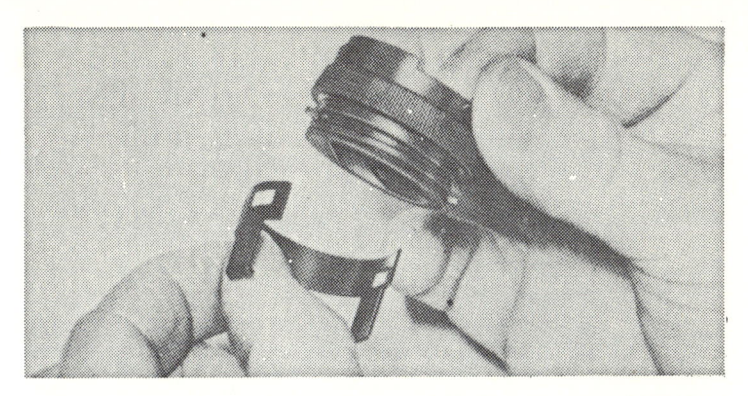

Fig. 10-8. Installing retarder coupling on Bendix high-speed clutch.

clutch (AB-303) and the drive-end expander (AB-306). The dentils must face each other. Place the bottom hook of the retarder spring (AB-312) in the groove and pry the spring on. Remove the assembly from the low-speed driver. Hook the coupling (AB-21) on the retarder spring of the high-speed clutch (AB-23). The lower window of the coupling should align with the low hook on the spiral spring (Fig. 10-8). Now hook the coupling into the slots provided in the low-speed driving clutch (AB-303) (see Fig. 10-9).

The drive-screw subassembly is next. Assemble the indexing spring (AB-26) over the sleeve of the high-speed driving screw (AB-318) or, if your dealing with an overdrive, (AB-418) with the three short lugs against the shoulder of the ball race (Fig. 10-10). The planet gears (AB- or MS-37) are fixed to the low-speed driving screw (AB-302) by pins (AB-30) which are set flush with or below the flange of the screw. Place the 11 uncaged 1/4 inch balls in the race of the driving screw. Grease liberally. You can temporarily locate the balls by using the low-speed driver as a pilot. Insert it upside down. Figure 10-11 shows how the drivers go together with the balls sandwiched between them.

Fig. 10-9. Low window on coupling aligns with low hook on spiral spring. (Courtesy Bendix Bicycle & Ignition Components Division)

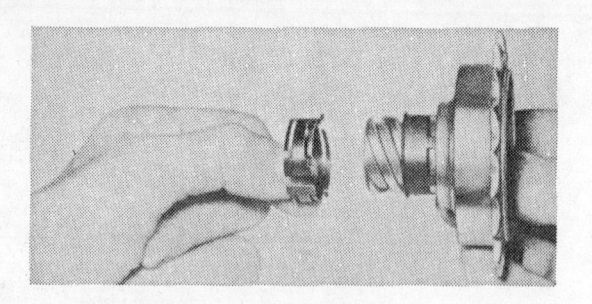

Fig. 10-10. Indexing spring assembly—lugs against ball race. (Courtesy Bendix Bicycle & Ignition Components Division)

The bearing (AB-16) is pressed on the anchor-end expander (AB-333) with the help of the dust cap (AB-331). This operation is shown in Fig. 10-12. Screw these parts on the axle until 1 1/8 inches of the axle protrudes. Install the dust cap and the brake arm (AB-310). Secure the locknut (BB-15).

Assembly of the hub is the last major step in the process. Insert the high-speed clutch (AB-23) and retarder subassembly (AB-345) into the hub as shown in Fig. 10-13. Insert

Fig. 10-11. Assembling the drivers. (Courtesy Bendix Bicycle & Ignition components Division)

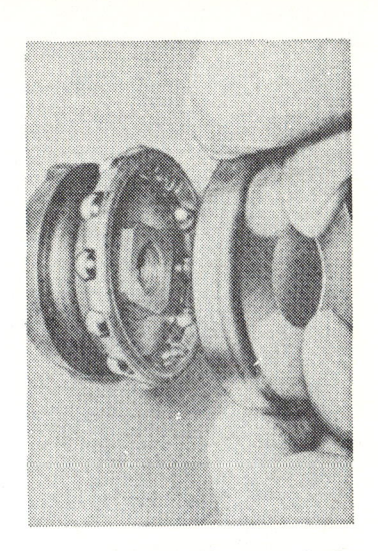

Fig. 10-12. Installing bearing retainers on the anchor-end expander with the aid of the dust cap. (Courtesy Bendix Bicycle & Ignition Components Division)

the brake shoes (AB-322) into the hub shell around the drive-end expander (AB-306).

Invert the assembly and clamp the arm side of the axle in a vise. Insert a large ball retainer (AB-16) into the hub shell with the balls down. Holding the drive screws (AB-318 and AB-328 or AB-418 and AB-428) for the overdrive transmission, insert them into the hub shell. Turn the parts clockwise until they seat (Fig. 10-14).

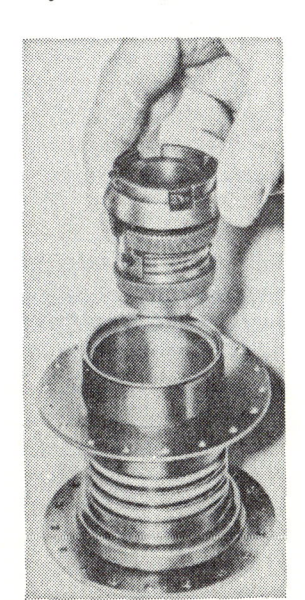

Fig. 10-13. Installing high-speed clutch and retarder subassembly into the hub shell. (Courtesy Bendix Bicycle & Ignition Components Division)

227

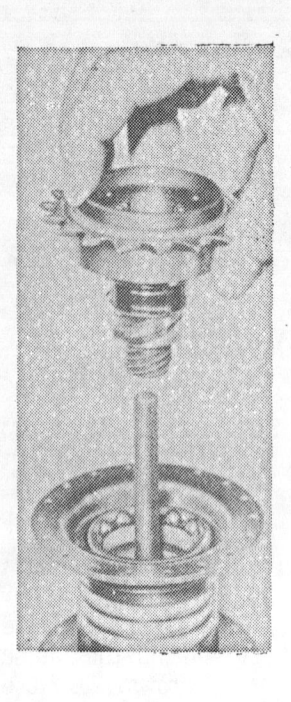

Fig 10-14. Drive screw installation. (Courtesy Bendix Bicycle & Ignition Components Division)

Place the small bearing retiner (AB-20) into the low-speed driver (AB-328) with the balls down. Turn the adjusting cone and sun gear (AB-7) on the axle until the sun gear touches the planet gears. Now turn the sun gear clockwise while at the same time turning the sprocket counterclockwise until the sun gear bottoms. Back the sun gear out 1/8 turn and secure it with the lock nut (AB-35). The rim of the wheel should have just a dab of side play. Adjust the sun gear as necessary.

STURMEY-ARCHER S3C

The S3C features a shoe-type coaster brake in combination with a three-speed planetary gear train. Low or first gear is an underdrive of 25 percent; normal or second is direct; and high or third gives a 33 1/3 percent overdrive. Sprockets are available in the usual Sturmey-Archer range—18 through 20 teeth with a 22 tooth grandma for hilly country.

Adjustment

As in all remote-controlled transmissions, the linkage must be periodically adjusted. Place the gear selector in "N" or direct drive. Turn the cable barrel (No. 3 in Fig. 10-15). Loosen the locknut (No. 2) and turn the adjustor barrel (No. 3) until the end of the indicator rod is dead level with the end of the axle. This can be seen through the inspection window in the right-hand axle nut.

It is no cause for concern that the indicator rod and coupling move outboard when the brake is applied in high gear. The clutch slides back over the ramps of the planet cage, moving the rod and coupling. When the brake is released, the cable adjustment returns to normal.

The hub-bearing clearance is correct when the wheel has just a trace of sideplay at the rim. If it is necessary to adjust the bearings, remove the brake arm clip and the indicator spindle. Loosen the axle nuts enough to slip the wheel out of the dropouts. Remove the left-hand axle nut, left-hand locknut, and the lockwasher. Turn the slotted adjustor nut as required to fix the amount of sideplay.

Replace the lockwasher securing it to the adjuster nut with a center punch. Replace the locknut and firm it snug. Install the wheel in the frame, tighten the axle nuts and brake-arm strap. Since removing and replacing the wheel almost invariably involves some change in chain tension, check the indicator linkage as previously described.

Troubleshooting

The most frequent cause of complaint is improper indicator-rod adjustment, followed by lack of lubrication. Oil with several drops of Sturmey-Archer lubricant through the hub lubricator. Do not use heavy grease or household oil.

- Juddering brake: Usually this fault can be traced to loose clip nuts.

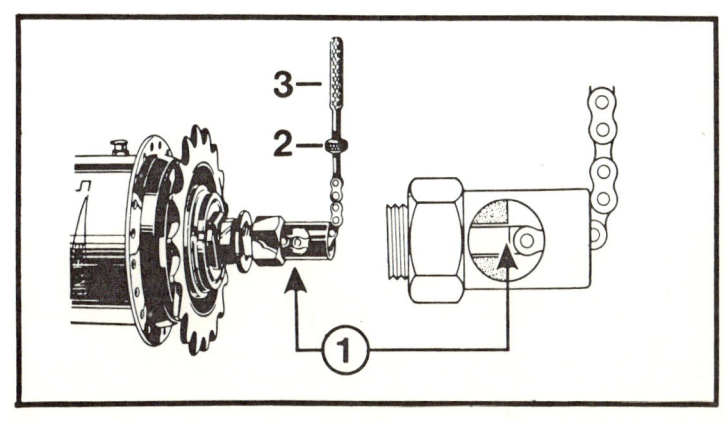

Fig. 10-15. S3C gear selector adjustment. (Courtesy Raleigh Industries Ltd.)

- Snatching brake: Should the braking action be erratic, oil the hub with a few drops of Sturmey-Archer oil.
- Squealing brake: Often this sympton is accompanied by a general decline in brake performance. The cure is to replace the shoes.
- No low gear: Assuming that the indicator-rod adjustment is correct, the problem may be caused by a distorted axle spring or by incorrect assembly of the low-gear pawls. They can be assembled upside down. Do not attempt to reform the spring—replace it instead.
- Slipping in low gear: One or more malfunctions may be involved here. The control cable can be kinked or abrased, the indicator coupling twisted, or the indicator rod out of adjustment. The right-hand cone may be positioned improperly on the axle, upsetting the special relationships inside the transmission. Another possibility is a worn or chipped sliding clutch.
- Transmission oscillates between low and normal (direct drive): Worn gear-ring pawls are the most likely culprit. Change both pawls.
- Slipping in normal gear (direct drive): Look for chipping and wear on the sliding clutch and gear-ring dogs. This difficulty is caused by incorrect shifting or chronic maladjustment. Replace the gear ring and/or the sliding clutch. The same symptom can be caused by an indicator rod not screwed fully into the axle key.
- Slipping in top gear: An incorrect right-hand cone adjustment can cause this problem. Other possibilities are worn pinion pins and a chipped or worn sliding clutch, as well as a distorted axle spring. At the risk of redundancy, allow me to repeat that the first thing to check is the indicator-rod adjustment and the control cable responsiveness.
- Hub turns stiffly: No sideplay at the hub bearings is the most likely source of this difficulty, followed by distorted and rubbing dust caps. Another possibility is a lack of lubrication or gum deposited on the mechanism by the use of improper oil. The dropouts must be perfectly parallel. Otherwise the transmission will be stressed and the parts may distort. The ball ring should have exactly 24 balls.
- Sluggish gear change: A Sturmey-Archer transmission almost snaps into gear when it is working correctly. Reluctance to shift may be caused by a distorted clutch spring, a bent axle, worn and sticking

links in the indicator linkage, an out-of-line cable pulley, or a binding cable.

Brake Service

It is not necessary or desirable to dismantle the entire hub to service the brakes. Many difficulties are simply the result of loose brake-arm clip nuts and can be corrected with the wheel in place. The brake band or shoes can be replaced by removing the wheel from the frame, and removing the left-hand fasteners (axle nut, lock nut, lockwasher, and slotted adjuster nut). Take out the brake-arm assembly and ball cage. Remove the brake band.

New brake bands should be pulled apart by hand to see that they are functional. If the band refuses to respond, give it a sharp crack on the bench to open the slot. Lubricate with generous amounts of Sturmey-Archer oil and install. The notches on the left-hand cone engage lugs on the brake band and on the actuating spring.

Assemble the wheel and test. If braking difficulties persist, the hub will have to be dismantled.

Hub Disassembly

Figure 10-16 is our reference picture. Remove the wheel from the frame as previously described. Begin disassembly from the right-hand (sprocket) side. Remove the gear-indicator coupling (No. 43) both axle nuts, and washers. Note the position of these washers for future reference.

Now go to the left or brake-arm side. Holding the axle by its flats (a Crescent wrench is ideal for this) loosen the left cone lucknut (No. 27). Take off the locknut and washer and back off the adjuster nut (No. 29) until it is clear of the brake arm. Use a dulled screwdriver to jar the nut free.

Moving to the right side, prevent the wheel from turning, and loosen the ball ring assembly (No. 20) with a hammer and punch. It has a normal right-hand thread (counterclockwise to loosen). Once the cup is loose, turn the hub over once again. Remove the adjuster nut (No. 29). The brake-arm assembly is now free and can be lifted out together with the ball cage (No. 8). With the axle held securely in a vise, remove the hub and wheel and set aside.

At this point the mechanism is held upright in the vise, stacked somewhat precariously like a three-decker ice cream cone. Work from the brake band (No. 10) down. Lift the band off, then remove the brake thrust plate or actuator (No. 12) by rotating it counterclockwise on the drive screw. Next comes the planet pawl ring assembly (No. 13).

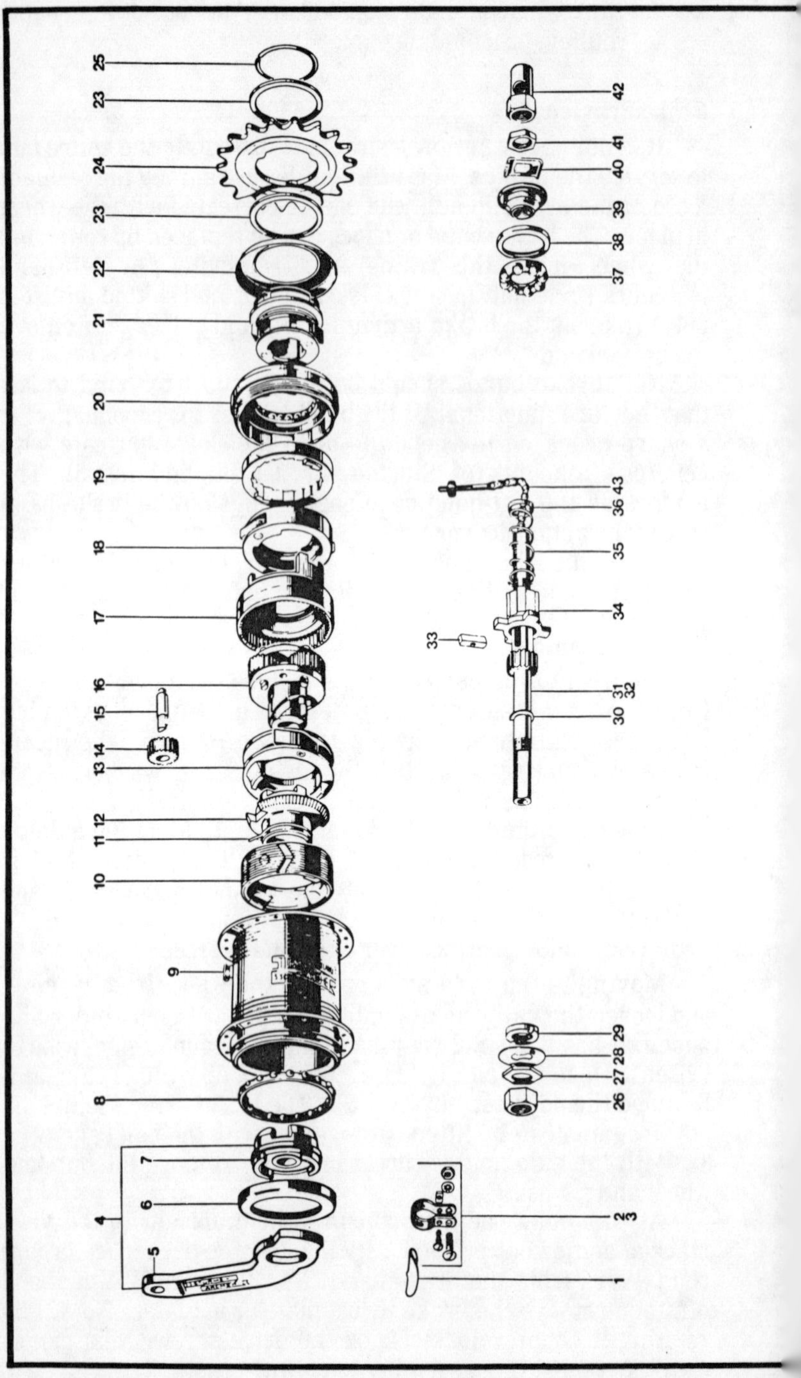
1
2
3
4
5
6
7
8
9
10
11
12
13
14
15
16
17
18
19
20
21
22
23
24
23
25
26
27
28
29
30
31
32
33
34
35
36
43
37
38
39
40
41
42

PHOTO No.	SALES No.	DESCRIPTION
1	HSH 401	Strengthening Pad
2	HCB 104	Brake Arm Clip – Sports
3	HCB 103	Brake Arm Clip – Roadster
4	HSH 446	Brake Arm & L.H. Cone Assembly
5	HSH 404	Brake Arm
6	HSH 447	Dust Cap for L.H. Cone
7	HSA 164	Cone – L.H.
8	HSA 106	Ball Retainer L.H.
9	HSH 448	Lubricator
10	HSH 407	Brake Band
11	HSH 408	Brake Actuating Spring
12	HSH 168	Brake Thrust Plate
13	HSA 111	Pawl Ring Assembly – for Planet Cage
13A	HSA 133	Pawl
13B	HSA 120	Pin See Assembly 13
13C	HSA 292	Spring
14	HSA 293	Planet Pinion
15	HSA 291	Pinion Pin
16	HSA 296	Planet Cage
17	HSA 307	Gear Ring
18	HSA 119	Pawl Ring Assembly – for Gear Ring
18A	HSA 133	Pawl
18B	HSA 253	Pin see Assembly 18
18C	HSA 304	Spring
19	HSA 308	Ratchet Ring
20		Ball Ring Assembly with Dust Cap – 24 ($\frac{3}{16}$″ diam.) Ball Bearings
21	HSA 311	Driver and Brake Operating Pawls

PHOTO No.	SALES No.	DESCRIPTION
21A	HSA 300	Pawl
21B	HSA 301	Pin see Assembly 21
21C	HSA 302	Spring
21D	HSA 303	Circlip
22	HSA 102	Dust Cap – Sprocket
23	HMW 127	Spacing Washer – for Sprocket
24	HSL 714-722	Sprocket Range 14T to 20T & 22T
25	HSL 721	Circlip for Sprocket
26	HMN 128	Axle Nut – L.H. side
27	HMN 335	Lock Nut
28	HMN 156	Lock Washer
29	HMN 334	Adjuster Nut
30	HSL 725	Circlip – for Securing Planet Cage
31	HSA 313	Axle 6″ (152 mm)
33	HSA 295	Key for Axle
34	HSA 294	Clutch
35	HSA 128	Clutch Spring
36	HSA 129	Spring Cap
37	HSA 284	Ball Retainer – for Driver – ($\frac{1}{4}$″ Diam.) Ball Bearings
38	HSA 102	Dustcap – for Driver Ball Retainer
39	HSA 257	Cone – R.H.
40	HMW 147	Lockwasher for Cone
41	HMN 132	Locknut – for R.H. Cone
42	HMN 129	Axle Nut R.H.
43	HSA 126	Gear Indicator Coupling – 6″ Axle (152 mm)

Fig. 10-16. Sturmey-Archer 2S3C hub. (Courtesy Raleigh Industries Ltd.)

233

Turn the assembly over, clamping the left end of the axle in the vise at the flats. Remove the cone locknut (No. 41) and lock washer (No. 40). Late production S3cs feature a nylon spring cap (No. 36). The metal cap offered no problem, but this one will not pass through the driver. A special technique is required.

Hold the ball retainer (No. 37) down while turning the driver assembly (No. 21) to the right. This will allow the spring (No. 35) to force the cup out. As the pawls clear the ball retainer, squeeze them in and lift the driver assembly clear of the spring and cap. Lift out the spring and the cap.

Nest, remove the pinion pins (No. 15) and planet pinion (No. 14). Once again, turn the axle over in the vise. Pry off the planet cage circlip (No. 30) and remove the planet cage (No. 16).

Inspection

Clean all parts in solvent and scrutinize each part with particular attention to:

- axle for straightness
- gear teeth
- bearing races
- ratchets and pawls
- pinion pins, sliding clutch, driver and gear-ring splines, planet-cage dogs, and cam surfaces
- contact surfaces of the brake thrust plate and gear and rachet ring
- dust caps for signs of contact
- brake arm fit in its recess in the left-hand cone. The brake arm is an interference fit and should be immobile in the cone recess. Damage usually takes the form of chipping of one or both parts
- actuator spring for distortion or loss of tension. Don't guess about this part: if you have any doubt that it is less than perfect, replace it

There is no point in removing the pawl and pawl pins from their respective rings. Replace as an assembly. (It is suggested, however, that you replace the old solid pawl pins with the newer hollow type.)

Assembly

As is usual with complex units, assembly is best done as a sequence of subassemblies.

Planet Cage. Hold the pawl ring so the pawl facing you is angled upwards. The parts relationship is shown in Fig. 10-17. Hold the spring (part of the assembly and not listed

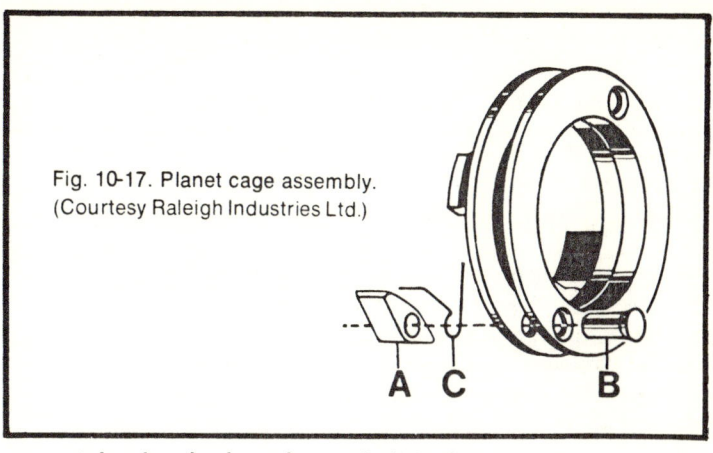

Fig. 10-17. Planet cage assembly.
(Courtesy Raleigh Industries Ltd.)

separately) by the bent leg and slide the other leg under the pin and to the right of the pawl. Press down the short end of the pawl and gently ease the spring over the corner of the pawl. Do the same for the others.

Gear Ring. This one is tricky. Hold the gear ring between your forefinger and thumb. Turn the pawl so that the inside of the pawl faces out. Hold the spring at its bend and slide it between the pawl and ring. Pull the spring through until it is seated against the pin. Slip the spring over the edge of the pawl so that the pawl is loaded in its normal operating position. See Fig. 10-18. Rivet the pawls, spreading the outboard ends to keep them in place.

Driver. Hold the driver with the inboard end facing you. Hold the spring by its bent leg and slide it between the pawl and driver. The long leg of the spring must be outside the driver. Turn pawl to its operative position. See Fig. 10-19.

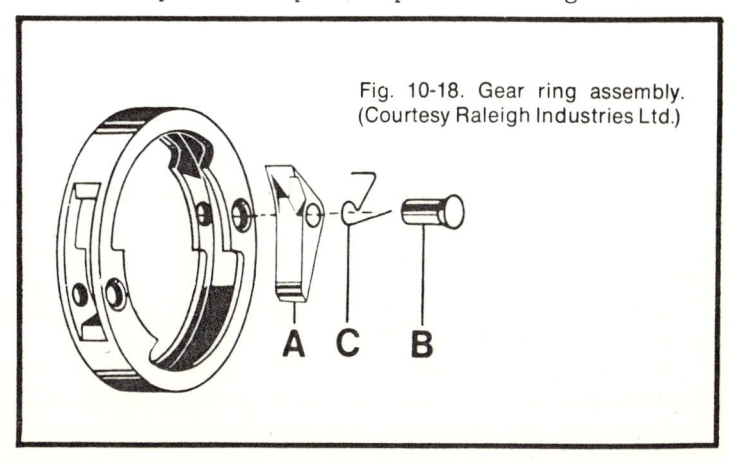

Fig. 10-18. Gear ring assembly.
(Courtesy Raleigh Industries Ltd.)

235

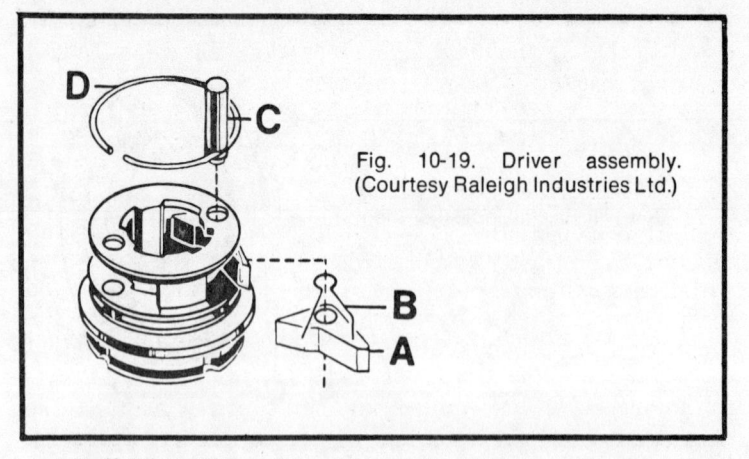

Fig. 10-19. Driver assembly. (Courtesy Raleigh Industries Ltd.)

Ball Ring. If need be, pry off the dust cap (Fig. 10-16, No. 22) being careful not to distort it and replace the bearings. The ball ring (No. 20) is loaded with 24 3-16- inch balls and should be packed with Shell Alvania No. 3 or the equivalent. Press the dust cap on, using a vise and hardwood blocks. Check for easy rotation of the balls after the cap is in place.

Brake Arm and Cone. Place the left-hand dust cap (Fig. 10-16, No. 8) over the left-hand cone (No. 7) and press the brake arm into the slots. The name "Sturmey Archer" stamped in the arm should be on the outboard side. Smear Shell Alvania No. 3 in the ball track of the left-hand cone (inside of the hub shell).

Final Assembly

Now that the subassemblies are together, we can proceed with final assembly of the transmission. Hold the right-hand end of the axle in the vise. Drop the planet cage (No. 16)—actuator thread uppermost—on the axle. Secure the cage with the circlip (No. 30). Reverse the axle in the vise, add the planet pinions (No. 14) and pins (No. 15), making certain that the D-shaped ends of the pins are facing downwards. The flat of the D is outwards.

Insert the axle key (No. 33) with the hole facing upwards into the axle slot, slide the clutch (No. 34), with the large diameter down, over the axle and key. The four clutch dogs should engage the planet pinion pins. Screw the gear-indicator coupling (No. 43) into the key.

Install gear ring (No. 17) and the previously assembled gear-ring pawl (No. 18). The heads of the pawl pins face upwards. Insert the ratchet ring (No. 19) into the right-hand ball ring (No. 20) and place these over the gear-ring assembly.

The tabs face downwards to engage the pawl ring. Install the ball ring (No. 20) holding the planet cage and turning the ball cup clockwise to check for free operation.

Fit the driver subassembly (No. 21) on hubs fitted with a metal spring cap. Pawls face counterclockwise. Turn clockwise until seated. Fit the clutch spring (No. 35) and cap (No. 36). Install the right-hand cone (No. 39) and run up finger tight. If the hub is fitted with a nylon spring cap, install the cap and spring first. Now install the driver and hold it down while fitting the right-hand cone. The cone should be finger tight and locked into position with washer (No. 40) and the locknut (No. 41). *Note:* Do not back off the cone more than 5/8 turn, as that would throw off the geometry of the hub.

Reverse the assembled unit in the vise. Install the planet-cage pawl-ring (No. 13) over the flats of the pinion pins. The dogs should face outwards. If the ring does not seat, ensure that the flat section of the D-shaped pin end is facing outwards and the pawl-ring dogs are seated on the brake-thrust plate (No. 12). The leg of the brake-actuating spring (No. 11) must face outwards. When the actuator is down on the pawl rings, but not engaged, turn the pawl ring counterclockwise until the dogs engage. Then turn counterclockwise to seat the actuator. Install the brake band (inner projections facing up) over the brake-thrust plate.

Remove the assembled mechanism from the vise. Hold the wheel horizontally and insert the assembled mechanism into the hub shell from below and screw in the right-hand ball ring (No. 20). Tighten with a hammer and blunted punch.

Fit the left-hand ball retainer (No. 8) with balls down, in the left-hand ball race. Fit the left-hand cone and brake-arm subassembly (No. 4). Note that the brake-band projections must engage the large slots in the cone—i.e., the spring leg is in narrow slot at 90 degrees to the large slot.

Screw the adjustor nut (No. 29) on the axle (finger tight). Fit lock washer (No. 28) and locknut (No. 27). Adjust for a trace of side play at the rim and none at the hub. Secure the adjuster nut after adjustment, and center punch lockwasher over the slot in the adjuster nut. Tighten the locknut.

Replace the wheel in the frame as described previously. The strengthening pad (1) is fitted to sports machines. Do not twist the brake arm sideways when tightening the clip. Adjust the gears.

SHIMANO 3.3.3.

The basic Shimano hub is the 3.3.3 which, as sold in this country, generally incorporates a coaster brake (Fig. 10-20). The transmission offers a 25 percent underdriver, direct drive,

Shimano Three Speed Hub with Coaster Brake

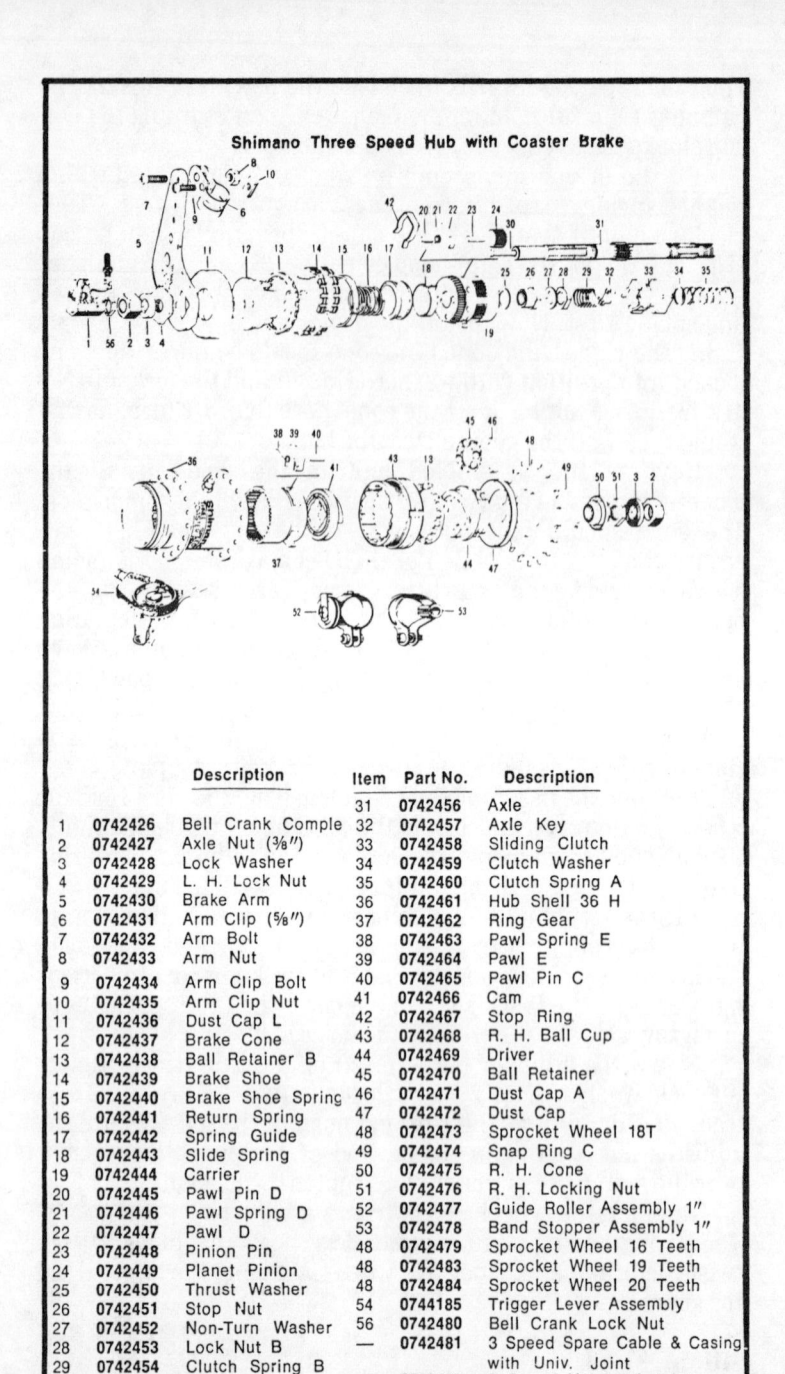

Item	Part No.	Description	Item	Part No.	Description
			31	0742456	Axle
1	0742426	Bell Crank Comple	32	0742457	Axle Key
2	0742427	Axle Nut (3/8")	33	0742458	Sliding Clutch
3	0742428	Lock Washer	34	0742459	Clutch Washer
4	0742429	L. H. Lock Nut	35	0742460	Clutch Spring A
5	0742430	Brake Arm	36	0742461	Hub Shell 36 H
6	0742431	Arm Clip (5/8")	37	0742462	Ring Gear
7	0742432	Arm Bolt	38	0742463	Pawl Spring E
8	0742433	Arm Nut	39	0742464	Pawl E
9	0742434	Arm Clip Bolt	40	0742465	Pawl Pin C
10	0742435	Arm Clip Nut	41	0742466	Cam
11	0742436	Dust Cap L	42	0742467	Stop Ring
12	0742437	Brake Cone	43	0742468	R. H. Ball Cup
13	0742438	Ball Retainer B	44	0742469	Driver
14	0742439	Brake Shoe	45	0742470	Ball Retainer
15	0742440	Brake Shoe Spring	46	0742471	Dust Cap A
16	0742441	Return Spring	47	0742472	Dust Cap
17	0742442	Spring Guide	48	0742473	Sprocket Wheel 18T
18	0742443	Slide Spring	49	0742474	Snap Ring C
19	0742444	Carrier	50	0742475	R. H. Cone
20	0742445	Pawl Pin D	51	0742476	R. H. Locking Nut
21	0742446	Pawl Spring D	52	0742477	Guide Roller Assembly 1"
22	0742447	Pawl D	53	0742478	Band Stopper Assembly 1"
23	0742448	Pinion Pin	48	0742479	Sprocket Wheel 16 Teeth
24	0742449	Planet Pinion	48	0742483	Sprocket Wheel 19 Teeth
25	0742450	Thrust Washer	48	0742484	Sprocket Wheel 20 Teeth
26	0742451	Stop Nut	54	0744185	Trigger Lever Assembly
27	0742452	Non-Turn Washer	56	0742480	Bell Crank Lock Nut
28	0742453	Lock Nut B	—	0742481	3 Speed Spare Cable & Casing with Univ. Joint
29	0742454	Clutch Spring B			
30	0742455	Push Rod	—	0742482	3 Speed Universal Joint

Fig. 10-20. The Shimano 3.3.3 hub and coaster brake. (Courtesy Browning)

and a 33 percent overdrive. In all, the mechanism is reminiscent of the Sturmey-Archer, although its designers claim some superiority in the shift mechanism.

Adjustment

The Shimano employs a bell crank rather than the trouble-prone chain. Put the shift trigger in second (normal) gear. A red "N" should appear at the window of the bell-crank housing (Fig. 10-21). If the mark is not centered, loosen the knurled locknut and turn the gear adjustment barrel. For large adjustments loosen the ferrule and move it along the chain stay. There should always be a generous thread in the cable barrel for mechanical strength.

Teardown

Figure 10-20 is our reference picture. Dismount the wheel and fix the assembly in a vise, sprocket up. Remove right-hand cone (No. 50) and lift the sprocket and clutch spring (No. 35) up and off. Next comes the sliding clutch (No. 33), ball retainer (No. 13) and cam (No. 41). This sequence is shown in Fig. 10-22. Lift off the hub carefully.

The next operation requires a special Shimano tool. The right-hand ball cup (No. 43) is threaded into the hub. Insert the tool and remove the cup, shim (if present), and ring gear (No. 37). Remove the axle key (No. 32) and spring (No. 29). Note the slot in the key faces away from the sprocket.

Turn the axle over and remove the locknut (No. 4). The parts are sequenced as shown in Fig. 10-23. Loosen the stop nut (No. 26), remove the non-turn washer (No. 27), locknut B (No. 28), spring guide (No. 17), and carrier (No. 19).

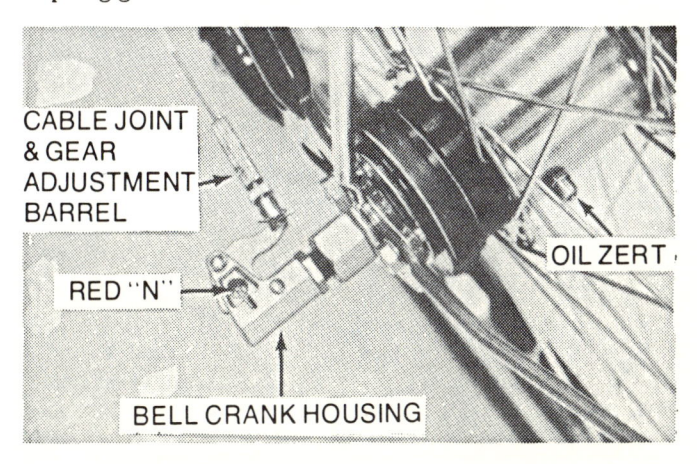

Fig. 10-21. Shimano adjustments. (Courtesy Browning)

Fig. 10-22. Shimano parts sequence, brake side. (Courtesy Browning)

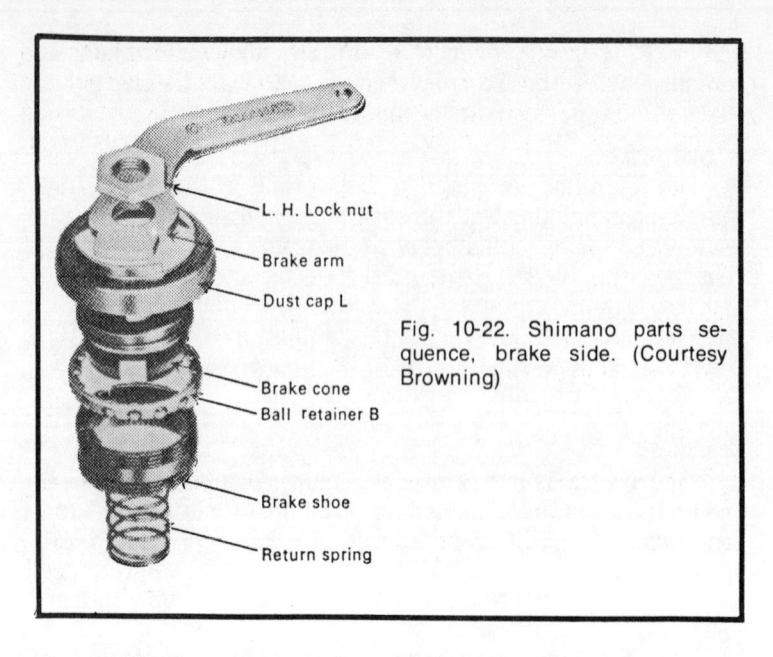

No further disassembly is possible. Clean all parts in solvent and dry with compressed air or a clean, lintless rag. Scrutinize each part with a jeweler's eye for wear. Inspect the bearing runs for brinnelling, pitting, and irregular tracking. Oval wear marks on the cones and cups mean that the bearings have been run loose or the axle is bent. Replace the slide spring (No. 18), pawl springs D (No. 21), and pawl springs E (No. 38) for the insurance value. Inspect the pawls for wear on their tips and the drive screw for chipping.

Coat all bearings, pinion and sun gears, and brake shoes with liberal amounts of light grease. Medium-grade (30W) motor oil should be applied to the other parts.

Assembly

With the axle mounted in a vise—push-rod hole—place the carrier and pinion assembly (No. 19) on the axle. The spring guide (No. 17) is next. It has dogs on its bottom surface which mesh with holes in the carrier. Place the slide spring (No. 18) over it. Add the stop nut, nonturn washer, and locknut B. The parts stack will look as it did in Fig. 10-23. Place the return spring (No. 16) over the stop nut. Insert retainer B (No. 13) over the brake cone (No. 12), with the retainer positioned as shown in the exploded view. The brake shoe (No. 14) indexes with grooves on the cone. Grease these parts if you haven't already.

Slip the return spring over the axle and install the cone and brake shoe. The brake cone has a narrow slot to accept the curved end of the slide spring. Be sure these parts are mated before going on. Assemble the dust cap (No. 11), brake arm (No. 5), and locknut (No. 4).

At this point we have to check the brake adjustment. The clearance between the edge of the brake shoe and the serrated portion of the carrier should be between 0.5 and 1 mm or, 0.02-0.04 inch. Measure with a feeler gauge. A 0.1 mm leaf should pass freely between the two parts with some resistance; a 0.2 mm leaf should be blocked. If the clearance is too great, tighten the locknut (No. 4); if too small, loosen it.

Turn the assembly over and mount it vertically in the vise, gripping it at the brake arm. Insert the clutch spring B (No.

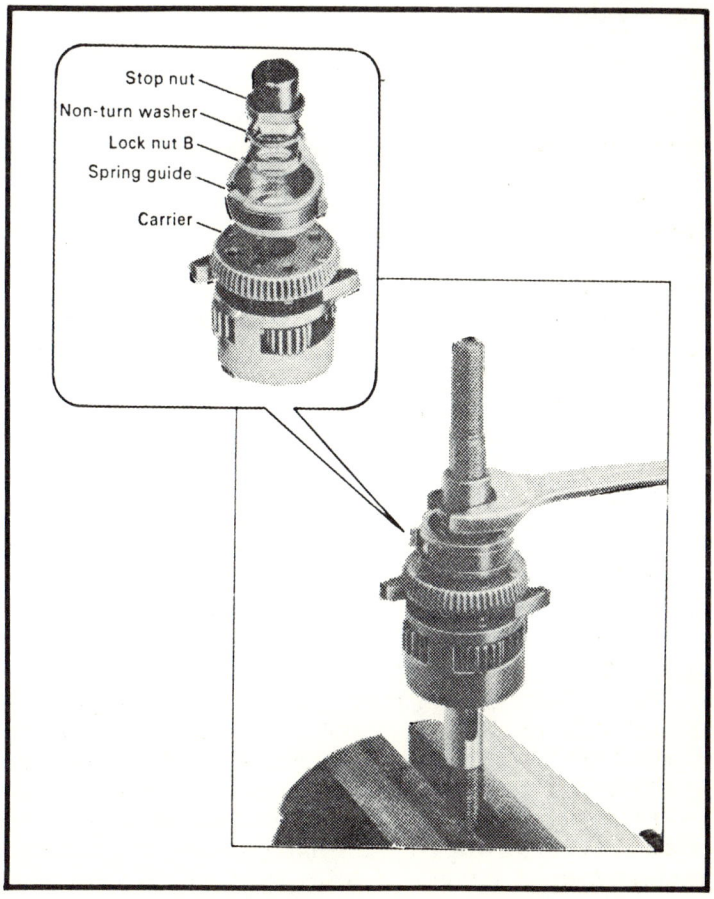

Fig. 10-23. Carrier and related parts. (Courtesy Browning)

29) and the axle key (No. 32). The key goes as shown in the drawing—ears down. Slide the hub home. Next insert the ring gear (No. 37) into the shell. Squeeze the pawls together so the parts mesh. Now thread the right-hand ball cup (No. 43) in behind it. Start the threads by hand and finish with the special tool. The sliding clutch (No. 33) follows. Turn it counterclockwise so it mates with pawl E (No. 39) of the ring gear. When in place it should be able to travel up and down on the axle.

The cam (No. 41) fits over the squared-off end of the clutch. Assemble the clutch washer (No. 34) and clutch spring A (No. 35) over the axle. The washer and spring end fit into a relief in the end of the clutch. Insert retainer B (No. 13), balls down. The driver (No. 44) and sprocket are next, followed by the right-hand cone (No. 50), locknut (No. 51), and axle fittings. Adjust the right-hand cone so that there is no play in the driver.

Changing sprockets is simple on this unit. Remove the snap ring using a small screwdriver as a pry bar. Protect your eyes and fingers since the snap ring can bite. The sprocket lifts off.

Three diameters are available: 18, 19, and 20 teeth. Table 10-1 gives the equivalent gearing:

Table 10-1. Shimano 33.3 Equivalent Gearing

Ratio	Sprocket 18T	19T	20T
High gear (1:1.33)	13.5T	14.2T	15T
Normal (1:1)	18T	19T	20T
Low gear	24T	25.3T	26.6T

As shown in the table if an 18 tooth wheel were fitted, high gear would be the same as having a sprocket with 13.5T. In low, the same sprocket would act like one with 24 teeth.

Install the wheel in the dropouts, secure the brake arm, and tighten the locknuts. The push rod should extend approximately 1/2 inch out of the axle as shown in Fig. 10-24. The bell crank is turned over the axle until it comes to rest against the stop screw (Fig. 10-25). The crank pivot should be in line with cable. Align it and tighten the locknut (Fig. 10-20, item 56) to make certain the crank stays put. Place the shift trigger in "N" and adjust the gears as described previously.

Fig. 10-24. The push rod should extend 1/2 inch out of the axle. (Courtesy Browning)

SHIMANO DISC BRAKE

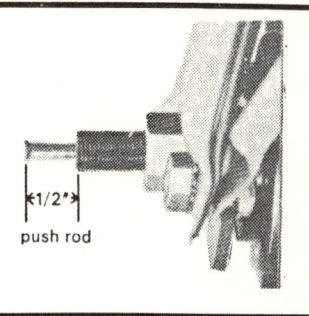

The Shimano disc brake is the most exciting news in bicycle brakes since the invention of the coaster brake. Disc brakes were originally developed for aircraft with the double aim of reducing landing distances and weight. Two types evolved: the fixed caliper and the floating caliper. Both have friction pads on either side of the disc which is mounted on the wheel and rotates with it. The fixed caliper variety energizes both sets of pads with individual hydraulic cylinders; the floating caliper type is mechanically simpler since only one pad set is energized. As this pad (or multiple-pad set) is energized, it makes contact with the disc. Since the caliper "floats," additional pressure on the pads displaces the caliper and causes the second (or fixed) set to come into action, sandwiching the disc between both sets. Disc brakes are widely used on domestic and foreign automobiles (the first American car to employ them was the all-but-forgotten Crosley Hotshot) and are becoming quite popular on motorcycles. All contempory designs use a floating caliper.

What are the advantages of this brake? Several at least in theory. The first is the ability of the brake to dissipate heat,

Fig. 10-25. Bell crank and stop screw. (Courtesy Browning)

and the disc compares very favorably with the drum, coaster, and other sheathed brake mechanisms. However, heat dissipation does not appear to be superior to that of a good rim brake. A second advantage is the ability to perform when wet. Both rim and disc brakes tend to throw water off the braking surface as the wheel turns, while the moped-derived drum brake used on some bicycles tends to trap water. The radial slots cut into the Shimano disc appear to function as water vents, rather than as cooling vents, and coupled with the distance of the disc from the pavement, helps give quicker wet stops on rain-puddled roadways.

Another advantage is the relative directness of the actuating mechanism in contrast to the levers and arms involved in a rim brake. The Shimano is not by any means simple, yet the action is very direct, with most of the members in simple compression.

The most convincing evidence thus far of the disc brake's superiority for bicycle applications is the results of a test run by the U.S. Testing Company in March, 1974.

In all, eleven bikes were tested by three riders whose weights ranged from 158 to 188 pounds. Six machines were equipped with Shimano disc brakes and Shimano Tourney center pulls on the front wheels. The others were equipped with Diacompe, Weimann 750 (Vainqueur 999), Altemburger, and Cherry center pulls. Freshly uncrated bikes were used with their brakes set to factory recommended clearances.

Each of the three riders rode all bikes. The first part of the test was to measure stopping distances on dry asphalt from 15 mph. The results are shown in Table 10-2. The second test was under wet conditions. The pavement was saturated and the

Table 10-2. Braking Test Results

	Disc Brake (Average of All Runs in Feet)	Rim Brake (Average of All Runs in Feet)
Dry Test		
Rider A (158.5 lbs)	10.69	15.84
Rider B (158 lbs)	6.98	13.03
Rider C (188.5 lbs)	11.56	16.97
Wet Test		
Rider A	21.46	48.37
Rider B	16.22	52.64
Rider C	20.91	56.36

pads were sprayed with water both before riding and as the machines approached the starting line. The results are interesting.

The U.S. Testing Company is an independent testing laboratory whose stock-in-trade is its reputation for honest, impartial evaluation. At the same time, the pros have not stood in line to buy this brake. Many say they have tried the disc and do not find any particular merit in it.

Adjustment

The adjustment procedure is somewhat different than for the typical rim brake in that the cable adjuster (Fig. 10-26, No. 17) only functions to add or remove cable slack at the handlebar lever. The brake adjustments involve the adjuster (No 15) and the bolts (Nos. 3, 4, adjusting and setting and 5).

Remove the bracket cover (No. 2) which is fixed by the Phillips screws (No. 1). Loosen the setting bolt (No. 5). It is secured by the locknut (No. 6). Turn the large adjuster (No. 15) clockwise with a pair of pliers until the wheel locks solid. Now turn the adjuster half a revolution counterclockwise. If the wheel is free to rotate, turn the setting bolt (No. 5) until it just touches holder A (No. 16). Tighten the locknut (No. 6).

Should the wheel drag, the problem involves misaligned pads. There are three adjustment bolts located on the bracket: two are identified as bolts A and are shown as No. 3, the lower bolt B is No. 4. Bolt A aligns the inboard pad horizontally with the disc; bolt B takes care of the vertical alignment. Loosen all bolts then tighten them very gradually until pad A and the disc plate are paralled. (See Fig. 10-27). After you are satisfied with the alignment, tighten the bolts evenly for optimum pad clearance. After each adjustment, spin the wheel to insure that it turns freely. Turn the setting bolt (No. 5) clockwise until it touches the holder lightly then tighten the locknut (No. 6).

The cable wire should be adjusted so that the pads contact the disc during the first third of handlebar-lever travel. Loosen the serrated locknut at the cable barrel (No. 17) and turn the barrel counterclockwise to tauten the cable wire.

Pad Replacement

After long service the pads wear beyond the point of adjustment. To replace the pads you will need the following:

- 6 mm socket wrench
- Phillips screwdriver
- 7 mm open-end wrench

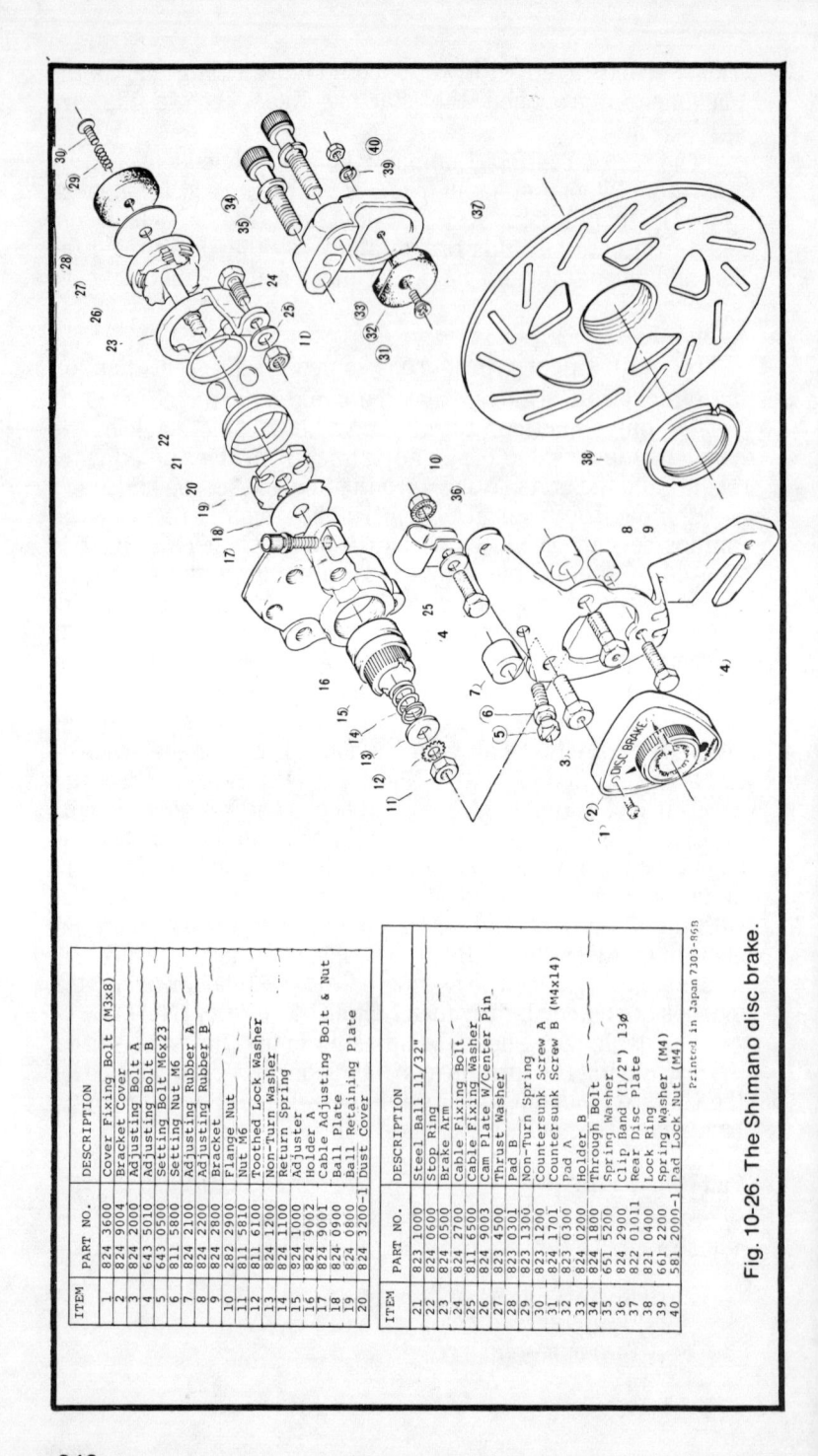

ITEM	PART NO.	DESCRIPTION
1	824 3600	Cover Fixing Bolt (M3x8)
2	824 9004	Bracket Cover
3	824 2000	Adjusting Bolt A
4	643 5010	Adjusting Bolt B
5	643 0500	Setting Bolt M6x23
6	811 5800	Setting Nut M6
7	824 2100	Adjusting Rubber A
8	824 2200	Adjusting Rubber B
9	824 2800	Bracket
10	282 2900	Flange Nut
11	811 5810	Nut M6
12	811 6100	Toothed Lock Washer
13	824 1200	Non-Turn Washer
14	824 1100	Return Spring
15	824 1000	Adjuster
16	824 9002	Holder A
17	824 9001	Cable Adjusting Bolt & Nut
18	824 0900	Ball Plate
19	824 0800	Ball Retaining Plate
20	824 3200-1	Dust Cover

ITEM	PART NO.	DESCRIPTION
21	823 1000	Steel Ball 11/32"
22	824 0600	Stop Ring
23	824 0500	Brake Arm
24	824 2700	Cable Fixing Bolt
25	811 6500	Cable Fixing Washer
26	824 9003	Cam Plate W/Center Pin
27	823 4500	Thrust Washer
28	823 0301	Pad B
29	823 1300	Non-Turn Spring
30	823 1200	Countersunk Screw A
31	823 1701	Countersunk Screw B (M4x14)
32	823 0300	Pad A
33	824 0200	Holder B
34	824 1800	Through Bolt
35	651 5200	Spring Washer
36	824 2900	Clip Band (1/2") 13∅
37	822 01011	Rear Disc Plate
38	821 0400	Lock Ring
39	661 2200	Spring Washer (M4)
40	581 2000-1	Pad Lock Nut (M4)

Printed in Japan 7303-869

Fig. 10-26. The Shimano disc brake.

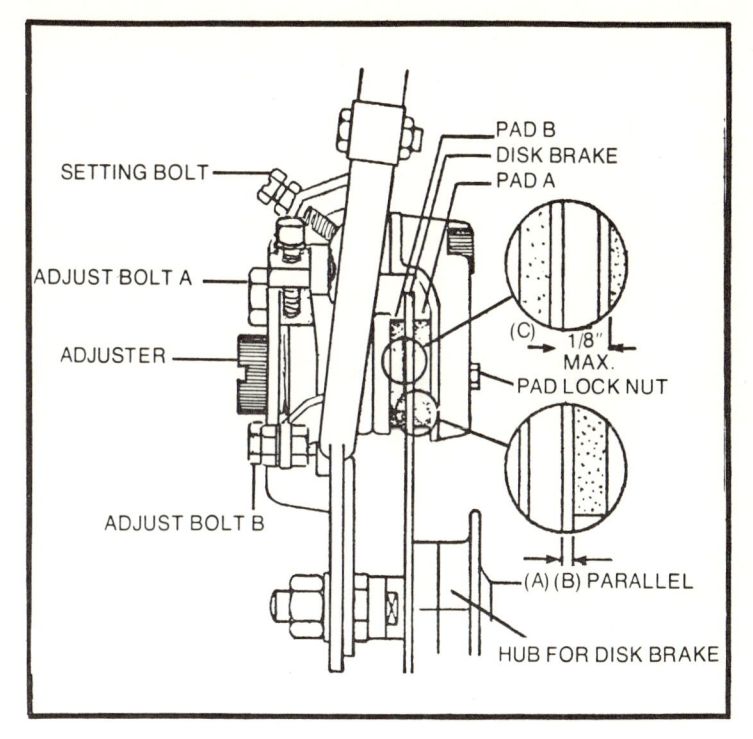

Fig. 10-27. Adjustment procedure for pad A.

Remove the wheel from the frame and with a 6 mm socket wrench, loosen the through bolts (No. 34) keeping the holders (No. 16 and 33) together.

Take the wheel out of the frame. Remove the through bolts with the socket wrench. Pad B (No. 28) can be removed when the countersunk screw (No. 30) is removed. Note the presence of the nonturn spring (No. 29) under the screw. Next remove the countersunk screw (No. 31) securing the A pad. It is backed up by a lockwasher (No. 39) and a nut (No. 40).

Place a new pad on each holder. Secure pad A by tightening the countersunk screw snugly against its nut and washer. Do the same for pad B, but after tightening the screw, give the pad a half-turn counterclockwise. This will provide space for the pad to float. The nonturn spring prevents the screw from vibrating loose.

Assemble the holders (Nos. 16 and 33), securing them with the through-bolts (No. 34). Attach the cover to the disc brake and mount the wheel on the frame. Then adjust as outlined previously.

11

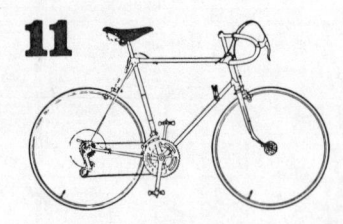

Hanger and Headsets

The hanger set consists of the pedals, chain wheels, crank (which may be a single forging or built up from a pair of cranks, axle, and attaching hardware), bearing, cups, cones or inner races, spacers, nuts and locknuts. The assembly is suspended from the bottom bracket and is sturdy enough to handle forces of several tons.

The hanger set needs occassional dismantling when bearings and races fail, or for cleaning and lubrication. Less than complete dismantling is required to replace or repair the external parts and to adjust the bearing end clearance.

AMERICAN PEDALS

American pedals are identified by the rubber inserts. The term American is something of a misnomer today since few pedals are still manufactured in this country. But it is descriptive in that these pedals, suitable for ordinary show leather, were and remain identified with domestic middle-weight bikes. In addition they are used on children's bikes, three- and five-speed machines, and on the less imposing ten-speeds.

The cheapest of these pedals are pressed and crimped together, making repair more trouble than it's worth. Middle and upper grades can be disassembled and, if you are very lucky, parts are available, but do not bank on it. (An exception is ball bearings which can be purchased without difficulty.)

Removal

Use a thin-section wrench to remove the pedal from the crank. Note: the left-hand pedal has a left-hand thread. The letter *L* is marked on the threaded end of the spindle where it passes through the crank. Turn clockwise to remove. The right pedal, marked *R*, has a standard right-hand thread.

Some persuasion may be required to loosen the left-hand pedal since it tightens with use. Soak with penetrating oil for several hours. Have someone hold the crank while you shock the wrench with a hammer. As brutal as this is and sounds, it is the only way to loosen some pedals. Enough heat to do the job will burn the chrome plating on the crank.

Inspect the threads carefully. You may find that the troublesome left-hand thread has been partially stripped by someone who assumed a standard thread. Repairs are not advised. It is cheaper and, in the long run, less trouble to replace the crank arm or crank.

Overhaul

Remove the pedals from the crank. Next, remove the two small nuts holding the frame and rubber pads to the spindle. The outer end of the frame doubles as the dust guard. Place the spindle upright in a vise with the jaws gripping the flats. Remove the locknut and washer (if fitted). Remove the cone. The cone will typically be slotted and a specially ground tool is useful, although you can do as well with a small screwdriver. Work on the slot on one side of the spindle and rotate counterclockwise. Be careful, for the bearings are loose and will be lost forever if you are not careful.

Holding the parts together, gingerly remove the spindle from the vise. Complete the disassembly over a large container to catch the rain of bearings.

Clean all parts, excepting the rubber pads, in solvent. Inspect for wear and the spindle for trueness. Mount the spindle in the vise as before. Coat the end of the barrel (the cylindrical part which fits over the spindle and is flared on the ends to accept the bearings) with grease. Place half of the bearings along the inner surface of the flare. The grease will hold the little buggers in place long enough to slip the barrel over the spindle. Place the remaining bearings in the upper or outboard flare. Tweezers help.

Thread the cone tightly over the spindle to seat the bearings, then back off until you have just a tiny amount of end play. Install the lock washer and locknut. The lock washer will be keyed to the spindle so that it does not turn when the locknut

Fig. 11-1 American pedal. (Courtesy Ware's Cycles)

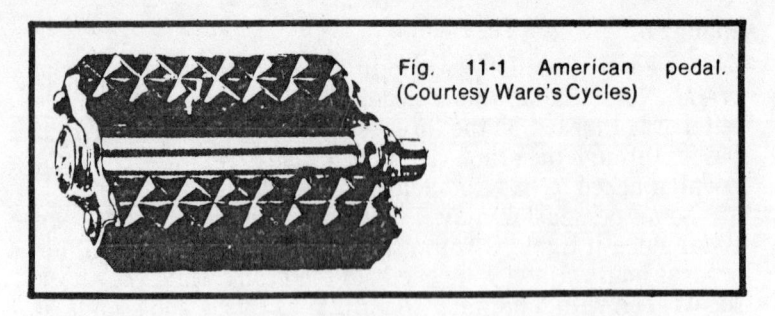

is tightened. After the locknut is tight, recheck the end clearance. Assemble the frame, tightening the nuts securely. Thread the pedal on the crank.

CONTINENTAL PEDALS

The term *continental* is as misleading as *American* when referring to pedals, since many continental types are made in the Orient. But this was the original European or rat trap pattern. Figure 11-2 illustrates one popular configuration. The pedal has serrations rather than rubber pads (which are slick when wet). The better rat traps are made of dural, while the cheaper types are of mild steel. A variation is the platform type without serrations, designed to be used with shoe cleats.

Overhaul

Overhaul procedures are almost identical to those for American pedals. The left-hand pedal is unthreaded by turning clockwise. The dust cap is threaded on any continental pedal pretending to quality, although a few use snap-on dust caps which must be pried off. Mount upright in a vise and remove the dust cap, locknut, lock washer, and cone from the outboard side. The bearings are loose. The outboard bearings can be retrieved with a magnet. Separation of the pedal frame and spindle is best done over a large container to catch the lower bearing set. Clean parts in solvent and inspect. Assemble with

Fig. 11-2. Rat trap pedal. (Courtesy Ware's Cycles)

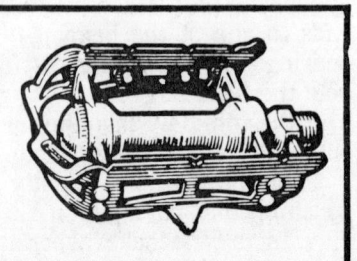

the aid of light grease. Place the lower bearings around the circumference of the flare, imbedded in the grease. Mount the spindle in the vise and gingerly slide the pedal barrel and frame over the spindle. Nervousness will be rewarded with the pitter-patter of little bearings bouncing over the floor. Insert the upper bearings in the outboard flare and thread the cone on the spindle. Tighten and back off a fraction of a turn. Check the adjustment. The pedal should spin freely over the spindle with very little up and down play. Install the lock washer and locknut. Tighten and check the clearance again.

AMERICAN CRANKS

There are three types of cranks in use today. The one-piece crank, combining both crankarms and the axle in a single forging, is known as the American or Astabula crank. It is found on many American bikes and on some of the imports. While one-piece cranks are subject to criticism because of the weight, they have the virtue of near indestructability.

Overhaul

As with all hanger sets, disassembly is from the left (chain wheeless) side. Remove the pedal. Proceed to the locknut, shown to the far left in Fig. 11-3. It, like the pedal, has a left-hand thread. Remove by turning clockwise. Behind the nut you will find a lock washer, keyed to a slot in the crank axle. The cone is slotted to accept a small screwdriver placed on either side of the crank. It may be stubborn and require the use of a punch. Turn it clockwise to loosen since it shares the same left-hand thread as the locknut.

The bearings are normally caged with this type of crank. On most bikes the crank, together with the fixed cone and the chain-wheel side bearing can be slipped out of the hanger at this point. High-rise bikes sometimes require that the chain-wheel side bearing cup be removed for clearance. Drive it out of the hanger with a long drift pin, working from the left side.

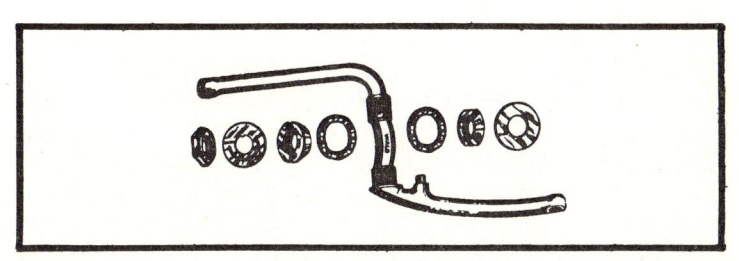

Fig. 11-3. American one-piece crankset. (Courtesy Action Accessories)

The chain wheel is secured by the stationary cone which has a normal right-hand thread. If it is necessary to remove the chain wheel, turn the cone using a large adjustable wrench. Some of these cones can be tight and you may have to mount the assembly in a vise. Position the jaws on the flats of the cone and rap the crank arms with a soft-faced mallet or hardwood block. There may be a spacer between the chain wheel and the cone.

Clean the parts in solvent and inspect paying particular attention to the cones and hanger cuts. If the bearing runs look like a rutted road, replace all friction surfaces—bearings, cones, and hubs. These parts are quite inexpensive. Check the balls for pitting and rust specks. The tiniest degree of rust is reason to replace the set. Lubricate generously with light grease. The correct way to do this is the messy way: Put a glob of grease in the center of your palm, and holding the bearing in your other hand, scrape the grease into the retainer. Work it into every crevice so that the bearings are saturated.

Assembly

Assemble, noting that the chain wheel has left and right sides. Tighten the left cone to seat the bearings and back off about 1/8 turn. The crank should spin freely. If it binds on one side, check to see that the hanger cups are fully home and square with the sides of the bracket. As with all bicycle bearings, you should have just a hair's breath of side play. Install the keyed washer and locknut, tightening the nut securely. Check the bearing clearance again. Install the pedals and chain guard.

COTTERED CRANKS

Cottered cranks are three-piece affairs, consisting of two crank arms and the axle. The arms are secured to the axle by tapered pins. These designs represent a compromise between the American crank and the more exotic cotterless variety. They are lighter than the former but, on the average, weaker than cotterless cranks.

Overhaul

Start from the left side, turning the pedal spindle clockwise to unthread it from the arm. While the pins look deceptively easy to remove (No. 2 in Fig. 11-4) alas, that is not the case. Hammering on them is virtually equivalent of hammering on the bearings. If you can stand the hassle of transporting the bike to a shop to have the pins pressed out, taking the bike home, then bringing it back when the work is

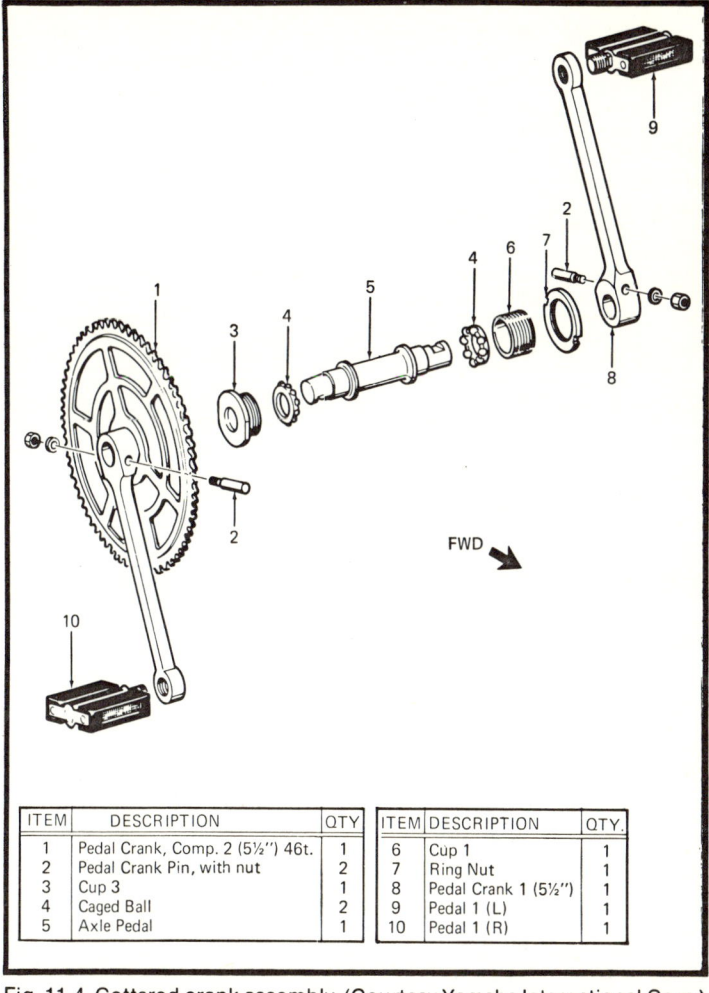

Fig. 11-4. Cottered crank assembly. (Courtesy Yamaha International Corp.)

ITEM	DESCRIPTION	QTY
1	Pedal Crank, Comp. 2 (5½") 46t.	1
2	Pedal Crank Pin, with nut	2
3	Cup 3	1
4	Caged Ball	2
5	Axle Pedal	1

ITEM	DESCRIPTION	QTY
6	Cup 1	1
7	Ring Nut	1
8	Pedal Crank 1 (5½")	1
9	Pedal 1 (L)	1
10	Pedal 1 (R)	1

completed to have the pins pressed back in, you are indeed patient. The pins can be driven out (with a soft-faced mallet) if you are careful to support the crankarms on blocks so that the shock is absorbed by the arm and not through the bearings. This is touchy and takes some ingenuity to design a proper cradle. Another alternative is to construct a tool similar to the press that bike mechanics use. Take a pair of Vise-Grips, preferably large ones, and place a wrench socket on the lower jaw. Position this below the pin. Squeeze hard. The upper jaw will drive the pin down, flush with the surface of the crankarm.

If necessary you can force the pin deeper with a ball bearing or spacer between it and the upper jaw. This is tedious, especially when it is so easy to drive that pin out, but much cheaper than investing in a V.A.R. Cobra press (if you can find one for sale).

The ring nut (No. 7 in the drawing) may have a right- or left-hand thread. Most have a left-hand thread and are turned clockwise to loosen. A C spanner is very useful here, but not absolutely essential (Fig. 11-5). You can use a punch and achieve the same result. The ring will not be mutilated if you make up a punch from a heavy copper or brass rod. Unthread the adjustable cup out of the bracket. This part is shown as No. 6 in Fig. 11-4. Some cups have flats to accept a wrench, others are pin-drive propositions. In most cases the bearings will be loose. Count the bearings in the cup then take a small magnet to retrieve those that have scattered themselves inside of the bottom bracket. Hold the axle up against the fixed cup (3), and the chain wheel side bearings in place. One loose set at a time is enough. Place the bearings in a container and withdraw the axle. You should have the same number of bearings on both sides. Do not turn the bike over until all bearings are accounted for. Should one decide to go up into the tubes, you will never find it. Clean the innards of the bracket with a brush and solvent. Inspect the fixed cup in place since it may be so tight that special tools and skills will be needed to remove it. Inspect the bearing path with the help of a strong light. The bearings may have described an ellipical path due to uneven pedal pressures. This is tolerable, but pitting and chipping are cause for replacement. The fixed cup is loosened by turning it clockwise for almost all bikes.

Inspect the bearings for pits, dull spots, and other blemishes. Abuse will sometimes bend the axle, a condition which can be detected by rolling it on a flat surface. Should you need to replace any parts, bring them with you to a bike dealer. The cups are very critical since there are three popular thread options. The English thread is 1.37 × 24 inches; the French is 35 × 1 inch; and the Italian is 36 × 24

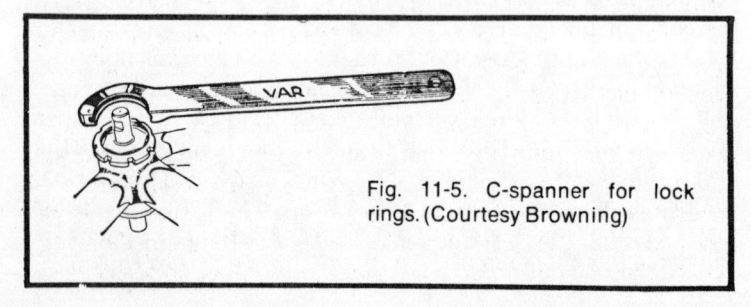

Fig. 11-5. C-spanner for lock rings. (Courtesy Browning)

mm. The last two are easy to confuse and appear to be interchangeable. However the cups will strip when tightened.

Assembly

Assemble in reverse order of the instruction given in the overhaul procedures. Be on the lookout for left-hand threads when threading the ring nut and pedals. Make sure all the balls are in the bearing cages.

COTTERLESS CRANKS

Cotterless cranks represent the highest state of the art. These cranks are the lightest of all and, in their most expensive versions, feature exotic touches such as titanium mounting bolts. Naturally such fine machinery requires special tools

Overhaul

Remove the pedals—turn the left spindle clockwise to loosen, the right, counterclockwise—and the dust cap. A 5 mm Allen wrench fits most including the Stronglight 93 illustrated in Fig. 11-6. Remove the mounting bolt (standard thread) with a socket, and retrieve the washer under it. The crankarms are fitted to a taper on the axle and must be removed with the appropriate puller. There are several thread combinations, so purchase the puller for your bike. The next drawing (Fig. 11-7) shows a three-piece professional puller. An amateur need not purchase the handle, since a large Crescent wrench will substitute. The outside body of the puller is threaded into the crankarm and tightened. The bolt is tightened against the axle, forcing the crankarm out and off. If the arm is particularly stubborn, tighten the bolt snug and rap it with a hammer. Repeat as needed. A lock ring holds the adjustable cone in place. On bikes built to the English standard the lock ring has a left-hand thread. European thread standards specify a right-hand thread. You can remove it with a soft punch as explained under Cottered Cranks or with the C-spanner illustrated in Fig. 11-5. If you plan to do much work on different models, it would be well to invest in a pair of lock ring pliers. Unlike the C-spanner, lock ring pliers fit all lock rings.

Place a cloth under the bottom bracket to catch the bearings and unthread the adjustable cup. Hold the axle in place so you have only one bearing set loose. Retrieve all bearings from the bottom bracket and count them. Remove the axle from the left and collect all of the right-side bearings. Count them. You should have the same number on both sides.

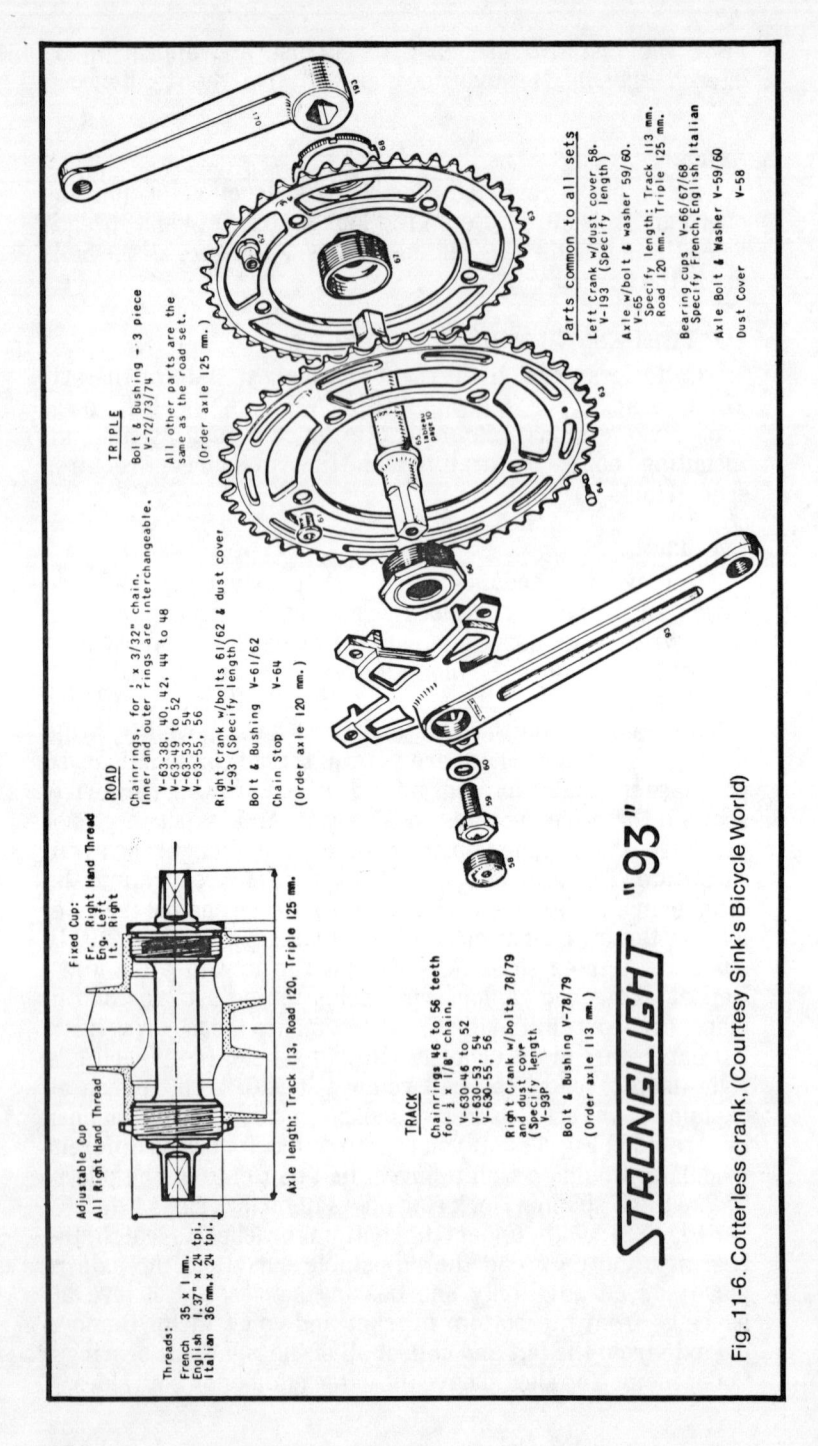

Fig. 11-6. Cotterless crank. (Courtesy Sink's Bicycle World)

Swab out the bracket with solvent and turn the bike up to inspect the inner surface of the fixed cup. We haven't taken it off because this job can be more effort than it's worth. The bearing run should be dead smooth and have a constant width. If the run is excessively wide or erratic, you have problems; maybe a bent axle or even a bent frame. Some eccentricity is allowed, so long as the bearings do not meander much off a circular path. Make the same careful inspection of the adjustable cone, and look at each bearing as if it were a pearl you found in a bowl of oyster soup. The smallest imperfection of any is justification to replace all of them. At least replace a complete set, being careful not to mix new and old bearings. The reason for this scrupulousness is that bearings are relatively inexpensive. New ones can do much to make the assembly live longer. Cotterless cranks and their components seem to be sold by the carat.

Assembly

Assemble from the left. Lay a bead of light grease along the inside of the fixed cup and place one set of bearings in the grease, roughly in line with each other. Do the same for the adjustable cup. Slip the axle home, and holding it in position, thread the loaded adjustable cup into the bracket. With luck, all of the bearings will stay in place and the bottom cup will seat. If not, do not use force. Take it off, find out why it refused to draw up, and repeat the operation. Tighten enough to cam the bearings in place and loosen 1/8 turn. Adjustment is correct when there is just an echo of lateral play and the axle turns easily. Install the lock ring and check the bearing adjustment again.

Install the crank arms, remembering that they are 180 degrees apart, and tighten the mounting bolt. Use discretion since it is possible to strip the threads on the bolt and/or axle.

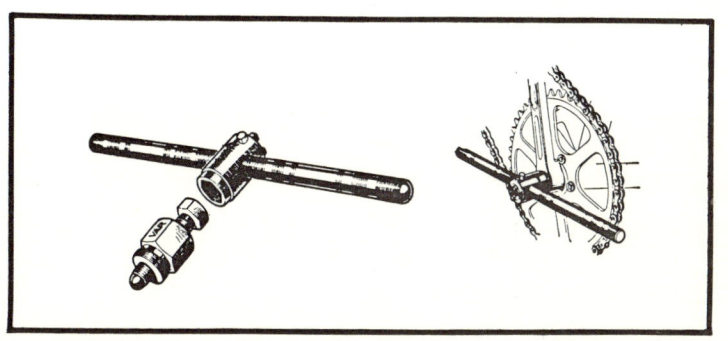

Fig. 11-7. Three-piece crank-arm puller. (Courtesy Browning)

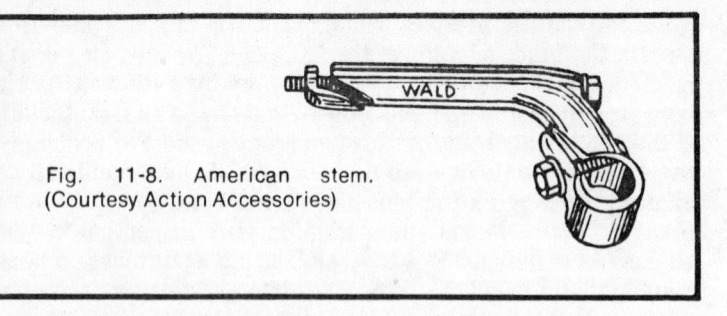

Fig. 11-8. American stem. (Courtesy Action Accessories)

Work the crank arm back and forth as you tighten. It is imperative that the axle be lined up with the square hole in the arm. Alloy arms will not straighten themselves as they are tightened. Small misalignments will cause the hole to enlarge and the arm to pound out under pedal pressure. The only cure is new parts.

AMERICAN HEADSETS

The headset is usually thought of as the replaceable parts—handlebar stem, bearings, cones, and related hardware. As is so often the case with bicycles, headsets fall into two broad family classifications: American and European. The former are designed for maximum durability at some cost in weight. The handlebar stems (goosenecks) are made of forged or stamped steel and feature caged ball bearings for easy maintenance. European headsets generally employ light alloy castings and loose balls. Another difference is in the shape of the wedges—American wedges act off center and imply that the fork stem be of adequate thickness to support the concentration of forces. European wedges are the full circle variety, gripping the internal diameter of the fork stem around its full circumference.

Adjusting American Headsets

American bikes manufactured through 1965 used 16 gauge tubing and an 0.875 inch diameter stem (Fig 11-8). Later bikes were heavier with 14 gauge tubing at the steering head. Consequently, the diameter of the handlebar stem was reduced to 0.833 inch. Both sizes are available, although the 0.875 inch is limited to 15/16 inch handlebars and the smaller stem to 1 inch bars. Conversion is possible—you can install a 0.833 inch stem in a 0.875 head with an adaptor sleeve available from Action Accessories.

In addition to stem and handlebar diameter, headsets are available in several lengths, although an extension of more than 2 inches above the steering head tube is not considered safe.

Stem. If the front wheel does not align with the stem, that is, if the handlebars are angled to one side, loosen the binder bolt slightly, with 1/2 or 9/16 inch box-end wrench. Open-ends tend to slip. Walk around to the front of the bike and holding the wheel between your legs, align the handlebars. You may have to use a soft mallet below the stem on the horizontal extension or overhang to break the wedge loose. If the expander bolt turns free, it has lost the wedge. Tap the stem up and out with your mallet, and turn the bike over to retrieve the wedge. Assemble the bolt and wedge into the stem, leaving plenty of slack and reassemble.

How tight should the stem be? Some riders like the security of a supertight stem, having had experience or premonitions of stem/fork parting. Others, perhaps the great majority, feel that the stem should be snug enough to withstand any ordinary road shocks, but should give in a crash. This is perhaps the best philosophy and one that prevents expander bolts from being sheared off by overtightening.

On the other hand, the bars should be as tight as you dare make them. They must support the whole weight of the rider when he stands up to get full power. Slipped bars mean a nasty accident. If you cannot seem to tighten the bars sufficiently, check for a stripped threads at the pinch bolt (usually on the stem and not on the relatively inexpensive bolt) and for wear on the bar serrations. Should the serrations be worn smooth, no amount of tightening will suffice to keep the bars from drooping under weight.

Inspect the stem for cracks and bends. Do not ride a bike with a cracked stem nor attempt to straighten one that has suffered impact damage.

Handlebars. American bars, sometimes lumped as longhorn or steerhorn bars, are available in various bends. The scout bar looks like old-fashioned motorcycle bars, with a sharp drop and horizontals extending far back and almost in parallel. Several varieties of highrise bars are offered for those who put questionable taste ahead of function. At any rate the bar should fall to the hands and should be angled up enough to clear the top tube and the riders knees.

Handlegrips. Handlegrips must be secure. Any movement is a prelude to an accident. Slippery or loose grips should be replaced. Do not try to salvage a loose set of grips by wrapping the bar with vinyl tape or by attempting to fix the grips with adhesives. If the latter course is successful (doubtful, and

Fig. 11-9. American head bearing set. (Courtesy Action Accessories)

failure may be sudden), you will have to cut the grips off should you need to replace the stem. Replace if the grip is torn so the end of the bar shows through.

Old grips may be removed with a pair of waterpump pliers, but some damage to the plastic will result, making them forever uncomfortable. A better way is to use compressed air. Insert the nozzle in the hole at one end and block the other with your thumb. Warning: Do not use air at over 30 psi, since it is possible for high-pressure air to penetrate the skin, and enter the bloodstream in the form of bubbles. This can be fatal. Force the nozzle against the near side grip and apply air. The opposite grip will blow off with some velocity. Do the same for the remaining one, this time stuffing the end of the bar with rags to contain the pressure.

Bearings and Related Hardware

American headset bearings look like the picture in Fig. 11-9. From the top the parts are: head locknut, key washer, head adjustable cone, bearing, head cup, head cup again (sometimes called set cones) bearing (also interchangeable), and lower fork or crown race.

The most common malady is excessive play between the bearings. You can detect this condition by lifting the front wheel off the ground by the handlebars. There should be no perceptible lag. Adjust by loosening the locknut—a large wrench is very useful to have at this time. An old-fashioned smooth-jawed monkey wrench is ideal, although you can invest in a head locknut wrench such as the one shown in Fig. 11-10. It will remove stubborn locknuts without scarring the flats and is slotted so you do not have to disassemble the handlebar stem. If all else fails, use a pair of Vise-Grips or water pump pliers. Turn counterclockwise enough to take the pressure off the adjustable cone.

The adjustable cone is knurled so that it can be turned with pliers. Try not to allow the pliers to slip. Tighten by turning clockwise. One or two revolutions should be enough to remove all up-and-down play. If the cone must be lowered more than a tiny fraction of an inch, back it off and inspect the bearing run. If it is pitted or meanders about on the cone, you should overhaul the headset.

Bearings which bind the fork are usually too tight, although the problem may be compounded by dried grease. In any event, loosen the locknut as described a moment ago, loosen the cone, and inspect the upper bearing. If it is gunky, try cleaning both bearings with derailleur cleaner. Spray both bearings around their circumference. Wipe off the afterspray and the oily dribble which will run down the fork and steering head. Lubricate with light grease from a tube applicator or dabble it on the bearings with a screwdriver blade. Reassemble.

Steering which is alternately tight and loose or steering which pops and crackles means one or more of the following:

- dented (brinnelled) bearing surfaces
- flattened or chipped bearings
- a bent fork stem
- or, horror of horrors, a bent steering head

A bent steering head fortunately very rare, particularly on American bikes which are built with the strength factor of

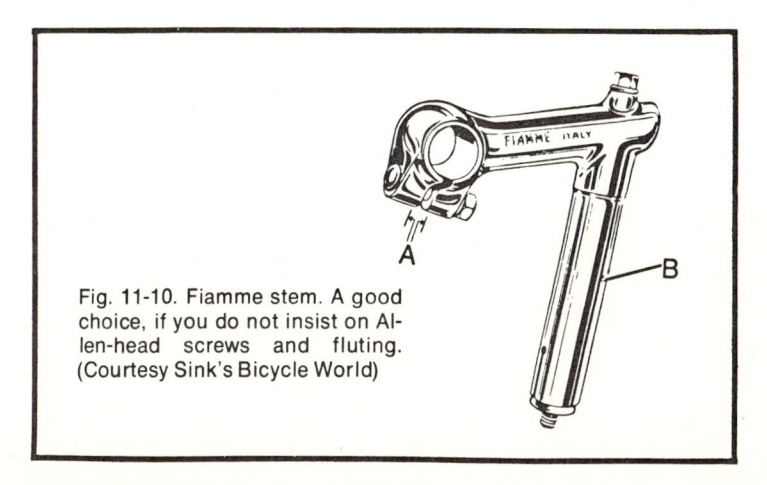

Fig. 11-10. Fiamme stem. A good choice, if you do not insist on Allen-head screws and fluting. (Courtesy Sink's Bicycle World)

Sherman tanks. But you should keep this possibility in the back of your mind should the overhaul prove unsuccessful.

Overhaul

Remove one handlegrip, loosen the pinch bolt, and slip the handbar out of the stem eye. Remove the stem. Holding the front wheel between your legs, remove the locknut, key washer, and adjustable (upper) cone, and upper bearing. It may be easier to remove the front wheel from the fork, although this step is not necessary unless you intend to replace the fork. Lift the bike frame up and over the fork stem. Remove the lower bearing.

The bearings may be held in their retainers so that they face outward, like jewels in a ring. Correct assembly is no problem since either side can be up. Wald bearings, original equipment on many bikes and the standard replacement parts carried by many bike shops, have the balls on one side of the retainer. The top set faces down and the lower set faces up as shown in Fig. 11-9.

Clean all parts in solvent and inspect with the same scrupulous attention that a banker gives to a blurred hundred dollar bill. Look for structural failures at the fork, stem, and handlebars. Cracks or obvious bends are calls for immediate replacement. The lower cone takes most of the beating, but do not attempt to remove it from the fork stem unless it is damaged. Scrub the bearings and the cups. You will have to raise the frame to check the lower cup.

The lower cone can be removed with the aid of a thin screwdriver blade. Pry it up on the stem, working around the circumference. Try not to scar the stem since nicks act as stress rises and can be a prelude to fatigue failure. If you should do some damage, burnish lightly with a file. Install a new cone with a tool designed for the purpose or with a length of pipe with an inner diameter slightly larger than the 1 inch diameter of the fork stem. It is important that the cone be driven on from the flat above the race. Naturally, pounding on the race will ruin it.

The cups are press fitted into the steering head tube and must be forced out. Tools are available to make this job easier, but, with care, you can drive them out and not damage the inside of the tube. Use a flat brass punch and a hammer. Install new cups with the help of a soft wooden block. Again, tools are available to press the cups into place, and the purchase of one of these is certainly justified if you plan to do much bike work.

Lubricate the bearings with light grease, making certain that the grease is packed into the crevices between the balls and retainer. Assemble and adjust as before.

EUROPEAN HEADSETS

These headsets do not have the general ruggedness of the American variety, although their materials and manufacturing tolerances are, in many cases, superior. Great care must be taken not to damage the components during repair operations. Consequently, I will specify tools to reduce the risk factor and to protect the finish. However, do not think that special tools are absolutely required. Headsets are not in the same class of sophistication as cotterless cranks. You can do a reasonably adequate job with a minimum of general-purpose tools, if you are patient and use common sense. The same techniques apply to both headset varieties. You can, for example, drive out Campagnolo cups with a dull screwdriver and replace them with a white pine 2 × 4 as a buffer against hammer blows.

Overhauling European Headsets

These headsets are subject to all of the ills described in the previous section. Good quality European bearings and cones last longer but alloy handlebars and stems are more subject to deformation from impact than the steel variety.

Handlebars. Alloy bars can be straightened in the aftermath of a collision, but this procedure is not recommended. The bars will never be true and will be much weaker at the site of the bend.

Taping is not difficult if you do one side at a time, using the other for a model. Remove the end plug. Ordinary plugs are held by simple friction and must be twisted off with pliers. Better quality plugs have an expansion element wedged by a central screw. Turn the screw counterclockwise to retract the wedge and give the plug a half-twist to loosen. One end of the tape is under the plug. Unwind the tape and lay it out with the sticky side up if you are using adhesive tape and intend to reuse it.

Position the handbrake in where it is reachable and comfortable. The classic method of taping is to begin near the stem, leaving some two or three inches of metal showing. Wrap two layers on top of the other to secure the rest of the coils. If you are using nonadhesive tape, you can tack the end with masking tape, although this expedient should not really be necessary. Continue to wrap the bar, overlapping each layer. Things get a little sticky on the bends—the inner layer will tend to bunch and crease unless you keep tension on the tape—and stickier around the brake lever. Several tries may be necessary to make a neat job of it. Wrap out to the end and leave some surplus to be pinned by the plug. Install the plug before the whole thing unwinds. Adhesive tape is easier to use and is suspect in some circles because of it. It's important to remove fingerprints from the bar first with alcohol or some TV tuner cleaner or some other solvent which does not leave a residue. You have an option on the direction of the lay. You can begin near the stem and work out to the bar end or, because the tape is adhesive, you can work from the end inward. As before, leave some surplus for the plug.

Stems. If the stem does not secure the handlebars, check the joint at the binder bolt. As the bolt is tightened the center of the stem is drawn together, tightening on the handlebar center. Several conditions may defeat this mechanism. The stem may elongate under tension from the binder bolt and the two faces of the broken circle meet (dimension *A* in Fig. 11-10). Tightening the binder bolt ceases to reduce the diameter of the circle. The best and surest recourse is to replace the stem; you could file the interfaces to obtain clearance, but this sort of economy is *not* recommended. This part of the stem has been overstressed and can break. The binder nut may slip and turn. The repair is to purchase another binder nut and bolt, preferably one with a recessed (Allen) head. Either the bolt or nut may strip.

Remove the stem by giving the expansion bolt a few turns counterclockwise. The bolt will climb up out of the stem. Tap it down with a mallet to free the expansion plug. Repeat the process as needed, but don't get carried away, since the plug will eventually unthread and drop down in the fork stem. A minor frustration, since you will have to turn the bike over and persuade the plug to fall out the top of the head tube.

The stem is as highly stressed and about as safety-related as any component on the bike. Inspect it carefully for evidence if impending failure, particularly if the stem is made of light alloy and fluted to reduce weight. Surface cracks may develop at the handlebar fitting or at the expansion plug. Discard any stem with these defects.

Replacement stems are available in various extensions or overhangs. No really trustworthy formula is available to determine which overhang is suitable for your torso length and arm reach, so you must experiment. TTT Record is one of several manufacturers who make an adjustable stem with a sliding extension for hard-to-fit riders.

Stem diameter is critical and has not been standardized. Many Japanese bikes employ a 21 mm stem, while Italian manufacturers favor 22 mm. Other countries use a hodgepodge of sizes clustering around 22 mm, but not identical with the Italian. The moral is to bring the old stem to your dealer for measurement. Sleeves, sometimes called shims, are available to compensate for gross misfits but should not be used unless it's absolutely necessary to keep the bike on the road. Better to search out obscure catalogs and wait for the mailman to bring a stem that fits.

Headset Bearings. Again there is the problem of national standards. The British standard is 1 inch × 24 threads, excepting that most British of makes, Raleigh. In its corporate wisdom Raleigh has used a finer thread on utility and middle grade headsets during the last decade. The American standard is the same as the English, while the French and Italians use what appears to be the same thread until you ruin the fork trying to tighten the cone. Pitch is almost identical, but thread profile differs.

To disassemble remove the stem and the locknut. As mentioned previously, an old-fashioned monkey wrench is a very serviceable tool for this chore, but you can use a large Crescent (adjustable wrench) or, better, a wrench designed for the purpose. The VAR locknut wrench shown in Fig. 11-11 is convenient (since the stem does not have to be removed to place the wrench) and will not damage the plating on the locknut. Turn counterclockwise. Some locknuts have serations as shown in the drawing of the Stronglight bearing set (Fig. 11-12). You can use a pair of waterpump pliers with the jaws wrapped in a shop rag to protect the finish of this high-quality example of the machinist's art, or you can purchase a tool for the job. Smooth-jawed pliers are available through dealers or from Browning which also may be used for the upper cone. The Campagnolo headset is shown in Fig. 11-13.

Remove the lock washer and with one hand steady the fork in the head tube. Otherwise the uncaged bearings will duck for cover. Remove the bearings with patience and sharp

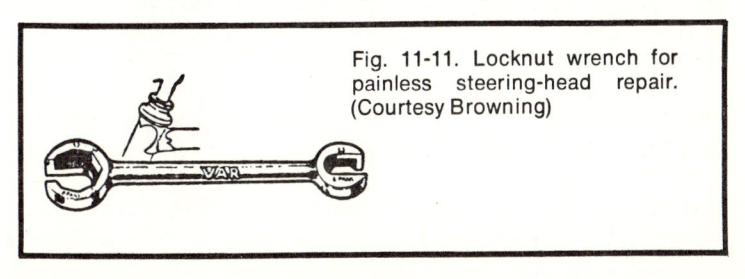

Fig. 11-11. Locknut wrench for painless steering-head repair. (Courtesy Browning)

Fig. 11-12. Stronglight headset.
(Courtesy Sink's Bicycle World)

fingernails or with a small magnet. Count them. A peculiarity of bicycles is that no matter where made, the bearings are to the inch standard. Most are 3/16 inch and easy to handle. A minority of brands use 1/8 inch bearings.

Without releasing the fork and the lower bearings, lay the bike on its side over a clean rag. Pull the fork out of the

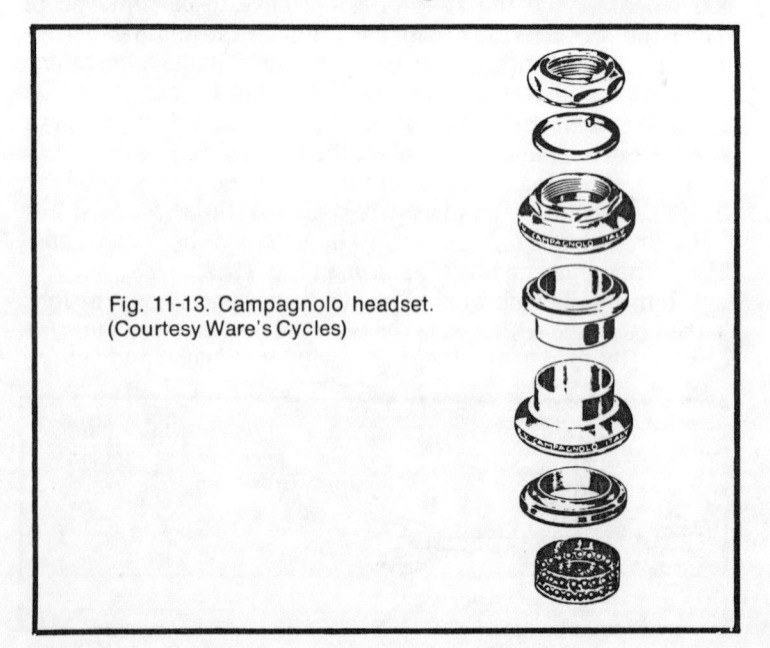

Fig. 11-13. Campagnolo headset.
(Courtesy Ware's Cycles)

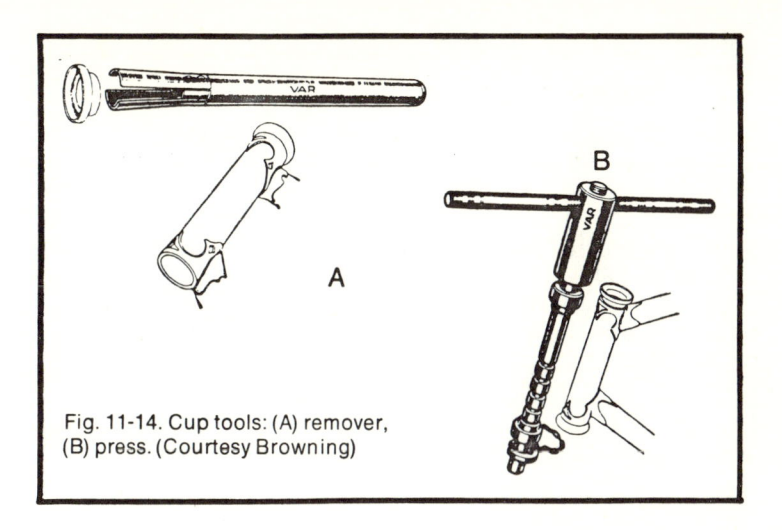

Fig. 11-14. Cup tools: (A) remover, (B) press. (Courtesy Browning)

steering tube, watching for bearings which stick and fall off once the fork is clear of the rag. Count them. In almost all cases the bearings will be the same size as the upper group.

Clean and inspect as outlined in the discussion of American headsets. Brinnelling, rust spots, and wobbly bearing runs are of course grounds for replacement since anti-friction bearings are most unforgiving. Leave the cups and lower race in place unless worn, cracked or otherwise unserviceable.

Should it be necessary to disturb these parts, at least think about the advisability of purchasing the proper tools. Removal is not critical (so long as you do not damage the fork or steering head tube in the process), but assembly is critical. Figure 11-14A illustrates a splayed driver for cup removal; Fig. 11-14B shows a press used to bring the cups home without damage. The next illustration (Fig. 11-15) is a lower race driver. It has one advantage—it fits.

After everything has been cleaned and scrutinized and you have purchased whatever parts you may need, it's time to

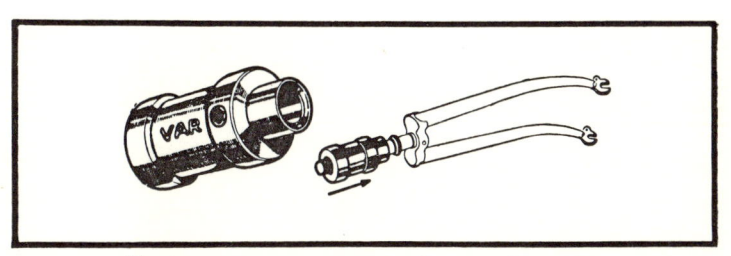

Fig. 11-15. Crown race driver. (Courtesy Browning)

267

begin assembly. If you have removed the cups, install with the largest at the bottom. The cups should seat squarely on the tube. With the bike upside down, lay a bead of light grease on the inner diameter of the cup and, with tweezers, inlay the bearings in the grease. The lower or crown race should be bottomed on the fork. Now with one movement slip the fork stem home. While steadying the fork, place the upper set of bearings around the periphery of the upper cup. A bearing dispenser helps. A plastic catsup or mustard bottle with the spout cut off just enough to pass a single bearing makes a good one. Thread the adjustable cone over the fork stem and snug it finger tight. Tighten a trifle more to seat the bearings while waggling the fork back and forth. Be patient and keep a picture in your mind of what will happen if a row of ball bearings is compressed too hard between the cones and cups. Loosen until you have just the tiniest bit up and down play. If all is right the forks will swing from lock to lock effortlessly.

Tighten the locknut and insert the handlebar stem. Notice the manner in which the expansion plug is keyed to the stem. Fix the stem into the steering tube to the proper depth for your saddle and riding preference. Align the handlebar by straddling the front wheel and rotating the bar and stem. Tighten the expansion bolt securely, but moderately.

FORKS

Available in a staggering array of sizes, threads, and forward bends or rakes, fork choice is critical to tune the bike to your riding style. As shown in Fig. 11-16 the fork stem meets the blades at the crown. The blades terminate in slots, or dropouts, for the front axle. Most forks sold today are of the tubular variety, with the most desirable of these made of high-quality steel such as Reynolds 531. Round blades may have tapered thicknesses to match stress and strength, or can

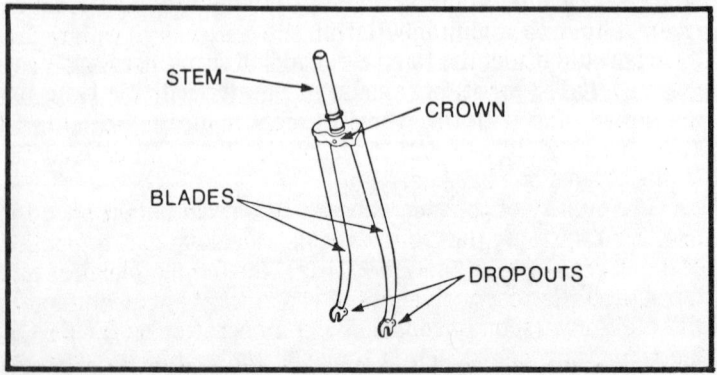

Fig. 11-16. Fork nomenclature.

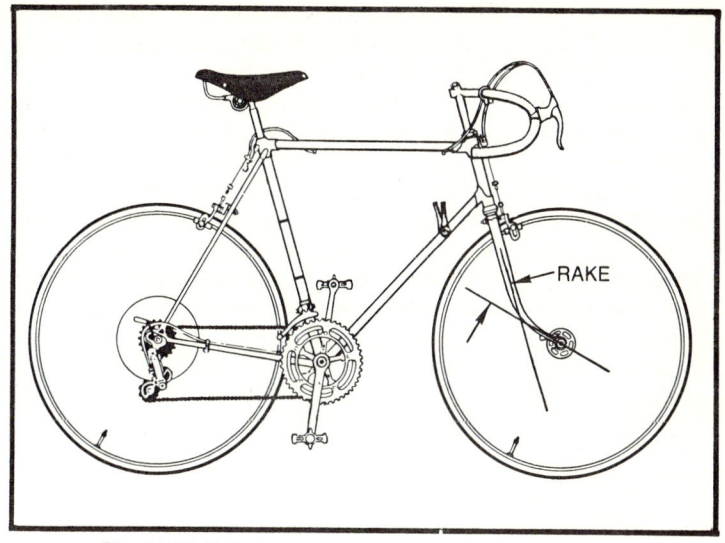

Fig. 11-17. Rake is the angle of bend in the fork blades.

be straight gauge. Oval forks are usually straight gauge, although it is possible to get blades with variable thicknesses from Reynolds.

American forks are not this subtle and are usually straight-gauged, mild steel affairs. The exception is solid forks which should be used on middle-weight frames only. These forks are very strong. In the event of accident most of the impact will be transferred to the frame. It is better to have the fork bend than the frame.

Most fork damage, other than fatigue failures and gaping welds at the crown, are caused by impact. You can check alignment with a known good wheel. If the wheel is true and straight axled, it should slip easily into the dropouts. Another check is to drop a plumb bob from the center of the stem. The string should bisect the fork with equal distance between it and the blades. The fork stem should be parallel with the blades at the crown, and with the wheel at right angles to your line of sight, you should see only near blade. If the other leads or trails, at least one has been bent.

The quality of the ride depends to a great extent upon the fork. How springly the front wheel is at least in part a function of the degree of rake (see Fig. 11-17), the tubing thickness and taper, and the responsiveness of the steel. Any misalignment will call for a (soon unconscious) compensation on the part of the rider, and one which is tiring at the end of the day. An unpleasant bike can often be civilized by a sagacious fork substitution. However, you should remember that rake has an effect on steering. Extending it cushions road shocks, while at the same time slowing the steering response. Conversely shortening the rake will, all things equal, tend to make the bike lively and as they say about sea-sensitive ships, tender. It should be noted that some manufacturers stock forks of extended blade length that will give the effect of changing the rake.

When purchasing a fork it is always wise to take the old one with you as a guide. If you order by mail, specify make, thread system (if known), wheel size, and stem height.

12

Wheels and Tires

A bicycle wheel is one of the most impressive structures known. Its symmetry is the first quality to attract the eye. This same quality is seen in works of many artists—from the Gettysburg Address to formal gardens of the eighteenth century. It is hardly a wonder that contemporary sculptors such as Fumio Yoshimura sometimes incorporate bicycle wheels into their displays.

The visual aspects of the wheel are entirely conditioned by its function (if we overlook the chrome plate). All man-made objects have some purpose. But these purposes are often quite broadly defined and compromised by other demands. Thus we have the phenomenon of streamlined electric can openers, trousers with bell bottoms (once meaningful for sailors who can kick their way out of them in the water), fiberglass fronts on Volkswagens to make them resemble Rolls-Royces or 1940-vintage Fords. And even the more serious objects are a package of compromises. Machine tools, even if the designer is not interested in "style" and market acceptability, should have rounded, easy-to-clean surfaces without sharp angles which would be unfriendly to the operator's hands and clothing. Airliner seats are designed to look massive and finished in neutral colors to give the passengers psychological support.

Wheelwrights care not a whit for secondary considerations. Their job is to build a wheel which will support a 200 pound man with enough of a safety margin to withstand an occasional drop off a curb.

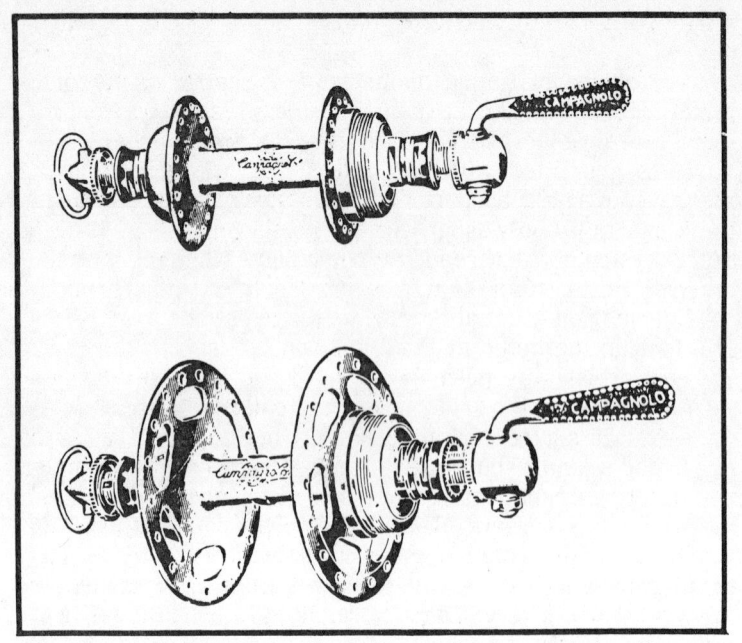

Fig. 12-1. Campagnolo small- and large-flange rear hubs. (Courtesy Ware's)

The play of forces on the wheel is dynamic. As the wheel turns it cycles through tension and relaxation periods, much like human musculature. The uppermost spoke or pair of spokes supports the weight of the rider and machine. As these spokes leave the 12 o'clock position, they relax. Braking and accelerating loads are taken by those spokes in the 3 and 9 o'clock positions. It is important to replace broken or bent spokes as the damage occurs, for the strength of the wheel is not an aggregrate of the total number of spokes. At some point in each revolution, each spoke bears almost complete responsibility for the integrity of the structure.

HUBS

Figure 12-1 illustrates a pair of Campagnolo hubs. These particular hubs are for the rear wheel and are threaded to accept British and Italian (1.370 inches × 24TPI) or French (34.7 × 1 mm) clusters. Hub diameters are measured from the centers of the spoke holes and range from 30 mm to 102.5 mm. The latter is something of a curiosity and is seen on certain exotica such as the Sturmey-Archer Dyno Hub. Normally when we speak of large flange hubs we mean something on the order of 53 mm. Medium or standard flange is nominally 48 mm, and small flange hubs are anything under this.

The choice of flange diameters is a matter of personal preference: the larger the flange, the more responsive the bike is and the more vibration is transmitted to the handlebars.

Hubs are fitted with two axle styles: the quick-release skewer illustrated as part of the Campagnolo hubs and the traditional nut-and-washer variety as shown in Fig. 12-2. A delux version of the threaded type employs wingnuts for easy removal. Best results seem to be had with the Gripfast brand.

Bearings on all quality hubs are cageless and usually are 3/16 inch in diameter at the front and 1/4 inch at the rear. However, this is by no means a hard and fast rule. Expect variations from 1/4 to 3/16 inch on the front.

About 20 sealed and precision-ground hubs a day leave Phil Wood's small shop in Los Gatos, California. These hubs are necessarily expensive, but are guaranteed to need no attention for five years. Racers and people who just like fine machinery under them find the investment worthwhile. The bearings are mated to the hub by means of Loc-Tite, an anaerobic adhesive. Stored in porous tubes, it dries and expands when air is excluded. This and the most rigid quality control this side of Project Apollo are the secrets of Phil Wood's success. Tests have shown that his hubs have a higher starting torque than those which are recognized as the world's best conventional types, but have only about 30 percent of the running torque.

Hub Adjustment

The bearings may be expected to develop play with use. There should be just a trace of side movement at the rim and no more. Failure to tighten the cones will soon wreck the

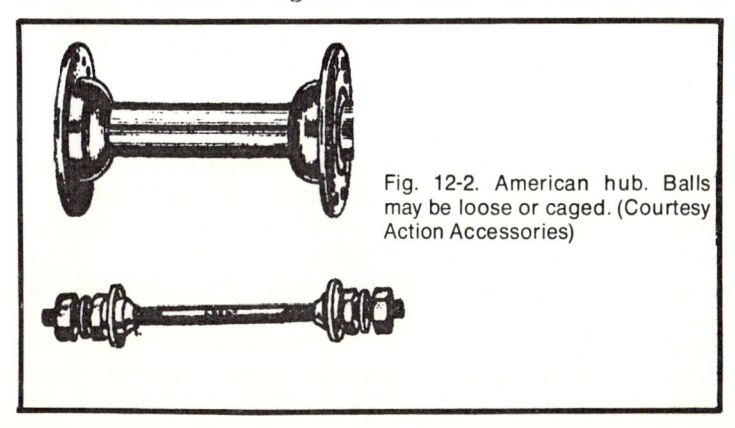

Fig. 12-2. American hub. Balls may be loose or caged. (Courtesy Action Accessories)

Fig. 12-3. Cone wrench. (Courtesy Browning)

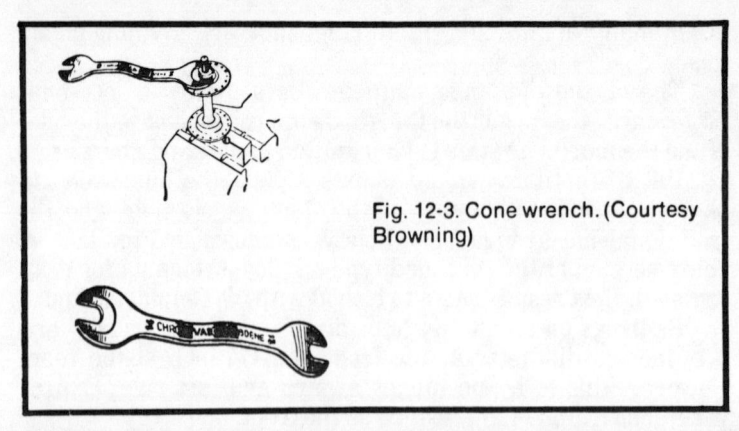

bearings and the cups. Cups on the cheaper hubs are integral. When they become pitted or brinneled, you have to buy another hub and go to the trouble of building a wheel. And while those on the more expensive hubs can be removed, the chore is not always painless. Nor are replacement parts readily available.

The cones should be adjusted with the wheel in the forks, because the tightening of the axle nuts will affect the cone adjustment. This means that you must purchase a cone wrench. Campagnolo makes the ultimate cone wrench just as they make the ultimate corkscrew, but these wrenches are hard to come by. Figure 12-3 shows a reasonable facsimile.

For the American utility hub, loosen the axle nuts enough to provide a bit of working clearance and use your special wrench to turn either one of the cones as required. Retighten the axle nuts and check. You may find that these nuts have loaded the assembly enough to bind the cones. If so, repeat the operation, this time anticipating the preload.

European hubs with axle nuts (sometimes called track nuts) should be installed in the dropouts and held by the right nut. Normally, the left-hand cone is adjustable and is identified by the slots in the cone. A few have the adjustable cone on the right. If your hub tightens in service, check with your dealer for the proper placement of the adjustable cone. If reversed, it is possible that the cone will thread itself deeper on the axle.

Many hubs have cone locknuts in addition to axle nuts (the hubs shown in Fig. 12-4 and 12-5 have this feature). The left locknut must be loosened before the left cone is turned. Use two wrenches, one to hold the cone stationary and the other to turn the locknut.

Quick-release cone adjustment can be a bit of a hassle. Remove the wheel from the frame. In order to keep the axle centered, it is a good idea to adjust both cones simultaneously. Using Fig. 12-5 as our reference, hold one locknut and crack the other counterclockwise to free its cone. You can also work from one side of the wheel at a time. Hold each cone and loosen its locknut. Adjust both cones equally; hold them from turning and seat their respective locknuts. Check the bearings clearance after this operation.

The springs (No. 1) should be placed with the large ends out, facing the dropouts. Campys have paired springs for a total of four on each skewer. These springs are assembled with the small ends together, large ends facing the dropouts and the hub flanges.

Adjustment of the quick-release is required if the axle remains loose when the handle is turned to full locked position, or if the handle binds before it reaches the limit of its travel. Unlock the lever and adjust the serrated adjustment nut (No. 8). The lever should point to the back of the bike when locked.

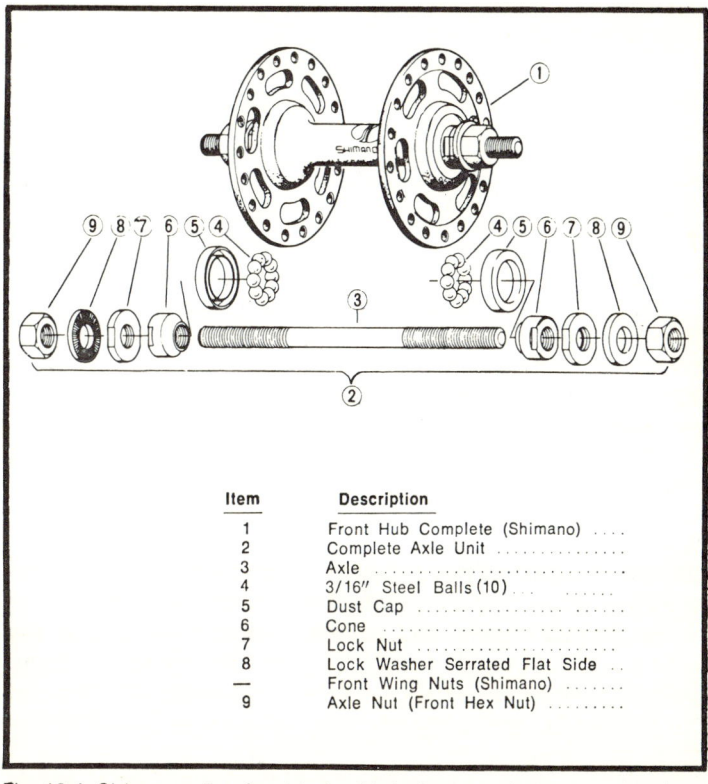

Item	Description
1	Front Hub Complete (Shimano)
2	Complete Axle Unit
3	Axle
4	3/16" Steel Balls (10)
5	Dust Cap
6	Cone
7	Lock Nut
8	Lock Washer Serrated Flat Side
—	Front Wing Nuts (Shimano)
9	Axle Nut (Front Hex Nut)

Fig. 12-4. Shimano alloy front hub with locknuts and without detachable cups.

Quick Release Axle

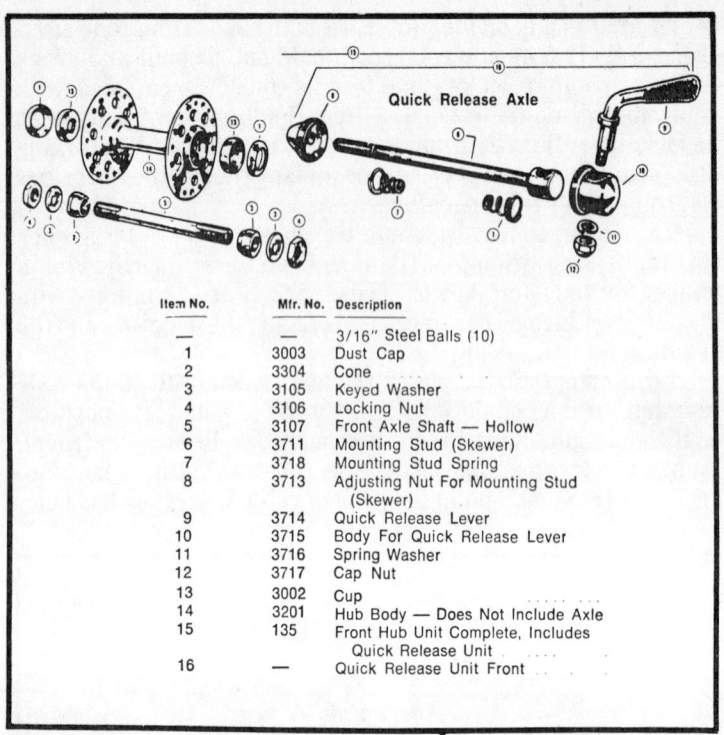

Item No.	Mfr. No.	Description
—	—	3/16" Steel Balls (10)
1	3003	Dust Cap
2	3304	Cone
3	3105	Keyed Washer
4	3106	Locking Nut
5	3107	Front Axle Shaft — Hollow
6	3711	Mounting Stud (Skewer)
7	3718	Mounting Stud Spring
8	3713	Adjusting Nut For Mounting Stud (Skewer)
9	3714	Quick Release Lever
10	3715	Body For Quick Release Lever
11	3716	Spring Washer
12	3717	Cap Nut
13	3002	Cup
14	3201	Hub Body — Does Not Include Axle
15	135	Front Hub Unit Complete, Includes Quick Release Unit
16	—	Quick Release Unit Front

Fig. 12-5. Normandy hub with locknuts and detachable cups. (Courtesy Browning)

Hub Repair

The axle assembly must be periodically taken apart, cleaned, and lubricated. Cyclists who want the best from their machines do this chore once a year and more frequently if riding in the wet. Serious competitors clean and inspect the hubs after each event.

Remove the wheel from the frame. Remove the sprocket cluster on rear wheels. Because of the usual location of the adjustable cone, the hub is taken down from the left side. The right side cone and locknut are not disturbed in order to keep the axle centered in the dropouts. Lay the wheel down on the bench or support it in a soft-jawed vise. Remove the left locknut, keyed washer, and adjustable cone. Remove the left side bearings. Loose bearings can be picked up with a small magnet or tweezers. If a dust cap is fitted (No. 1) pry it off with a pocket knife or small screwdriver. Try not to distort the cap.

Holding the wheel at the axle (to prevent the right side bearings from escaping), turn it over and remove the axle together with the cone and locknut. Remove the dust cap if present and retrieve the bearings.

Clean the hub and associated parts with solvent and lubricate. Oil will generate less friction than grease, but must be replenished frequently. Most riders use a light grease on the order of Lubriplate 5555. Working from the right side, set the bearings in a film of grease. There should be an equal number of loose bearings on both sides, filling the cup, but not touching each other. Retainers should be greased with particular care that all of the cavities are packed. The messy way is the best way: put a glob of grease on your palm and holding the retainer with your other hand, work it back and forth into the grease, packing the lubricant tightly into the ring. Lay the wheel on its left side, place the bearings and install the axle and cone assembly. Insert the dust cap with the help of a softwood block. If a dust cap is not fitted to your hub, be very careful to hold the wheel by the axle when you turn it over to do the other bearings. If the axle drops out the balls will not be far behind.

Do the same for the left side. Install the cone, keyed washer, and locknut. Adjust as described in the foregoing section.

If the bearings are pitted, rusted, or show telltale flat spots, they must be replaced. It is always a good idea to replace the cones as well and, if possible, the cups (No. 13). Outright failure of these parts will be shown by a wavy, irregular, and possibly chipped bearing track. Unfortunately, not all hubs have replaceable cups; for those that do, the cups may be only sporadically available. Remove the cups by driving them out with a dulled punch from behind. Clean the cup boss, and bottom the replacements with a softwood block. Bearings are standard items, purchases by diameter. Caged bearings are stamped with a code on the retainer.

SPOKES

Spokes come in a variety of sizes and styles. The length of the spoke required depends upon a number of variables, including:

- the diameter of the rim
- the diameter of the flange
- the spoke pattern (the number of crosses)
- the number of spokes
- the type and manufacture of the rim
- the manufacture of the spoke nipple

Fig. 12-6. Spike nonmenclature.

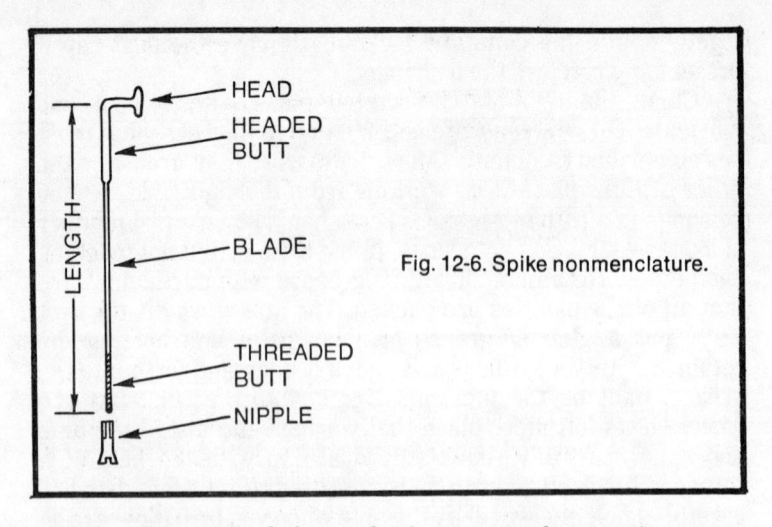

The diameter of the spoke is expressed as a wire-gauge number. The lower the number, the thicker the spoke. Fourteen gauge or 0.080 inch is the most popular size. The better spokes are single or doublebutted. That is, the diameter of the blade is reduced by cold rolling. The metal is compressed, increasing the tensile strength of the blade. Butted spokes are catalogued with both gauge numbers as for example, 15/17 or 14/16.

Spokes are made of medium carbon or stainless steel. The latter is not as reliable as medium carbon, but is very rust resistant and is certainly a good choice for an all-weather bike. So-called rustless spokes are carbon steel and are galvanized. Eventually, the zinc coat looses its integrity and the spoke rusts. Chromed spokes have a cosmetic appeal, but require a careful maintenance to keep them shiny. Nor are these spokes particularly reliable. Chrome plating has adverse affects on steel, which can only be overcome by heating the part in an oven for several hours to drive the entrapped hydrogen out of the metal. I do not know how many, if any, spoke manufacturers bother to do this.

The number of spokes to the wheel varies from a low of 20 for sprint racers to 40 for British three-speed and tandem drive wheels. The three-speed traditionally has 32 spokes on the front wheel, while the Continental approach is 36/36.

RIMS

Rims are available in aluminum alloy or steel. The oldest type—still surviving on stirrup-braked machines—is the Westwood rim. It has been almost completely replaced by the

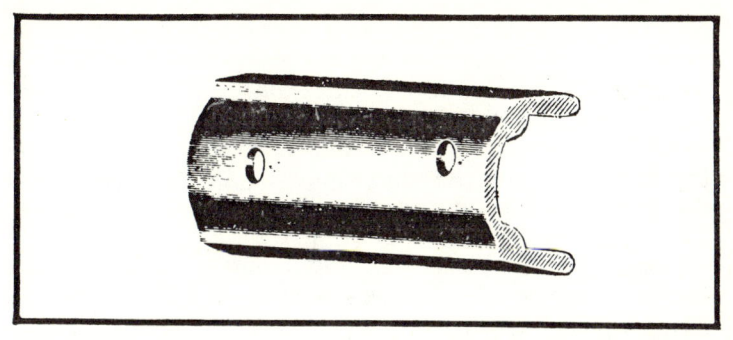

Fig. 12-7. Westrick pattern in alloy. (Courtesy Sink's Bicycle World)

slab-sided Endrick rim, which was designed for caliper brakes. The Westrick rim is a variation of the Endrick with vertical inner flanges. An alloy example of the Westric pattern is shown in Fig. 12-7. Other patterns abound, including two in-house Schwinn types.

Rims designed for tubular (sew-up) tires do not, of course, require the flange. These rims are made of extruded alloy which have been in times past filled with a wood reinforcement, or which have eyelet cups around the spoke holes.

WHEEL REPAIRS

Spokes loosen with use, and periodic spoke tightening is one of the chores associated with bike riding. A correctly laced wheel has the spoke ends even with the slots at the base of the nipples. This is to give working clearance for on-bike adjustments. You should be able to turn the spokes two full revolutions before making contact with the base tape. You will need a spoke wrench (Fig. 12-8) and, on an older bike, some penetrating oil. Ideally you should oil the nipples several days before you tighten the spokes to allow the oil time to work down the threads. Be careful not to spill any on the tires since bike tires do not take kindly to petroleum.

Raise the wheel off the ground and spin it. Sight between the side of the rim and the fork tubes (or the brake calipers) to

Fig. 12-8. Spoke wrench. Other wrenches are available, including adjustable models. (Courtesy Browning)

detect gross wobble. Tap each spoke lightly with a thin wrench. Each should give the same sharp ping. Dull notes mean loose spokes as does a wheel which is noticeably out of true. Tighten the loose spokes a quarter of a turn at a time. It may help to loosen them a bit first to break any corrosion on the threads. Tighten the spokes until they begin to sing, but do not overtighten. In other words, do not stretch the spokes to their limit of elasticity.

Local deformations of the rim, caused by hitting sharp obstacles, can be more or less smoothed out with the help of a large pair of water-pump (Channel-Lock) pliers. Simply squeeze the rim back into shape. The same results can be had by rapping the raised portion of the rim with a leather mallet. It must be emphasized that the kind of deformations discussed in this paragraph are local in nature and are not the gentle curves and bows which can be corrected by spoke adjustments. This damage is the direct result of narrowly focused impacts, and not the result of generalized wear and tear.

Spoke-correctable damage is of three varieties: the wheel may lose concentricity (it may become egg-shaped); the wheel may develop an excessive horizontal runout (it may wobble), or the wheel may take on a vertical offset (the hub becomes displaced to the side relative to the rim). Unless the wheel has been grossly abused or routine spoke tightening neglected, none of these conditions is absolute. Middle and upper middle-grade bikes out of the crate exhibit these characteristics to some degree. Even the most expensive bikes may employ proprietary rims which are not going to be true unless the builder takes the time to make them so.

How much runout is acceptable? Yamaha suggests 1/4 inch as a reasonable figure for its Moto-Bike. Perfectionists have been known to incorporate a dial indicator in their truing stands so that wheel dimensions can be read within 0.0001 inch. The prudent owner will make some compromise between these two extremes, particularly since few if any riders could detect a runout of less than 1/4 inch.

WHEEL ALIGNMENT—REPAIR

Figure 12-9 illustrates a professional wheel truing stand which carries a dealer price of $50.00. An amateur can build a workable substitute for pennies from an old fork (assuming that the fork is true) and an aircraft-type stainless steel hose clamp. These clamps are available from auto parts jobbers in various diameters. Secure the clamp to one fork tube and mount a suitable pointer in it. An Allen wrench is ideal since it

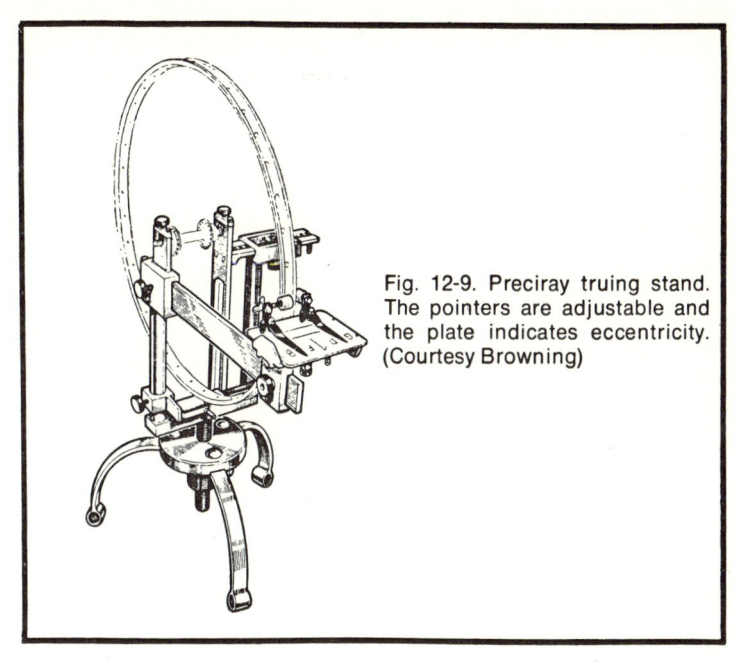

Fig. 12-9. Preciray truing stand. The pointers are adjustable and the plate indicates eccentricity. (Courtesy Browning)

is bent in a right angle. The long leg is held to the fork tube by the clamp; the short leg is positioned close to the rim. Some riders prefer to use chalk or soft crayon as a marker.

Remove the wheel from the frame, dismount the tire and tube, and remove the rim tape. Place the wheel in the stand and check that the spokes sound off smartly when struck. Of course, all spokes must be in place and none obviously bent. The rim must not be crimped or severely twisted. Check the lateral runout (wobble) first since this sort of deformation is chronic. Spoked wheels are very vulnerable to side forces. With your pointer establish the true center of the wheel. Chances are there will be one or two irregularities in the wheel. Tighten the spokes on the opposite side of the irregularities to pull that portion of the rim back to the center line. See Figure 12-10. It may be necessary to loosen spokes on the near side. Repeat this process until the wheel is reasonably wobble-free. Next, place the pointer across the outer diameter of the rim. Spin the wheel. You will have no difficulty in spotting any eccentricity. Loosen the spokes on both sides of the flat spot and tighten those on the long diameter of the "egg." Recheck for wobble. Offset is more difficult, especially when we realize that derailleur rear wheels have a designed-in offset to accommodate the sprocket cluster. In almost all cases, offset disturbances will be local and you will easily be

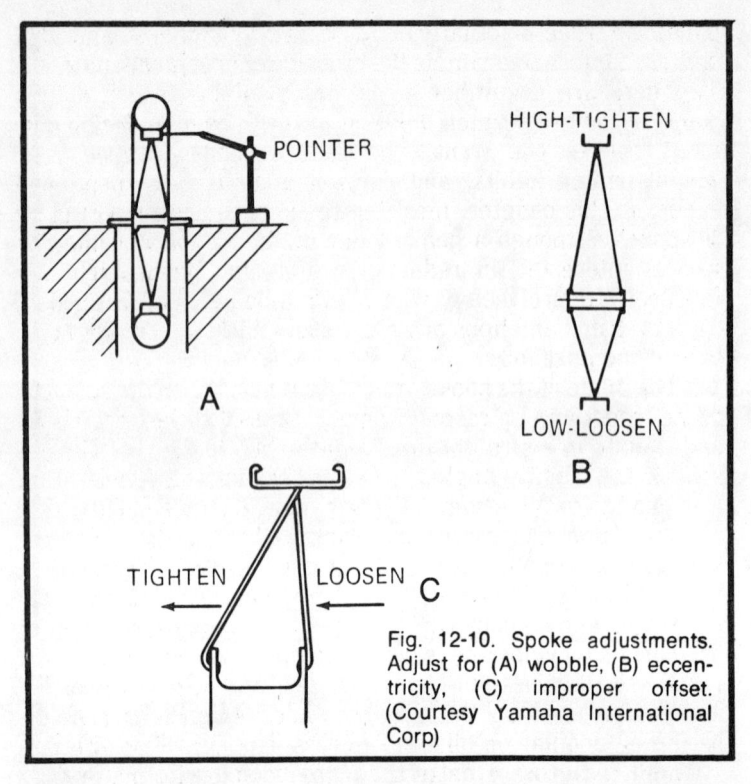

Fig. 12-10. Spoke adjustments. Adjust for (A) wobble, (B) eccentricity, (C) improper offset. (Courtesy Yamaha International Corp)

able to recognize the variation from the original or average setting. If you are nearly finished and the wheel suddenly springs out of alignment, rest assured that you have overtightened the spokes. Loosen them all the same amount and begin again.

Wheel alignment is an art and requires some patience and no little fortitude. The principle is grandly simple—loosen the spokes on the convex side of the wobble and tighten those on the concave side, as viewed from the hub. But the application is muddied by the possibility (no, the probability) that all three kinds of dislocation are present at the same bump. The best advice is to work systematically, tackling one aspect of the problem in turn. With practice, you will be able to align a wheel to within factory specifications in five minutes or less.

WHEEL BUILDING

In one respect, wheel building is easier than aligning a badly warped rim. This is because you are presumably working with new, unstressed components whose response to the turn of the spoke wrench is predictable and uniform. And building a wheel—actually building a wheel—from a handful of spokes, a hub, and a rim, is the pinnacle of bike mechanics.

There are a number of options available to you at this point. If you are scratch building, you will have to decide how many spokes you want. The decision depends upon your weight, riding habits, and parts availability. As mentioned earlier in this chapter, most ten-speed rims are supported by 36 spokes, although a heavy rider might opt for 40 while one who is interested in reducing weight and particularly the flywheel effect of heavy wheels could be satisfied with 28 or even 24. Rims and hubs are available with 20 to 40 spoke holes in increments of four.

The angle of the spokes has a great bearing on the strength of the wheel and its responsiveness. Cross 0 spokes are radial and radiate in a straight line from the hub to the rim. Cross 1 spokes are slightly angled to resist braking and accelerating loads and to provide some strength margin for side loads. This and other popular crosses are illustrated in Fig. 12-11. Cross 2 lacing is sometimes used for the front wheel of lightweight bikes, although it is not the pattern one would choose for touring or knockabout riding. Cross 3 is standard on most of the world's bicycles and is a good compromise between weight (each cross extends the spoke length) and strength. Cross 4 spokes are used on the driving wheel of tandems and are becoming popular on bike moto-cross machines. For ultimate strength the cross 4 pattern can be beefed with heavy-duty straight-gauge spokes, tied and soldered at the crosses.

Wheel building is a minor art form and must be practiced before one becomes even passably proficient at it. It is a good idea to start with a front wheel so there will be no hassle with the wheel dish or offset. Use a good quality alloy rim, it would also be wise to use Robergel spokes instead of some other, less forgiving brand. Decide on the spoke gauge—a function of your weight, riding style, and experience. Most wheels are laced with 14 or 15 gauge spokes (14/16 and 15/16 butted). Spoke tables have been published, but most are less than completely satisfactory and are no substitute for measuring the actual length of the spokes in a wheel with the same hub and rim.

The hub is an unwieldy object when festooned with spokes. One way to tame it is to lay a couple of 2 × 4s on the bench to support the flange. Observe the holes in the hub. Some hubs have countersunk (beveled) holes on one or both sides. The spoke head must be away from the bevel. Otherwise the spoke will fail since the sharp edge of the hole acts as a stress riser. The standard rim has two rows of staggered holes. The holes on each side are for spokes radiating from that side of the flange.

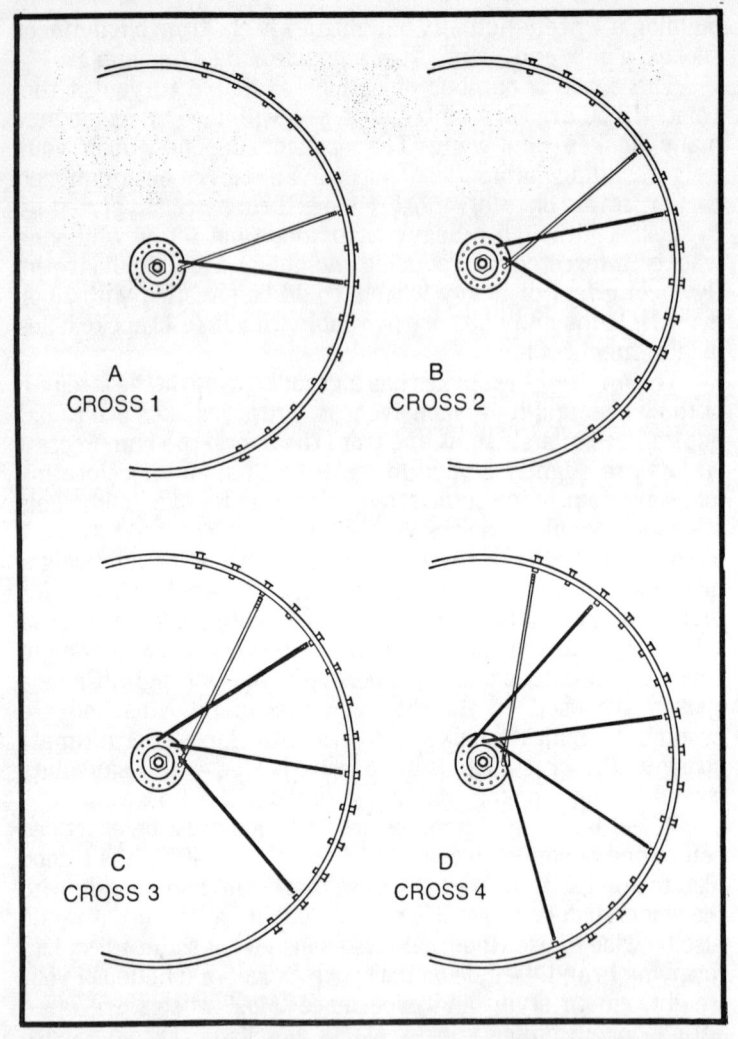

Fig. 12-11. Spoke patterns: (A) cross 1, (B) cross 2, suitable for front wheel, light duty, (C) cross 3, most popular for front and rear wheels, and (D) cross 4, rear wheels, heavy duty.

Dip the threaded end of each spoke in oil to make assembly and adjustment easier. Try threading a spoke through one of the holes in the hub flange. If it sticks, ream the hole slightly oversized with a 3/32 inch drill. Heavy spokes may require the next larger drill size.

I will assume that you want to lace a cross 3, 36-spoke rim. Divide the spokes into four equal groups of nine. Insert the first group, head outwards, into every other hole on one side of the hub. The first spoke goes near the valve stem hole. The next spoke goes into the fourth hole from this one. Spoke, skip three, spoke.

Install the second set of nine on the same side of the hub. This time the heads should face inwards with the curve riding on the bevel. These spokes oppose the direction on the first set. The cross 3 pattern requires that each of our second set goes over two spokes and under the third. Secure each spoke on the near side rim hole. If you do this correctly you will have all the holes on one side filled—half with heads in and half with heads out—and all the rim spoke holes on the same side filled as well.

Repeat the process for the other side of the wheel. Start at a flange hole adjacent to but on the opposite side of the first spoke installed. It will terminate one spoke hole from the valve hole with the head of the spoke on the outside of the flange. Every fourth hole on the rim is filled with a spoke from this set. The last set is inserted from the inside of the hub, head in, and crossed over two spokes and under one.

Points to remember:

- Always start with the valve stem hole as a reference.
- Install the spokes with the head out on each side before you install the head-in spokes. This simplifies the work.
- Crossed wheels are biased over and under. That is, cross 1 is over a spoke, cross 3 is over two and under one, cross 4 is over three and under one.

The next operation is to align the wheel. Put the wheel in a truing stand and tighten all nipples equally. Run the nipples up to the third or fourth thread from the end of the butt. You can use a screwdriver for this preliminary work. Now tighten each nipple one complete turn with a wrench. Repeat this until all slack is taken up but without stressing the spokes enough that they sing.

Check the offset between the hub and rim. Front wheels have zero offset with the hub and rim in a straight line; rear wheels on derailleur-equipped bikes require offset to center the wheel in the frame. This is achieved by deliberately over-torquing the spokes on the cluster side. This is unfortunate because the right side spokes are prone to fatigue and because the angle is such that the wheel is prone to damage from side forces. The angle on the cluster side may be as shallow as four or five degrees compared to an angle of seven or eight degrees for undished wheels. There are several methods of determining offset. One way to find the center of the rim is to mount it on the truing stand, and set the pointer to the center of the rim. Remove the wheel from the stand and install it reversed. Any change in the location of the center of the rim is twice the error in the offset. The rim should track an identical center no matter how it is mounted in the stand. Another way is to slip a steel pocket rule between two spokes. Find the center of the hub and take a bead through the valve stem hole over the hub center and to the center of the rim on the far side. The center of the rim can be laid off with help of a rule or calipers as half the distance between two adjacent spoke holes. I realize this sounds awfully complicated, but without special equipment, this is the way it is done.

Offset is adjusted by tightening the spokes on either side of the wheel. Tighten each one the same amount and no more than half turn at a time. To obtain the required offset on derailleur wheels, you will have to tighten the cluster side spokes half again as tight as those on the right side. Even more differential, approaching twice as much tension, is needed to dish the wheel for a six plate cluster.

Once the offset is approximated, you can proceed with wheel alignment as described in the previous section. Remove the side-to-side wobble first, while keeping spoke tension as constant as you can on both sides for symmetrical wheels and keeping the differential with dished wheels. Then correct the inevitable eccentricity and go back over each check again. Final tightening is very critical. Do not overdo it, and do not localize tension by tightening each spoke in turn. Do the job in several passes, passing over three or four spokes each time around until you tighten each one. If, as mentioned before, the wheel goes "sprong" and folds in on itself, you have overtightened the spokes. It is impossible to give verbal instructions on how tight is enough. If it helps, Yamaha suggests no more than 25 inch-pounds minimum for symmetrical wheels. An equally ineffectual instruction is to say that the spokes should just begin to find their voice, but not touch the high notes.

TIRES

There are two basic bicycle tires; *clincher* and *tubular*. Each type is best suited for specific uses, although the purist may argue this.

Clincher tires are by far the most popular. The tire has a lip or bead which expands under pressure to grip the flanges of the rim. Since the bead is reinforced by steel wire, these tires are sometimes called *wire-on's* to distinguish them from tubulars. The general characteristics of clinchers are a fairly high rolling resistance (mitigated somewhat by the advent of gumwalls), poor feedback, and good puncture resistance. These tires are available in a large number of tread styles, although the typical bike shop will stock only those utilitarian patterns suitable for commuting and casual touring. The cords are generally nylon and the tire itself made of Butyl or some other synthetic.

Clincher Tire Inflation. As with any pneumatic tire pressure is critical. Most clincher tires use the American standard Schrader valve, of the type which is compatible to filling station air lines (for good or ill) and conventional air pumps. The size of the tire (e.g., 27 × 1 3/8) and, in most cases, the recommended pressure is marked on the sidewall. Experienced riders can sense if a clincher is underinflated, although few can detect slight, but critical over-inflation. The following table is a rough guide. Heavy or very light riders may wish to vary from these figures by five or six pounds per squre inch (psi).

Table 12-1. Recommended Clincher Tire Pressure

Tire Size	Pressure
16 × 1 3/8	40 psi
16 × 1.75	35 psi
20 × 1 3/8	40 psi
20 × 1.75	35 psi
20 × 2.125	35 psi
24 × 2.125	35 psi
26 × 1 3/8	45 psi
26 × 1.75	35 psi
26 × 2.125	40 psi
27 × 1 1/4	80 psi

Filling station air lines deliver air at high pressures and volumes and are almost guaranteed to explode your tires. The "one-armed bandit" type of regulator with the crank and musical bell is the safest type to use, although the accuracy of these units may be on the order of plus or minus ten percent. A number of clincher tires have that European speciality, the Presta valve. You will need an adapter to fill these tires from American pumps.

Clincher Tire Damage. Clincher tires are relatively rugged, but can suffer a variety of ills. Flat spots on the tread are common on coaster braked machines and are caused by wheel lockup. Wear on the sidewall is caused by rubbing against the fork or frame tubes or by maladjusted rim brakes. A tire which is worn in this manner is quite dangerous and

Fig. 12-12. Removing the tire without tools. (Courtesy Yamaha International)

should be discarded. Rim cuts—grooves at the base of the sidewall—have a number of causes. Chronic underinflation will damage the sidewalls around the whole circumference of the tire; rust on the rim usually leaves a local rip with rough and jagged edges; impact damage may show as a rupture on the flank of the sidewall or as a rim cut. Impact damage may not tear the outer skin of the tire but may only be seen as a bulge in the sidewall when the tire is inflated. The cords have broken and a blowout is imminent. Other damage can be seen from the inside of the tire. Star-shaped breaks behind the bead or sidewalls are the signatures of contact with sharp objects; ragged and torn beads mean someone has used a tire tool improperly or worse yet, has used a screwdriver in lieu of a tire tool; separated cords are the result of too much flexing, and soon saw their way through the tube.

Clincher Tire Repair. Fixing a flat is one of those humble chores associated with cycling and is probably good for one's spiritual development. Attack the problem immediately. Do not ride a bike with a flat, nor, if you care about your tires, should you even push it. Dismount and try to inflate the tire with your pump. If you're lucky the leak is a small one and you will be able to get home without further ado. Assuming you can get the pressure up, place a drop of spittle on your finger and smear it over the top of the valve stem. Bubbles mean that the valve core is leaking. You can tighten it with a screwdriver-type valve cap which you have thoughtfully brought along. If you do not have one of these caps (they're not standard bike tubes), thread the existing cap tightly over the stem and hope for the best.

If this doesn't work, you'll have to repair the tube on the roadside. Remove the wheel and unscrew the valve core. With your fingers, work the bead to part it from the rim. There are several ways of removing the tube. Tires with pliable sidewalls can be rolled from the rim, together with the tube. Unfortunately, the usual clincher tire is more stubborn than this and requires some judicious prybar work. Insert a tire tool (*not* a screwdriver) between the bead and the rim at the point farthest away from the valve stem. Be very careful not to pinch the tube between the bead and tool. Pry up and down, unseating this section of the bead. Hold the tool in place, or if you have one of the notched types, slip it over a spoke. Take the second tire tool and perform the same operation at a point close to the first. Don't stress the bead anymore than you have to. Slip the first tool out from under the bead while holding pressure on the second. Place it near the second, take a fresh bite, and unseat this portion of the bead. As more and more of the bead is dismounted the work will go easier and faster. With the bead on one side completely off the rim, push the valve stem up and gently tug on the tube. Once the stem is clear, the tube will slither out. Alternatively, you can leave the tube secured by the valve stem and inflate it on the wheel. Put enough pressure in it to detect the puncture.

Small leaks can best be detected by removing the tube and holding it under water (Fig. 12-13). Mark the leak with chalk or insert a twig in the hole (Fig. 12-14).

Cold-patch kits should be part of every cyclist's tool inventory. The directions for use vary in detail between brands, but essentially the procedure is this:

- Clean the leak area with sandpaper or with the "cheese grater" supplied with the kit (Fig. 12-15). Some kits would have you clean the area with gasoline or lighter fluid.
- Apply a thin coat of rubber cement (Fig. 12-16).

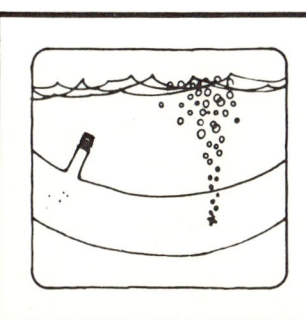

Fig. 12-13. The bubble test. (Courtesy Raleigh Industries Ltd.)

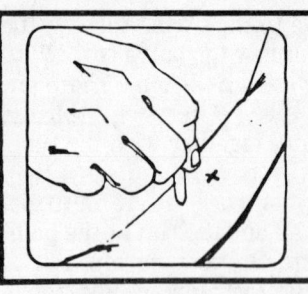

Fig. 12-14. Marking the puncture. (Courtesy Raleigh Industries Ltd.)

- Peel off the backing tape on one of the patches supplied in the kit.
- Apply it to the puncture, newly exposed edge down (Fig. 2-17). If possible, roll the edges since most patch failures work progressively inward from lifted edges.
- Dust the exposed portion of the patch with chalk or talc to prevent sticking.
- Inspect the tire. The foreign object which caused the puncture may still be in the casing.

Install the tube after making sure the rim tape has not slipped and covered the valve-stem hole. Pull the valve stem through first. Gently work the rest of the tube around the rim and up into the casing. Partially inflate the tube, just enough to get the wrinkles out of it. Check the position of the valve stem—it should be straight, in line with the spokes. Work the bead over the tube with your hands. If you must employ a tire iron, be very careful not to pinch the tube. Insert the tip of the iron just enough to lever the bead over the rim. Squeeze the sidewalls together to see that the tube is on the inside of the tire and not peeking out between the casing and the rim.

Inflate the tire slowly. Some cyclists inflate to half pressure and then depress the valve stem as a precaution against tube pinching.

Fig. 12-15. Roughing the surface for better patch adhesion. (Courtesy Raleigh Industries Ltd.)

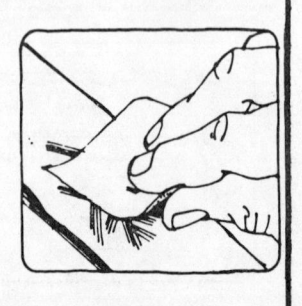

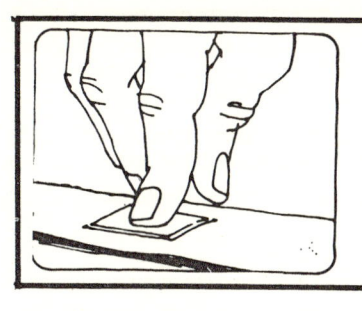

Fig. 12-16. Applying the rubber cement. (Courtesy Raleigh Industries Ltd.)

Tubular Tires

Tubulars are necessary for racing and are preferred by some tourists. The ride is so much better with tubulars that once on them it is difficult to go back to clinchers, even though tubulars are expensive, demand more or less constant attention, and have an almost magnetic attraction for thorns, nails, and bits of glass. Flats are, however, quick to repair, and a spare can be folded (tread out, stem at the bend) and hung behind the seat.

Various weights are offered from 4 ounce racing covers to 15 ounce training tires. If you choose tubulars for ordinary knockabout riding, by all means specify the heavier training type. Various tread patterns are available, with the universal type as the best choice for the nonprofessional. (The same logic applies to tube types.) Butyl rubber holds pressure better the natural rubber in the lighter tires. This can be a convenience on a long trip, although you should bleed the tires at night to preserve their tubular elasticity.

Tire Inflation. Pressure requirements vary inversely as the weight of the tire. Most tubulars should be inflated to at least 90 psi as checked with an accurate gauge. The remarks made earlier concerning the inaccuracy of filling-station gauges are particularly true for pressures near the top of the scale. Invest in an accurate gauge and a good pump such as the Zefal competition or the all-metal Ad-Hoc.

Fig. 12-17. Applying the patch. (Courtesy Raleigh Industries Ltd.)

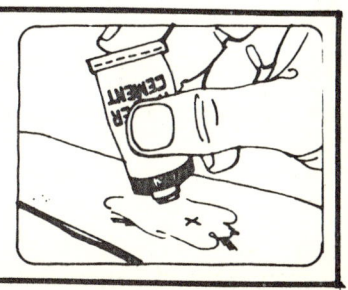

Fig. 12-18. Tubular repair kit. (Courtesy Sink's Bicycle World)

Tubular Tire Repair. Whenever possible, one should avoid making tubular repairs on the road. Figure 12-18 shows a typical repair kit. Instead, use your spare. Make sure there is enough cement on the rim to hold the tire. It may be necessary to remove all traces of the old cement with solvent and lightly sand the rim. (Number 600 wet-or-dry paper is ideal.) Spread on two coats of cement on the rim and one on the casing with a brush or, if you don't mind the mess, with your finger. Tires cemented with Tubasti and Pastali brands can be mounted several times without reapplication. Once the tire is mounted, spin the wheel and gently nudge the tire into alignment.

To repair a tubular, dip the mounted tire in water and watch for bubbles. Do not be misled—the bubbles emerge at the point of least resistance which may be remote from the actual site of the leak. Be particularly suspicious of bubbles which escape around the valve stem. Once you are satisfied that you have located the area of the leak, deflate the tire and gently push it off the rim, being careful that you do not displace the rim tape. Push the valve stem up and clear of the rim. The tire should slip off easily.

Carefully lift the rim tape from the affected section without cutting it. You will see a crisscross pattern of threads. Mark the tube with chalk on either side of the leak area, which for practical purposes means an incision of about six inches. Cut the threads and pull out the tube. Partially inflate and locate the puncture. Apply a cold patch as described in the previous section and dust with chalk to prevent the patch from adhering to the inner walls of the casing. Check the casing for damage. Sew up the tire, using the holes already there. Be certain your chalk marks align since it is very easy to get a pucker in the tire. Glue the rim tape back and mount the tire by hand, beginning at the valve stem and working progressively around the rim on both sides of the stem. You may have to stretch the tire to get it on the rim.

Index

A

Accessories ... 105
Adjustment of brakes ... 116
American cranks ... 251
   assembly ... 252
   overhaul ... 251
American headsets ... 258
   adjusting ... 258
   bearings ... 260
   handlebars ... 259
   handlegrips ... 259
   overhaul ... 262
American pedals ... 248
   overhaul ... 249
   removal ... 249
Appearance ... 92
Archer, James ... 24
Assembly ... 217

B

Bendix automatic
   assembly ... 217
   transmission-brake ... 212
   troubleshooting ... 213
Bendix coaster brakes ... 205
Bendix yellow and blue
   band brakes ... 218
   overhaul ... 223
   subassemblies ... 223
   troubleshooting ... 218
Bicycles
   activists ... 39
   brands ... 74
   changing attitudes ... 33
   environmentally sound ... 34
   first show ... 14
   Institute of America,
     exercises for safety ... 97
   Institute of America,
     rules for safety ... 95
   technology ... 70
   varieties ... 75
   warranties ... 72
   where to buy ... 73
Bikes,
   in harmony with mass transit ... 39
Bikeways ... 35
Blocks, brake ... 122
Bottom bracket and crank adjustments ... 105
Brakes ... 91
   adjustment ... 104, 116
   assembly ... 211
   Bendix automatic transmission brake ... 212
   Bendix yellow and blue band ... 218
   blocks ... 122
   cables ... 124
   center pull ... 114
   coaster ... 205
   disassembly ... 210
   hub ... 204
   levers ... 123
   rim ... 113
   Shimano disk ... 242
   side pull ... 114
   stirrup ... 125
   troubleshooting ... 207
Brands of bicycles ... 74

C

Cable
   adjustments ... 143
   and twist grip ... 167
   for brakes ... 124
Celerifere, bicycle forerunner ... 10
Celeripede, bicycle forerunner ... 10
Center pull vs side pull ... 114
Chain
   jumps ... 148
   tension ... 147
Characteristics
   of different bicycles ... 76
Circulatory system and exercise ... 50
Clincher tire
   damage ... 287
   inflation ... 287
   repair ... 288
Cluster removal ... 134
Cottered cranks ... 252
   assembly ... 255
   overhaul ... 252
Cotterless cranks ... 255
   assembly ... 257
   overhaul ... 255
Components of the bicycle ... 79
Continental pedals ... 25
Overhaul ... 250
Control levers ... 138
Crank
   and bottom bracket adjustments ... 105
   American ... 251
   and cranksets ... 90
   cottered ... 252
   cotterless ... 255
Crank and hub
   installation ... 163
   operating principles ... 161
   teardown ... 166
   transmissions ... 157
   troubleshooting ... 168
Cycling, exercise ... 47

D

Derailleur
   chains ... 153
   chain maintenance ... 154
   chain stretch ... 155
   freewheels ... 129
   gear ratio ... 127
   nomenclature ... 129
   shifting ... 129
   transmissions ... 127
   troubleshooting ... 139
Dublin study ... 46
Dynohub ... 201
   assembly ... 203
   teardown ... 203
   troubleshooting ... 201

E

European headsets ... 263
   bearings ... 265
   forks ... 268
   handlebars ... 263
   ovrhauling ... 263
   stems ... 264
Exercise
   how to get started ... 54
   programs ... 48

F

Flags ... 110
Frames ... 80
   adjustments ... 103
   construction ... 83
   fit ... 87
   materials ... 80
Freewheels ... 129
   overhaul ... 136
Front changers ... 149
   adjustment ... 150
   overhaul ... 152
   troubleshooting ... 150

G

Gears ... 91
   ratio ... 127

H

Handlebars ... 89
   adjustments ... 102
Headsets
   American ... 258
   European ... 263
Headstems ... 89
Health
   and exercise ... 44
   and psychology ... 52
Helmets ... 110
Hubs ... 272
   adjustment ... 273
   brakes ... 204
   repair ... 276
Hub and crank
   installation ... 163
   operating principles ... 161
   teardown ... 166
   transmissions ... 157
   troubleshooting ... 168

L

Lamps ... 107
Lawson, chain drive ... 18
league of American Wheelmen ... 42
Le Long, cross country ... 26
Levers ... 138
   of brakes ... 123
Lucas, bicycle headlamp ... 23

M

Michaux, Pierre ... 11
Models 70 and 70-J ... 206
Murphy, speed record ... 27

P

Parking ... 39
Pedals ... 90
   American ... 248
   Continental ... 250
Planetary transmissions ... 168
Pope ... 29
Psychology of health ... 52
Purchasing of bicycle ... 73

R

Rear changers ... 138
Reflectors ... 108
Reflexes ... 97
Respiration, and exercise ... 50
Rims ... 278
   brakes ... 113

S

Saddles ... 89
   adjustments ... 101
Security ... 111
Shifting ... 129
Shimano 3.3.3. ... 237
   adjustment ... 239

293

    assembly 240
    teardown 239
Shimano disc
    adjustment 245
    brake 242
    pad replacement 245
Side pull vs center pull 114
Spokes 277
Sportshift changers 173
Sprocket alignment 144
Starley, bicycle manufacturer ..14
Stevens, cross country 26
Stirrup brakes 125
Stroke adjustments 146
Sturmey-Archer
    assembly 180
    automatic 192
    automatic assembly 196
    automatic teardown 193
    five-speed 181
    five-speed adjustment .183
    five-speed, assembly ..189
    five-speed, teardown ..188
    five-speed, troubleshooting
   184
    hubs 174
    hub, teardown 177
    transmission 171
Sturmey-Archer S3C 228
    adjustment 228
    assembly 234
    ball ring 236
    brake arm and cone 236
    brake service 231
    driver 235

    final assembly 236
    gear ring 235
    hub disassembly 231
    inspection 234
    planet cage 234
    troubleshooting 229
Sturmey, Henry 24

T

TCC 41
Technology of bicycles 70
Thomson, pneumatic tire 25
Tires 88, 271, 286
    tubular 291
Touring
    bikeways 61
    bikes 56
    cooking out 66
    inspection 67
    planning 59
    sleeping accommodations .65
    what to carry 57
    what to wear 68
Tracking 145
Transmissions
    adjustments 105
    derailleur 127
    hub and crank 157
    planetary 168
    Sturmey-Archer 171
Trigger changers 171
Troubleshooting, derailleur ..139
Tubular tires 291

    inflation 291
    repair 292
Twist grip
    and cable 167
    changers 172
Types of bicycles 75

V

Velocipedes, Michaux family ...11

W

Warranties, on bicycles 72
Weight loss and exercise 50
Wheels 87, 271
    adjustments 104
    alignment 280
    building 282
    repairs 279

Y

Yellow and blue subassamblies 223
    assembly 224
    brake arm 223
    clutch expander 224
    driver 224
    inspection 224

Z

Zimmerman, racing 27